	ㄱ K(G)	ㄴ N	ㄷ T(D)	ㄹ R(L)	ㅁ M	ㅂ P(B)
ㅏ a	가 K(G)a	나 Na	다 T(D)a	라 R(L)a	마 Ma	바 P(B)a
ㅑ ya	갸 K(G)ya	냐 Nya	댜 T(D)ya	랴 R(L)ya	먀 Mya	뱌 P(B)ya
ㅓ ŏ	거 K(G)ŏ	너 Nŏ	더 T(D)ŏ	러 R(L)ŏ	머 Mŏ	버 P(B)ŏ
ㅕ yŏ	겨 K(G)yŏ	녀 Nyŏ	뎌 T(D)yŏ	려 R(L)yŏ	며 Myŏ	벼 P(B)yŏ
ㅗ o	고 K(G)o	노 No	도 T(D)o	로 R(L)o	모 Mo	보 P(B)o
ㅛ yo	교 K(G)yo	뇨 Nyo	됴 T(D)yo	료 R(L)yo	묘 Myo	뵤 P(B)yo
ㅜ u	구 K(G)u	누 Nu	두 T(D)u	루 R(L)u	무 Mu	부 P(B)u
ㅠ yu	규 K(G)yu	뉴 Nyu	듀 T(D)yu	류 R(L)yu	뮤 Myu	뷰 P(B)yu
ㅡ ŭ	그 K(G)ŭ	느 Nŭ	드 T(D)ŭ	르 R(L)ŭ	므 Mŭ	브 P(B)ŭ
ㅣ i	기 K(G)i	니 Ni	디 T(D)i	리 R(L)i	미 Mi	비 P(B)i

Alphabet

(*McCune-Reischauer System*)

ㅇ	ㅈ	ㅊ	ㅋ	ㅌ	ㅍ	ㅎ
ng	Ch(J)	Ch'	K'	T'	P'	H
아	자	차	카	타	파	하
A	Ch(J)a	Ch'a	K'a	T'a	P'a	Ha
야	쟈	챠	캬	탸	퍄	햐
Ya	Ch(J)ya	Ch'ya	K'ya	T'ya	P'ya	Hya
어	저	처	커	터	퍼	허
Ŏ	Ch(J)ŏ	Ch'ŏ	K'ŏ	T'ŏ	P'ŏ	Hŏ
여	져	쳐	켜	텨	펴	혀
˙Yŏ	Ch(J)yŏ	Ch'yŏ	K'yŏ	T'yŏ	P'yŏ	Hyŏ
오	조	초	코	토	포	호
O	Ch(J)o	Ch'o	K'o	T'o	P'o	Ho
요	죠	쵸	쿄	툐	표	효
Yo	Ch(J)yo	Ch'yo	K'yo	T'yo	P'yo	Hyo
우	주	추	쿠	투	푸	후
U	Ch(J)u	Ch'u	K'u	T'u	P'u	Hu
유	쥬	츄	큐	튜	퓨	휴
Yu	Ch(J)yu	Ch'yu	K'yu	T'yu	P'yu	Hyu
으	즈	츠	크	트	프	흐
Ŭ	Ch(J)ŭ	Ch'ŭ	K'ŭ	T'ŭ	P'ŭ	Hŭ
이	지	치	키	티	피	히
i	Ch(J)i	Ch'i	K'i	T'i	P'i	Hi

gateway to

SPEAKING

KOREAN

Practical Text
for
Foreigners
by
The Association of
Foreign Language
Propagation

MOONYELIM
SEOUL, KOREA

GATEWAY TO
SPEAKING KOREAN

Copyright © 1993
First, Revised Edition
Issued September · 10. · 1994
Editor : by The Association of
　　　　Foreign Language
　　　　Propagation
Publisher : Kim Sung—Uck
Published by The Moonyelim
#201 Moonye B/D 195—21 Kunja-dong, Sungdong-gu,
Seoul, 133—150, Korea
Phone : (02) 499—1281~2
Fax : (02) 499—1283
Price : 8,500 Won
　　　　Registerd as 2—110 with the
　　　　Ministry of Culture and
　　　　Public Information of KOREA
　　　　ISBN : 89—7482—003—X

FOREWORD

Frankly speaking, the Korean language is not one of the important international languages which are used widely in the world. And it can be said that national power has played a big and important role in disseminating languages.

The case of Japan well proves this. Even though Japan is a small island nation, and the use of its language was limited to Japan in the past, there are now a considerable number of people in other countries who study Japanese. This tendency can be attributed to the ever increasing national power of Japan.

Overcoming the past vicious circles of history and many tra gedies, the Korean people are now making strenuous efforts to modernize their country in political, social, cultural and economic areas. Korea has enjoyed more than five thousand year's tradition and history. In the near future, Korea will play a leading part in world affairs.

These days, there is an increasing number of people who want to study the Korean language. This can be interpreted as meaning that Korea has begun to occupy an important place in the world.

This conversation is published to help in the study of the Korean language. The best way to learn a foreign language is to make oneself familiar with the simple and easy daily words of the language. By memorizing single phrases and sentences and by trying to using them, you can more easily learn the Korean language.

This book includes practical and necessary phrases and words, which are spoken daily by native Korean people.

It consists of four parts ; in the first, the basic expressions of Korean are introduced, in the second part, the most necessary phrases and sentences, in the third, practical sentences used in daily life, and in the last part, dailogue−style sentences.

The McCune−Reischauer System of romanization of Korean words is used. But it is not a complete system and they say the pronunciation of Korean words is hard to record correctly and completely in the Roman alphabet. For example, the pronunciation of the word "flower" is romanized "*kkot.*" But when it is used in a sentence such as "the flower is pretty", the pronunciation is recorded as "*kko-ch'ŭn ye-ppŭ-da.*" Thus this book tries to record Korean words "as pronounced" in Roman alphabet, whether they are used in phrases or in sentences. But for reference, the McCune−Reischauer System is carried on the back page of this book.

This book is written only for the practical use. If you want to improve your knowledge of the Korean language after using this book, you must seek another special book on the Korean language. Anyhow, we hope that you will become much interested in the Korean language and speech through the help of this handy conversation book.

1992. 9. 30.

INTRODUCTION

People study languages for various reasons. Scholars want to read documents relating to the countries in which they are interested. Diplomats want to be able to comnunicate with officials of the countries to which they are assigened. And travellers want to understand the people whom they visit. The present work is an attempt to fulfill this last need.

Books to help the visitor understand the Korean language are rather rare, and most of them are now out of date. This is a great pity, since Korea is taking an increasingly important role in world trade and in tourism. The present work is therefore particularly welcome.

This is a practical book for the person who needs to communicate on a practical, everyday level. It concentrates on the situations in which the foreign visitor will find himself in visits of relatively brief duration.

One of this book's more valuable features is that it introduces the reader to Hangul, the Korean alphabet. This is easy to learn as easy as ABC, as it were and is the best way to learn Korean pronunciation, since even the best system of Romanization can represent Korean sounds only approximately. Hangul, the only known alphabet deliberately devised to convey a language, represents the sounds of Korean with precision, and enables the learner to grasp the sounds of the language with ease.

Koreans are warm and hospitable people, and always willing to make allowances for the ignorance of foreigners. But the foreigner who is willing to take the trouble to learn their language will find himself much more richly rewarded than the casual tourist. So welcome to Korea *Annyong hashimnikka* !

Grafton K. Mintz

Former Fulbright Professor,

Staff Member

of The Korea Times

Contents

Part I (Basic Expressions)

9

Part II (Necessary Phrase)

Part III (Practical Sentences)

Part IV（Dialogue）

General Remarks on Korean Language

Invented and promulgated by King Sejong, the fourth monarch of the Yi Dynasty in 1446, Hangul, or the Korean alphabet, originally had 28 letters. But four letters of the original 28, ㆁ, ㆆ, △, disappeared from use throughout the long history of more than 500 years, and at present, only 24 letters are in use.

Included in the Ural—Altaic language family, the Korean language shows a strong tendecy of vocal harmony and in sentences, the words follow the order of subject, predicate and the modifier. And particles and auxiliary verbs are added occasionally to major words.

The Korean letters are phonetic symbols, not hieroglyphs. And unlike other Oriental languages, the Korean language tends to be weak in logical expression, but it has an abundant vocabulary of sensitive and emotional expressions. Thus, the abundance of onomatopoeic, simulation, adjective and exclamatory words are distinguishing characteristics of the Korean language.

As already mentioned, there are 24 letters in the Korean alphabet, ten vowels as medials and fourteen consonants used both as initial and final letters. Beside these, there are also double consonants, formed by and based on the original single consonants.

The individual letter has a phonetic value and independent form, and two or more letters are written together as syllables in the same fashion as in Latin.

It is very helpful to foreign readers that they note the spelling rules and the manner in which the symbols are combined to make syllables and words.

The original ten vowels are ㅏ, ㅑ, ㅓ, ㅕ, ㅗ, ㅛ, ㅜ, ㅠ, ㅡ, ㅣ. The vowels ㅏ, ㅓ, and ㅣ, modify or compounding to form the sounds ; ㅐ, ㅔ, ㅒ, ㅖ, ㅘ, ㅝ, ㅢ, are those modified by the ㅣ, ㅘ, ㅝ, are these compounded with the ㅏ, ㅓ, respectively ; ㅙ, ㅞ, are these modified by the ㅏ, ㅓ, ㅣ, in compound.

ㅏ (아 ; *a*) ········· 아버지(*a-bŏ-ji*——father)

　　　　　　　아 침(*a-ch'im*——morning)

　　　　　　　아름다운(*a-rŭm-da-un*——beautiful)

ㅑ (야 ; *ya*) ······ 야 망(*ya-mang*——ambition)

　　　　　　　야 당(*ya-dang*——opposition party)

　　　　　　　야 수(*ya-su*——wild animal)

ㅓ (어 ; *ŏ*) ········· 어머니(*ŏ-mŏ-ni*——mother)

　　　　　　　어 부(*ŏ-bu*——fisherman)

　　　　　　　어 른(*ŏ-rŭn*——adult)

ㅕ (여 ; *yŏ*) ······ 여 자(*yŏ-ja*——woman)

　　　　　　　여 름(*yŏ-rŭm*——summer)

　　　　　　　여 우(*yŏ-u*——fox)

ㅗ (오 ; *o*) ········· 오 늘(*o-nŭl*——today)

　　　　　　　오 후(*o-hu*——afternoon)

　　　　　　　오 월(*o-wŏl*——May)

ㅛ (요 ; *yo*) ······ 요 술(*yo-sul*——magic)

　　　　　　　요 람(*yo-ram*——cradle)

　　　　　　　요 새(*yo-sae*——fortress)

ㅜ (우 ; *u*) ········· 우 정(*u-jŏng*——friendship)

　　　　　　　우 주(*u-ju*——universe)

　　　　　　　우체국(*u-ch'e-guk*——post office)

ㅠ (유 ; *yu*) ······ 유 월(*yu-wŏl*——June)

　　　　　　　유 산(*yu-san*——inheritance)

유치원(*yu-ch'i-wŏn*——kindergarten)

一(으 ; *ŭ*)········ 으 뜸(*ŭ-ttŭm*——first, best)

으름장(*ŭ-rŭm-tchang*——threat)

으스스(*ŭ-sŭ-sŭ*——chilly)

ㅣ(이 ; *i*)········ 이 름(*i-rŭm*——name)

이 민(*i-min*——immigration)

이 별(*i-byŏl*——separation)

The fourteen consonants have their own names. In each case, the first syllable expresses the letter's sound when used as an initial letter, and the second syllable its sound when used as a final letter. Its sound as an initial letter and its sound as a final letter coupled together constitute the following names.

ㄱ(기역 ; *ki-yŏk* ; *k*,*g*)······ 가 위(*ka-wi*——scissors)

고구마(*ko-gu-ma*——sweet potato)

구 월(*ku-wŏl*——September)

기 차(*ki-ch'a*——train)

개 울(*kae-ul*——stream)

ㄴ(니은 ; *ni-ŭn* ; *n*)········ 누 나(*nu-na*——sister)

나 라(*na-ra*——country)

노 래(*no-rae*——song)

나 무(*na-mu*——tree)

노 인(*no-in*——old man)

ㄷ(디귿 ; *ti-gŭt* ; *t*,*d*)······ 도 시(*to-si*——city)

다 방(*ta-bang*——coffee shop)

다 리(*ta-ri*——bridge, legs)

대 학(*tae-hak*——college, university)

다 섯(*ta-sŏt*——five)

15

ㄹ(리을 ; *ri-ŭl* ; *r, l*) ········ 라디오(*ra-di-o*——radio)

리 듬(*ri-dŭm*——rhythm)

라일락(*ra-il-lak*——lilac)

렌 즈(*ren-jŭ*——lens)

루 비(*ru-bi*——ruby)

ㅁ(미음 ; *mi-ŭm* ; *m*) ······ 마 음(*ma-ŭm*——mind)

미 움(*mi-um*——hatred)

미 국(*mi-guk*——America)

모 험(*mo-hŏm*——adventure)

무 늬(*mu-nŭi*——pattern)

ㅂ(비읍 ; *pi-ŭp* ; *p, b*) ······ 보 리(*po-ri*——barley)

바 다(*pa-da*——sea)

밤 (*pam*——night)

부 인(*pu-in*——wife)

봄 (*pom*——spring)

ㅅ(시옷 ; *si-ot* ; *s, sh*) ······ 사 랑(*sa-rang*——love)

사 월(*sa-wŏl*——April)

시 민(*si-min*——citizen)

수 명(*su-myŏng*——longevity)

식 당(*sik-ttang*——restaurant)

ㅇ(이응 ; *i-ŭng* ; *ng*) ······ 아버지(*a-bŏ-ji*——father)

오 늘(*o-nŭl*——today)

오 후(*o-hu*——afternoon)

어머니(*ŏ-mŏ-ni*——mother)

유 월(*yu-wŏl*——June)

ㅈ(지읒 ; *chi-ŭt* ; *ch, j*) ······ 자동차(*cha-dong-ch'a*——automobile)

자 유(*cha-yu*——freedom)

조 심(*cho-sim*——caution)

주 먹(*chu-mŏk*——fist)

주전자(*chu-jŏn-ja*——kettle)

ㅊ(치읓 ; *ch'i-ŭt* ; *ch'*)··· 추 억(*ch'u-ŏk*——memory)

처 녀(*ch'ŏ-nyŏ*——virgin)

초록색(*ch'o-rok-ssaek*——green)

초가집(*ch'o-ga-jip*——thatched house)

추 석(*ch'u-sŏk*——Thanksgiving)

ㅋ(키읔 ; *k'i-ŭk* ; *k'*)······ 코끼리(*k'o-kki-ri*——elephant)

코 (*k'o*——nose)

키다리(*k'i-da-ri*——tall man)

쿠 폰(*k'u-p'on*——coupon)

큰 집(*k'ŭn-jip*——large house)

ㅌ(티읕 ; *t'i-ŭt* ; *t'*)········ 토 끼(*t'o-kki*——rabbit)

태평양(*t'ae-p'yŏng-yang*——the Pacific)

태 양(*t'ae-yang*——sun)

토 지(*t'o-ji*——land)

투 쟁(*t'u-jaeng*——struggle)

ㅍ(피읖 ; *p'i-ŭp* ; *p'*)······ 파 도(*p'a-do*——wave)

파 산(*p'a-san*——bankruptcy)

패 배(*p'ae-bae*——defeat)

포 도(*p'o-do*——grape)

포 로(*p'o-ro*——prisoner of war)

ㅎ(히읗 ; *hi-ŭng* ; *h*)······ 하 늘(*ha-nŭl*——sky)

하 인(*ha-in*——servant)

호 수(*ho-su*——lake)

호랑이(*ho-rang-i*——tiger)

호 텔(*ho-t'el*——hotel)

In forming words, the fourteen consonants have both initial and final positions. And except ㅇ(*i-ŭng*), ㅊ(*ch'i-ŭt*) and ㅋ(*k'i-ŭk*), other double consonants are made by combining the above basic symbols.

For example, the consonants, ㄱ, ㄴ, ㄷ, ㄹ, ㅁ, ㅂ, ㅅ, ㅈ, ㅌ, ㅍ, ㅎ can be combined as such double consonants ㄲ, ㄸ, ㅃ, ㅆ, ㅉ, ㄶ, ㄺ, ㄳ, ㄻ, ㄼ, ㄾ, ㄿ, ㅀ, ㅄ, and so forth.

ㄵ, ㄺ, ㅄ, ㄳ, and etc, are not used between vowels.

Except ㄲ, ㄸ, ㅃ, ㅆ, and ㅉ, all the double consonants take only the final position. But the double consonants ㄲ and ㅆ are used either initially or finally. The double consonants should be strictly distinguished from the single ones, because the two have quite different sounds.

ㄲ .... (쌍기역 ; *ssang-gi-yŏk* ; *kk*)

꼭두각시(*kkok-ttu-gak-ssi*——puppet)
꿈 (*kkum*——dream)
끼 다(*kki-da*——to insert)
낚 다(*nak-tta*——to catch)
밖 (*pak*——outside)

ㄸ .... (쌍디귿 ; *ssang-di-gŭt* ; *tt*)

딸 (*ttal*——daughter)
떡 (*ttŏk*——cake)
떨어지다(*ttŏ-rŏ-ji-da*——to drop)
뛰 다(*ttwi-da*——to run)
팔 뚝(*p' al-ttuk*——arm)

ㅃ .... (쌍비읍 ; *ssang-bi-ŭp* ; *pp*)

빠 지 다(*ppa-ji-da*——to drown)
빵 (*ppang*——bread)
뻐 꾸 기(*ppŏ-kku-gi*——cuckoo)
뽑 다(*ppop-tta*——to select, to pick)

ㅆ .... (쌍시옷 ; *ssang-si-ot* ; *ss*)

싸 움(*ssa-um*——fight)
썰 다(*ssŏl-da*——to slice)
쑥 (*ssuk*——mugwort)
있 다(*it-tta*——to be)

ㅉ ················· (쌍지읒 ; *ssang-ji-ŭt* ; *tch*)

ㅉ 개 다(*tcha-gae-da*──to divide)

ㅉ 집 기(*tcha-jip-kki*──spinning)

쫓 다(*tchot-tta*──to follow)

찐 빵(*tchin-ppang*──steamed bread)

철 쭉 꽃(*ch'ŏl-tchuk-kkot*──azalea)

ㄳ(*k*)····················· 몫 (*mok*──share)

삯 (*sak*──wage)

ㄵ(*n*)····················· 앉 다(*an-tta*──to sit)

얹 다(*ŏn-tta*──to put something on)

ㄶ(*n*)····················· 괜 찮 다(*kwaen-ch'an-t'a*──to be all right)

많 다(*man-t'a*──many)

ㄺ(*k*, *l*)················· 밝 다(*pak-tta*──to be bright)

붉 다(*puk-tta*──to be red)

맑 게(*mal-kke*──clear)

ㄻ(*m*)···················· 삶 다(*sam-tta*──to boil)

옮 기 다(*om-gi-da*──to move)

젊 다(*chŏm-tta*──to be young)

ㄼ(*l*, *p*)················· 얇 다(*yal-tta*──thin)

여 덟(*yŏ-dŏl*──eight)

짧 다(*tchal-tta*──short)

밟 다(*pap-tta*──step)

ㄽ(*l*)······················· 외 곬(*oe-gol*──single way)

ㄾ(*l*)······················· 핥 다(*hal-t'a*──to lick)

ㄿ(*p*)····················· 읊 다(*ŭp-tta*──to recte)

ㅀ(*l*)······················· 뚫 다(*ttul-t'a*──to punch)

싫 다(*sil-t'a*──to dislike)

옳 다(*ol-t'a*──right)

잃 다(*il-t'a*──to lose)

ㅄ(*p*)····················· 값 (*kap*──price)

19

PART I

Basic Expressions

I

1. I am···

Na-nŭn ···im-ni-da.
나는 ···입니다.

2. I am a boy.

Na-nŭn so-nyŏn-im-ni-da.
나는 소년입니다.

3. I am a teacher.

Na-nŭn sŏn-saeng-im-ni-da.
나는 선생입니다.

4. I am Kim Po-sung.

Na-nŭn kim-bo-sŏng-im-ni-da.
나는 김보성입니다.

5. I am 30 years old.

Na-nŭn sŏ-rŭn sal-im-ni-da.
나는 서른 살입니다.

6. I am Korean.

Na-nŭn han-guk ssa-ram-im-ni-da.
나는 한국 사람입니다.

7. I am young.

Na-nŭn chŏm-ssŭm-ni-da.
나는 젊습니다.

You

1. You are···

Tang-si-nŭn ···im-ni-da.
당신은 ···입니다.

2. You are a girl.

Tang-si-nŭn so-nyŏ-im-ni-da.
당신은 소녀입니다.

3. You are a soldier.

Tang-si-nŭn ku-nin-im-ni-da.
당신은 군인입니다.

---

1. *"chŏ-nŭn"* is politer than *"na-nŭn"* Both mean "I."
2. *"tang-sin"* and *"nŏ,"* *"kŭ nam-ja"* and *"kŭ sa-ram,"* and *"kŭ-nyŏ"* and *"kŭ yŏ-ja"* have the same meaning.

boy(*so-nyŏn*)···소년   girl(*so-nyŏ*)···소녀
teacher(*sŏn-saeng*)···선생   soldier(*ku-nin*)···군인
people(*sa-ram*)···사람   Korea(*han-guk*)···한국

4. You are American.	*Tang-si-nŭn mi-guk ssa-ram-im-ni-da.*
	당신은 미국 사람입니다.
5. You are my friend.	*Tang-si-nŭn na-ŭi ch'in-gu-im-ni-da.*
	당신은 나의 친구입니다.
6. You are old.	*Tang-si-nŭn nŭl-gŏt-ssŭm-ni-da.*
	당신은 늙었습니다.
7. You are right.	*Tang-si-ni ol-ssŭm-ni-da.*
	당신이 옳습니다.

He   *He*

1. He is···	*Kŭ-nŭn ···im-ni-da.*
	그는 ···입니다.
2. He is a professor.	*Kŭ-nŭn kyo-su-im-ni-da.*
	그는 교수입니다.
3. He is old.	*Kŭ-nŭn nŭl-gŏt-ssŭm-ni-da.*
	그는 늙었습니다.
4. He is my uncle.	*Kŭ-nŭn na-ŭi sam-ch'on-im-ni-da.*
	그는 나의 삼촌입니다.
5. He is a man.	*Kŭ-nŭn nam-ja-im-ni-da.*
	그는 남자입니다.
6. He is an actor.	*Kŭ-nŭn pae-u-im-ni-da.*
	그는 배우입니다.

---

3. When *"sip-ssi-o"* is added to the end of a verb, it indicates politeness. For example, *"ka-sip-ssi-o"* is politer than *"ka-si-o,"* and *"po-sip-ssi-o"* than *"po-si-o."*

America *(mi-guk)*···미국	England *(yŏng-guk)*···영국
friend *(ch'in-gu)*···친구	uncle *(a-jŏ-ssi)*···아저씨
professor *(kyo-su)*···교수	man *(nam-ja)*···남자

She

She

1. She is···

Kŭ-nyŏ-nŭn ···im-ni-da.
그녀는 ···입니다.

2. She is a nurse.

Kŭ-nyŏ-nŭn kan-ho-sa-im-ni-da.
그녀는 간호사입니다.

3. She is pretty.

Kŭ-nyŏ-nŭn ye-ppŭm-ni-da.
그녀는 예쁩니다.

4. She is my mother.

Kŭ-nyŏ-nŭn na-ŭi ŏ-mŏ-ni-im-ni-da.
그녀는 나의 어머니입니다.

5. She is a woman.

Kŭ-nyŏ-nŭn yŏ-ja-im-ni-da.
그녀는 여자입니다.

6. She is polite.

Kŭ-nyŏ-nŭn yam-jŏn-ham-ni-da.
그녀는 얌전합니다.

It

It

1. It is···

Kŭ-gŏ-sŭn ···im-ni-da.
그것은 ···입니다.

2. It is a pencil.

Kŭ-gŏ-sŭn yŏn-p'il-im-ni-da.
그것은 연필입니다.

3. It is big.

Kŭ-gŏ-sŭn k'ŭm-ni-da.
그것은 큽니다.

4. It is expensive.

Kŭ-gŏ-sŭn pi-ssam-ni-da.
그것은 비쌉니다.

---

4. Grown-ups call their mothers "*ŏ-mŏ-ni*," but children say "*ŏm-ma*."
5. In the Korean language, there is no clear distinction in the expression of singularity and plurality.

nurse (*kan-ho-sa*)···간호사
pretty (*ye-ppŭn*)···예쁜
auntie (*a-ju-mŏ-ni*)···아주머니
woman (*yŏ-ja*)···여자
expensive (*pi-ssan*)···비싼

father (*a-bŏ-ji*)···아버지
mother (*ŏ-mŏ-ni*)···어머니
pencil (*yŏn-p'il*)···연필
big (*k'ŭn*)···큰

25

5. It is my book.   *Kŭ-gŏ-sŭn na-ŭi ch'aek-im-ni-da.*
그것은 나의 책입니다.

6. It is wonderful.   *Hul-ryung-ham-ni-da.*
훌륭합니다.

7. It is rainy.   *Pi-ga om-ni-da.*
비가 옵니다.

8. It is dark.   *Ŏ-dup-ssŭm-ni-da.*
어둡습니다.

9. It is ten o'clock.   *Yŏl-ssi-im-ni-da.*
열시입니다.

10. It is too short.   *Nŏ-mu tchal-ssŭm-ni-da.*
너무 짧습니다.

They   *They*

1. They are…   *Kŭ-dŭ-rŭn …im-ni-da.*
그들은 …입니다.

2. They are children.   *Kŭ-dŭ-rŭn a-i-dŭl-im-ni-da.*
그들은 아이들입니다.

3. They are students.   *Kŭ-dŭ-rŭn hak-ssaeng-dŭl-im-ni-da.*
그들은 학생들입니다.

4. They are scholars.   *Kŭ-dŭ-rŭn hak-tcha-im-ni-da.*
그들은 학자입니다.

---

6. Usage of "my" and "our" is frequently confused. For example, Koreans say "our father" for "my father," and "our house" for "my house."

7. Both "*yŏ-gĭ*" and "*i-n*" mean "here," and "*kŏ-gĭ*" and "*kŭ ko-se*" mean "there".

book(*ch'aek*)…책
short(*tchal-tta*)…짧다
children(*a-i-dŭl*)…아이들
student(*hak-ssaeng*)…학생
animal(*tong-mul*)…동물
wonderful(*hul-lyung-han*)…훌륭한

rainy(*pi-ga nae-ri-nŭn*)…비가 내리는
cloudy(*hŭ-rin*)…흐린
dark(*ŏ-dup-tta*)…어둡다
light(*pak-tta*)…밝다

26

5. They are my pupils. *Kŭ-dŭ-rŭn na-ŭi hak-ssaeng-dŭl-im-ni-da.*
그들은 나의 학생들입니다.

6. They are my friends. *Kŭ-dŭ-rŭn na-ŭi ch'in-gu-im-ni-da.*
그들은 나의 친구입니다.

7. They are rich. *Kŭ-dŭ-rŭn pu-ja-im-ni-da.*
그들은 부자입니다.

This / *This*

1. This is··· *I-gŏ-sŭn ···im-ni-da.*
이것은 ···입니다.

2. This is my house. *I-gŏ-sŭn u-ri chip-im-ni-da.*
이것은 우리 집입니다.

3. This is a lily. *I-gŏ-sŭn pae-k'ap-kko-ch'im-ni-da.*
이것은 백합꽃입니다.

4. This is my wallet. *I-gŏ-sŭn na-ŭi chi-gap-im-ni-da.*
이것은 나의 지갑입니다.

5. This is your hat. *I-gŏ-sŭn tang-sin mo-ja-im-ni-da.*
이것은 당신 모자입니다.

6. These are ants. *I-gŏ-sŭn Kae-mi-im-ni-da.*
이것은 개미입니다.

7. These are flowers. *I-gŏ-sŭn kko-ch'im-ni-da.*
이것은 꽃입니다.

That / *That*

1. That is··· *Chŏ-gŏ-sŭn ···im-ni-da.*
저것은 ···입니다.

---

pupil(*hak-ssaeng*)···학생
house(*chip*)···집
notebook(*su-ch'ŏp*)···수첩
purse(*chi-gap*)···지갑

attenging school(*t'ong-hak*)···통학
rich(*pu-ja*)···부자
hat(*mo-ja*)···모자

2. That is my umbrella.	*Chŏ-gŏ-sŭn na-ŭi u-san-im-ni-da.* 저것은 나의 우산입니다.
3. That is Mt. Namsan.	*Chŏ-gŏ-sŭn nam-san-im-ni-da.* 저것은 남산입니다.
4. That is wonderful.	*A-ju hul-lyung-ham-ni-da.* 아주 훌륭합니다.
5. That is the Chosun Hotel.	*Chŏ-gŏ-sŭn cho-sŏn ho-t'el-im-ni-da.* 저것은 조선 호텔입니다.
6. That is Han river.	*Chŏ-gŏ-sŭn han-gang-im-ni-da.* 저것은 한강입니다.
7. Those are flies.	*Chŏ-gŏt-ttŭ-rŭn p'a-ri-im-ni-da.* 저것들은 파리입니다.

Here

Here

1. Here is…	*Yŏ-gi …it-ssŭm-ni-da.* 여기 …있습니다.
2. Here is your dictionary.	*Yŏ-gi tang-sin sa-jŏ-ni it-ssŭm-ni-da.* 여기 당신 사전이 있습니다.
3. Here is your name.	*Yŏ-gi tang-sin i-rŭ-mi it-ssŭm-ni-da.* 여기 당신 이름이 있습니다.
4. Come here.	*I-ri o-se-yo.* 이리 오세요.
5. It is 20 miles from here to Suwon.	*Yŏ-gi-sŏ su-wŏn-kka-ji-nŭn i-sim ma-il-im-ni-da.* 여기서 수원까지는 이십 마일입니다.

---

umbrella(*u-san*)…우산
rainwater(*pin-mul*)…빗물
dictionary(*sa-jŏn*)…사전
name(*i-rŭm*)…이름

come(*o-da*)…오다
here(*i kot*)…이 곳
mile(*ma-il*)…마일

28

6. Here is the place.

Yŏ-gi-ga kŭ ko-sim-ni-da.
여기가 그 곳입니다.

7. Here is my house.

Yŏ-gi na-ŭi chi-bi it-ssŭm-ni-da.
여기 나의 집이 있습니다.

8. Here we go.

Kap-ssi-da.
갑시다.

There

There

1. There is…

Kŏ-gi …it-ssŭm-ni-da.
거기 …있습니다.

2. There is my car.

Kŏ-gi na-ŭi ch'a-ga it-ssŭm-ni-da.
거기 나의 차가 있습니다.

3. There is a famous temple.

Kŭ ko-se yu-myŏng-han chŏ-ri it-ssŭm-ni-da.
그 곳에 유명한 절이 있습니다.

4. Look over there.

Chŏ-tcho-gŭl pa-ra po-a-ra.
저쪽을 바라 보아라.

5. I will be there soon.

Kot kŭ ko-se ka-get-ssŭm-ni-da.
곧 그 곳에 가겠습니다.

6. There are many people.

Kŭ ko-se sa-ram-dŭ-ri man-ssŭm-ni-da.
그 곳에 사람들이 많습니다.

7. There are students in the classroom.

Kyo-si-re-nŭn hak-ssaeng-dŭ-ri it-ssŭm-ni-da.
교실에는 학생들이 있습니다.

---

car(*ch'a*)…차
place(*chang-so*)…장소
tower(*t'ap*)…탑
go(*ka-da*)…가다

famous(*yu-myŏng-han*)…유명한
church(*kyo-hoe*)…교회
temple(*chŏl*)…절
look(*po-da*)…보다

Mr. , Miss, Mrs.	*Mr. , Miss, Mrs.*

1. Mr. Kim.

Kim kun

김 군.

2. Miss Park.

Pak yang.

박 양.

3. Mrs. Ahn.

An yŏ-sa.

안 여사.

4. Kim is a high school boy.

Kim ku-nŭn ko-dŭng hak-kkyo hak-ssaeng-im-ni-da.

김 군은 고등 학교 학생입니다.

5. Miss Park is a secretary.

Pak yang-ŭn pi-sŏ-im-ni-da.

박 양은 비서입니다.

6. Mrs. Ahn is a wife of professor Lee.

An yŏ-sa-nŭn i kyo-su-ŭi pu-in-im-ni-da.

안 여사는 이 교수의 부인입니다.

7. Mr. Park is a son of Mrs. Kim.

Pak kku-nŭn kim yŏ-sa-ŭi a-dŭl-im-ni-da.

박 군은 김 여사의 아들입니다.

8. Miss Kim is a daughter of Prof. Kim.

Kim yang-ŭn kim kyo-su-ŭi ttal-im-ni-da.

김 양은 김 교수의 딸입니다.

---

8. "Mr." and "Miss" in English are also used by Koreans with the same pronunciation.

classroom(*kyo-sil*) ⋯교실
middle school boy(*chung-hak-ssaeng*) ⋯중학생
Mr.(*mi-sŭ-t'ŏ*) ⋯미스터
Miss(*mi-ssŭ*) ⋯미쓰
Mrs.(*mi-ssi-jŭ*) ⋯미씨즈

high school boy(*ko-dŭng hak-ssaeng*) ⋯고등 학생
wife(*pu-in*) ⋯부인
secretary(*pi-sŏ*) ⋯비서
son(*a-dŭl*) ⋯아들
daughter(*ttal*) ⋯딸

Who

1. Who ?

2. Who are you ?

3. Who is she ?

4. She is my daughter.

Who

Nu-gu ?
누구 ?

Tang-si-nŭn nu-gu-im-ni-kka ?
당신은 누구입니까 ?

Kŭ-nyŏ-nŭn nu-gu-im-ni-kka ?
그녀는 누구입니까 ?

Kŭ a-i-nŭn na-ŭi ttal-im-ni-da.
그 아이는 나의 딸입니다.

Whom

1. Whom ?

2. For Whom did you buy it ?

3. Whom do you like best ?

4. I like Miss Kim best.

5. To whom did you give it ?

Whom

Nu-gu-rŭl ?
누구를 ?

Nu-gu-rŭl wi-hae tang-si-nŭn kŭ-gŏ-sŭl sat-ssŭm-ni-kka ?
누구를 위해 당신은 그것을 샀습니까 ?

Nu-gu-rŭl tang-si-nŭn ka-jang cho-a-ham-ni-kka ?
누구를 당신은 가장 좋아합니까 ?

Na-nŭn kim yang-ŭl ka-jang cho-a-ham-ni-da.
나는 김 양을 가장 좋아합니다.

Nu-gu-e-ge kŭ-gŏ-sŭl chu-ŏt-ssŭm-ni-kka ?
누구에게 그것을 주었습니까 ?

---

9. When "*kka?*" is added at the end of a verb, it becomes interrogative.
   For example ; "*kam-ni-kka?*"(Do you go ?), "*pom-ni-kka?*"(Do you see ?)
   buy(*sa-da*)…사다   toll(*ul-li-da*)…울리다
   like(*cho-a-ha-da*)…좋아하다   lowest(*ch'oe-jŏ*)…최저
   best(*ch'oe-go*)…최고

6. For whom the bell to-
lls ?

*Nu-gu-rŭl wi-ha-yŏ chong-ŭn ul-li-
na ?*
누구를 위하여 종은 울리나 ?

Whose

1. Whose ?

Whose

Nu-gu-ŭi ?
누구의 ?

2. Whose article ?

Nu-gu-ŭi ki-sa-ji ?
누구의 기사지 ?

3. Whose magazine is
this ?

*I-gŏ-sŭn nu-gu-ŭi chap-tchi-ch'aek-
im-ni-kka ?*
이것은 누구의 잡지책입니까 ?

4. That is my magazine.

*Kŭ-gŏ-sŭn na-ŭi chap-tchi-ch'aek-im-
ni-da.*
그것은 나의 잡지책입니다.

5. Whose pencil is this ?

*I-gŏ-sŭn nu-gu-ŭi yŏn-p'il-im-ni-
kka ?*
이것은 누구의 연필입니까 ?

6. Whose picture do you
like best ?

*Nu-gu-ŭi kŭ-ri-mŭl ka-jang cho-a-
ha-sim-ni-kka ?*
누구의 그림을 가장 좋아하십니
까 ?

Which

1. Which ?

Which

Ŏ-nŭ kŏt ?
어느 것 ?

---

article(*ki-sa*)…기사
magazine(*chap-tchi*)…잡지
picture-book(*kŭ-rim-ch'aek*)…그림책

bell(*chong*)…종
hue(*saek-ch'ae*)…색채

2. Which is the best?   *Ŏ-nŭ kŏ-si ka-jang chot-ssŭm-ni-kka?*

어느 것이 가장 좋습니까?

3. Which way will you go?   *Tang-si-nŭn ŏ-nŭ kil-lo ka-si-get-ssŭm-ni-kka?*

당신은 어느 길로 가시겠습니까?

4. I will go this way.   *Na-nŭn i kil-lo ka-get-ssŭm-ni-da.*

나는 이 길로 가겠습니다.

5. Which is yours?   *Ŏ-nŭ kŏ-si tang-si-nŭi kŏ-sim-ni-kka?*

어느 것이 당신의 것입니까?

6. Which do you like best?   *Ŏ-nŭ kŏ-sŭl ka-jang cho-a-ha-sim-ni-kka?*

어느 것을 가장 좋아하십니까?

What

What

1. What?   *Mu-ŏt?*

무엇?

2. What is your name?   *Tang-si-nŭi i-rŭ-mŭn mu-ŏ-sim-ni-kka?*

당신의 이름은 무엇입니까?

3. What is the name of this street?   *I ki-rŭi i-rŭ-mŭn mu-ŏ-sim-ni-kka?*

이 길의 이름은 무엇입니까?

4. What do you do?   *Tang-si-nŭn mu-ŏ-sŭl ham-ni-kka?*

당신은 무엇을 합니까?

5. I am a colleage student.   *Na-nŭn tae-hak-ssaeng-im-ni-da.*

나는 대학생입니다.

---

villa(*pyŏl-tchang*)…별장
college student(*tae-hak-ssaeng*)…대학생

shorter road(*chi-rŭm-kkil*)…지름길
way(*kil*)…길

6. What shall I do ?   *Ŏ-ttŏ-k'e ha-myŏn cho-ŭl-kka-yo ?*
어떻게 하면 좋을까요 ?

7. What do you mean by that ?   *Mu-sŭn ttŭ-sim-ni-kka ?*
무슨 뜻입니까 ?

Where   *Where*

1. Where ?   *Ŏ-di ?*
어디 ?

2. Where is your home ?   *Tang-si-nŭi chi-bŭn ŏ-di im-ni-kka ?*
당신의 집은 어디 입니까 ?

3. Where is Mt. Halla ?   *Hal-la-sa-nŭn ŏ-di it-ssŭm-ni-kka ?*
한라산은 어디 있습니까 ?

4. Where are you going ?   *Tang-si-nŭn ŏ-di-rŭl ka-sim-ni-kka ?*
당신은 어디를 가십니까 ?

5. Where do you come from ?   *Ko-hyang-i ŏ-di im-ni-kka ?*
고향이 어디 입니까 ?

6. That's where it is.   *Kŭ-gŏ-si pa-ro chŏ-gi-e it-ssŭm-ni-da.*
그것이 바로 저기에 있습니다.

7. Where do you live ?   *Ŏ-di sa-sim-ni-kka ?*
어디 사십니까 ?

When   *When*

1. When ?   *Ŏn-je ?*
언제 ?

2. When can you come ?   *Tang-si-nŭn ŏn-je o-sil ssu it-ssŭm-ni-kka ?*
당신은 언제 오실 수 있습니까 ?

---

live(*sal-da*)…살다   question(*chil-mun*)…질문
mean(*ttŭt-t'a-da*)…뜻하다   street(*kil*)…길

3. When is your birthday?

Tang-si-nǔi saeng-i-rǔn ǒn-je-im-ni-kka?

당신의 생일은 언제입니까?

4. When did the Korean War break out?

Han-guk chǒn-jaeng-ǔn ǒn-je nat-ssǔm-ni-kka?

한국 전쟁은 언제 났습니까?

5. Till when?

Ǒn-je-kka-ji?

언제까지?

6. When can you stay until?

Ǒn-je-kka-ji mǒ-mul-get-ssǔm-ni-kka?

언제까지 머물겠습니까?

7. It is cold when it snows.

Nu-ni nae-ri-myǒn ch'up-ssǔm-ni-da.

눈이 내리면 춥습니다.

8. I'll go when I've had dinner.

Sik-ssa-rǔl kkǔn-nae-go ka-get-ssǔm-ni-da.

식사를 끝내고 가겠습니다.

How

How

1. How?

Ǒl-ma-na?

얼마나?

2. How much?

Ǒl-ma-im-ni-kka?

얼마입니까?

3. How far?

Ǒl-ma-na mǒm-ni-kka?

얼마나 멉니까?

4. How old are you?

Myǒt ssal-im-ni-kka?

몇 살입니까?

---

birthday(*saeng-il*)…생일
war(*chǒn-jaeng*)…전쟁
invitation(*ch'o-dae*)…초대
powder(*ka-ru*)…가루
far(*mǒl-li*)…멀리

stay(*mǒ-mul-da*)…머물다
cold(*ch'u-un*)…추운
snow(*nun*)…눈
dinner(*sik-ssa*)…식사
break(*pu-su-da*)…부수다

5. How is she now?　　　*Kŭ-nyŏ-nŭn chi-gŭm ŏ-ttŏt-ssŭm-ni-*
　　　　　　　　　　　　　　　kka?
　　　　　　　　　　　　그녀는 지금 어떻습니까?

6. How well does she　*Kŭ-nyŏ-nŭn ŏl-ma-na no-rae-rŭl chal*
　sing?　　　　　　　　　　　*pu-rŭm-ni-kka?*
　　　　　　　　　　　　그녀는 얼마나 노래를 잘 부릅니
　　　　　　　　　　　　까?

7. How long?　　　　　*Ŏl-ma-na o-rae toe-ŏt-ssŭm-ni-kka?*
　　　　　　　　　　　　얼마나 오래 되었습니까?

8. How do you mean?　*Mu-sŭn ttŭ-sŭ-ro kŭ-rŏ-k'e mal-*
　　　　　　　　　　　　　　ssŭm-ha-sim-ni-kka?
　　　　　　　　　　　　무슨 뜻으로 그렇게 말씀하십니
　　　　　　　　　　　　까?

9. How do you like Ko-　*Han-gu-gŭn ŏ-ttŏt-ssŭm-ni-kka?*
　rea?　　　　　　　　　　한국은 어떻습니까?

10. How beautiful!　　　*Ch'am a-rŭm-dap-ssŭm-ni-da!*
　　　　　　　　　　　　참 아름답습니다!

Why　　　　　　　　　*Why*

1. Why?　　　　　　　　*Ŏ-tchae-sŏ? Wae?*
　　　　　　　　　　　　어째서?　　왜?

2. Why not?　　　　　　*Ŏ-tchae-sŏ kŭ-rŏ-ch'i a-nŭn-ga?*
　　　　　　　　　　　　어째서 그렇지 않은가?

3. Why do birds sing?　*Sae-dŭ-rŭn wae no-rae-ham-ni-kka?*
　　　　　　　　　　　　새들은 왜 노래합니까?

---

old(*nŭl-gŭn*) … 늙은　　　　　long(*o-rae*) … 오래
sing(*no-rae-ha-da*) … 노래하다　beautiful(*a-rŭm-da-un*) … 아름다운
well(*chal*) … 잘　　　　　　　fire(*pul*) … 불
hear(*tŭt-tta*) … 듣다　　　　　burn(*t'a-da*) … 타다
noise(*so-ri*) … 소리

4. I don't know why you are here.

Na-nŭn tang-si-ni wae yŏ-gi in-nŭn-ji-rŭl mo-rŭ-get-tta.

나는 당신이 왜 여기 있는지를 모르겠다.

5. This is why I came here.

I-gŏ-si nae-ga yŏ-gi on i-yu-im-ni-da.

이것이 내가 여기 온 이유입니다.

6. Why don't you go there?

Wae kŭ ko-se ka-ji an-ssŭm-ni-kka?

왜 그 곳에 가지 않습니까?

7. Why not speak to him about it?

Kŭ-gŏ-se tae-hae-sŏ wae kŭ-e-ge mal-ha-ji an-ssŭm-ni-kka?

그것에 대해서 왜 그에게 말하지 않습니까?

Can

1. Can.

···Hal ssu it-tta.

···할 수 있다.

2. Can I help you?

Nae-ga tang-si-nŭl to-ul ssu it-ssŭm-ni-kka?

내가 당신을 도울 수 있습니까?

3. Can I go there?

Nae-ga kŏ-gi-e kal ssu it-ssŭm-ni-kka?

내가 거기에 갈 수 있습니까?

4. I can speak Korean.

Na-nŭn han-gung-ma-rŭl hal ssu it-ssŭm-ni-da.

나는 한국말을 할 수 있습니다.

---

speak(*mal-ha-da*)···말하다
help(*top-tta*)···돕다

tomorrow(*nae-il*)···내일

5. Can I see you tomorrow?

Na-nŭn nae-il tang-si-nŭl man-nal ssu it-ssŭm-ni-kka?

나는 내일 당신을 만날 수 있습니까?

6. Can you hear that noise?

Chŏ so-ri-ga tŭl-lim-ni-kka?

저 소리가 들립니까?

7. Can you play the piano?

P'i-a-no-rŭl ch'il ssu it-ssŭm-ni-kka?

피아노를 칠 수 있습니까?

May

May

1. May.

…Hae-do cho-t'a.

…해도 좋다.

2. May I ask you?

Na-nŭn tang-si-ne-ge mu-rŏ-bwa-do chot-ssŭm-ni-kka?

나는 당신에게 물어봐도 좋습니까?

3. May I do this?

Na-nŭn i-gŏ-sŭl hae-do chot-ssŭm-ni-kka?

나는 이것을 해도 좋습니까?

4. You may smoke here.

Tang-si-nŭn i ko-se-sŏ tam-bae-rŭl p'i-wŏ-do cho-t'a.

당신은 이 곳에서 담배를 피워도 좋다.

5. You may go home.

Nŏ-nŭn chi-be ka-do cho-t'a.

너는 집에 가도 좋다.

6. It may be true.

A-ma sa-si-ril kkŏ-sim-ni-da.

아마 사실일 것입니다.

---

see(*po-da*)…보다
play(*nol-da*)…놀다
smoke(*tam-bae p'i-u-da*)…담배 피우

다
true(*sa-si-rŭi, chin-si-rŭi*)…사실의, 진실의

7. I hope he may succeed.

Kŭ-ga sŏng-gong-ha-gi-rŭl pim-ni-da.

그가 성공하기를 빕니다.

If

If

1. If···

Ma-nya-ge···.

만약에···.

2. If you wish,

Ma-nya-ge tang-si-ni pa-ran-da-myŏn,

만약에 당신이 바란다면,

3. If I fail,

Ma-nya-ge nae-ga sil-p'ae-han-da-myŏn,

만약에 내가 실패한다면,

4. If I only know,

Ma-nya-ge nae-ga al-gi-man haet-tta-myŏn,

만약에 내가 알기만 했다면,

5. There are too many 'ifs' in his speech.

Kŭ-ŭi mal sso-ge-nŭn nŏ-mu ma-ni ma-nya-ge-ga it-tta.

그의 말 속에는 너무 많이 만약에가 있다.

6. If he comes, I will tell him.

Kŭ-ga o-myŏn i-ya-gi ha-get-ssŭm-ni-da.

그가 오면 이야기 하겠습니다.

7. If in doubt, I ask.

Ŭi-mu-ni na-myŏn na-nŭn mut-ssŭm-ni-da.

의문이 나면 나는 묻습니다.

---

hope(*pil-da*)···빌다
success(*sŏng-gong*)···성공
wish(*pa-ra-da*)···바라다
fail(*sil-p'ae-ha-da*)···실패하다

speech(*mal*)···말
feel(*nŭ-kki-da*)···느끼다

advise(*ch'ung-go*)···충고

8. If this should be true, that will be wrong.

Ma-nil i-gŏ-si sa-si-ri-ra-myŏn kŭ-gŏ-si t'ŭl-lun-ni-da.

만일 이것이 사실이라면 그것이 틀립니다.

Because

Because

1. Because,

··· *TTae-mu-ne,*

··· 때문에,

2. Because I love you,

Na-nŭn tang-si-nŭl sa-rang-ha-gi ttae-mu-ne,

나는 당신을 사랑하기 때문에,

3. I can't go because I'm busy.

Na-nŭn pa-ppŭ-gi ttae-mu-ne kal ssu-ga ŏp-tta.

나는 바쁘기 때문에 갈 수가 없다.

4. Because you are young,

Nŏ-nŭn chŏm-kki ttae-mu-ne,

너는 젊기 때문에,

5. I didn't go out because of the rain.

Pi ttae-mu-ne na-nŭn pak-kke na-ga-ji a-nat-tta.

비 때문에 나는 밖에 나가지 않았다.

6. You should not despise a man because he is poor.

Ka-nan-ha-da-go hae-sŏ sa-ra-mŭl ŏp-ssin-yŏ-gyŏ-sŏ-nŭn an-doem-ni-da.

가난하다고 해서 사람을 업신여겨서는 안됩니다.

---

despise(*ŏp-ssin-yŏ-gi-da*)···업신여기다
young(*chŏl-mŭn*)···젊은
rain(*pi*)···비

wrong(*t'ŭl-lin*)···틀린
poor(*ka-nan-han*)···가난한

A few, Few

A few, Few	*A few, Few*
1. A few,	*Myŏt kkae-ŭi,* 몇 개의,
2. In a few days,	*Myŏ-ch'il a-ne,* 며칠 안에,
3. Only a few people,	*Tan-ji myŏn myŏng-ŭi sa-ram,* 단지 몇 명의 사람,
4. He has a few frends.	*Kŭ-nŭn myŏt sa-ra-mŭi ch'in-gu-ga* *it-tta(ka-ji-go it-tta).* 그는 몇 사람의 친구가 있다(가지고 있다).
5. few,	*Kŏ-ŭi ŏm-nŭn,* 거의 없는,
6. few people,	*Myŏt sa-ram-do ŏm-nŭn,* 몇 사람도 없는,
7. A man of few words,	*Kŏ-ŭi ma-ri ŏm-nŭn sa-ram,* 거의 말이 없는 사람,
8. She has few friends.	*Kŭ-nyŏ-nŭn kŏ-ŭi ch'in-gu-ga ŏp-tta* *(ka-ji-go it-tchi an-t'a).* 그녀는 거의 친구가 없다(가지고 있지 않다).
9. He is a man of few wo-rds.	*Kŭ-nŭn kŏ-ŭi ma-ri ŏm-nŭn sa-ram-* *im-ni-da.* 그는 거의 말이 없는 사람입니다.
10. Give me a few pencils.	*Yŏn-p'il myŏt kkae chu-sip-ssi-o.* 연필 몇 개 주십시오.

A little, Little

A little, Little	*A little, Little*
1. Little,	*Cha-gŭn, Cho-gŭm,*

---

few(*myŏt kkae-ŭi*)…몇 개의   word(*mal*)…말

2. A little drop of water,

작은, 조금,
Mu-rūi cho-gūm,
물의 조금,

3. A little girl,

Cha-gŭn so-nyŏ,
작은 소녀,

4. There is a little hope.

Yak-kka-nŭi hŭi-mang-ŭn it-tta.
약간의 희망은 있다.

5. Give me a little mutton.

Yang-go-gi-rŭl cho-gŭm chu-sip-ssi-o.
양고기를 조금 주십시오.

6. I hardly know.

Na-nŭn kŏ-ŭi mo-rŭn-da.
나는 거의 모른다.

7. He has very little sense.

Kŭ-nŭn kŏ-ŭi chi-ga-gi ŏp-tta.
그는 거의 지각이 없다.

8. May I have a little bit of money?

Ton chom chu-si-ryŏm-ni-kka?
돈 좀 주시렵니까?

9. Wait a little.

Cham-kkan-man ki-da-ri-sip-ssi-o.
잠깐만 기다리십시오.

10. I have but little money.

To-ni cho-gŭm-bak-kke ŏp-ssŭm-ni-da.
돈이 조금밖에 없습니다.

11. Little things amuse little mind.

Chŏ-nŭn ha-ch'a-nŭn i-re hŭng-mi-rŭl nŭ-kkim-ni-da.
저는 하찮은 일에 흥미를 느낍니다.

---

hope(*hi-mang*)…희망
interest(*hŭng-mi*)…흥미
mutton(*yang-go-gi*)…양고기
sense(*chi-gak*)…지각
many(*ma-ni*)…많이
abundance(*p'ung-bu*)…풍부

wait(*ki-da-ri-da*)…기다리다
amusement(*chŭl-gŏ-um*)…즐거움
mind(*ma-ŭm*)…마음
money(*ton*)…돈
busy(*pa-ppŭn*)…바쁜

Much	**Much**
1. Much,	*Ma-ni,* 많이,
2. How much,	*Ŏl-ma-na ma-ni, (ŏl-ma-im-ni-kka ?)* 얼마나 많이, (얼마입니까?)
3. Much water.	*Ma-nŭn mul.* 많은 물.
4. I don't drink much wine.	*Na-nŭn su-rŭl ma-ni ma-si-ji an-nŭn-da.* 나는 술을 많이 마시지 않는다.
5. I do not see much of him.	*Na-nŭn kŭ-rŭl pyŏl-lo man-na-ji an-nŭn-da.* 나는 그를 별로 만나지 않는다.
6. He is not so much a scholar as a writer.	*Kŭ-nŭn hak-tcha-ra-gi-bo-da-nŭn, o-hi-ryŏ chak-kka-im-ni-da.* 그는 학자라기보다는, 오히려 작가입니다.
7. You work too much.	*Tang-si-nŭn nŏ-mu i-rŭl ha-sim-ni-da.* 당신은 너무 일을 하십니다.
8. This is much better of the two.	*I-tcho-gi hwŏl-ssin chot-ssŭm-ni-da.* 이쪽이 훨씬 좋습니다.
9. I thought as much.	*Saeng-ga-k'an tae-ro-im-ni-da.* 생각한 대로입니다.
10. It is too much.	*Nŏ-mu man-ssŭm-ni-da.* 너무 많습니다.

---

10. There is little difference between "much" and "many," in the Korean language.

much(*ma-ni*)···많이   scholar(*hak-tcha*)···학자

Many

1. Many,

   Ma-ni,

   많이,

2. How many,

   Ŏl-ma-na ma-ni,

   얼마나 많이,

3. Many planes,

   Ma-nŭn pi-haeng-gi,

   많은 비행기,

4. There are many children in the playground.

   Un-dong-jang-e-nŭn ma-nŭn a-i-dŭ-ri it-ssŭm-ni-da.

   운동장에는 많은 아이들이 있습니다.

5. Many people think so.

   Kŭ-rŏ-k'e saeng-ga-k'a-nŭn sa-ram-dŭ-ri man-ssŭm-ni-da.

   그렇게 생각하는 사람들이 많습니다.

6. How many students are there in the classroom?

   Kyo-si-re-nŭn hak-ssaeng-dŭ-ri myŏn myŏng-i-na it-ssŭm-ni-kka?

   교실에는 학생들이 몇 명이나 있습니까?

7. How many times do you go there?

   Myŏt ppŏ-ni-na kŭ ko-se kat-ssŭm-ni-kka?

   몇 번이나 그 곳에 갔습니까?

8. Many of us were tired.

   Tae-da-su-ŭi u-ri-dŭ-rŭn p'i-ro-haet-ssŭm-ni-da.

   대다수의 우리들은 피로했습니다.

Than

1. Than,

   …Po-da,

---

scholarship(*hak-ssik*)…학식
plane(*pi-haeng-gi*)…비행기
think(*saeng-ga-k'a-da*)…생각하다

playground(*un-dong-jang*)…운동장
landing(*ch'ang-nyuk*)…착륙
tire(*p'i-ro-han*)…피로한

2. More than,
…보다,
…*Po-da ma-nŭn,*
…보다 많은,

3. Less than,
…*Po-da chŏ-gŭn,*
…보다 적은,

4. I am older than you.
Na-nŭn tang-sin-bo-da na-i-ga man-ssŭm-ni-da.
나는 당신보다 나이가 많습니다.

5. I am taller than you.
Na-nŭn tang-sin-bo-da k'i-ga k'ŭm-ni-da.
나는 당신보다 키가 큽니다.

6. I love Miss Kim more than Miss Lee.
Na-nŭn i yang-bo-da kim yang-ŭl tŏ sa-rang-ham-ni-da.
나는 이 양보다 김 양을 더 사랑합니다.

7. I know you better than him.
Kŭ-bo-da-nŭn nae-ga tang-si-nŭl tŏ chal am-ni-da.
그보다는 내가 당신을 더 잘 압니다.

8. He is no happier than before.
Kŭ-nŭn chŏn-bo-da cho-gŭm-do haeng-bo-k'a-ji an-ssŭm-ni-da.
그는 전보다 조금도 행복하지 않습니다.

9. I am wiser than to believe that.
Na-nŭn kŭ-gŏ-sŭl mi-dŭl man-k'ŭm pa-bo-nŭn a-nim-ni-da.
나는 그것을 믿을 만큼 바보는 아닙니다.

---

easy(*swi-un*)…쉬운
action(*hwal-ttong*)…활동
happy(*haeng-bo-k'an*)…행복한

than(*po-da*)…～보다
jolly(*yu-k'wae-han*)…유쾌한
matter(*mun-je*)…문제

10. I have no other friends beside you.

*Tang-sin-bak-kke-nŭn   ch'in-gu-ga
öp-ssŭm-ni-da.*

당신밖에는 친구가 없습니다.

Very

Very

1. Very,

Mae-u,

매우

2. Very good,

Mae-u chot-ssŭm-ni-da.

매우 좋습니다.

3. Very much,

Mae-u ma-ni,

매우 많이,

4. Thank you very much.

Mae-u kam-sa-ham-ni-da.

매우 감사합니다.

5. Do your very best.

Ch'oe-sŏ-nŭl ta-ha-sip-ssi-o.

최선을 다하십시오.

6. That's a very easy matter for me.

*Kŭ-gŏ-sŭn mae-u swi-un mun-je-im-
ni-da.*

그것은 매우 쉬운 문제입니다.

7. He is the very picture of his father.

*Kŭ-nŭn a-bŏ-ji-rŭl kkok tal-mat-
ssŭm-ni-da.*

그는 아버지를 꼭 닮았습니다.

8. The very idea of it is disgusting.

*Kŭ-gŏ-sŭn saeng-gang-man hae-do
ki-bu-ni na-ppŭm-ni-da.*

그것은 생각만 해도 기분이 나쁩
니다.

9. I was very pleased.

Tae-dan-hi ki-ppŏt-ssŭm-ni-da.

대단히 기뻤습니다.

10. It is the very last thing

Kŭ-gŏ-sŭn chŏn-hyŏ ttŭt-ppa-kkŭi i-

---

before(*chŏ-ne*)…전에
believe(*mit-tta*)…믿다

idea(*saeng-gak*)…생각
disgusting(*pul-k'wae-han*)…불쾌한

I expected.	*ri-yŏt-ssŭm-ni-da.*
	그것은 전혀 뜻밖의 일이었습니다.

Be

Be

1. Be.	*···I-da.*
	···이다.
2. I am a reporter.	*Na-nŭn ki-ja-im-ni-da.*
	나는 기자입니다.
3. You are a soldier.	*Tang-si-nŭn ku-nin-im-ni-da.*
	당신은 군인입니다.
4. She is an actress.	*Kŭ-nyŏ-nŭn pae-u-im-ni-da.*
	그녀는 배우입니다.
5. I am happy.	*Na-nŭn haeng-bo-k'am-ni-da.*
	나는 행복합니다.
6. Where is Mt. Paektu?	*Paek-ttu-sa-nŭn ŏ-di it-ssŭm-ni-kka ?*
	백두산은 어디 있습니까?
7. Seoul is the capital of Korea.	*Seŏ-u-rŭn han-gu-gŭi su-do-im-ni-da.*
	서울은 한국의 수도입니다.
8. Be ambitious.	*P'o-bu-rŭl ka-ji-sip-ssi-o.*
	포부를 가지십시오.
9. Be silent.	*Cho-yong-hi ha-sip-ssi-o.*
	조용히 하십시오.
10. Her beauty was her	*Kŭ-nyŏ-nŭn mi-mo-ttae-mu-ne p'a-*

---

please⟨*mi-an-han*⟩···미안한
expect⟨*ki-dae-ha-da*⟩···기대하다
reporter⟨*ki-ja*⟩···기자
talkative⟨*su-da-sŭ-rŏp-tta*⟩···수다스럽
　다

actress⟨*yŏ-bae-u*⟩···여배우
capital⟨*su-do*⟩···수도
ambition⟨*p'o-bu*⟩···포부
silence⟨*ch'im-muk*⟩···침묵
confidence⟨*si-nyong*⟩···신용

ruin.	*myŏl-haet-tta.*
	그녀는 미모때문에 파멸했다.
11. Two tines two is four.	*Tul ko-p'a-gi tu-rŭn ne-si-da.*
	둘 곱하기 둘은 넷이다.
12. When is the children's Day?	*Ŏ-ri-ni-na-rŭn ŏn-je-im-ni-kka?*
	어린이날은 언제입니까?
13. It is on the 5th of May.	*O-wŏl o-il-im-ni-da.*
	오월 오일입니다.
14. To live is to fight.	*Sal-mūn t'u-jaeng-i-da.*
	삶은 투쟁이다.
15. To be or not to be, that is the question.	*Sa-nŭ-nya chung-nŭ-nya, kŭ-gŏ-si mun-je-ro-da.*
	사느냐 죽느냐, 그것이 문제로다.
16. Be here at five.	*Ta-sŏt-ssi-e i-ri-ro o-sip-ssi-o.*
	다섯시에 이리로 오십시오.

Come

Come

1. Come.	*O-da.*
	오다.
2. Come here.	*I-ri o-se-yo.*
	이리 오세요.
3. I come from Seoul.	*Na-nŭn seŏ-ul ch'ul-ssin-im-ni-da.*
	나는 서울 출신입니다.
4. The bus is coming.	*Pŏ-sŭ-ga om-ni-da.*
	버스가 옵니다.

---

11. There are a number of foreign words, which are used by Koreans with slight changes in pronunciation. For example; bus, drive, truck, love, letter, table, necktie, piano, canvas, paint, vacation,…

ruin(*p'a-myŏl*)…파멸	children's day(*ŏ-ri-ni-nal*)…어린이날
divorce(*p'a-gyŏng*)…파경	peace(*p'yŏng-hwa*)…평화
twice(*tu pŏn*)…두 번	materiality(*yu-hyŏng*)…유형

5. Blue is coming into fashion.

Ch'ŏng-sae-gi yu-haeng-ha-go it-ssŭm-ni-da.

청색이 유행하고 있습니다.

6. Beyond the Alps is Italy.

Al-p'ŭ-sŭ-rŭl nŏ-mŭ-myŏn i-t'ae-ri-im-ni-da.

알프스를 넘으면 이태리입니다.

7. Come and see me.

Nol-lŏ o-sip-ssi-o.

놀러 오십시오.

8. No harm will come to you.

Tang-si-ne-gen hae-ga ŏp-ssŭl kkŏ-sim-ni-da.

당신에겐 해가 없을 것입니다.

9. Yellow is coming into fashion.

Hwang-sae-gi yu-haeng-ha-gi si-ja-k'aet-ssŭm-ni-da.

황색이 유행하기 시작했습니다.

10. A smile comes to her lips.

Kŭ-nyŏ-ŭi ip-ssu-re mi-so-ga ttŏ-ol-lat-ssŭm-ni-da.

그녀의 입술에 미소가 떠올랐습니다.

11. Does he come from Seoul?

Kŭ-nŭn seŏ-ul ch'ul-ssin-im-ni-kka?

그는 서울 출신입니까?

12. Things will be right.

Mo-dŭn i-ri ta chal toel kkŏ-sim-ni-da.

모든 일이 다 잘 될 것입니다.

13. All happy things come to those who wait.

Ki-da-ri-nŭn cha-e-ge po-gi om-ni-da.

기다리는 자에게 복이 옵니다.

14. Years came and

Hae-ga pa-kkwi-go tto pa-kkwi-ŏt-

---

blue(*ch'ŏng-saek*)…청색
harm(*hae*)…해
yellow(*hwang-saek*)…황색

fashion(*yu-haeng*)…유행
lip(*ip-ssul*)…입술
smile(*mi-so*)…미소

went.

ssŭm-ni-da.
해가 바뀌고 또 바뀌었습니다.

Go

Go

1. Go.

Ka-da.
가다.

2. Let's go for a drive.

Tŭ-ra-i-bŭ-rŭl hap-ssi-da.
드라이브를 합시다.

3. I'm going to church.

Na-nŭn kyo-hoe-e kam-ni-da.
나는 교회에 갑니다.

4. It is time to go.

Kal si-gan-im-ni-da.
갈 시간입니다.

5. I am going to go fishing.

Nak-ssi-rŭl ha-rŏ kal-lyŏ-go ham-ni-da.
낚시를 하러 갈려고 합니다.

6. Let's go to bed early this evening.

O-nŭl chŏ-nyŏ-gŭn il-tchik chap-ssi-da.
오늘 저녁은 일찍 잡시다.

7. This road goes to Seoul.

I ki-run seŏ-ul-lo ka-nŭn kil-im-ni-da.
이 길은 서울로 가는 길입니다.

8. Who goes there !

Nu-gu-ya!
누구야 !

9. The pain has gone now.

Ko-t'ong-ŭn i-je ka-bŏ-ryŏt-tta.
고통은 이제 가버렸다.

10. The flowers are dead.

KKo-ch'ŭn chyŏt-ssŭm-ni-da.
꽃은 졌습니다.

11. I will go by train.

Ki-ch'a-ro ka-get-ssŭm-ni-da.

---

fishing(*nak-ssi*)…낚시
evening(*chŏ-nyŏk*)…저녁

train(*ki-ch'a*)…기차
pain(*ko-t'ong*)…고통

12. I will go on foot.

기차로 가겠습니다.
Kŏ-rŏ ka-get-ssŭm-ni-da.
걸어 가겠습니다.

13. She is going on seventeen.

Kŭ-nyŏ-nŭn yŏl-il-gop ssa-ri toe-ŏ kam-ni-da.
그녀는 열일곱 살이 되어 갑니다.

14. How goes it with you?

Yo-sae ŏ-ttŏt-ssŭm-ni-kka?
요새 어떻습니까?

15. My watch goes well.

Nae si-gye-nŭn chal kam-ni-da.
내 시계는 잘 갑니다.

16. We are here today and gone tomorrow.

U-ri-nŭn o-nŭl i cha-ri-e it-tchi-man, nae-i-rŭn chu-gŭl mok-ssum-im-ni-da.
우리는 오늘 이 자리에 있지만, 내일은 죽을 목숨입니다.

Have

Have

1. Have

Ka-ji-da.
가지다.

2. I have···

Na-nŭn ···ka-ji-go it-tta.
나는 ···가지고 있다.

3. I have money.

Na-nŭn to-ni it-tta(ka-ji-go it-tta).
나는 돈이 있다(가지고 있다).

4. Have you any questions?

Ta-rŭn chil-mu-ni it-ssŭm-ni-kka?
다른 질문이 있습니까?

5. I have to do something.

Na-nŭn hae-ya hal li-li it-tta.
나는 해야 할 일이 있다.

6. I had a bath.

Na-nŭn mo-gyo-gŭl haet-tta.

---

foot (*ta-ri*)···다리
watch (*si-gye*)···시계

bath (*mo-gyok*)···목욕

나는 목욕을 했다.

7. Have a cigarette.

Tam-bae-rŭl p'i-u-sip-ssi-o.

담배를 피우십시오.

8. Will you have another cup of tea?

Ch'a-rŭl han chan tŏ ma-si-get-ssŭm-ni-kka?

차를 한 잔 더 마시겠습니까?

9. Did you have good time?

Chŭl-gŏ-un si-ga-nŭl po-naet-ssŭm-ni-kka?

즐거운 시간을 보냈습니까?

10. This house has five rooms.

I chi-bŭn ta-sŏt kkae-ŭi pang-i it-ssŭm-ni-da.

이 집은 다섯 개의 방이 있습니다.

11. I hope you will have a nice time in Korea.

Na-nŭn tang-si-ni han-gu-ge-sŏ chŭl-gŏ-un si-ga-nŭl po-nae-gi-rŭl pa-ram-ni-da.

나는 당신이 한국에서 즐거운 시간을 보내기를 바랍니다.

12. This room has five windows.

I pang-ŭn ch'ang-mu-ni ta-sŏt kkae it-ssŭm-ni-da.

이 방은 창문이 다섯 개 있습니다.

13. Do you often catch cold?

Kam-gi-ga cha-ju tŭ-sim-ni-kka?

감기가 자주 드십니까?

14. The well has little water.

Kŭ u-mu-re-nŭn kŏ-ŭi mu-ri ŏp-ssŭm-ni-da.

그 우물에는 거의 물이 없습니다.

15. She has a good memory.

Kŭ-nyŏ-nŭn ki-ŏng-nyŏ-gi chot-ssŭm-ni-da.

그녀는 기억력이 좋습니다.

16. Have you done it?

Kŭ-gŏ-sŭl haet-ssŭm-ni-kka?

---

well(*u-mul*)…우물

그것을 했습니까?

Let

1. Let

2. Let's go.

3. Let me see.

4. Let's swim.

5. The house lets for 300,
   000 won a month.

6. I will let you go.

7. Let me hear you sing.

8. Let me alone.

9. This is the room to
   let.

10. Let him through the
    gate.

11. Let bygones be bygo-
    nes.

Let

…Ha-ge ha-da.
…하게 하다.

Kap-ssi-da.
갑시다.

Po-yŏ chu-sip-ssi-o.
보여 주십시오.

Su-yŏng-ŭl hap-ssi-da.
수영을 합시다.

*Kŭ chi-bŭn han ta-re sam-sim-man
   wŏ-ne se non-nŭn-da.*
그 집은 한 달에 삼십만 원에 세
놓는다.

*Na-nŭn nŏ-rŭl ka-do-rok hae chu-get-
   tta.*
나는 너를 가도록 해 주겠다.

No-rae-rŭl tŭl-lyŏ chu-sip-ssi-o.
노래를 들려 주십시오.

Hon-ja it-kke nae-bŏ-ryŏ tu-sip-ssi-o.
혼자 있게 내버려 두십시오.

I-gŏ-si se-no-ŭl pang-im-ni-da.
이것이 세놓을 방입니다.

*Kŭ-rŭl tae-mu-nŭ-ro t'ong-gwa-si-
   k'yŏ-ra.*
그를 대문으로 통과시켜라.

*Chi-nan i-rŭn hŏ-mul-ch'i ma-sip-
   ssi-o.*

---

month(*tal*)…달   gate(*mun*)…문

지난 일은 허물치 마십시오.

Always

Always

1. Always.

Hang-sang. Ŏn-je-na. Nŭl.

항상. 언제나. 늘.

2. I always love you.

Na-nŭn hang-sang nŏ-rŭl sa-rang-han-da.

나는 항상 너를 사랑한다.

3. I always wake up at six.

Na-nŭn nŭl yŏ-sŏt-ssi-e cha-mi kkaen-da.

나는 늘 여섯시에 잠이 깬다.

4. I will always follow you.

Na-nŭn hang-sang tang-si-nŭl tta-rŭ-get-tta.

나는 항상 당신을 따르겠다.

5. You must always be honest.

Nŏ-nŭn hang-sang chŏng-ji-k'ae-ya-man han-da.

너는 항상 정직해야만 한다.

6. The rich is not always happy.

Pu-ja-ra-go hang-sang haeng-bo-k'an-gŏn a-nim-ni-da.

부자라고 항상 행복한건 아닙니다.

7. The poor is not always miserable.

Pin-ja-ra-go hang-sang ko-t'ong-sŭ-rŏ-un-gŏn a-nim-ni-da.

빈자라고 항상 고통스러운건 아닙니다.

8. Miseries always follow in the wake of war.

Chŏn-jaeng twi-e-nŭn hang-sang pul-haeng-i tta-rŭn-da.

전쟁 뒤에는 항상 불행이 따른다.

9. You always make me cry.

Tang-si-nŭn hang-sang na-rŭl ul-lin-da.

honest(*chŏng-ji-k'an*)…정직한   miserable(*ko-t'ong-sŭ-rŏn*)…고통스런

당신은 항상 나를 울린다.

10. The sun always rises from the east.

T'ae-yang-ŭn hang-sang tong-tcho-ge-sŏ ttŭn-da.

태양은 항상 동쪽에서 뜬다.

Affirmative expressions

Kŭng-jŏng-jŏk p'yo-hyŏn

긍정적 표현

1. Yes.

Ne. Ye. Kŭ-rŏt-ssŭm-ni-da.

네. 예. 그렇습니다.

2. Oh, yes.

Oh, kŭ-rŏt-ssŭm-ni-da.

오, 그렇습니다.

3. Of course.

Mul-lon-im-ni-da.

물론입니다.

4. Sure.

Kŭ-rŏ-k'o mal-go-yo.

그렇고 말고요.

5. Certainly.

Kŭ-rŏ-k'o mal-go-yo.

그렇고 말고요.

6. Good.

Chot-ssŭm-ni-da.

좋습니다.

7. Very nice.

Mae-u chot-ssŭm-ni-da.

매우 좋습니다.

8. All right.

Kwaen-ch'an-ssŭm-ni-da.

괜찮습니다.

9. I think so.

Kŭ-rŏ-k'e saeng-ga-k'am-ni-da.

그렇게 생각합니다.

10. I agree with you.

Tang-sin-gwa tong-gam-im-ni-da.

---

cry(*ul-da*)…울다
certainly(*a-ma-do*)…아마도
nice(*cho-ŭn*)…좋은
agree(*tong-gam-ha-da*)…동감하다
present(*hyŏn-jae*)…현재

course(*kwa-jŏng*)…과정
instead(*tae-si-ne*)…대신에
direct(*chik-tchŏp*)…직접
past(*kwa-gŏ*)…과거
future(*mi-rae*)…미래

	당신과 동감입니다.
11. Yes, indeed.	*Ne, a-mu-ryŏ-mŭn-yo.*
	네, 아무렴은요.
12. Yes, I see.	*Ye, al-get-ssŭm-ni-da.*
	예, 알겠습니다.
13. That's true.	*Kŭ-ge sa-sil-im-ni-da.*
	그게 사실입니다.
14. I have no doubt about that.	*Kŭ-gŏ-se kwan-hae-sŏ-nŭn ŭi-sim-hal yŏ-ji-ga ŏp-ssŭm-ni-da.*
	그것에 관해서는 의심할 여지가 없습니다.
15. Yes, with pleasure.	*Ne, a-ju ki-kkŏ-i.*
	네, 아주 기꺼이.

Negative expressions   *Pu-jŏng-jŏk p'yo-hyŏn*
부정적 표현

1. No.	*A-ni-o. A-nim-ni-da.*
	아니오. 아닙니다.
2. Perhaps not.	*A-ma-do a-nim-ni-da.*
	아마도 아닙니다.
3. Of course not.	*Mul-lon a-ni-ji-yo.*
	물론 아니지요.
4. I don't think so.	*Kŭ-rŏ-k'e saeng-ga-k'a-ji an-ssŭm-ni-da.*
	그렇게 생각하지 않습니다.
5. I don't agree with you.	*Ch'an-sŏng-ha-ji an-ssŭm-ni-da.*
	찬성하지 않습니다.
6. Never.	*Kyŏl-k'o a-nim-ni-da.*

---

assent(*ch'an-sŏng*)…찬성   worry(*kŏk-tchŏng-ha-da*)…걱정하다
contrary(*pan-dae*)…반대   repentance(*hu-hoe*)…후회

결코 아닙니다.

7. Not yet. *A-jik mŏ-rŏt-ssŭm-ni-da.*

아직 멀었습니다.

8. On the contrary. *Pan-dae-im-ni-da.*

반대입니다.

9. Far from it. *Tang-ch'i-do an-ssŭm-ni-da.*

당치도 않습니다.

10. Don't worry about that. *Kŏk-tchŏng-ha-ji ma-sip-ssi-o.*

걱정하지 마십시오.

Exclamation *Kan-t'an* 감탄

1. Oh ! *Oh !*

오 !

2. Oh, no ! *Oh, i i-rŭl !*

오, 이 일을 !

3. Oh, dear ! *Ŏ-mŏ-na !*

어머나 !

4. What ! *Mwŏ-ra-go !*

뭐라고 !

5. What a pity ! *Ka-yŏp-kke-do !*

가엾게도 !

6. Really ! *Chŏng-ma-ri-ya !*

정말이야 !

7. Oh, bother ! *E-i, kwi-ch'a-na !*

에이, 귀찮아 !

8. Thank God ! *A-i-gu ko-ma-wŏ-ra !*

아이구 고마워라 !

---

glad(*ki-ppŭn*)…기쁜
lucky(*un cho-ŭn*)…운 좋은
excellent(*hul-lyung-han*)…훌륭한

bravo(*yong-gam-han*)…용감한
shame(*pu-kkŭ-rŏ-un*)…부끄러운
cowardice(*pi-gŏp*)…비겁

9. How happy I am !　　　*Ŏl-ma-na haeng-bo-k'an-ji!*
　　　　　　　　　　　　얼마나 행복한지 !

10. How lucky !　　　　*Ch'am u-ni cho-k'u-na!*
　　　　　　　　　　　　참 운이 좋구나 !

11. I am so glad.　　　　*Ch'am ki-ppŭm-ni-da.*
　　　　　　　　　　　　참 기쁩니다.

12. Excellent !　　　　　*Hul-lyung-ha-gu-na!*
　　　　　　　　　　　　훌륭하구나 !

13. Bravo !　　　　　　　*Yong-gam-ha-gu-na!*
　　　　　　　　　　　　용감하구나 !

14. Wonderful !　　　　　*Mŏt-tchi-gu-na!*
　　　　　　　　　　　　멋지구나 !

15. Well done !　　　　　*Chal-haet-kku-na!*
　　　　　　　　　　　　잘했구나 !

16. Alas !　　　　　　　　*Tŭ-di-ŏ!*
　　　　　　　　　　　　드디어 !

17. Beautiful !　　　　　　*A-rŭm-dap-kku-na!*
　　　　　　　　　　　　아름답구나 !

18. Hell !　　　　　　　　*Pi-rŏ-mŏ-gŭl!*
　　　　　　　　　　　　빌어먹을 !

19. Damn it !　　　　　　*U-ra-jil kkŏt ka-t'ŭ-ni!*
　　　　　　　　　　　　우라질 것 같으니 !

20. Shame on you !　　　*P'a-ryŏm-ch'i-han cha-sik!*
　　　　　　　　　　　　파렴치한 자식 !

21. What a shame !　　　*Ch'ang-p'i-ha-gu-na!*
　　　　　　　　　　　　창피하구나 !

22. Get out !　　　　　　*Na-ga!*
　　　　　　　　　　　　나가 !

23. What a nuisance !　　*Si-kkŭ-rŏp-kku-na!*

---

nuisance(*so-ran-han*)···소란한

시끄럽구나 !

24. I'm ashamed of you !　*Ch'am chǒng-ttǒ-rǒ-ji-nǔn-gu-na !*
참 정떨어지는구나 !

25. Go to hell !　*Chi-o-ge-na kal cha-sik !*
지옥에나 갈 자식 !

Thanks, Apologies　*Kam-sa, Sa-gwa*
감사, 사과

1. Tank you.　*Kam-sa-ham-ni-da. Ko-map-ssǔm-ni-da.*
감사합니다. 고맙습니다.

2. Thank you so much.　*Mae-u kam-sa-ham-ni-da.*
매우 감사합니다.

3. Don't mention about it.　*Kǔ yae-gi-nǔn ha-ji ma-sip-ssi-o.*
그 얘기는 하지 마십시오.

4. Please forget it.　*Che-bal kǔ-gǒ-sǔn i-jǒ pǒ-ri-sip-ssi-o.*
제발 그것은 잊어 버리십시오.

5. Please don't worry.　*Che-bal sin-gyǒng-ssǔ-ji ma-sip-ssi-o.*
제발 신경쓰지 마십시오.

6. I'm sorry.　*Mi-an-ham-ni-da.*
미안합니다.

7. Excuse me.　*Sil-lye-ham-ni-da.*
실례합니다.

8. Pardon me.　*Yong-sǒ-ha-sip-ssi-o.*
용서하십시오.

9. I beg your pardon.　*Yong-sǒ-ha-sip-ssi-o.*
용서하십시오.

---

mention(*ǒn-gǔ-p'a-da*)…언급하다　　forget(*i-jǒ-bǒ-ri-da*)…잊어버리다
hell(*chi-ok*)…지옥　　recollection(*hoe-sang*)…회상
apology(*sa-gwa*)…사과

10. I'm very sorry for what I have done.

Che-ga chŏ-ji-rŭn i-re tae-dan-hi mi-an-ham-ni-da.

제가 저지른 일에 대단히 미안합니다.

Uncertainty expressions

Pul-hwak-ssil-han p'yo-hyŏn

불확실한 표현

1. Perhaps.

A-ma-do.

아마도.

2. Perhaps so.

A-ma-do kŭ-rŏl kkŏ-sim-ni-da.

아마도 그럴 것입니다.

3. I suppose so.

Kŭ-rŏ-ri-ra saeng-gak-doem-ni-da.

그러리라 생각됩니다.

4. I guess so.

Kŭ-rŏ-ri-ra ch'u-ch'ŭk-doem-ni-da.

그러리라 추측됩니다.

5. I dare say it is.

A-ma kŭ-rŏl kkŏ-sim-ni-da.

아마 그럴 것입니다.

6. It's quite probable.

I-ssŭm-ji-k'an il-im-ni-da.

있음직한 일입니다.

7. I hope so.

Kŭ-rŏ-k'e toe-gil pa-ram-ni-da.

그렇게 되길 바랍니다.

8. It's quite possible.

Ka-nŭng-han il-im-ni-da.

가능한 일입니다.

9. I doubt it.

Ŭi-sim-sŭ-rŏp-ssŭm-ni-da.

의심스럽습니다.

10. It can't be true.

Sa-si-ril ssu-ga ŏp-ssŭm-ni-da.

사실일 수가 없습니다.

---

suppose(*saeng-ga-k'a-da*)…생각하다
guess(*ch'u-ch'ŭ-k'a-da*)…추측하다
true(*chin-sil-han*)…진실한

probable(*i-ssŭm-ji-k'an*)…있음직한
possible(*ka-nŭng-han*)…가능한
doubt(*ŭi-sim*)…의심

PART II

Necessary Phrase

Greetings(I)	*In-sa*(인사)··· *I*
1. Good morning?	*An-nyŏng-ha-sim-ni-kka?*
	안녕하십니까?
2. Good evening?	*An-nyŏng-ha-sim-ni-kka?*
	안녕하십니까?
3. Good night.	*An-nyŏng-hi chu-mu-sip-ssi-o.*
	안녕히 주무십시오.
4. Hello!	*Yŏ-bo-se-yo!*
	여보세요!
5. How are you?	*Ŏ-ttŏ-sim-ni-kka?*
	어떠십니까?
6. Fine. Thank you.	*Mo-du mu-go-ham-ni-da. Kam-sa-ham-ni-da.*
	모두 무고합니다. 감사합니다.
7. How is your family?	*Ka-jok-dŭl-do an-nyŏng-ha-sim-ni-kka?*
	가족들도 안녕하십니까?
8. Thank you. My family are all very well.	*Kam-sa-ham-ni-da. Ka-jok-dŭl-do mo-du mu-go-ham-ni-da.*
	감사합니다. 가족들도 모두 무고합니다.
9. How is your father?	*A-bŏ-ji-kke-sŏ-nŭn ŏ-ttŏ-sim-ni-kka?*
	아버지께서는 어떠십니까?
10. My father is well.	*A-bŏ-ji-kke-sŏ-do mu-go-ha-sim-ni-*

12. "*An-nyŏng-ha-sim-ni-kka?*" can be used usually throughout the day as a cordial greeting. But in the morning "*Chin-ji chap-ssu-syŏt-ssŭm-ni-kka?*" (Have you had breakfast?)
is frequently used to seniors. And for the night's greeting, there is "*An-nyŏng-hi chu-mu-sip-ssi-o,*" which means "sleep well."

greeting(*in-sa*)···인사   family(*ka-jok*)···가족
fine(*cho-ŭn*)···좋은   bad(*na-ppŭn*)···나쁜

아버지께서도 무고하십니다.

11. How is your mother's health ?

Ŏ-mŏ-ni-ŭi kŏn-gang-ŭn ŏ-ttŏ-sim-ni-kka ?

어머니의 건강은 어떠십니까 ?

12. Please remember me to your mother.

Ŏ-mŏ-ni-e-ge an-bu chŏn-hae chu-sip-ssi-o.

어머니에게 안부 전해 주십시오.

13. Give my best regards to your brother.

Hyŏng-nim-e-ge an-bu chŏn-hae chu-sip-ssi-o.

형님에게 안부 전해 주십시오.

14. How goes it ?

Chae-mi-ga ŏ-ttŏt-ssŭm-ni-kka ?

재미가 어떻습니까 ?

15. How kind of you !

I-rŏ-k'e ch'in-jŏl-hal tchu-ri-ya !

이렇게 친절할 줄이야 !

16. How about your health ?

Kŏn-gang-ŭn ŏ-ttŏt-ssŭm-ni-kka ?

건강은 어떻습니까 ?

17. Let's get busy and finish this job.

Cha, ki-u-nŭl nae-sŏ i i-rŭl kkŭn-naep-ssi-da.

자, 기운을 내서 이 일을 끝냅시다.

Greetings (Ⅱ)

In-sa (인사) ··· *Ⅱ*

1. How are you, Mr. Kim ?

An-nyŏng-ha-sim-ni-kka ?　Kim hyŏng.

안녕하십니까 ? 김 형.

2. How are you, Miss Park ?

An-nyŏng-ha-sim-ni-kka ? Pak yang.

안녕하십니까 ? 박 양.

---

remember(*ki-ŏ-k'a-da*) ··· 기억하다
regard(*chŏn-ha-da*) ··· 전하다
promise(*yak-ssok*) ··· 약속

health(*kŏn-gang*) ··· 건강
separation(*i-byŏl*) ··· 이별

3. I am very well.   *Mu-go-ham-ni-da.*
무고합니다.

4. I am glad to see you.   *Man-na poe-ŏ pan-gap-ssŭm-ni-da.*
만나 뵈어 반갑습니다.

5. Long time since I last met you.   *Man-na-boen chi-ga ch'am o-rae toe-ŏt-ssŭm-ni-da.*
만나뵌 지가 참 오래 되었습니다.

6. Indeed, it has been a long time.   *Ch'a-mŭ-ro o-raen-man-im-ni-da.*
참으로 오랜만입니다.

7. I'm glad to have met you.   *Man-na poep-kke toen kŏ-sŭl ki-ppŭ-ge yŏ-gi-go it-ssŭm-ni-da.*
만나 뵙게 된 것을 기쁘게 여기고 있습니다.

8. How is your school?   *Hak-kkyo-nŭn ŏ-ttŏt-ssŭm-ni-kka?*
학교는 어떻습니까?

9. How is your business?   *Sa-ŏ-bŭn ŏ-ttŏt-ssŭm-ni-kka?*
사업은 어떻습니까?

10. Fairly good.   *Chal twae-gam-ni-da.*
잘 돼갑니다.

11. May I join you?   *Chŏ-do han mok kki-wŏ chu-si-get-ssŭm-ni-kka?*
저도 한 몫 끼워 주시겠습니까?

12. Not so good.   *Sin-t'ong-ch'i an-ssŭm-ni-da.*
신통치 않습니다.

13. That's all right.   *Kwen-ch'an-ssŭm-ni-da.*
괜찮습니다.

14. I'm very pleased that   *O-sin-da-ni mae-u ki-ppŭm-ni-da.*

---

last(*ma-ji-mak*)…마지막
meet(*man-na-da*)…만나다
kind(*ch'in-jŏl-han*)…친절한

business(*sa-ŏp*)…사업
fairly(*chal*)…잘

you will come.	오신다니 매우 기쁩니다.
15. When can I meet you?	*Ŏn-je man-nal ssu it-ssŭl-kka-yo?* 언제 만날 수 있을까요?
16. Come any time.	*A-mu-ttae-na o-sip-ssi-o.* 아무때나 오십시오.
17. I will call on you Monday.	*Wŏ-ryo-i-re ch'a-ja poep-kket-ssŭm-ni-da.* 월요일에 찾아 뵙겠습니다.
18. Good. I will see you then.	*Chot-ssŭm-ni-da. Kŭ-ttae poep-kket-ssŭm-ni-da.* 좋습니다. 그때 뵙겠습니다.
19. I'm sorry to bother you.	*Pang-hae-rŭl hae-sŏ choe-song-ham-ni-da.* 방해를 해서 죄송합니다.
20. We are delight you could come.	*Wa chu-syŏ-sŏ mae-u ki-ppŭm-ni-da.* 와 주셔서 매우 기쁩니다.
21. I hope I haven't bothered you much.	*Ma-nŭn p'ye-rŭl kki-ch'ŏ-dŭ-ri-ji a-nan-nŭn-ji mo-rŭ-get-ssŭm-ni-da.* 많은 폐를 끼쳐드리지 않았는지 모르겠습니다.
22. Not at all.	*Ch'ŏn-man-e-yo. Kŭ-rŏ-ch'i an-ssŭm-ni-da.* 천만에요. 그렇지 않습니다.
23. I will show you to the banquet room.	*Yŏn-hoe-jang-ŭ-ro an-nae-ha-get-ssŭm-ni-da.* 연회장으로 안내하겠습니다.

---

bother(*p'ye-rŭl kki-ch'i-da*)…폐를 끼치다
again(*ta-si*)…다시

invite(*ch'o-ch'ŏng-ha-da*)…초청하다
banquet hall(*yŏn-hoe-jang*)…연회장

24. Thank you for your hospitality. *Hwan-dae-e kam-sa-ham-ni-da.*
환대에 감사합니다.

25. Good-bye. *An-nyŏng-hi ka-sip-ssi-o.*
안녕히 가십시오.

26. Good-bye. See you Monday. *An-nyŏng-hi kye-sip-ssi-o. Wŏ-ryo-i-re poep-kket-ssŭm-ni-da.*
안녕히 계십시오. 월요일에 뵙겠습니다.

27. Please come again. *TTo o-sip-ssi-o.*
또 오십시오.

28. Please speak more distinctly. *Chom-dŏ myŏng-hwa-k'a-ge mal-ssŭm-hae chu-sip-ssi-o.*
좀더 명확하게 말씀해 주십시오.

29. Please speak more clearly. *Chom-dŏ ttok-tto-k'i mal-ssŭm-hae chu-sip-ssi-o.*
좀더 똑똑히 말씀해 주십시오.

30. Please speak more slowly. *Chom-dŏ ch'ŏn-ch'ŏn-hi mal-ssŭm-hae chu-sip-ssi-o.*
좀더 천천히 말씀해 주십시오.

Introduction *So-gae*(소개)

1. How do you do? *An-nyŏng-ha-sim-ni-kka?*
안녕하십니까?

2. What's your name, please? *Sŏng-ha-mi mu-ŏ-si-jyo?*
성함이 무엇이죠?

3. My name is Kim Po-ram. *Che i-rŭ-mŭn kim-bo-ram-im-ni-da.*
제 이름은 김보람입니다.

4. This is Miss Yun A- *I pu-nŭn yun-a-rŭm yang-im-ni-da.*

---

13. "*ch'un-ch'u*" is used when one asks a senior or aged people's age.
hospitality(*hwan-dae*)…환대   introduction(*so-gae*)…소개
typist(*t'a-i-p'i-sŭ-t'ŭ*)…타이피스트

67

rum.

5. Do you have your name card ?

이 분은 윤아름 양입니다.

Myŏng-ha-mi it-ssŭm-ni-kka?

명함이 있습니까 ?

6. Yes. Here is my name card.

Ne. Yŏ-gi che myŏng-ha-mi it-ssŭm-ni-da.

네. 여기 제 명함이 있습니다.

7. Excuse me. I don't have my name card now.

Choe-song-ham-ni-da.   Chi-gŭm myŏng-ha-mŭl ka-ji-go it-tchi an-ssŭm-ni-da.

죄송합니다. 지금 명함을 가지고 있지 않습니다.

8. May I introduce Miss Park Po-ra ?

Pak-bo-ra yang-ŭl so-gae-hal-kka-yo?

박보라 양을 소개할까요 ?

9. She works with the Dong-A Trading Company as a typist.

Kŭ-nyŏ-nŭn tong-a sang-sa-e-sŏ t'a-i-p'i-sŭ-t'ŭ-ro il-ha-go it-ssŭm-ni-da.

그녀는 동아 상사에서 타이피스트로 일하고 있습니다.

10. It was nice to have seen you.

Tang-si-nŭl man-na poe-ŏ ch'am pan-gap-ssŭm-ni-da.

당신을 만나 뵈어 참 반갑습니다.

11. How old are you ?

Myŏt ssal-im-ni-kka?

몇 살입니까 ?

12. I am 25 years old.

Sŭ-mul-da-sŏt ssal-im-ni-da.

스물다섯 살입니다.

13. Must you go so soon ?

Kŭ-rŏ-k'e ppal-li ka-ya ham-ni-kka?

그렇게 빨리 가야 합니까 ?

14. I hope we can meet again sometime.

Ŏn-je tto man-na-boel ssu it-kkil pa-ram-ni-da.

언제 또 만나뵐 수 있길 바랍니다.

---

interview(*tae-myŏn*)…대면   name card(*myŏng-ham*)…명함

15. See you later.	*TTo man-nap-ssi-da.*
	또 만납시다.
16. Please take care of yourself.	*Cho-sim-ha-sip-ssi-o.*
	조심하십시오.
17. What are you talking about?	*Mu-sŭn mal-ssŭm-i-sim-ni-kka?*
	무슨 말씀이십니까?
18. What is the matter with you?	*Mu-sŭn yong-mu-i-sim-ni-kka?*
	무슨 용무이십니까?
19. What is she?	*Kŭ yŏ-ja-bu-nŭn ŏ-ttŏn sa-ram-im-ni-kka?*
	그 여자분은 어떤 사람입니까?
20. Please contact him through telephone.	*Chŏn-hwa-ro kŭ-wa yŏl-la-k'a-sip-ssi-o.*
	전화로 그와 연락하십시오.

Time　　　　　　　*Si-gan*(시간)

1. What time is it?　　*Myŏt ssi-im-ni-kka?*
　　　　　　　　　　몇 시입니까?

2. It is one o'clock.　　*Han-si-im-ni-da.*
　　　　　　　　　　한시입니다.

3. It is five fifteen.　　*Ta-sŏt-ssi sip-o-bun-im-ni-da.*
　　　　　　　　　　다섯시 십오분입니다.

4. It is a quarter to six.　*Yŏ-sŏt-ssi sip-o-bun chŏn-im-ni-da.*
　　　　　　　　　　여섯시 십오분 전입니다.

5. It is half past three.　*Se-si pan-im-ni-da.*

---

14. When time is mentioned, "*pan*" and "thirty minutes" have the same meaning.

time(*si-gan*)…시간　　　　　　talking(*tae-hwa*)…대화
minute(*pun*)…분　　　　　　　contact(*yŏl-rak*)…연락
sometime(*ŏn-je-in-ga*)…언제인가　care(*cho-sim*)…조심
compromise(*t'a-hyŏp*)…타협　　second(*ch'o*)…초(of time)

세시 반입니다.

6. It is ten minutes past seven.

Il-gop-ssi si-ppun-im-ni-da.

일곱시 십분입니다.

7. Do you have time?

Si-ga-ni it-ssŭm-ni-kka?

시간이 있습니까?

8. This watch keeps good time.

I si-gye-nŭn si-ga-ni chal mat-ssŭm-ni-da.

이 시계는 시간이 잘 맞습니다.

9. My watch is five minutes slow.

Nae si-gye-nŭn o-bu-ni nŭt-ssŭm-ni-da.

내 시계는 오분이 늦습니다.

10. This clock is three minutes fast.

I si-gye-nŭn sam-bu-ni ppa-rŭm-ni-da.

이 시계는 삼분이 빠릅니다.

11. What time do you usually get up in the morning?

A-ch'i-me po-t'ong myŏt ssi-e i-rŏ-nam-ni-kka?

아침에 보통 몇 시에 일어납니까?

12. I get up at six in the morning.

Na-nŭn a-ch'im yŏ-sŏt-ssi-e i-rŏ-nam-ni-da.

나는 아침 여섯시에 일어납니다.

13. It takes about thirty minutes to go from my home to the office.

U-ri chi-be-sŏ sa-mu-sil-kka-ji ka-nŭn-de-nŭn yak sam-si-ppu-ni kŏl-lim-ni-da.

우리 집에서 사무실까지 가는데는 약 삼십분이 걸립니다.

14. What time do you have lunch?

Myŏt ssi-e chŏm-si-mŭl mŏk-ssŭm-ni-kka?

---

office (*sa-mu-sil*)…사무실
bed (*ch'im-dae*)…침대
quarter (*sa-bu-nŭi il*)…사분의 일 (or *sip-o-bun*)

quickly (*ppal-li*)…빨리
slow (*ch'ŏn-ch'ŏn-hi*)…천천히
morning (*a-ch'im*)…아침
lunch (*chŏm-sim*)…점심

몇 시에 점심을 먹습니까?

15. What time do you go to bed?

Myŏt ssi-e cham-ni-kka?

몇 시에 잡니까?

16. I will wait for you until ten o'clock.

Yŏl-ssi-kka-ji tang-si-nŭl ki-da-ri-get-ssŭm-ni-da.

열시까지 당신을 기다리겠습니다.

17. I will be back here by five in the afternoon.

O-hu ta-sŏt-ssi-kka-ji i-ri-ro o-get-ssŭm-ni-da.

오후 다섯시까지 이리로 오겠습니다.

18. Church bells ring at four thirty.

Kyo-hoe-jong-ŭn ne-si pa-ne ul-lim-ni-da.

교회종은 네시 반에 울립니다.

19. Time and tide wait for no man.

Se-wŏ-rŭn sa-ra-mŭl ki-da-ri-ji an-ssŭm-ni-da.

세월은 사람을 기다리지 않습니다.

Days of the Week

Chu-il(주일)

1. What day of the week is it?

Mu-sŭn yo-il-im-ni-kka?

무슨 요일입니까?

2. It is Monday.

Wŏ-ryo-il-im-ni-da.

월요일입니다.

3. The first day of the week is Sunday.

Chu-i-rŭi ch'ŏt-tchae-na-rŭn i-ryo-il-im-ni-da.

주일의 첫째날은 일요일입니다.

4. What is the last day of

Chu-i-rŭi ma-ji-mang na-rŭn mu-ŏ-

---

15. The names of the week days originated from Chinese characters which mean sun, moon, fire, water, tree, gold and earth.

afternoon(*o-hu*) … 오후   first day(*ch'ŏn-nal*) … 첫날

the week?	*sim-ni-kka?*
	주일의 마지막 날은 무엇입니까?
5. It is Saturday.	*T'o-yo-il-im-ni-da.*
	토요일입니다.
6. Sunday is a holiday.	*I-ryo-i-rŭn hu-il-im-ni-da.*
	일요일은 휴일입니다.
7. Saturday is a half holi-day in Korea.	*Han-gu-ge-sŏ t'o-yo-i-rŭn pan-gong-il-im-ni-da.*
	한국에서 토요일은 반공일입니다.
8. How many days are there in a week?	*Il-tchu-i-rŭn myŏ ch'i-ri it-ssŭm-ni-kka?*
	일주일은 몇 일이 있습니까?
9. There are seven days.	*Ch'i-ri-ri it-ssŭm-ni-da.*
	칠일이 있습니다.
10. May I come again next Wednesday?	*Ta-ŭm su-yo-i-re ta-si-wa-do chot-ssŭm-ni-kka?*
	다음 수요일에 다시와도 좋습니까?
11. I am going to go to Seoul next Thursday.	*Ta-ŭm mo-gyo-i-re seŏ-u-rel kal-lyŏ-go ham-ni-da.*
	다음 목요일에 서울엘 갈려고 합니다.
12. Korean daily newspa-pers are published	*Han-guk sin-mun-dŭ-rŭn mae-il pal-haeng-doem-ni-da.*

---

last day(*ma-ji-mang nal*)…마지막 날
holiday(*hyu-il*)…휴일
Monday(*wŏ-ryo-il*)…월요일
Tuesday(*hwa-yo-il*)…화요일
Wednesday(*su-yo-il*)…수요일
Thursday(*mo-gyo-il*)…목요일
Friday(*kŭ-myo-il*)…금요일

Saturday(*t'o-yo-il*)…토요일
Sunday(*i-ryo-il*)…일요일
holidays(*hyu-ga*)…휴가
next(*ta-ŭm*)…다음
full year(*il-tchu-nyŏn*)…일주년
week(*il-tchu-il*)…일주일
lifetime(*il-ssaeng*)…일생

every day.

한국 신문들은 매일 발행됩니다.

13. The USIS Library is open Monday through Saturday except Wednesday.

Yu-es-ai-es to-sŏ-gwa-nŭn su-yo-i-rŭl che-we-ha-go-nŭn wŏ-ryo-i-re-sŏ t'o-yo-il-kka-ji yŏm-ni-da.

『유. 에스. 아이. 에스』 도서관은 수요일을 제외하고는 월요일에서 토요일까지 엽니다.

14. What do you do on Sunday?

I-ryo-i-re-nŭn mu-ŏ-sŭl ha-sim-ni-kka?

일요일에는 무엇을 하십니까?

15. I go to church on Sunday.

Na-nŭn i-ryo-i-re kyo-hoe-rŭl kam-ni-da.

나는 일요일에 교회를 갑니다.

16. Last Tuesday was my 26th birthday.

Chi-nan hwa-yo-i-rŭn na-ŭi sŭ-mul-lyŏ-sŏt ppŏn-tchae saeng-il-i-yŏt-ssŭm-ni-da.

지난 화요일은 나의 스물여섯 번째 생일이었습니다.

17. Some stores are closed every first Sunday of the month.

Myŏn-myŏt ka-ge-dŭ-rŭn wŏl-tchung ch'ŏt i-ryo-i-rŭn mu-rŭl tat-ssŭm-ni-da.

몇몇 가게들은 월중 첫 일요일은 문을 닫습니다.

18. May 8 is the Parents Day.

O-wŏl p'a-ri-rŭn ŏ-bŏ-i-ŭi nal-im-ni-da.

오월 팔일은 어버이의 날입니다.

19. He works a fortyhour

Kŭ-nŭn il-tchu-i-re sa-sip si-gan i-

---

publish(*pal-haeng-ha-da*)…발행하다
everyday(*mae-il*)…매일
library(*to-sŏ-gwan*)…도서관

newspaper(*sin-mun*)…신문
daily newspaper(*il-gan-ji*)…일간지

in a week.	*rŭl ham-ni-da.*
	그는 일주일에 사십 시간 일을 합니다.
20. There are several weekly magazines in Korea.	*Han-gu-ge-nŭn myŏt kkae-ŭi chu-gan-ji-ga it-ssŭm-ni-da.*
	한국에는 몇 개의 주간지가 있습니다.

Months of the Year   *Tal*(달)

1. How many months are there in a year?	*Il nyŏ-ne-nŭn myŏt tta-ri-na it-ssŭm-ni-kka?*
	일 년에는 몇 달이나 있습니까?
2. There are twelve months in a year.	*Il nyŏ-ne-nŭn yŏl-ttu ta-ri it-ssŭm-ni-da.*
	일 년에는 열두 달이 있습니다.
3. January is the coldest month.	*I-rwŏ-rŭn ka-jang ch'u-un tal-im-ni-da.*
	일월은 가장 추운 달입니다.
4. August is the hottest month.	*P'a-rwŏ-rŭn ka-jang tŏ-un tal-im-ni-da.*
	팔월은 가장 더운 달입니다.

---

magazine(*chap-tchi*)…잡지
year(*nyŏn*)…년
moon(*tal*)…달
one year(*il nyŏn*)…일 년
January(*i-rwŏl*)…일월
Feburuary(*i-wŏl*)…이월
March(*sam-wŏl*)…삼월
April(*sa-wŏl*)…사월
May(*o-wŏl*)…오월
June(*yu-wŏl*)…유월

July(*ch'i-rwŏl*)…칠월
August(*p'a-rwŏl*)…팔월
September(*ku-wŏl*)…구월
October(*si-wŏl*)…시월
November(*sip-i-rwŏl*)…십일월
December(*sip-i-wŏl*)…십이월
hot(*tŏ-un*)…더운
sunrise(*il-ch'ul*)…일출
sunset(*il-mol*)…일몰

5. There are 30 or 31 days in a month.

Han ta-re-nŭn sam-sip il tto-nŭn sam-sip-i ri-ri it-ssŭm-ni-da.

한 달에는 삼십 일 또는 삼십일 일이 있습니다.

6. February has only 28 days.

I-wŏ-re-nŭn tan-ji i-sip-p'a ri-ri it-ssŭm-ni-da.

이월에는 단지 이십팔 일이 있습니다.

7. Spring begins in the first part of April.

Po-mŭn sa-wŏl ch'o-e si-jak-doem-ni-da.

봄은 사월 초에 시작됩니다.

8. When do cherry blossoms bloom?

Pŏt-kko-ch'ŭn ŏn-je p'im-ni-kka?

벚꽃은 언제 핍니까?

9. They bloom in mid April.

Sa-wŏl chung-su-ne p'im-ni-da.

사월 중순에 핍니다.

10. In Korea, the best months of the year are September and October.

Han-gu-ge-sŏ ka-jang cho-ŭn ta-rŭn ku-wŏl-gwa si-wŏl-im-ni-da.

한국에서 가장 좋은 달은 구월과 시월입니다.

11. June comes before July.

Yu-wŏ-rŭn ch'i-rwŏl chŏ-ne om-ni-da.

유월은 칠월 전에 옵니다.

12. The 3·1 Independe-

Sa-mil tong-nip un-dong ki-nyŏ-mi-

---

16. The names of the months formed by preceding the Arabic numbers 1 to 12 to "*wŏl*," which means "month" in Chinese character.

begin(*si-ja-k'a-da*) … 시작하다   cherry(*pŏt-kkot*) … 벚꽃
sunlight(*haet-ppit*) … 햇빛   bloom(*p'i-da*) … 피다
sunrise(*hae-do-ji*) … 해돋이   fall(*chi-da*) … 지다
sultry(*mu-dō-un*) … 무더운   blossom(*kkot-ssong-i*) … 꽃송이
sunny side(*yang-ji-tchok*) … 양지쪽   moisture(*sŭp-kki*) … 습기
movement(*un-dong*) … 운동   indeqendence(*tong-nip*) … 독립

nce Movement Day falls on the first day of March.

rŭn sam-wŏl i-ril-im-ni-da.

삼일 독립 운동 기념일은 삼월 일일입니다.

13. August 15 is the Liberation Day of Korea.

P'a-rwŏl sip-o-i-rŭn kwang-bok-tchŏl-im-ni-da.

팔월 십오일은 광복절입니다.

14. When did you come to Korea?

Ŏn-je han-gu-ge o-syŏt-ssŭm-ni-kka?

언제 한국에 오셨습니까?

15. I came here last May.

Chi-nan o-wŏ-re wat-ssŭm-ni-da.

지난 오월에 왔습니다.

16. In which month were you born?

Tang-si-nŭn ŏ-nŭ ta-re ch'ul-ssaeng-haet-ssŭm-ni-kka?

당신은 어느 달에 출생했습니까?

17. I was born in November.

Na-nŭn sip-i-rwŏl tta-re ch'ul-ssaeng-haet-ssŭm-ni-da.

나는 십일월 달에 출생했습니다.

18. When does your summer vacation begin?

Tang-si-nŭi ha-gye pang-ha-gŭn ŏn-je si-ja-k'am-ni-kka?

당신의 하계 방학은 언제 시작합니까?

19. It starts at the end of July and ends in September.

Ch'i-rwŏl ma-re si-ja-k'ae-sŏ, ku-wŏ-re kkŭn-nam-ni-da.

칠월 말에 시작해서, 구월에 끝납니다.

20. After a long drought and unusually warm weather, the month of April has stepped in.

O-raen ka-mum-gwa i-sang na-no-ni chi-nan twi, sa-wŏl-lo chŏ-bŏ-dŭ-rŏt-ssŭm-ni-da.

오랜 가뭄과 이상 난온이 지난 뒤, 사월로 접어들었습니다.

---

vacation(*pang-hak*)…방학   drought(*ka-mum*)…가뭄

Seasons

1. How many seasons are there in a year?

2. There are four seasons. They are spring, summer, antumn and winter.

3. Last winter was comparatively warm.

4. What season do you prefer?

5. I like fall and spring seasons.

6. Which season do you like best?

7. I like autumn best.

Kye-jŏl(계절)

Il nyŏ-ne-nŭn myŏt kkye-jŏ-ri it-ssŭm-ni-kka?

일 년에는 몇 계절이 있습니까?

Ne kye-jŏ-ri it-ssŭm-ni-da. Pom, yŏ-rŭm, ka-ŭl, kyŏ-ul-im-ni-da.

네 계절이 있습니다. 봄, 여름, 가을, 겨울입니다.

Chi-nan kyŏ-u-rŭn pi-gyo-jŏk tta-ttŭt-t'aet-ssŭm-ni-da.

지난 겨울은 비교적 따뜻했습니다.

Tang-si-nŭn ŏ-nŭ kye-jŏ-rŭl cho-a-ham-ni-kka?

당신은 어느 계절을 좋아합니까?

Na-nŭn ka-ŭl-gwa po-mŭl cho-a-ham-ni-da.

나는 가을과 봄을 좋아합니다.

Tang-si-nŭn ŏ-nŭ kye-jŏ-rŭl ka-jang cho-a-ha-sim-ni-kka?

당신은 어느 계절을 가장 좋아하십니까?

Na-nŭn ka-ŭ-rŭl ka-jang cho-a-ham-ni-da.

나는 가을을 가장 좋아합니다.

---

17. The early part of the month is called "*ch'o-sun,*" the middle part "*chung-sun,*" and the end "*ha-sun.*" Thesewords also originated from Chinese characters.

spring(*pom*)···봄
summer(*yŏ-rŭm*)···여름
autumn(*ka-ŭl*)···가을
winter(*kyŏ-ul*)···겨울

warm weather(*na-non*)···난온
step in(*chŏ-bŏ-dŭl-da*)···접어들다
comparatively(*pi-gyo-jŏk*)···비교적
season(*kye-jŏl*)···계절

8. When does the summer begin in Korea ?

Han-gu-ge-sŏ-nŭn yŏ-rŭ-mi ŏn-je si-jak-doem-ni-kka ?

한국에서는 여름이 언제 시작됩니까 ?

9. Usually, it begins from June.

Po-t'ong, yu-wŏl-bu-t'ŏ si-jak-doem-ni-da.

보통, 유월부터 시작됩니다.

10. In Korea, the rainy season lasts from the end of June to the early part of August.

Han-gu-ge-sŏ-nŭn chang-ma-ga yu-wŏl mal-bu-t'ŏ p'a-rwŏl ch'o-kka-ji kye-sok-doem-ni-da.

한국에서는 장마가 유월 말부터 팔월 초까지 계속됩니다.

11. Isn't it a lovely day ?

Ch'am a-rŭm-da-un nal-ssi-ga a-nim-ni-kka ?

참 아름다운 날씨가 아닙니까 ?

12. Yes, it is neither too cold nor too warm.

Ne, ch'up-tchi-do an-k'o, tŏp-tchi-do an-ssŭm-ni-da.

네, 춥지도 않고, 덥지도 않습니다.

13. Autumn sky of Korea is well known throughout the world.

Han-gu-gŭi ka-ŭl ha-nŭ-rŭn se-gye-jŏ-gŭ-ro chal al-lyŏ-jyŏ it-ssŭm-ni-da.

한국의 가을 하늘은 세계적으로 잘 알려져 있습니다.

14. Really, spring has come around the corner.

Chŏng-mal-lo po-mi ka-kka-i wat-ssŭm-ni-da.

정말로 봄이 가까이 왔습니다.

15. In spring, every thing seems to come to life

Po-me-nŭn man-mu-ri ta-si so-saeng-ha-nŭn kŏt kat-ssŭm-ni-da.

---

rainy season(*chang-ma-ch'ŏl*) … 장마철
corner(*ku-sŏk*) … 구석

everything(*mo-dŭn kŏt*) … 모든 것
flood(*hong-su*) … 홍수

again.

봄에는 만물이 다시 소생하는 것 같습니다.

16. The seasons are pretty early this year, isn't it?

Ol-hae-nŭn kye-jŏ-ri cho-gŭm i-rŭm-ni-da. Kŭ-rŏ-ch'i an-ssŭm-ni-kka?

올해는 계절이 조금 이릅니다. 그렇지 않습니까?

17. It seems about two weeks faster than the average year.

P'yŏng-nyŏn-bo-da yak i-ju-il ppa-rŭn kŏt kat-ssŭm-ni-da.

평년보다 약 이주일 빠른 것 같습니다.

18. Let us prepare a lunch box and go out somewhere on this fine spring day.

To-si-ra-gŭl chun-bi-hae-sŏ i hwa-ch'ang-han pom-na-re ŏ-di-ro na-gap-ssi-da.

도시락을 준비해서 이 화창한 봄날에 어디로 나갑시다.

19. Summer weather is quite unpredictable.

Yŏ-rŭm-na-rŭi nal-ssi-nŭn chŏng-mal ye-ch'ŭ-k'al ssu-ga ŏp-ssŭm-ni-da.

여름날의 날씨는 정말 예측할 수가 없습니다.

20. Where's my umbrella? It is raining outside.

Na-ŭi u-sa-ni ŏ-di it-ssŭm-ni-kka? Pak-kke-nŭn pi-ga om-ni-da.

나의 우산이 어디 있습니까? 밖에는 비가 옵니다.

21. How long does the so-called Jang-ma last in

So-wi chang-ma-ra-nŭn kŏ-si han-gu-ge-sŏ-nŭn ŏl-ma-na o-rae kye-

---

forward (*~ŭl hyang-hae-sŏ*)…~을 향해서
unpredictable (*ye-ch'ŭ-k'al ssu ŏm-nŭn*)…예측할 수 없는

average (*p'yŏng-gyun*)…평균
umbrella (*u-san*)…우산
hail (*u-bak*)…우박
drizzle (*i-sŭl-bi*)…이슬비

Korea ?

sok-doem-ni-kka ?

소위 장마라는 것이 한국에서는
얼마나 오래 계속됩니까 ?

22. The rainy season usually lasts about two weeks, but sometimes it lasts much longer than a month.

Chang-ma-nŭn po-t'ong yak i-ju-il kye-sok-doe-nŭn-de, ŏ-ttŏn ttae-nŭn han tal i-sang kye-sok-doe-nŭn ttae-do it-ssŭm-ni-da.

장마는 보통 약 이주일 계속되는데,
어떤 때는 한 달 이상 계속되는
때도 있습니다.

23. Autumn comes after summer.

Ka-ŭ-rŭn yŏ-rŭm ta-ŭ-me om-ni-da.

가을은 여름 다음에 옵니다.

24. Summer seems to have gone.

Yŏ-rŭ-mŭn chi-na-gan kŏt-ch'ŏ-rŏm po-im-ni-da.

여름은 지나간 것처럼 보입니다.

25. Autumn is a good season for reading.

Ka-ŭ-rŭn tok-ssŏ-e cho-ŭn kye-jŏl-im-ni-da.

가을은 독서에 좋은 계절입니다.

26. Autumn is known as a season when the sky is high and the horse becomes fat.

Ka-ŭ-rŭn ha-nŭ-ri nop-kko, ma-ri sal-tchi-nŭn kye-jŏl-lo al-lyŏ-jyŏ it-ssŭm-ni-da.

가을은 하늘이 높고, 말이 살찌는
계절로 알려져 있습니다.

27. Autumn is also a season of harvest.

Ka-ŭ-rŭn tto-han ch'u-su-ŭi kye-jŏl-im-ni-da.

가을은 또한 추수의 계절입니다.

28. What is Thanksgiving ?

Ch'u-sŏ-gi-ran mu-ŏ-sim-ni-kka ?

추석이란 무엇입니까 ?

---

reading(*tok-ssŏ*)…독서
sky(*ha-nŭl*)…하늘
horse(*mal*)…말

festival(*ch'uk-tche*)…축제
harvest(*ch'u-su*)…추수

29. It is similar to Thanksgiving and it is obser-
ved on the 15th day of
August by lunar calen-
dar during Autumn.

*Kŭ myŏng-jŏ-rŭn sŏ-gu na-ra-ŭi
ch'u-su kam-sa-jŏl-gwa pi-sŭt-t'a-
myŏ, ka-ŭl chung ŭm-nyŏ-gŭ-ro p'
a-rwŏl sip-o-i-re se-ge toem-ni-da.*

그 명절은 서구 나라의 추수 감사
절과 비슷하며, 가을 중 음력으로
팔월 십오일에 세게 됩니다.

30. This has been a se-
vere winter so far.

*Chi-gŭm-kka-ji ch'am ch'u-un kyŏ-u-
ri-ŏt-ssŭm-ni-da.*

지금까지 참 추운 겨울이었습니다.

31. I think this has been
the coldest winter I've
ever experienced in
Korea.

*Ol kyŏ-u-rŭn nae-ga han-gu-ge-sŏ
kyŏk-kkŏ-ttŏn ka-jang ch'u-un kyŏ-
u-ri-ra-go saeng-ga-k'am-ni-da.*

올 겨울은 내가 한국에서 겪었던
가장 추운 겨울이라고 생각합니
다.

32. This morning, it was
six degrees below zero
centigrade.

*O-nŭl a-ch'i-mŭn sŏp-ssi yŏng-ha yuk
tto-yŏt-ssŭm-ni-da.*

오늘 아침은 섭씨 영하 육 도였습
니다.

33. Spring is the blooming
season.

*Sa-wŏ-rŭn kkot-p'i-nŭn kye-jŏl-im-
ni-da.*

사월은 꽃피는 계절입니다.

34. In Autumn, the leaves
fall.

Ka-ŭ-re-nŭn ip-p'i chim-ni-da.

가을에는 잎이 집니다.

35. The baseball season

Ya-gu si-jŭ-ni si-jak-doe-ŏt-ssŭm-ni-

---

western country(*sŏ-gu na-ra*)…서구
나라
lunar(*ŭm-nyŏk*)…음력
zero(*yŏng*)…영

leaf(*ip*)…잎
curage(*yong-gi*)…용기
terrible(*mu-sŏ-un*)…무서운

| starts. | *da.* |
| | 야구 시즌이 시작되었습니다. |

Weather

Il-gi(일기)

1. It's a nice day, isn't it?

Cho-ŭn nal-ssi-im-ni-da. Kŭ-rŏ-ch'i an-ssŭm-ni-kka?

좋은 날씨입니다. 그렇지 않습니까?

2. Yes, it is.

Ne, chŏng-mal-im-ni-da.

네, 정말입니다.

3. How's the weather to-day?

O-nŭ-rŭn nal-ssi-ga ŏ-ttŏt-ssŭm-ni-kka?

오늘은 날씨가 어떻습니까?

4. The weather is fine.

Nal-ssi-ga chot-ssŭm-ni-da.

날씨가 좋습니다.

5. The weather is terrible.

Nal-ssi-ga na-ppŭm-ni-da.

날씨가 나쁩니다.

6. It's cloudy.

Ku-rŭ-mi kkyŏt-ssŭm-ni-da.

구름이 꼈습니다.

7. It's raining.

Pi-ga om-ni-da.

비가 옵니다.

8. It looks like rain.

Pi-ga ol kkŏt kat-ssŭm-ni-da.

비가 올 것 같습니다.

9. It's warm.

TTa-ttŭt-t'am-ni-da.

따뜻합니다.

10. It's hot.

Tŏp-ssŭm-ni-da.

덥습니다.

11. It's very hot.

Mae-u tŏp-ssŭm-ni-da.

매우 덥습니다.

---

cloud(*ku-rŭm*)···구름   raincoat(*pi-ot*)···비옷

12. It's cold.
Ch'up-ssŭm-ni-da.
춥습니다.

13. It's very cold.
Mae-u ch'up-ssŭm-ni-da.
매우 춥습니다.

14. It's snowing.
Nu-ni om-ni-da.
눈이 옵니다.

15. It's windy.
Pa-ra-mi pum-ni-da.
바람이 붑니다.

16. It's very windy.
Pa-ra-mi mop-ssi pum-ni-da.
바람이 몹시 붑니다.

17. Windy day, isn't it?
Pa-ra-mi pul-jyo?
바람이 불죠?

18. It's dusty.
Mŏn-ji-ga il-da.
먼지가 일다.

19. It's a lovely day.
A-rŭm-da-un nal-ssi-im-ni-da.
아름다운 날씨입니다.

20. The air is dry.
Kong-gi-ga kŏn-jo-ham-ni-da.
공기가 건조합니다.

21. In Korea, we have a lot of rain in the summer.
Han-gu-ge-sŏ-nŭn yŏ-rŭ-me pi-ga ma-ni om-ni-da.
한국에서는 여름에 비가 많이 옵니다.

22. We have cold weather in the winter.
Kyŏ-u-re-nŭn nal-ssi-ga ch'am-ni-da.
겨울에는 날씨가 찹니다.

23. What's the weather forecast for tomorrow?
Nae-il il-gi ye-bo-nŭn ŏ-ttŏt-ssŭm-ni-kka?

---

wind(*pa-ram*)…바람
dust(*mŏn-ji*)…먼지
dry(*kŏn-jo-han*)…건조한

air(*kong-gi*)…공기
weather(*nal-ssi*)…날씨
forecast(*ye-bo*)…예보

24. The radio announcement says it will be rainy tomorrow.

내일 일기 예보는 어떻습니까?
Ra-di-o pang-song-ŭn nae-il pi-ga o-ri-ra-go ham-ni-da.
라디오 방송은 내일 비가 오리라고 합니다.

25. I'm afraid it'll be rainy tomorrow.

Nae-i-rŭn pi-ga ol kkŏt kat-ssŭm-ni-da.
내일은 비가 올 것 같습니다.

26. It's cloudy this morning.

O-nŭl a-ch'i-men ku-rŭ-mi kkyŏt-ssŭm-ni-da.
오늘 아침엔 구름이 꼈습니다.

27. Do you think it's going to rain today?

Tang-si-nŭn o-nŭl pi-ga o-ri-ra-go saeng-ga-k'am-ni-kka?
당신은 오늘 비가 오리라고 생각합니까?

28. Yes, I think so.

Ne, kŭ-rŏ-t'a-go saeng-ga-k'am-ni-da.
네, 그렇다고 생각합니다.

29. I don't like to walk in mud.

Na-nŭn chin-hŭk sso-gŭl kŏn-nŭn kŏ-sŭl si-rŏ-ham-ni-da.
나는 진흙 속을 걷는 것을 싫어합니다.

30. It is not windy at all.

Chŏn-hyŏ pa-ra-mi pul-ji an-ssŭm-ni-da.
전혀 바람이 불지 않습니다.

31. In winter, it's very easy to catch cold.

Kyŏ-u-re-nŭn kam-gi-ga tŭl-gi swip-ssŭm-ni-da.
겨울에는 감기가 들기 쉽습니다.

32. In rainy day, we have

Pi o-nŭn na-re-nŭn u-sa-nŭl ka-jyŏ

---

mud(*chin-hŭk*)…진흙
radio(*ra-di-o*)…라디오

announcement(*pal-p'yo*)…발표
catch(*chap-tta*)…잡다

to carry umbrella.

ka-ya ham-ni-da.

비오는 날에는 우산을 가져 가야
합니다.

33. We are going to have bad weather again.

Ta-si nal-ssi-ga na-ppa-jil kkŏt kat-ssŭm-ni-da.

다시 날씨가 나빠질 것 같습니다.

34. Cloudy day, isn't it?

Na-ri mop-ssi hŭ-ryŏt-ssŭm-ni-da.

날이 몹시 흐렸습니다.

35. According to radio broadcasting, there will be a typhoon this afternoon.

Ra-di-o pang-song-e ŭi-ha-myŏn, o-nŭl o-hu-e t'ae-p'ung-i pul kkŏt kat-ssŭm-ni-da.

라디오 방송에 의하면, 오늘 오후에
태풍이 불 것 같습니다.

36. I am afraid of thunder and lightning.

Na-nŭn ch'ŏn-dung-gwa pŏn-gae-rŭl mu-sŏ-wŏ-ham-ni-da.

나는 천둥과 번개를 무서워합니다.

37. The weather suddenly has changed.

Nal-ssi-ga kap-tcha-gi pyŏn-haet-ssŭm-ni-da.

날씨가 갑자기 변했습니다.

38. Nasty day, isn't it?

Ko-yan nal-ssi-im-ni-da.

고얀 날씨입니다.

39. Last night, the moon and stars were shining.

Chi-nan pa-me-nŭn tal-gwa pyŏ-ri pin-nat-ssŭm-ni-da.

지난 밤에는 달과 별이 빛났습니다.

40. Nice day, isn't it?

Cho-ŭn nal-ssi-im-ni-da.

좋은 날씨입니다.

41. Young boys and girls

Chŏl-mŭn so-nyŏn-gwa so-nyŏ-dŭ-

---

carry(*un-ban-ha-da*)…운반하다
broadcasting(*pang-song*)…방송
thunder(*ch'ŏn-dung*)…천둥

lightning(*pŏn-gae*)…번개
typhoon(*t'ae-p'ung*)…태풍
shine(*pin-na-da*)…빛나다

like to walk under the moonlight.	*rŭn tal-bit a-rae-sŏ san-ppo-ha-gi-rŭl cho-a-ham-ni-da.*
	젊은 소년과 소녀들은 달빛 아래서 산보하기를 좋아합니다.
42. High school girls like the full moon.	*Yŏ-ja ko-dŭng hak-ssaeng-dŭ-rŭn po-rŭm-tta-rŭl cho-a-ham-ni-da.*
	여자 고등 학생들은 보름달을 좋아합니다.
43. Men are afraid of storms and floods.	*Sa-ram-dŭ-rŭn p'ok-p'ung-gwa hong-su-rŭl mu-sŏ-wŏ-ham-ni-da.*
	사람들은 폭풍과 홍수를 무서워합니다.
44. Peoples are afraid of avalanche in winter and flood in summer.	*Sa-ram-dŭ-rŭn kyŏ-u-re-nŭn nun-sa-t'ae-rŭl mu-sŏ-wŏ-ha-go, yŏ-rŭ-me-nŭn hong-su-rŭl mu-sŏ-wŏ-ham-ni-da.*
	사람들은 겨울에는 눈사태를 무서워하고, 여름에는 홍수를 무서워합니다.
45. It is raining cats and dogs.	*Ŏk-ssu-ga-ch'i pi-ga om-ni-da.*
	억수같이 비가 옵니다.

Name And Age   *I-rŭm, Na-i*(이름, 나이)

1. What is your name?   *Tang-si-nŭi i-rŭ-mŭn mu-ŏ-sim-ni-kka?*

당신의 이름은 무엇입니까?

---

18. *"sŏng-ham"* or *"chon-ham"* is politer than *"i-rŭm."*

full moon(*po-rŭm-ttal*)···보름달	fog(*an-gae*)···안개
storm(*p'ok-p'ung*)···폭풍	avalanche(*nun-sa-t'ae*)···눈사태
shadow(*kŭ-rim-ja*)···그림자	moonlight(*tal-bit*)···달빛

2. My name is Kim Tu-ri.

Na-ŭi i-rŭ-mŭn kim-du-ri-im-ni-da.

나의 이름은 김두리입니다.

3. What is your father's name?

Tang-sin a-bŏ-ji-ŭi sŏng-ha-mŭn mu-ŏ-sim-ni-kka?

당신 아버지의 성함은 무엇입니까?

4. My father's name is Kim Saem-to.

Na-ŭi a-bŏ-ji sŏng-ha-mŭn kim-saem-t'ŏ-im-ni-da.

나의 아버지 성함은 김샘터입니다.

5. How old are you?

Myŏt ssal-im-ni-kka?

몇 살입니까?

6. I am 30 years old.

Na-nŭn sŏ-rŭn sal-im-ni-da.

나는 서른 살입니다.

7. How old do you think I am?

Nae-ga myŏt ssa-ri-ra-go saeng-ga-k'a-sim-ni-kka?

내가 몇 살이라고 생각하십니까?

8. You look younger.

Tang-si-nŭn chŏl-mŏ po-im-ni-da.

당신은 젊어 보입니다.

9. Can you guess my age?

Nae na-i-rŭl ma-ch'il ssu it-ssŭm-ni-kka?

내 나이를 맞칠 수 있습니까?

10. You are probably forty years old.

Tang-si-nŭn a-ma ma-hŭn sa-ril kkŏ-sim-ni-da.

당신은 아마 마흔 살일 것입니다.

11. You don't look forty years old.

Tang-si-nŭn ma-hŭn sal-lo po-i-ji an-ssŭm-ni-da.

당신은 마흔 살로 보이지 않습니다.

---

19. In Korea, the family name comes before one's given name.

12. What is his family name ?

Kŭ-ŭi sŏng-i mu-ŏ-sim-ni-kka?
그의 성이 무엇입니까 ?

13. His family name is Kim. There are many Kims and Lees in Korea.

Kŭ-ŭi sŏng-ŭn kim-ssi-im-ni-da. Han-gu-ge-nŭn ma-nŭn kim-ssi-wa i-ssi-ga it-ssŭm-ni-da.
그의 성은 김씨입니다. 한국에는 많은 김씨와 이씨가 있습니다.

14. What are the most popular family names in Korea ?

Han-gu-ge-sŏ ka-jang hŭn-han sŏng-ssi-dŭ-rŭn mu-ŏ-sim-ni-kka?
한국에서 가장 흔한 성씨들은 무엇입니까 ?

15. Kim, Lee and Park are the most popular family names in Korea.

Kim-ssi, i-ssi, pak-ssi-dŭ-rŭn han-gu-ge-sŏ ka-jang hŭn-han sŏng-ssi-dŭl-im-ni-da.
김씨, 이씨, 박씨들은 한국에서 가장 흔한 성씨들입니다.

16. What's your Christian name ?

Tang-si-nŭi se-re-myŏng-ŭn mu-ŏ-sim-ni-kka?
당신의 세례명은 무엇입니까 ?

17. My Christian name is John.

Na-ŭi se-re-myŏng-ŭn yo-han-im-ni-da.
나의 세례명은 요한입니다.

18. He is just my age.

Kŭ-nŭn na-ŭi yŏn-bae-im-ni-da.
그는 나의 연배입니다.

19. When I was your age, I succeeded in the examination.

Ne na-i ttae-e na-nŭn kŭ si-hŏ-me hap-kkyŏ-k'aet-tta.
네 나이 때에 나는 그 시험에 합격했다.

---

religion(*chong-gyo*)…종교   Christian name(*se-re-myŏng*)…세례명

20. Worry and illness age a man.

Kŭn-sim-gwa pyŏng-i sa-ra-mŭl nŭl-kke-ham-ni-da.

근심과 병이 사람을 늙게합니다.

Family

Ka-jok(가족)

1. How many family members do you have?

Tang-si-nŭn ka-jo-gi myŏ-ch'i-sim-ni-kka?

당신은 가족이 몇이십니까?

2. I have seven.

Il-gop-im-ni-da.

일곱입니다.

3. Do you have a father?

A-bŏ-ji-ga kye-sim-ni-kka?

아버지가 계십니까?

4. Yes, I have.

Ne, kye-sim-ni-da.

네, 계십니다.

5. Do you have a grandmother?

Hal-mŏ-ni-ga kye-sim-ni-kka?

할머니가 계십니까?

6. How many children do you have?

A-i-dŭ-ri myŏ-ch'i-sim-ni-kka?

아이들이 몇이십니까?

7. I have three children.

Se a-i-ga it-ssŭm-ni-da.

세 아이가 있습니다.

8. I have two sons and one daughter.

Tu a-dŭl-gwa ttal ha-na-ga it-ssŭm-ni-da.

두 아들과 딸 하나가 있습니다.

9. Do you have a wife?

Pu-i-ni kye-sim-ni-kka?

---

20. When the word "wife" is mentioned, "*a-nae*" is used for one's own wife and "*pu-in*" for another's wife, And aged people call their wives "*ma-nu-ra.*"

examination(*si-hŏm*)···시험	number(*su*)···수
worry(*kŭn-sim*)···근심	grandmother(*hal-mŏ-ni*)···할머니
illness(*pyŏng*)···병	collective life(*kong-dong saeng-hwal*)···공동 생활
cause(*wŏ-nin*)···원인	

부인이 계십니까?

10. Yes, indeed. I love my wife.

Mul-lon-i-ji-yo. Na-nŭn a-nae-rŭl sa-rang-ham-ni-da.

물론이지요. 나는 아내를 사랑합니다.

11. What is your husband's profession?

Tang-sin nam-p'yŏ-nŭi chi-gŏ-bŭn mu-ŏ-sim-ni-kka?

당신 남편의 직업은 무엇입니까?

12. He is a professor at Seoul National University.

Seŏ-ul tae-hak-kkyo-ŭi kyo-su-im-ni-da.

서울 대학교의 교수입니다.

13. I am going to get married when I graduate from college.

Chŏ-nŭn tae-hak-kkyo-rŭl cho-rŏ-p'al ttae kyŏl-hon-hal-lyŏ-go ham-ni-da.

저는 대학교를 졸업할 때 결혼하려고 합니다.

14. Are you engaged?

Ya-k'on-ha-syŏt-ssŭm-ni-kka?

약혼하셨습니까?

15. My fiance is operating a business firm in Seoul.

Na-ŭi ya-k'on-ja-nŭn seŏ-u-re-sŏ sa-ŏp-ch'e-rŭl u-nyŏng-ha-go it-ssŭm-ni-da.

나의 약혼자는 서울에서 사업체를 운영하고 있습니다.

16. How many cousins do

Tang-si-nŭn sa-ch'o-ni myŏ-ch'i-na

---

cousin(*sa-ch'on*)…사촌
husband(*nam-p'yŏn*)…남편
university(*tae-hak-kkyo*)…대학교
marry(*kyŏl-hon-ha-da*)…결혼하다
graduate(*cho-rŏ-p'a-da*)…졸업하다
college(*tae-hak*)…대학

engage(*ya-k'on-ha-da*)…약혼하다
fiance(*ya-k'on-ja*)…약혼자
operate(*u-nyŏng-ha-da*)…운영하다
business firm(*sa-ŏp-ch'e*)…사업체
occupation(*chi-gŏp*)…직업

90

you have? *it-ssŭm-ni-kka?*

당신은 사촌이 몇이나 있습니까?

17. The soldier is my nephew. *Kŭ ku-ni-nŭn chŏ-ŭi cho-k'a-im-ni-da.*

그 군인은 저의 조카입니다.

18. My niece is a typist. *Na-ŭi cho-k'a-tta-rŭn t'a-i-p'i-sŭ-t'ŭ-im-ni-da.*

나의 조카딸은 타이피스트입니다.

19. Generally, Koreans have large families. *Il-ban-jŏ-gŭ-ro han-guk sa-ram-dŭ-rŭn tae-ga-jo-gŭl kŏ-nŭ-rim-ni-da.*

일반적으로 한국 사람들은 대가족을 거느립니다.

20. Sometimes, more than two generations of the same family live together. *Ka-kkŭm, ka-t'ŭn ka-jok tu-se tae i-sang-i ka-ch'i sam-ni-da.*

가끔, 같은 가족 두세 대 이상이 같이 삽니다.

Numerals   *Su*(수)

1. There are seven days in a week. *Il-tchu-i-re-nŭn ch'i ri-ri it-ssŭm-ni-da.*

일주일에는 칠 일이 있습니다.

2. There are twelve months in a year. *Il nyŏ-ne-nŭn yŏl-ttu ta-ri it-ssŭm-ni-da.*

일 년에는 열두 달이 있습니다.

---

nephew(*cho-k'a*)…조카
son-in-law(*sa-wi*)…사위
niece(*cho-k'a-ttal*)…조카딸
uncle(*sam-ch'on*)…삼촌
maternal uncle(*woe-suk*)…외숙
one(*ha-na*)…하나
two(*tul*)…둘

three(*set*)…셋
four(*net*)…넷
five(*ta-sŏt*)…다섯
six(*yŏ-sŏt*)…여섯
seven(*il-gop*)…일곱
eight(*yŏ-dŏl*)…여덟
nine(*a-hop*)…아홉

3. One minute has sixty seconds.

Il-bu-nŭn yuk-sip-ch'o-im-ni-da.
일분은 육십초입니다.

4. Two and three are five.

Tul tŏ-ha-gi se-sŭn ta-sŏt-im-ni-da.
둘 더하기 셋은 다섯입니다.

5. Ten plus five is fifteen.

Yŏl tŏ-ha-gi to-sŏ-sŭn yŏl-da-sŏt-im-ni-da.
열 더하기 다섯은 열다섯입니다.

6. Five times three is fifteen.

Ta-sŏt ko-p'a-gi se-sŭn yŏl-da-sŏt-im-ni-da.
다섯 곱하기 셋은 열다섯입니다.

7. Twenty minus seven is thirteen.

Sŭ-mu-re-sŏ il-go-bŭl ppae-myŏn yŏl-set-im-ni-da.
스물에서 일곱을 빼면 열셋입니다.

8. Six divided by two is three.

Yŏ-sŏ-sŭl tul-lo na-nu-myŏn set-im-ni-da.
여섯을 둘로 나누면 셋입니다.

9. How many books do you have?

Tang-si-nŭn ch'ae-gŭl myŏt kkwŏ-ni-na ka-ji-go it-ssŭm-ni-kka?
당신은 책을 몇 권이나 가지고 있습니까?

10. Please count the apples.

Sa-gwa-rŭl se-ŏ po-sip-ssi-o.
사과를 세어 보십시오.

11. There are 365 days in a year.

Il nyŏ-ne-nŭn sam-baeng-yuk-sip-o i-ri it-ssŭm-ni-da.
일 년에는 삼백육십오 일이 있습

---

ten(*yŏl*)…열
eleven(*yŏl-ha-na*)…열하나
twelve(*yŏl-ttul*)…열둘
thirteen(*yŏl-set*)…열셋
fourteen(*yŏl-net*)…열넷

fifteen(*yŏl-da-sŏt*)…열다섯
sixteen(*yŏl-lyŏ-sŏt*)…열여섯
twenty(*sŭ-mul*)…스물
count(*se-da*)…세다

니다.

12. How many students are in this class?

I hak-kkŭ-be-nŭn myŏn myŏng-ŭi hak-ssaeng-i it-ssŭm-ni-kka?

이 학급에는 몇 명의 학생이 있습니까?

13. There are sixty five students in this class.

I hak-kkŭ-be-nŭn ye-sun-da-sŏn myŏng-ŭi hak-ssaeng-i it-ssŭm-ni-da.

이 학급에는 예순다섯 명의 학생이 있습니다.

14. Let's buy ten peaches and five water melons.

Yŏl kkae-ŭi pok-ssung-a-wa ta-sŏt kkae-ŭi su-ba-gŭl sap-ssi-da.

열 개의 복숭아와 다섯 개의 수박을 삽시다.

15. How much does it cost?

Ŏl-ma-im-ni-kka?

얼마입니까?

16. It's 50,000 won.

O-man wŏn-im-ni-da.

오만 원입니다.

17. How many people are there in the auditorium?

Kang-dang-e-nŭn myŏn myŏng-ŭi sa-ram-dŭ-ri it-ssŭm-ni-kka?

강당에는 몇 명의 사람들이 있습니까?

18. Thousands and thousands peoples gatherea in the auditorium.

Su-ch'ŏn myŏng-ŭi sa-ram-dŭ-ri kang-dang-e mo-yŏt-ssŭm-ni-da.

수천 명의 사람들이 강당에 모였

---

wild rose(*hae-dang-hwa*)…해당화
water melon(*su-bak*)…수박
sea gull(*kal-mae-gi*)…갈매기
beach(*hae-byŏn*)…해변
sand(*mo-rae*)…모래

gather(*mo-i-da*)…모이다
million(*paek*)…백
thousand(*ch'ŏn*)…천
ten thousand(*man*)…만

19. Every summer, millions and millions peoples go to beach for swimming.

습니다.

Mae-nyŏn yŏ-rŭm, su-baeng ma-nŭi sa-ram-dŭ-ri su-yŏng-ŭl ha-rŏ pa-dat-kka-ro kam-ni-da.

매년 여름, 수백 만의 사람들이 수영을 하러 바닷가로 갑니다.

20. What's the population of Korea?

Han-gu-gŭi in-gu-nŭn ŏl-ma-im-ni-kka?

한국의 인구는 얼마입니까?

21. The population of Korea is over fifty million.

Han-gu-gŭi in-gu-nŭn o-ch'ŏn-ma-ni nŏm-ssŭm-ni-da.

한국의 인구는 오천만이 넘습니다.

22. What's the population of Seoul?

Seŏ-u-rŭi in-gu-nŭn ŏl-ma-im-ni-kka?

서울의 인구는 얼마입니까?

23. It's more than twelve million.

Ch'ŏn-i-baeng-man i-sang-im-ni-da.

천이백만 이상입니다.

24. It is three hundred twenty miles from Seoul to Pusan.

Seŏ-ul-ssŏ pu-san-kka-ji-nŭn sam-baek-i-sim ma-il-im-ni-da.

서울서 부산까지는 삼백이십 마일입니다.

25. How much does it cost to fly from Seoul to Pusan?

Seŏ-ul-ssŏ pu-san-kka-ji pi-haeng-gi-ro ka-nŭn-de ŏl-ma-im-ni-kka?

서울서 부산까지 비행기로 가는데 얼마입니까?

26. It costs forty thousands and two hundreds won.

Sa-man i-baek wŏn-im-ni-da.

사만 이백 원입니다.

---

fly(*nal-da*)…날다
wing(*nal-gae*)…날개

population(*in-gu*)…인구

27. What is the rental price of this room?

I pang-ŭi set-tto-nŭn ŏl-ma-im-ni-kka?

이 방의 셋돈은 얼마입니까?

28. It's 300,000 won per month.

Han ta-re sam-sim-man wŏn-im-ni-da.

한 달에 삼십만 원입니다.

29. Many bridges were built during the New Community Movement.

Sae-ma-ŭl un-dong-ŭ-ro ma-nŭn ta-ri-ga no-yŏ-jyŏt-ssŭm-ni-da.

새마을 운동으로 많은 다리가 놓여졌습니다.

30. GNP growth of Korea in 1990 marked 5,500 dollars.

Ch'ŏn-gu-baek-gu-sim-nyŏ-ne han-gu-gŭi chi-en-p'i sŏng-jang-yu-rŭn o-ch'ŏn-o-baek ppu-rŭl ki-ro-k'aet-tta.

천구백구십년에 한국의 『지. 엔. 피』성장률은 오천오백 불을 기록했다.

Color

Saek(색)

1. What is the color of this shirt?

I syŏ-ch'u-ŭi sae-gŭn mu-ŏ-sim-ni-kka?

이 셔츠의 색은 무엇입니까?

2. It's white.

Ha-yan-saek-im-ni-da.

하얀색입니다.

3. Sky is blue.

Ha-nŭ-rŭn p'u-rŭm-ni-da.

---

price(*kap*)…값
interest(*i-ja*)…이자
build(*se-u-da*)…세우다
growth(*sŏng-jang*)…성장
mark(*p'yo-si*)…표시

selection(*sŏn-t'aek*)…선택
color(*saek*)…색
shirt(*syŏ-ch'ŭ*)…셔츠
white(*hin*)…흰
blue(*p'u-rŭn*)…푸른

하늘은 푸릅니다.

4. The color of sunflower is yellow.

Hae-ba-ra-gi-ŭi sae-gŭn no-rang-im-ni-da.

해바라기의 색은 노랑입니다.

5. Give me the red pencil.

Pul-gŭn yŏn-p'i-rŭl chu-sip-ssi-o.

붉은 연필을 주십시오.

6. The color of my father's hair is grey.

U-ri a-bŏ-ji mŏ-ri-sae-gŭn hoe-saek-im-ni-da.

우리 아버지 머리색은 회색입니다.

7. What is the color of Korean flag?

T'ae-gŭk-kki-ŭi sae-gŭn mu-ŏ-sim-ni-kka?

태극기의 색은 무엇입니까?

8. There are red, blue and black colors in Korean flag.

T'ae-gŭk-kki-e-nŭn pul-gŭn-saek, p'u-rŭn-saek, kŏ-mŭn-sae-gi it-ssŭm-ni-da.

태극기에는 붉은색, 푸른색, 검은색이 있습니다.

9. What is the color of grass?

P'u-rŭn mu-sŭn saek-im-ni-kka?

풀은 무슨 색입니까?

10. It's green.

Ch'o-rok-ssaek-im-ni-da.

초록색입니다.

11. A brown rabbit is running.

Kal-ssae-gŭi t'o-kki-ga ttwi-go it-ssŭm-ni-da.

갈색의 토끼가 뛰고 있습니다.

12. Which color do you like?

Tang-si-nŭn ŏ-nŭ sae-gŭl cho-a-ha-sim-ni-kka?

---

yellow(*no-ran*)…노란
red(*ppal-gan*)…빨간
hair(*mŏ-ri-k'a-rak*)…머리카락
grey(*hoe-saek*)…회색

flag(*kuk-kki*)…국기
black(*kŏ-mŭn*)…검은
navy blue(*kon-saek*)…곤색
grass(*p'ul*)…풀

당신은 어느 색을 좋아하십니까?

13. I like violet.

Na-nŭn po-ra-sae-gŭl cho-a-ham-ni-da.

나는 보라색을 좋아합니다.

14. In winter, we have white snow.

Kyŏ-u-re-nŭn ha-yan nu-ni om-ni-da.

겨울에는 하얀 눈이 옵니다.

15. What is the color of rainbow?

Mu-ji-gae-ŭi sae-gŭn mu-ŏ-sim-ni-kka?

무지개의 색은 무엇입니까?

16. "Scarlet Letter" is a name of a wellknown novel.

Chu-hong kŭl-ssi-nŭn yu-myŏng-han so-sŏl i-rŭm-im-ni-da.

"주홍 글씨"는 유명한 소설 이름입니다.

17. Darkness is expressed with black color.

Ŏ-du-mŭn kŏ-mŭn-sae-gŭ-ro p'yo-hyŏn-doem-ni-da.

어둠은 검은색으로 표현됩니다.

18. In our garden, there are many red, white and yellow flowers.

U-ri chŏng-wŏ-ne-nŭn su-ma-nŭn pul-gŭn-saek, ha-yan-saek, no-ran-sae-gŭi kkot-ttŭ-ri it-ssŭm-ni-da.

우리 정원에는 수많은 붉은색, 하얀색, 노란색의 꽃들이 있습니다.

---

green(*nok-ssaek*)···녹색
brown(*kal-ssaek*)···갈색
scarlet(*chu-hong-saek*)···주홍색
indigo(*nam-saek*)···남색
violet(*po-ra-saek*)···보라색
pink(*pun-hong-saek*)···분홍색
classification(*pul-lyu*)···분류

rainbow(*mu-ji-gae*)···무지개
rose-colored(*chang-mi-bi-ch'ŭi*)···장미빛의
darkness(*ŏ-dum*)···어둠
garden(*chŏng-wŏn*)···정원
rabit(*t'o-kki*)···토끼
run(*ttwi-da*)···뛰다

PART III

Practical Sentences

At the Airport

Kong-hang-e-sŏ (공항에서)

1. Where's the Korean Air Line counter ?

   Tae-han hang-gong-sa-ŭi k'a-un-t'ŏ-nŭn ŏ-di it-ssŭm-ni-kka ?

   대한 항공사의 『카운터』는 어디 있습니까 ?

2. Right over there.

   Chŏ-tchok-im-ni-da.

   저쪽입니다.

3. Let me have your passport.

   P'ae-sŭ-p'o-t'ŭ-rŭl po-yŏ chu-sip-ssi-o.

   『패스포트』를 보여 주십시오.

4. Here it is.

   Yŏ-gi it-ssŭm-ni-da.

   여기 있습니다.

5. What is the purpose of your visit to Korea ?

   Han-gu-gŭl pang-mun-han mok-tchŏ-gŭn mu-ŏ-sim-ni-kka ?

   한국을 방문한 목적은 무엇입니까 ?

6. For sightseeing tour.

   Kwan-gwang yŏ-haeng-ŭl wi-hae-sŏ-im-ni-da.

   관광 여행을 위해서입니다.

7. How long are you going to stay in Korea ?

   Han-gu-ge ŏl-ma-na o-raet-ttong-an mŏ-mu-rŭ-si-get-ssŭm-ni-kka ?

   한국에 얼마나 오랫동안 머무르시겠습니까 ?

8. About one month.

   Yak han tal ttong-an-im-ni-da.

   약 한 달 동안입니다.

9. Do you have anything

   Sin-go-hal kkŏ-si it-ssŭm-ni-kka ?

---

airport(*kong-hang*)…공항
passport(*p'ae-sŭ-p'o-t'ŭ*)…패스포트
purpose(*mok-tchŏk*)…목적

sightseeing(*kwan-gwang*)…관광
visit(*pang-mun-ha-da*)…방문하다

to declare?	신고할 것이 있습니까?
10. I have nothing to declare.	*Sin-go-hal kkŏ-si ŏp-ssŭm-ni-da.* 신고할 것이 없습니다.
11. What does this trunk contain?	*I ka-bang-e-nŭn mu-ŏ-si it-ssŭm-ni-kka?* 이 가방에는 무엇이 있습니까?
12. This is a gift for my Korean friends.	*I-gŏ-sŭn na-ŭi han-guk ch'in-gu-dŭ-rŭl wi-han sŏn-mul-im-ni-da.* 이것은 나의 한국 친구들을 위한 선물입니다.
13. Please fill in this card.	*I k'a-dŭ-rŭl chŏ-gŏ chu-sip-ssi-o.* 이 카드를 적어 주십시오.
14. Is this all right?	*Toet-ssŭm-ni-kka?* 됐습니까?
15. Shall I weigh your baggage?	*Tang-si-nŭi chi-mŭl ta-ra pol-kka-yo?* 당신의 짐을 달아 볼까요?
16. Do I weigh all my baggage?	*Na-ŭi chi-mŭl mo-du ta-ra-ya ham-ni-kka?* 나의 짐을 모두 달아야 합니까?
17. No, except your hand baggage.	*A-nim-ni-da. So-ne tŭ-sin chi-mŭn che-oe-ham-ni-da.* 아닙니다. 손에 드신 짐은 제외합니다.
18. Are they over weight?	*Mu-ge-ga nŏ-mŏn-na-yo?* 무게가 넘었나요?
19. Would you mind wat-	*Nae chi-mŭl pwa chu-si-ji an-k'et-*

---

ching my luggage?

ssŭm-ni-kka?

내 짐을 봐 주시지 않겠습니까?

20. Which bag will you check?

Ŏ-nŭ ka-bang-ŭl hwak-in-ha-si-get-ssŭm-ni-kka?

어느 가방을 확인하시겠습니까?

21. I want this bag to be checked.

I ka-bang-ŭl pu-t'a-k'a-get-ssŭm-ni-da.

이 가방을 부탁하겠습니다.

22. Don't rush to come back. I am not going anywhere. I will stay here till you come back.

Ch'ŏn-ch'ŏn-hi ta-nyŏ o-sip-ssi-o. Na-nŭn a-mu-de-do an ka-yo. Tang-si-ni to-ra-ol ttae-kka-ji na-nŭn yŏ-gi it-kket-ssŭm-ni-da.

천천히 다녀 오십시오. 나는 아무 데도 안 가요. 당신이 돌아올 때 까지 나는 여기 있겠습니다.

23. I hope you will have good days in Korea.

Han-gu-ge-sŏ chŭl-gŏ-un na-rŭl po-nae-si-gil pa-ram-ni-da.

한국에서 즐거운 날을 보내시길 바랍니다.

24. Thank you for coming to see me.

Ma-jung-ŭl na-wa chu-syŏ-sŏ kam-sa-ham-ni-da.

마중을 나와 주셔서 감사합니다.

25. Thank you for coming to see me off.

Hwan-song-ŭl na-wa chu-syŏ-sŏ kam-sa-ham-ni-da.

환송을 나와 주셔서 감사합니다.

26. I will take you to the hotel.

Ho-t'el-kka-ji mo-syŏ tŭ-ri-get-ssŭm-ni-da.

---

check(*chŏm-gŏm*)…점검　　　　　bag(*ka-bang*)…가방
briefcase(*son-kka-bang*)…손가방

호텔까지 모셔 드리겠습니다.

At the hotel

1. Can I have a room please?
2. How many of you are there?
3. I want a single room without bath.

4. I wish to have a room with a bath.

5. Do you have a reservation?
6. How many nights are you going to stay?

7. Is this all the baggage you have?

8. Have you a better room than this?

Ho-t'e-re-sŏ(호텔에서)

Pang-i it-ssŭm-ni-kka?
방이 있습니까?
Myŏt ssa-ram-i-sim-ni-kka?
몇 사람이십니까?
Mo-gyok-t'ang-i ŏm-nŭn sing-gŭl ru-mŭl pu-t'a-k'am-ni-da.
목욕탕이 없는 『싱글 룸』을 부탁합니다.

Mo-gyok-t'ang-i ttal-lin pang-ŭl pu-t'a-k'am-ni-da.
목욕탕이 딸린 방을 부탁합니다.
Ye-ya-gŭl ha-syŏt-ssŭm-ni-kka?
예약을 하셨습니까?
Myŏn nal ppa-mi-na mŏ-mu-rŭ-si-get-ssŭm-ni-kka?
몇 날 밤이나 머무르시겠습니까?
I-gŏ-si tang-si-ni ka-jyŏ o-sin chi-mŭi chŏn-bu-im-ni-kka?
이것이 당신이 가져 오신 짐의 전부입니까?
I-gŏt-ppo-da tŏ cho-ŭn pang-i it-ssŭm-ni-kka?
이것보다 더 좋은 방이 있습니까?

---

motel(*mo-t'el*)···모텔
room(*pang*)···방
single(*ha-na-ŭi*)···하나의

bath(*mo-gyok-t'ang*)···목욕탕
reservation(*ye-yak*)···예약

9. I want a room with a nice view.

Chŏn-mang-i cho-ŭn pang-ŭl wŏn-ham-ni-da.

전망이 좋은 방을 원합니다.

10. I'll take this room.

I pang-ŭ-ro ha-get-ssŭm-ni-da.

이 방으로 하겠습니다.

11. What is the charge for this room?

I pang kkap-ssŭn ŏl-ma-im-ni-kka?

이 방 값은 얼마입니까?

12. Send up my luggage.

Nae chi-mŭl ol-lyŏ-da chu-sip-ssi-o.

내 짐을 올려다 주십시오.

13. Bring me some letter paper and envelopes.

P'yŏn-ji-ji-wa pong-t'u myŏt tchang-man ka-jyŏ-da chu-sip-ssi-o.

편지지와 봉투 몇 장만 가져다 주십시오.

14. When is the checking out time?

Suk-ppak kye-san si-ga-nŭn ŏn-je-im-ni-kka?

숙박 계산 시간은 언제입니까?

15. This is the key for your room.

I-gŏ-si tang-sin pang yŏl-ssoe-im-ni-da.

이것이 당신 방 열쇠입니다.

16. Please don't drain the bathtub after you have taken the bath.

Mo-gyo-gŭl ha-sin ta-ŭm, t'ang-ŭi mu-rŭl hŭl-lyŏ pŏ-ri-ji ma-syŏt-ssŭ-myŏn ko-map-kket-ssŭm-ni-da.

목욕을 하신 다음, 탕의 물을 흘려 버리지 마셨으면 고맙겠습니다.

17. This is used as a wash cloth and a bath towel.

I su-gŏ-nŭn mo-mŭl ttang-nŭn de-wa mo-mŭl mal-li-nŭn de ssŭ-yŏ-

---

view⟨*kwang-gyŏng*⟩…광경
envelope⟨*pong-t'u*⟩…봉투
paper⟨*chong-i*⟩…종이

luggage⟨*chim*⟩…짐
entrusting⟨*pu-t'ak*⟩…부탁
key⟨*yŏl-ssoe*⟩…열쇠

jim-ni-da.

이 수건은 몸을 닦는 데와 몸을 말리는 데 쓰여집니다.

18. With this, you wipe the dust from your face and hands.

I-gŏ-sŭ-ro ŏl-gul-gwa so-nŭi mŏn-ji-rŭl ssi-sŏ nae-nŭn kŏ-sim-ni-da.

이것으로 얼굴과 손의 먼지를 씻어내는 것입니다.

19. We serve meals at any time.

A-mu-ttae-na sik-ssa-rŭl tŭ-rim-ni-da.

아무때나 식사를 드립니다.

20. May I take your order?

Chu-mu-nŭl pa-dŭl-kka-yo?

주문을 받을까요?

21. Is there anything else I can do for you?

Tang-si-nŭl to-wa-dŭ-ril i-ri it-ssŭl-kka-yo?

당신을 도와드릴 일이 있을까요?

22. May I clean your room now?

Chi-gŭm pang-ŭl so-je-hal-kka-yo?

지금 방을 소제할까요?

23. May I prepare your bed now?

Chi-gŭm ch'im-gu-rŭl chun-bi-hal-kka-yo?

지금 침구를 준비할까요?

24. Do you accept traveller's checks?

Yŏ-haeng-ja su-p'yo-do pat-ssŭm-ni-kka?

여행자 수표도 받습니까?

25. Where is the Chosun Hotel?

Cho-sŏn ho-t'e-rŭn ŏ-di it-ssŭm-ni-kka?

조선 호텔은 어디 있습니까?

26. It is in Sokong-dong.

So-gong-dong-e it-ssŭm-ni-da.

---

meal(*sik-ssa*)…식사
order(*chu-mun*)…주문
accept(*pat-tta*)…받다

traveller(*yŏ-haeng-ja*)…여행자
bathroom(*yok-ssil*)…욕실
delivery(*pae-dal*)…배달

소공동에 있습니다.

27. Where are you staying?

Tang-si-nŭn ŏ-di mŏ-mu-rŭ-go kye-sim-ni-kka?

당신은 어디 머무르고 계십니까?

28. It is the YMCA Hotel.

Wai-em-ssi-ei ho-t'el-im-ni-da.

『와이. 엠. 씨. 에이』 호텔입니다.

29. Don't wake me tomorrow morning.

Nae-il a-ch'im kkae-u-ji ma-sip-ssi-o.

내일 아침 깨우지 마십시오.

30. Please wake me up at seven tomorrow morning.

Nae-il a-ch'im il-gop-ssi-e na-rŭl kkae-wŏ chu-sip-ssi-o.

내일 아침 일곱시에 나를 깨워 주십시오.

31. Please give these clothes to the laundry and have them washed.

I o-sŭl se-t'ak-ppu-e-ge chu-ŏ, ppal-ge ha-yŏ chu-sip-ssi-o.

이 옷을 세탁부에게 주어, 빨게 하여 주십시오.

32. When can I pick up the clean clothes?

Ŏn-je ppal-lae-rŭl ka-jyŏ kal-kka-yo?

언제 빨래를 가져 갈까요?

33. Where can I get my haircut?

Ŏ-di-sŏ mŏ-ri-rŭl kkak-kkŭl ssu it-ssŭl-kka-yo?

어디서 머리를 깎을 수 있을까요?

34. There is a barbershop on the third floor.

Sam-ch'ŭng-e i-bal-sso-ga it-ssŭm-ni-da.

삼층에 이발소가 있습니다.

35. How much for a haircut only?

Mŏ-ri-man kkang-nŭn-de ŏl-ma-im-ni-kka?

머리만 깎는데 얼마입니까?

---

disturb(*koe-ro-p'i-da*)⋯괴롭히다
clothes(*ot*)⋯옷
laundryman(*se-t'ak-ppu*)⋯세탁부

clean(*ch'ŏng-so-ha-da*)⋯청소하다
barbershop(*i-bal-sso*)⋯이발소
washer(*se-t'ak-kki*)⋯세탁기

36. How much for haircut, shave and shampoo ?

Mŏ-ri kkak-kko, myŏn-do-ha-go, se-bal-kka-ji ha-nŭn-de ŏl-ma-im-ni-kka ?

머리 깎고, 면도하고, 세발까지 하는데 얼마입니까 ?

37. If you pay 30,000 won it will cover everything.

Sam-man wŏn-man nae-si-myŏn mo-du toem-ni-da.

삼만 원만 내시면 모두 됩니다.

38. At what time will breakfast be ready ?

Myŏt ssi-e a-ch'i-mŭl chun-bi-hal-kka-yo ?

몇 시에 아침을 준비할까요 ?

39. When are you checking out ?

Ŏn-je kye-san-ha-si-get-ssŭm-ni-kka ?

언제 계산하시겠습니까 ?

40. Here is your bill.

Yŏ-gi kye-san-sŏ-ga it-ssŭm-ni-da.

여기 계산서가 있습니다.

On the street

Kŏ-ri-e-sŏ (거리에서)

1. Can you help me, please ?

Chom to-wa-ju-si-get-ssŭm-ni-kka ?

좀 도와주시겠습니까 ?

2. Where's the bus station ?

PPŏ-ssŭ chŏng-gŏ-jang-ŭn ŏ-di im-ni-kka ?

버스 정거장은 어디 입니까 ?

3. Turn right at the intersection.

Kyo-ch'a-ro-e-sŏ   pa-rŭn-tcho-gŭ-ro to-ra-ga-sip-ssi-o.

교차로에서 바른쪽으로 돌아가십시오.

---

shampoo (*se-bal*)…세발
shave (*myŏn-do-ha-da*)…면도하다
bill (*kye-san-sŏ*)…계산서

terminal (*chŏng-gŏ-jang*)…정거장
breakfast (*a-ch'im sik-ssa*)…아침 식사
calculation (*kye-san*)…계산

4. I want to go to the Seoul Sejong Cultural Center.

Se-jong mun-hwa hoe-gwa-ne ka-go sip-ssŭm-ni-da.

세종 문화 회관에 가고 싶습니다.

5. Please tell me the way to Kwanghwa-mun.

Kwang-hwa-mu-nŭ-ro ka-nŭn ki-rŭl ka-rŭ-ch'yŏ chu-sip-ssi-o.

광화문으로 가는 길을 가르쳐 주십시오.

6. Where's the nearest telephone ?

Ka-jang ka-kka-un chŏn-hwa-nŭn ŏ-di it-ssŭm-ni-kka ?

가장 가까운 전화는 어디 있습니까 ?

7. Walk for a hundred meters.

Paeng mi-t'ŏ-rŭl kŏ-rŏ ka-sip-ssi-o.

백 미터를 걸어 가십시오.

8. Can you tell me where the Capitol Building is ?

Chung-ang-ch'ŏng-i ŏ-di in-nŭn-ji ka-rŭ-ch'yŏ chu-si-get-ssŭm-ni-kka ?

중앙청이 어디 있는지 가르쳐 주시겠습니까 ?

9. How do I get to the Korea International Telecommunications Office ?

Ŏ-ttŏ-k'e ha-myŏn kuk-tche chŏn-sin-gu-ge kal ssu it-ssŭl-kka-yo ?

어떻게 하면 국제 전신국에 갈 수 있을까요 ?

10. How far from here ?

Yŏ-gi-sŏ ŏl-ma-na mŏm-ni-kka ?

여기서 얼마나 멉니까 ?

11. How long will it take ?

Ŏl-ma-na kŏl-lim-ni-kka ?

얼마나 걸립니까 ?

12. Let me ask that gentleman.

Chŏ pu-ne-ge nae-ga mu-rŏ-bwa tŭ-ri-jyo.

저 분에게 내가 물어봐 드리죠.

13. How far is Taejon from here ?

Yŏ-gi-sŏ tae-jŏn-kka-ji-nŭn ŏl-ma-na mŏm-ni-kka ?

---

nearest 〈*ka-jang ka-kka-un*〉…가장 가까운

여기서 대전까지는 얼마나 멉니
까 ?

14. It's about 50 miles from here.

Yŏ-gi-sŏ yak o-sim ma-il-im-ni-da.

여기서 약 오십 마일입니다.

15. How long does it take from here to Suwon by taxi ?

T'aek-ssi-ro yŏ-gi-sŏ su-wŏn-kka-ji ŏl-ma-na kŏl-rim-ni-kka ?

택시로 여기서 수원까지 얼마나
걸립니까 ?

16. It will take one and half hour to reach there by taxi.

T'aek-ssi-ro kŏ-gi-kka-ji ka-nŭn-de han si-gan pa-ni kŏl-lil kkŏ-sim-ni-da.

택시로 거기까지 가는데 한 시간
반이 걸릴 것입니다.

17. How far is Kwang-hwamun from here ?

Yŏ-gi-sŏ kwang-hwa-mu-nŭn ŏl-ma-na mŏm-ni-kka ?

여기서 광화문은 얼마나 멉니까 ?

18. It's within ten minutes distance on foot.

To-bo-ro si-ppun i-nae-ŭi kŏ-ri-im-ni-da.

도보로 십분 이내의 거리입니다.

19. Will you show me the way to Myong-dong ?

Myŏng-dong-ŭ-ro ka-nŭn ki-rŭl ka-rŭ-ch'yŏ chu-si-get-ssŭm-ni-kka ?

명동으로 가는 길을 가르쳐 주시
겠습니까 ?

20. Go straight and then, turn to the right.

TTok-ppa-ro ka-si-da-ga pa-rŭn-tcho-gŭ-ro to-ra-ga-sip-ssi-o.

똑바로 가시다가 바른쪽으로 돌아
가십시오.

21. Is this the right road

I-gŏ-si chong-no-ro ka-nŭn pa-rŭn

---

within(*a-ne*)…안에
reach(*to-ch'ak*)…도착

turn(*tol-da*)…돌다
depart(*ch'ul-bal-ha-da*)…출발하다

to Chong-no?

kil-im-ni-kka?

이것이 종로로 가는 바른 길입니까?

22. Yes. I am going to the same direction. May I guide you?

Kŭ-rŏt-ssŭm-ni-da. Chŏ-do ka-t'ŭn pang-hyang-ŭ-ro kam-ni-da. An-nae-hae tŭ-ril-kka-yo?

그렇습니다. 저도 같은 방향으로 갑니다. 안내해 드릴까요?

23. Can I go there on foot?

Kŭ ko-sŭl to-bo-ro kal ssu it-ssŭm-ni-kka?

그 곳을 도보로 갈 수 있습니까?

24. Yes, you can. But I would recommend you to take a bus.

Ne, to-bo-ro kal ssu it-ssŭm-ni-da. Kŭ-rŏ-na ppŏ-ssŭ-rŭl t'a-go ka-si-nŭn p'yŏ-ni nat-kket-ssŭm-ni-da.

네, 도보로 갈 수 있습니다. 그러나 버스를 타고 가시는 편이 났겠습니다.

25. Does this bus go to Chongnyang-ni direct?

I ppŏ-ssŭ-nŭn kot-tchang ch'ŏng-nyang-ni-ro kam-ni-kka?

이 버스는 곧장 청량리로 갑니까?

26. No. You have to transfer at Tongdaemun.

A-nim-ni-da. Tong-dae-mun-sŏ ka-ra t'a-syŏ-ya ham-ni-da.

아닙니다. 동대문서 갈아 타셔야 합니다.

27. Does this bus stop at

I ppŏ-ssŭ-nŭn nam-dae-mun-sŏ

---

direction(*pang-hyang*)…방향
recommend(*ch'u-ch'ŏn-ha-da*)…추천
  하다
side(*yŏp*)…옆

back(*twi*)…뒤
straight(*kot-tchang*)…곧장
front(*ap*)…앞
recommendation(*ch'u-ch'ŏn*)…추천

	Namdaemun ?	*sŏm-ni-kka ?* 이 버스는 남대문서 섭니까?
28.	Go around this South Gate and head straight to come south until you to the Seoul Railroad Station. The Daewoo Center is right across from this station.	*I nam-dae-mu-nŭl to-ra-sŏ kot-tchang nam-tcho-gŭ-ro ka-myŏn seŏ-ul-lyŏ-gi na-o-nŭn-de, kŭ kŏn-nŏ-p'yŏ-ne tae-u ssen-t'ŏ-ga it-ssŭm-ni-da.* 이 남대문을 돌아서 곧장 남쪽으로 가면 서울역이 나오는데, 그 건너 편에 대우 센터가 있습니다.
29.	Where I do get off for the Tower Hotel ?	*T'a-wŏ ho-t'e-rŭl ka-ja-myŏn ŏ-di-sŏ nae-rim-ni-kka ?* 타워 호텔을 가자면 어디서 내립 니까?
30.	Do you know this address ?	*I chu-so-rŭl a-si-get-ssŭm-ni-kka ?* 이 주소를 아시겠습니까?
31.	How can I find out ?	*Ŏ-ttŏ-k'e ch'a-jŭl ssu it-ssŭl-kka-yo ?* 어떻게 찾을 수 있을까요?
32.	Would you show me how to get this address ?	*I chu-so-ro ka-nŭn pŏ-bŭl ka-rŭ-ch'yŏ chu-si-get-ssŭm-ni-kka ?* 이 주소로 가는 법을 가르쳐 주시 겠습니까?
33.	Why don't you ask that policeman ?	*Chŏ kyŏng-gwan-e-ge mu-rŏ po-sip-ssi-o.* 저 경관에게 물어 보십시오.
34.	Could you draw me a brief map for this address ?	*I chu-so-ro ka-nŭn yak-tto-rŭl kŭ-ryŏ chu-si-get-ssŭm-ni-kka ?* 이 주소로 가는 약도를 그려 주시

---

transfer(*ka-ra t'a-da*)…갈아 타다
search for(*ch'at-tta*)…찾다

address(*chu-so*)…주소
sketch map(*yak-tto*)…약도

겠습니까?

35. Let me draw a brief map.

Yak-tto-rŭl kŭ-ryŏ tŭ-ri-get-ssŭm-ni-da.

약도를 그려 드리겠습니다.

36. You can easily find it.

Tang-si-nŭn swip-kke ch'a-jŭl ssu it-ssŭm-ni-da.

당신은 쉽게 찾을 수 있습니다.

37. You'll find the bank on your right.

Ŭn-haeng-i o-rŭn-tcho-ge po-il kkŏ-sim-ni-da.

은행이 오른쪽에 보일 것입니다.

38. Walk for three blocks.

Se pŭ-rŏ-gŭl kŏ-rŏ ka-sip-ssi-o.

세 브럭을 걸어 가십시오.

39. You'll see a big signboard there.

Tang-si-nŭn kŏ-gi-e-sŏ ha-na-ŭi k'ŏ-da-ran kan-p'a-nŭl pol ssu it-ssŭl kkŏ-sim-ni-da.

당신은 거기에서 하나의 커다란 간판을 볼 수 있을 것입니다.

40. You'll see a post office on the right.

Tang-si-nŭn pa-rŭn-tcho-gŭ-ro u-ch'e-gu-gŭl pal-gyŏn-hal kkŏ-sim-ni-da.

당신은 바른쪽으로 우체국을 발견할 것입니다.

41. Where are you from?

Ŏ-di-sŏ o-syŏt-ssŭm-ni-kka?

어디서 오셨습니까?

42. What country are you from?

Ŏ-nŭ na-ra-e-sŏ o-syŏt-ssŭm-ni-kka?

어느 나라에서 오셨습니까?

43. I am from America.

Mi-gu-ge-sŏ wat-ssŭm-ni-da.

미국에서 왔습니다.

---

draw(*kŭ-ri-da*)…그리다
map(*chi-do*)…지도

country(*na-ra*)…나라
signboard(*kan-p'an*)…간판

44. I am from Pusan.　*Pu-sa-ne-sŏ wat-ssŭm-ni-da.*
부산에서 왔습니다.

45. Let me get off over there.　*Chŏ-gi-sŏ nae-ryŏ chu-sip-ssi-o.*
저기서 내려 주십시오.

At the Restaurant　*Sik-ttang-e-sŏ*(식당에서)

1. What is the most famous Chinese restaurant in Korea !
Han-gu-ge-sŏ chung-guk ŭm-si-gŭ-ro ka-jang yu-myŏng-han sik-ttang-ŭn ŏ-nŭ sik-ttang-im-ni-kka !
한국에서 중국 음식으로 가장 유명한 식당은 어느 식당입니까 !

2. The Asowon is a famous for Chinese food.
A-sŏ-wŏ-nŭn chung-guk ŭm-si-gŭ-ro yu-myŏng-ham-ni-da.
아서원은 중국 음식으로 유명합니다.

3. Where can I have western food ?
Ŏ-di-sŏ sŏ-yang ŭm-si-gŭl mŏ-gŭl ssu it-ssŭl-kka-yo ?
어디서 서양 음식을 먹을 수 있을까요 ?

4. You can have various western food in the hotel restaurants.
Tang-si-nŭn ho-t'el sik-ttang-e-sŏ yŏ-rŏ ka-ji sŏ-yang ŭm-si-gŭl mŏ-gŭl ssu it-ssŭm-ni-da.
당신은 호텔 식당에서 여러 가지 서양 음식을 먹을 수 있습니다.

5. A table for five please.　*O in-yong sik-t'a-gŭl pu-t'a-k'am-ni-da.*

---

restaurant(*sik-ttang*)…식당
famous(*yu-myŏng-han*)…유명한
chinese food(*chung-guk ŭm-sik*)…중국 음식

westen food(*sŏ-yang ŭm-sik*)…서양 음식
various(*yŏ-rŏ ka-ji*)…여러 가지

오 인용 식탁을 부탁합니다.

6. This table is reserved. *I sik-t'a-gŭn ye-yak-doe-ŏt-ssŭm-ni-da.*

이 식탁은 예약되었습니다.

7. Would you mind moving from here to that chair? *Yŏ-gi-sŏ chŏ ŭi-ja-ro om-gyŏ chu-si-get-ssŭm-ni-kka?*

여기서 저 의자로 옮겨 주시겠습니까?

8. This is a very comfortable place. *I ko-sŭn mae-u p'yŏ-nan-han chang-so-im-ni-da.*

이 곳은 매우 편안한 장소입니다.

9. Can I see the menu? *Me-nyu-rŭl pol ssu it-ssŭl-kka-yo?*

메뉴를 볼 수 있을까요?

10. Here's the menu. *Yŏ-gi me-nyu-ga it-ssŭm-ni-da.*

여기 메뉴가 있습니다.

11. This is today's special. *I-gŏ-si o-nŭ-rŭi t'ŭk-ppyŏl ŭm-sik-im-ni-da.*

이것이 오늘의 특별 음식입니다.

12. What do you want to have? *Mu-ŏ-sŭl tŭ-si-get-ssŭm-ni-kka?*

무엇을 드시겠습니까?

13. What do you want to drink? *Mu-ŏ-sŭl ma-si-get-ssŭm-ni-kka?*

무엇을 마시겠습니까?

14. I will have komtang. *Kom-t'ang-ŭl mŏk-kket-ssŭm-ni-da.*

곰탕을 먹겠습니다.

15. I will try naengmyon. *Naeng-myŏ-nŭl mŏ-gŏ po-get-ssŭm-*

---

comfortable(*p'yŏ-nan-han*)…편안한
menu(*me-nyu*)…메뉴
special(*t'ŭk-ppyŏl-han*)…특별한
reserve(*ye-yak*)…예약

drink(*ma-si-da*)…마시다
bottle(*pyŏng*)…병
usual(*po-t'ong*)…보통

ni-da.

냉면을 먹어 보겠습니다.

16. I shall have the steak.

Sŭ-t'e-i-k'ŭ-rŭl   mŏk-kket-ssŭm-ni-da.

스테이크를 먹겠습니다.

17. What is the specialty of this house?

I chi-bŭi chŏn-mu-nŭn mu-ŏ-sim-ni-kka?

이 집의 전문은 무엇입니까?

18. What are you going to order, Mr. Kim?

Kim hyŏng, mu-ŏ-sŭl chu-mun-ha-sil-lyŏ-go ham-ni-kka?

김형, 무엇을 주문하실려고 합니까?

19. Please bring a bottle of Jinro.

Chil-lo han pyŏng-man chu-sip-ssi-o.

진로 한 병만 주십시오.

20. How about another drink, please?

Han chan tŏ ha-si-get-ssŭm-ni-kka?

한 잔 더 하시겠습니까?

21. Please one more beer.

Maek-tchu han pyŏng-man tŏ chu-sip-ssi-o.

맥주 한 병만 더 주십시오.

22. How do you like your eggs, up or turned over?

Kye-ra-nŭn ŏ-ttŏ-k'e tŭ-si-get-ssŭm-ni-kka? Han-tchong-man i-k'il-kka-yo, yang-tchok tta i-k'il-kka-yo?

계란은 어떻게 드시겠습니까? 한 쪽만 익힐까요, 양쪽 다 익힐까요?

23. Will you have soup?

Ku-gŭl tŭ-si-get-ssŭm-ni-kka?

국을 드시겠습니까?

24. It smells good!

Naem-sae ch'am chot-ssŭm-ni-da!

---

wheat flour(*mil-ga-ru*)…밀가루
egg(*kye-ran*)…계란
soup(*kuk*)…국

rice(*pap*)…밥
bread(*ppang*)…빵

냄새 참 좋습니다!

25. Will you have more rice?

Pa-búl tŏ tū-si-get-ssŭm-ni-kka?
밥을 더 드시겠습니까?

26. Won't you have more meat?

Ko-gi-rŭl tŏ ha-ji an-k'et-ssŭm-ni-kka?
고기를 더 하지 않겠습니까?

27. How do you like your coffee, with cream and sugar?

K'ŏ-p'i-nŭn ŏ-ttŏ-k'e tū-si-get-ssŭm-ni-kka? K'ŭ-rim-gwa sŏl-t'ang-ŭl t'a-si-get-ssŭm-ni-kka?
커피는 어떻게 드시겠습니까? 크림과 설탕을 타시겠습니까?

28. I'll have my coffee black.

Pŭl-laek k'ŏ-p'i-ro ha-get-ssŭm-ni-da.
블랙 커피로 하겠습니다.

29. I want apple pie with icecream.

A-i-sŭ-k'ŭ-ri-mŭl pa-rŭn ae-p'ŭl p'a-i-rŭl wŏn-ham-ni-da.
아이스크림을 바른 애플 파이를 원합니다.

30. Would you mind passing me that plate?

Chŏ chŏp-ssi-rŭl chi-bŏ chu-si-ji an-k'et-ssŭm-ni-kka?
저 접시를 집어 주시지 않겠습니까?

31. please hurry up.

PPal-li hae chu-sip-ssi-o.
빨리 해 주십시오.

32. This naengmyon is terribly hot.

I naeng-myŏ-nŭn chi-do-k'a-ge maep-ssŭm-ni-da.
이 냉면은 지독하게 맵습니다.

---

meat(*ko-gi*)…고기
coffee(*k'ŏ-p'i*)…커피
cream(*k'ŭ-rim*)…크림

sugar(*sŏl-t'ang*)…설탕
tea(*hong-ch'a*)…홍차

33. Korean kimchi is tasteful.

Han-guk kim-ch'i-nŭn ma-si it-ssŭm-ni-da.

한국 김치는 맛이 있습니다.

34. Have you ever tried Jinro? It is much stronger than Japanese sake.

Chil-lo-rŭl ma-syŏ-bon chŏ-gi it-ssŭm-ni-kka? Il-bon sul-bo-da tŏ to-k'am-ni-da.

진로를 마셔본 적이 있습니까? 일본 술보다 더 독합니다.

35. Please bring the check.

Kye-san-sŏ-rŭl ka-jyŏ o-sip-ssi-o.

계산서를 가져 오십시오.

36. Here it is, sir. It all comes to eight thousand and five hundred won.

Yŏ-gi it-ssŭm-ni-da. Mo-du p'al-ch'ŏn-o-baek wŏn-i na-wat-ssŭm-ni-da.

여기 있습니다. 모두 팔천오백 원이 나왔습니다.

Telephone Call

Chŏn-hwa-gŏl-gi(전화걸기)

1. Have you a telephone?

Chŏn-hwa-ga it-ssŭm-ni-kka?

전화가 있습니까?

2. May I use your telephone?

Chŏn-hwa-rŭl sa-yong-hae-do chot-ssŭm-ni-kka?

전화를 사용해도 좋습니까?

3. Hello.

Yŏ-bo-se-yo.

여보세요.

4. This is Park kkot-nim speaking.

Pak-kkon-nim-im-ni-da.

박꽃님입니다.

5. May I speak to Mr.

Kim-su-dong ssi-wa t'ong-hwa-hal

---

hurry(*ppal-li*)…빨리
call charge(*t'ong-hwa-ryo*)…통화료
content(*nae-yong*)…내용

telephone(*chŏn-hwa*)…전화
telephone traffic(*t'ong-hwa-ryang*)…통화량

Kim Su-dong?	*ssu i-ssŭl-kka-yo?* 김수동 씨와 통화할 수 있을까요?
6. Who's calling please?	*Nu-gu-si-jyo?* 누구시죠?
7. Just moment please.	*Cham-kkan-man ki-da-ri-sip-ssi-o.* 잠깐만 기다리십시오.
8. Your friend is on the phone.	*Ch'in-gu-bu-nŭi chŏn-hwa-im-ni-da.* 친구분의 전화입니다.
9. She is not here right now.	*Kŭ-nyŏ-nŭn chi-gŭm yŏ-gi an kye-sim-ni-da.* 그녀는 지금 여기 안 계십니다.
10. He's in conference now.	*Kŭ-nŭn chi-gŭm hoe-ŭi chung-im-ni-da.* 그는 지금 회의 중입니다.
11. Please try again.	*Ta-si kŏ-sip-ssi-o.* 다시 거십시오.
12. What is your telephone number?	*Tang-si-nŭi chŏn-hwa pŏn-ho-nŭn mu-ŏ-sim-ni-kka?* 당신의 전화 번호는 무엇입니까?
13. My telephone number is 776—3971.	*Na-ŭi chŏn-hwa pŏn-ho-nŭn ch'il-baek-ch'il-ssip-yuk-kku-gŭi sam-ch'ŏn-gu-baek-ch'il-ssip-il-bŏn-im-ni-da.* 나의 전화 번호는 칠백칠십육국의 삼천구백칠십일번입니다.
14. Would you ring me the	*O-baek-gu-sip-sam-gu-gŭi ku-ryuk-*

---

moment(*sun-gan*)…순간
conference(*hoe-ŭi*)…회의
try(*no-ryŏ-k'a-da*)…노력하다

ring(*ul-li-da*)…울리다
occupied(*pa-ppŭn*)…바쁜
spare time(*han-ga-han*)…한가한

119

number 593－9657.

o-ch'il chom tae chu-sip-ssi-o.

오백구십삼국의 구육오칠 좀 대
주십시오.

15. The line is busy.
Please try again.

*T'ong-hwa chung-im-ni-da. Ta-si
han pŏn kŏ-rŏ chu-sip-ssi-o.*

통화 중입니다. 다시 한 번 걸어
주십시오.

16. I'm sorry. You have
the wrong number.

*Mi-an-ham-ni-da. Chŏn-hwa pŏn-
ho-ga t'ŭl-ryŏt-ssŭm-ni-da.*

미안합니다. 전화 번호가 틀렸습니
다.

17. I can't hear you very
well. Please speak lou-
der.

*Chal tŭl-li-ji an-ssŭm-ni-da. Chom-
dŏ k'ŭn so-ri-ro yae-gi-ha-sip-ssi-
o.*

잘 들리지 않습니다. 좀더 큰 소
리로 얘기하십시오.

18. Who is this speaking,
please ?

Nu-gu-si-jyo?

누구시죠 ?

19. This is Miss Kim's
speaking. I'm Mr.
Park's secretary.

*Pak sŏn-saeng-ni-mŭi pi-sŏ-in mi-ssŭ
kim-im-ni-da.*

박 선생님의 비서인 미쓰 김입니다.

20. Will Mr. Park be back
soon ?

*Pak sŏn-saeng-ŭn kot to-ra-o-sim-ni-
kka?*

박 선생은 곧 돌아오십니까 ?

21. I expect him sometime
this evening.

*O-nŭl chŏ-nyŏk-ttae-tchŭm to-ra-o-sil
kkŏ-sim-ni-da.*

오늘 저녁때쯤 돌아오실 것입니다.

22. May I take your me-
ssage ?

*Chŏn-hal mal-ssŭm-i-ra-do it-ssŭm-
ni-kka?*

---

wrong(*chal-mot-ttoen*)…잘못된
loud(*k'ŭ-ge*)…크게

secretariat(*pi-sŏ-sil*)…비서실
message(*so-sik*)…소식

전할 말씀이라도 있습니까?

23. Shall I have him call you when he comes back?

Kŭ pu-ni to-ra-o-si-myŏn taek-e-ge chŏn-hwa-ha-si-ra-go mal-ssŭm tŭ-ril-kka-yo?

그 분이 돌아오시면 댁에게 전화 하시라고 말씀 드릴까요?

24. Yes, please do. My phone number is 776-2895.

Kŭ-rŏ-k'e hae chu-sip-ssi-o. Che chŏn-hwa pŏn-ho-nŭn ch'il-baek-ch'il-ssip-yuk-kku-gŭi i-p'al-gu-o-im-ni-da.

그렇게 해 주십시오. 제 전화 번호는 칠백칠십육국의 이팔구오입니다.

25. Please ask Mr. Park to come to the phone.

Pak sŏn-saeng-e-ge chŏn-hwa chom pa-dŭ-ra-go mal-ssŭm-hae chu-sip-ssi-o.

박 선생에게 전화 좀 받으라고 말씀해 주십시오.

26. Who is speaking, please?

Nu-gu-sim-ni-kka?

누구십니까?

27. I can't hear you very well. Will you please speak a little more loudly?

Chal an-dŭl-lim-ni-da. Chom-dŏ k'ŭn so-ri-ro mal-ssŭm-hae chu-sip-ssi-o.

잘 안들립니다. 좀더 큰 소리로 말씀해 주십시오.

28. There's no one here by that name.

Kŭ-rŏn i-rŭ-mŭl ka-jin sa-ra-mŭn yŏ-gi-e ŏp-ssŭm-ni-da.

그런 이름을 가진 사람은 여기에 없습니다.

---

contact(*yŏl-lak*)…연락   safety(*an-bu*)…안부

29. What number have you dialed?

Myŏt ppŏ-nŭl kŏ-syŏt-ssŭm-ni-kka?

몇 번을 거셨습니까?

30. I'm afraid you've dialed the wrong number.

Pŏn-ho-rŭl chal-mot tol-li-sin kŏt kat-ssŭm-ni-da.

번호를 잘못 돌리신 것 같습니다.

31. Do you make many long distance calls?

Chang-gŏ-ri chŏn-hwa-rŭl ma-ni kŏ-sim-ni-kka?

장거리 전화를 많이 거십니까?

32. Please call someone who speaks English.

Yŏng-ŏ-rŭl hal ssu in-nŭn sa-ra-mŭl pul-lŏ chu-sip-ssi-o.

영어를 할 수 있는 사람을 불러 주십시오.

33. In case of emergency you can call police on 112.

Wi-gŭ-p'an kyŏng-u-en chŏn-hwa pŏn-ho il-il-i-ro kyŏng-ch'a-rŭl pu-rŭl ssu it-ssŭm-ni-da.

위급한 경우엔 전화 번호 일일이로 경찰을 부를 수 있습니다.

34. Thank you for calling.

Chŏn-hwa-rŭl kŏ-rŏ chu-syŏ-sŏ kam-sa-ham-ni-da.

전화를 걸어 주셔서 감사합니다.

35. I'll call you again.

Ta-si kŏl-get-ssŭm-ni-da.

다시 걸겠습니다.

36. You can use public telephone on the street.

Kŏ-ri-e-sŏ-nŭn kong-jung chŏn-hwa-rŭl sa-yong-hal ssu-ga it-ssŭm-ni-da.

거리에서는 공중 전화를 사용할

---

urgent(*kŭ-p'an*)…급한
firstaid medicine(*ku-gŭp-yak*)…구급약
police(*kyŏng-ch'al*)…경찰

emergent(*wi-gŭ-p'an*)…위급한
mistake(*sil-ssu*)…실수
ambulance(*ku-gŭp-ch'a*)…구급차

수가 있습니다.

Shopping

Mul-gŏn-sa-gi(물건사기)

1. How much is it ?
   Ŏl-ma-im-ni-kka ?
   얼마입니까 ?

2. How much are these all together ?
   I-gŏt mo-du ŏl-ma-im-ni-kka ?
   이것 모두 얼마입니까 ?

3. That's too expensive.
   Nŏ-mu pi-ssam-ni-da.
   너무 비쌉니다.

4. Can you make it a little cheaper ?
   Chom ssa-ge hal ssu ŏp-ssŭm-ni-kka ?
   좀 싸게 할 수 없습니까 ?

5. If you reduce the price, I'll buy it.
   Kap-ssŭl chom kka-kka chu-sin-da-myŏn sa-get-ssŭm-ni-da.
   값을 좀 깎아 주신다면 사겠습니다.

6. We have fixed prices.
   U-ri-nŭn chŏng-ch'al-tche-im-ni-da.
   우리는 정찰제입니다.

7. Does this price include tax ?
   I-gŏ-sŭn se-gŭ-mŭl p'o-ham-han kap-ssim-ni-kka ?
   이것은 세금을 포함한 값입니까 ?

8. This is tax free.
   I-gŏ-sŭn se-gŭm myŏn-je-im-ni-da.
   이것은 세금 면제입니다.

9. What kind of material is this ?
   I-gŏ-sŭn mu-sŭn chae-ryo-im-ni-kka ?
   이것은 무슨 재료입니까 ?

10. This is foreign made.
    I-gŏ-sŭn woe-guk-tche-im-ni-da.
    이것은 외국제입니다.

---

material(*chae-ryo*)…재료
avenue(*kil*)…길
shopping(*mul-gŏn-sa-gi*)…물건사기
costly(*pi-ssan*)…비싼

cheaper(*ssa-ge*)…싸게
reduce(*kkak-tta*)…깎다
tax free(*se-gŭm myŏn-je*)…세금 면제
foreign(*woe-gu-gŭi*)…외국의

11. This is made-in-America. *I-gŏ-sŭn mi-guk-tche-im-ni-da.*
이것은 미국제입니다.

12. This is Korean-made. *I-gŏ-sŭn han-guk-tche-im-ni-da.*
이것은 한국제입니다.

13. What color do you like? *Mu-sŭn sae-gŭl cho-a-ha-sim-ni-kka?*
무슨 색을 좋아하십니까?

14. I think this is what you have in mind. *I-gŏ-si tang-sin ma-ŭ-me tŭl mul-gŏ-ni-ra-go saeng-ga-k'am-ni-da.*
이것이 당신 마음에 들 물건이라고 생각합니다.

15. I want to see a necktie. *Nek-t'a-i-rŭl po-go sip-ssŭm-ni-da.*
넥타이를 보고 싶습니다.

16. What size? *Mu-sŭn ssa-i-jŭ-i-ji-yo?*
무슨 사이즈이지요?

17. I want to buy a present my for friend. *Ch'in-gu-e-ge chul sŏn-mu-rŭl ha-na sa-go sip-ssŭm-ni-da.*
친구에게 줄 선물을 하나 사고 싶습니다.

18. Would you like to go shopping with me? *Chŏ-ha-go syo-p'ing-ŭl ka-ji a-nŭ-si-get-ssŭm-ni-kka?*
저하고 쇼핑을 가지 않으시겠습니까?

19. Let's go to the Shinsegye Department Store for shopping. *Syo-p'ing-ha-rŏ sin-se-gye pae-k'wa-jŏ-me kap-ssi-da.*
쇼핑하러 신세계 백화점에 갑시다.

20. There is a large selec- *Cho-ŭn mul-gŏ-ni ma-ni ku-bi-doe-ŏ*

---

guidance(*an-nae*)…안내
exhibition(*chi-nyŏl*)…진열
size(*sa-i-jŭ*)…사이즈

necktie(*nek-t'a-i*)…넥타이
store(*sang-jŏm*)…상점

tion of fine goods.

좋은 물건이 많이 구비되어 있습니다.

it-ssŭm-ni-da.

21. How about the Hyundai Department store ?

Hyŏn-dae pae-k'wa-jŏ-mŭn ŏ-ttŏt-ssŭm-ni-kka ?

현대 백화점은 어떻습니까 ?

22. Do you have more of these ?

I-rŏn kŏt-ttŭ-ri tŏ it-ssŭm-ni-kka ?

이런 것들이 더 있습니까 ?

23. It is too expensive. Are there any cheaper one than this ?

Nŏ-mu pi-ssam-ni-da. I-gŏt-ppo-da ssan kŏ-si ŏp-ssŭm-ni-kka ?

너무 비쌉니다. 이것보다 싼 것이 없습니까 ?

24. Give me this.

I-gŏ-sŭ-ro chu-sip-ssi-o.

이것으로 주십시오.

25. Give me two of these.

I-gŏ-sŭ-ro tu kae chu-sip-ssi-o.

이것으로 두 개 주십시오.

26. I can't afford to buy such an expensive good.

Na-nŭn kŭ-rŏ-k'e pi-ssan mul-gŏ-nŭl sal yŏ-yu-ga ŏp-ssŭm-ni-da.

나는 그렇게 비싼 물건을 살 여유가 없습니다.

27. Would you wrap them up ?

Kŭ-gŏl ssa-ju-si-get-ssŭm-ni-kka ?

그걸 싸주시겠습니까 ?

28. Can you deliver them to my house ?

Kŭ-gŏl u-ri chi-bŭ-ro pae-dal-hae chu-sil ssu it-ssŭm-ni-kka ?

그걸 우리 집으로 배달해 주실 수 있습니까 ?

---

selection*(sŏn-t'aek)*…선택
afford*(yŏ-yu-ga it-tta)*…여유가 있다
delay*(yŏn-ch'ak)*…연착
go against*(ŏ-gi-da)*…어기다

wrapping*(p'o-jang)*…포장
distribution*(pae-dal)*…배달
mailing*(u-song)*…우송
damage*(son-sang)*…손상

29. Please deliver them to this address.

Kŭ-gŏ-sŭl i chu-so-ro pae-dal-hae chu-sip-ssi-o.

그것을 이 주소로 배달해 주십시오.

30. The pen costs five thousand won.

Kŭ p'e-nŭn o-ch'ŏn wŏn-im-ni-da.

그 펜은 오천 원입니다.

31. I'm looking for a white shirt, and my neck size is 15.

Na-nŭn ha-yan syŏ-ch'ŭ-rŭl ch'at-kko it-ssŭm-ni-da. Chŏ-ŭi mok ssa-i-jŭ-nŭn sip-o-im-ni-da.

나는 하얀 셔츠를 찾고 있습니다. 저의 목 사이즈는 십오입니다.

32. Give me two pounds of beef.

I p'a-un-dŭ-ŭi soe-go-gi-rŭl chu-sip-ssi-o.

이 파운드의 쇠고기를 주십시오.

33. I want some canned goods.

T'ong-jo-rim-han mul-gŏ-nŭl wŏn-ham-ni-da.

통조림한 물건을 원합니다.

34. Where can I buy Korean souvenirs?

Ŏ-di-sŏ han-gu-gŭi ki-nyŏm-mul-dŭ-rŭl sal ssu it-ssŭl-kka-yo?

어디서 한국의 기념물들을 살 수 있을까요?

35. The Tongdae-mun Market is a famous shopping place in Korea.

Tong-dae-mun si-jang-ŭn han-gu-ge-sŏ i-rŭm-nan syo-p'ing chang-so-im-ni-da.

동대문 시장은 한국에서 이름난 쇼핑 장소입니다.

36. Let's go out for shopping.

Syo-p'ing-ha-rŏ na-gap-ssi-da.

쇼핑하러 나갑시다.

---

beef(*soe-go-gi*)…쇠고기　　market(*si-jang*)…시장
souvenir(*ki-nyŏm-mul*)…기념물　　diffuseness(*san-man*)…산만

Invitation and Visiting

1. Are you free this evening?

2. I'd like to invite you to dinner this evening.

3. Yes, I'd love to go.

4. I'm sorry. I'd love to come but I have another engagement.

5. Thank you for your invitation but I have another appintment.

6. It will be my great pleasure to go with you.

7. I will be free on Sun-

Ch'o-dae-wa pang-mun (초대와 방문)

O-nŭl chŏ-nyŏk si-ga-ni it-ssŭm-ni-kka?

오늘 저녁 시간이 있습니까?

O-nŭl chŏ-nyŏk sik-ssa-e tang-si-nŭl ch'o-dae-ha-go sip-ssŭm-ni-da.

오늘 저녁 식사에 당신을 초대하고 싶습니다.

Ne, ka-get-ssŭm-ni-da.

네, 가겠습니다.

Mi-an-ham-ni-da. Ka-go-nŭn sip-tchi-man, ta-rŭn yak-sso-gi it-ssŭm-ni-da.

미안합니다. 가고는 싶지만, 다른 약속이 있습니다.

Ch'o-dae-hae chu-syŏ-sŏ ko-map-ssŭm-ni-da-man, ta-rŭn yak-sso-gi i-mi it-ssŭm-ni-da.

초대해 주셔서 고맙습니다만, 다른 약속이 이미 있습니다.

Tang-sin-gwa ham-kke ka-ge-doen kŏ-sŭn na-ŭi k'ŏ-da-ran ki-ppŭm-im-ni-da.

당신과 함께 가게된 것은 나의 커다란 기쁨입니다.

I-ryo-i-re-nŭn si-ga-ni it-ssŭm-ni-

---

guest(son-nim)···손님
call(pang-mun)···방문

convenient(p'yŏn-han)···편한
pleasure(ki-ppŭm)···기쁨
ease(al-lak)···안락

127

day.

8. I am not free on Saturday evening.

9. If you don't mind, come over to my house.

10. What time will be convenient for you?

11. How about seven o'clock tomorrow evening?

12. Is Mr. Kim at home?

13. Pardon me. Are you Mr. James?

14. Yes. I am glad to see you.

15. My husband has told me about you.

da.
일요일에는 시간이 있습니다.

T'o-yo-il chŏ-nyŏ-ge-nŭn si-ga-ni ŏp-ssŭm-ni-da.
토요일 저녁에는 시간이 없습니다.

Kwaen-ch'a-nŭ-si-da-myŏn u-ri chi-bŭ-ro o-sip-ssi-o.
괜찮으시다면 우리 집으로 오십시오.

Myŏt ssi-ga p'yŏn-ha-si-get-ssŭm-ni-kka?
몇 시가 편하시겠습니까?

Nae-il chŏ-nyŏk il-gop-ssi-ga ŏ-ttŏt-ssŭm-ni-kka?
내일 저녁 일곱시가 어떻습니까?

Kim sŏn-saeng-ŭn chi-be kye-sim-ni-kka?
김 선생은 집에 계십니까?

Choe-song-ham-ni-da.   Che-im-sŭ ssi-i-si-jyo?
죄송합니다. 제임스 씨이시죠?

Kŭ-rŏt-ssŭm-ni-da.   Man-na-boe-ŏ pan-gap-ssŭm-ni-da.
그렇습니다. 만나뵈어 반갑습니다.

Nam-p'yŏn-kke-sŏ tang-si-ne kwan-han yae-gi-rŭl ha-syŏt-ssŭm-ni-da.
남편께서 당신에 관한 얘기를 하셨습니다.

---

pardon(*yong-sŏ-ha-da*)…용서하다   afraid(*tu-ryŏ-un*)…두려운

16. Please come in and wait. He shall be back soon.

Tŭ-rŏ-o-syŏ-sŏ ki-da-ri-sip-ssi-o. Kot to-ra-o-sil kkŏm-ni-da.

들어오셔서 기다리십시오. 곧 돌아오실 겁니다.

17. I am sorry I kept you waiting.

Ki-da-ri-ge hae-sŏ choe-song-ham-ni-da.

기다리게 해서 죄송합니다.

18. I'm sorry to have kept you waiting for such a long time.

Nŏ-mu o-rae ki-da-ri-ge hae-sŏ choe-song-ham-ni-da.

너무 오래 기다리게 해서 죄송합니다.

19. I am afraid I came a little early.

Cho-gŭm il-tchik on kŏt kat-ssŭm-ni-da.

조금 일찍 온 것 같습니다.

20. Let's sit down and have a talk.

An-jŭ-syŏ-sŏ yae-gi-na chom na-nu-si-jyo.

앉으셔서 얘기나 좀 나누시죠.

21. Make yourself at home.

Ŏ-ryŏp-kke saeng-ga-k'a-ji ma-sip-ssi-o.

어렵게 생각하지 마십시오.

22. Would you like to take off your coat?

K'o-t'ŭ-rŭl pŏ-sŭ-si-get-ssŭm-ni-kka?

코트를 벗으시겠습니까?

23. Would you mind waiting for a few minutes?

Chom ki-da-ryŏ chu-syŏ-ya-get-ssŭm-ni-da.

좀 기다려 주셔야겠습니다.

24. We Koreans exchange name cards when we

U-ri-dŭl han-gu-gi-nŭn ch'ŏ-ŭm man-nan sa-ram-gwa myŏng-ha-

---

coat(*k'o-t'ŭ*)⋯코트

early(*il-tchik*)⋯일찍

coat lapels(*k'o-t'ŭ-git*)⋯코트깃

decision(*kyŏl-tchŏng*)⋯결정

meet each other for the first time.

mūl kyo-hwan-ham-ni-da.

우리들 한국인은 처음 만난 사람과 명함을 교환합니다.

25. It has Korean on one side and English on the other.

Han myŏ-nūn han-gung-mal-lo, twin-myŏ-nūn yŏng-ŏ-ro toe-ŏ it-ssŭm-ni-da.

한면은 한국말로, 뒷면은 영어로 되어 있습니다.

26. This comes in very handy.

I-gŏ-sŭn mae-u p'yŏl-li-ham-ni-da.

이것은 매우 편리합니다.

27. Let me put down my phone number there.

Kŏ-gi-e chŏn-hwa pŏn-ho-rŭl chŏ-gŏ tŭ-ri-get-ssŭm-ni-da.

거기에 전화 번호를 적어 드리겠습니다.

28. Whrer is the wash room?

Hwa-jang-si-rŭn ŏ-di-im-ni-kka?

화장실은 어디 입니까?

29. Whould you like something to drink?

Mu-ŏt tchom ma-si-get-ssŭm-ni-kka?

무엇 좀 마시겠습니까?

30. Do you mind if I smoke?

Tam-bae chom p'i-wŏ-do cho-ŭl-kka-yo?

담배 좀 피워도 좋을까요?

31. Please pass me the salt.

So-gŭm chom kŏn-ne chu-sip-ssi-o.

소금 좀 건네 주십시오.

32. The food is delicious.

Ŭm-si-gi mat it-ssŭm-ni-da.

음식이 맛 있습니다.

33. It's very nice of you to invite me.

Chŏ-rŭl ch'o-dae-hae chu-syŏ-sŏ mae-u chŭl-gŏp-ssŭm-ni-da.

저를 초대해 주셔서 매우 즐겁습니다.

---

rest room(*pyŏn-so*)…변소   calling card(*myŏng-ham*)…명함

34. I ehjoyed this evening very much.

O-nŭl chŏ-nyŏk mae-u chŭl-gŏ-wŏt-ssŭm-ni-da.

오늘 저녁 매우 즐거웠습니다.

35. See you tomorrow.

Kŭ-rŏm, nae-il tto man-nap-ssi-da.

그럼, 내일 또 만납시다.

36. See you next week.

Kŭ-rŏm, ta-ŭm chu-i-re tto man-nap-ssi-da.

그럼, 다음 주일에 또 만납시다.

37. See you the day after tomorrow.

Mo-re tto man-nap-ssi-da.

모레 또 만납시다.

38. See you tomorrow at school.

Nae-il hak-kkyo-e-sŏ man-nap-ssi-da.

내일 학교에서 만납시다.

39. Where shall we meet?

Ŏ-di-sŏ man-nal-kka-yo?

어디서 만날까요?

40. Let's meet at the tea room Solmae in front of the Capitol Building.

Chung-ang-ch'ŏng ap sŏl-mae ta-bang-e-sŏ man-nap-ssi-da.

중앙청 앞 설매 다방에서 만납시다.

41. I'm sorry I'm late.

Nŭ-jŏ-sŏ mi-an-ham-ni-da.

늦어서 미안합니다.

42. Sorry to kept you waiting.

Ki-da-ri-ge hae-sŏ choe-song-ham-ni-da.

기다리게 해서 죄송합니다.

43. Are you going to stop over in Inchon this time?

I-bŏ-ne-nŭn in-ch'ŏ-ne ch'e-jae-ha-sim-ni-kka?

이번에는 인천에 체재하십니까?

44. He called on her three

Kŭ-nŭn pu-sa-ne ch'e-jae chung, kŭ-

---

enjoy (*chŭl-gi-da*)…즐기다
vicinity (*kŭn-bang*)…근방
tea room (*ta-bang*)…다방

late (*nŭ-jŭn*)…늦은
gift (*sŏn-mul*)…선물
satisfication (*man-jok*)…만족

times during his stay in Pusan.

nyŏ-rŭl se pŏn pang-mun-haet-ssŭm-ni-da.

그는 부산에 체재 중, 그녀를 세 번 방문했습니다.

45. I must be going now.

Cha, i-je ka-ya-get-ssŭm-ni-da.

자, 이제 가야겠습니다.

46. I'd like to be excused now.

Chŏ-nŭn i-man sil-rye-ha-get-ssŭm-ni-da.

저는 이만 실례하겠습니다.

47. I will show you to the front entrance.

Hyŏn-gwa-nŭ-ro   an-nae-ha-get-ssŭm-ni-da.

현관으로 안내하겠습니다.

48. Thank you. Good night.

Kam-sa-ham-ni-da.   An-nyŏng-hi kye-sip-ssi-o.

감사합니다. 안녕히 계십시오.

49. Thank you. See you again.

Kam-sa-ham-ni-da. TTo poep-kket-ssŭm-ni-da.

감사합니다. 또 뵙겠습니다.

Travel

1. When do you want to make a tour?

2. I am going to travel next week.

3. Where are you going?

Yŏ-haeng(**여행**)

Ŏn-je   kwan-gwang-ŭl   ha-si-get-ssŭm-ni-kka?

언제 관광을 하시겠습니까?

Na-nŭn ta-ŭm chu-i-re yŏ-haeng-ŭl hal-lyŏ-go ham-ni-da.

나는 다음 주일에 여행을 할려고 합니다.

Ŏ-di-ro ka-sim-ni-kka?

어디로 가십니까?

---

travel(*yŏ-haeng*)…여행   tour(*yŏ-haeng*)…여행

4. I am going to visit the Pulguksa temple in Kyongju.

Kyŏng-ju-e in-nŭn pul-guk-ssa-el kal-lyŏ-go ham-ni-da.

경주에 있는 불국사엘 갈려고 합니다.

5. May I accompany you on the tour?

Chŏ-do ham-kke ka tŭ-ril-kka-yo?

저도 함께 가 드릴까요?

6. Here's a complete timetable for train and express bus services between Seoul and Kyongju.

I-gŏ-si seŏ-ul kyŏng-ju-ga-nŭi ki-ch'a-wa ko-sok ppŏ-ssŭ-ŭi wan-jŏn-han si-gan-p'yo-im-ni-da.

이것이 서울 경주간의 기차와 고속 버스의 완전한 시간표입니다.

7. Are you going alone?

Hon-ja ka-sim-ni-kka?

혼자 가십니까?

8. No. I'm going with my Korean friends.

A-nim-ni-da. Han-guk ch'in-gu-wa ham-kke kam-ni-da.

아닙니다. 한국 친구와 함께 갑니다.

9. Are you traveling by train?

Ki-ch'a-ro yŏ-haeng-ha-sim-ni-kka?

기차로 여행하십니까?

10. No. We are going by express bus.

A-nim-ni-da. Ko-sok ppŏ-ssŭ-ro kam-ni-da.

아닙니다. 고속 버스로 갑니다.

11. We are going to fly.

Pi-haeng-gi-ro kal-lyŏ-go ham-ni-da.

비행기로 갈려고 합니다.

12. I'm going to tour Cheju-do island.

Che-ju-do-rŭl yŏ-haeng-hal-lyŏ-go ham-ni-da.

제주도를 여행할려고 합니다.

13. I'm going to travel by

Pae-ro yŏ-haeng-hal-lyŏ-go ham-ni-

---

alone(*hon-ja*)…혼자
fly(*nal-da*)…날다

round trip(*il-tchu yŏ-haeng*)…일주 여행

boat.

da.

배로 여행할려고 합니다.

14. Don't fail to see Mt. Halla.

Hal-la-sa-nŭl kkok po-sip-ssi-o.

한라산을 꼭 보십시오.

15. What time will the plane leave?

Myŏt ssi-e pi-haeng-gi-ga ttŏ-nam-ni-kka?

몇 시에 비행기가 떠납니까?

16. The plane will leave at two thirty.

Pi-haeng-gi-nŭn tu-si pa-ne ttŏ-nal kkŏ-sim-ni-da.

비행기는 두시 반에 떠날 것입니다.

17. Is the plane leaving on time?

Pi-haeng-gi-nŭn chŏng-si-e ttŏ-nam-ni-kka?

비행기는 정시에 떠납니까?

18. Please show me your ticket.

P'yo-rŭl po-yŏ chu-sip-ssi-o.

표를 보여 주십시오.

19. We will stay in Cheju island about one week.

U-ri-nŭn yak il-tchu-il-gan che-ju-do-e mŏ-mu-rŭ-ryŏ-go ham-ni-da.

우리는 약 일주일간 제주도에 머무르려고 합니다.

20. It will take about eight hours to sail from pusan to Cheju.

Pu-sa-ne-sŏ che-ju-do-kka-ji pae-ro ka-nŭn-de yak yŏ-dŏl ssi-ga-ni kŏl-rim-ni-da.

부산에서 제주도까지 배로 가는데 약 여덟 시간이 걸립니다.

21. When does the train leave for Pusan?

Ki-ch'a-nŭn ŏn-je pu-sa-nŭ-ro ttŏ-nam-ni-kka?

기차는 언제 부산으로 떠납니까?

22. Where is the ticket of-

Mae-p'yo-si-rŭn ŏ-di it-ssŭm-ni-kka?

---

boat (*po-t'ŭ*)…보트
yacht (*yo-t'ŭ*)…요트

ticket (*ch'a-p'yo*)…차표
leave (*ttŏ-na-da*)…떠나다

fice ?

23. Two first class tickets to Pusan, please.

Pu-san-haeng il-ttŭng ch'a-p'yo tu chang-man chu-sip-ssi-o.

매표실은 어디 있습니까?

부산행 일등 차표 두 장만 주십시오.

24. Has this train a sleeping-car ?

I ki-ch'a-nŭn ch'im-dae-ch'a-ga it-ssŭm-ni-kka ?

이 기차는 침대차가 있습니까?

25. Is this the train for Pusan ?

I-gŏ-si pu-san-haeng ki-ch'a-im-ni-kka ?

이것이 부산행 기차입니까?

26. Please get on board, the train leaves in a few minutes.

Cha t'a-sip-ssi-o. Ki-ch'a-nŭn myŏt ppun nae-e ttŏ-nam-ni-da.

자 타십시오. 기차는 몇 분 내에 떠납니다.

27. Where is the express bus terminal for Chonju ?

Chŏn-ju-ro ka-nŭn ko-sok ppŏ-ssŭ chŏng-gŏ-jang-ŭn ŏ-di im-ni-kka?

전주로 가는 고속 버스 정거장은 어디 입니까?

28. It is near Shinbanpo.

Sin-ban-p'o kŭn-ch'ŏ-im-ni-da.

신반포 근처입니다.

29. Will you draw me a brief map to reach the Hae-insa temple ?

Hae-in-sa-ro ka-nŭn yak-tto-rŭl kŭ-ryŏ chu-si-get-ssŭm-ni-kka ?

해인사로 가는 약도를 그려 주시겠습니까?

30. Where is the famous Pulguksa temple ?

Yu-myŏng-han pul-guk-ssa-nŭn ŏ-di it-ssŭm-ni-kka?

---

sleeping-car(*ch'im-dae-ch'a*) … 침대차
railway(*sŏl-lo*) … 선로
attention(*chu-ŭi*) … 주의

board(*sŭng-ch'a*) … 승차
reserved seat(*chwa-sŏk chi-jŏng*) … 좌석 지정

유명한 불국사는 어디 있습니까?

31. Is there an accommodation facility on Mt. Sorak?

Sŏ-rak-ssa-ne-nŭn suk-ppak si-sŏ-ri it-ssŭm-ni-kka?

설악산에는 숙박 시설이 있습니까?

32. I'll see you off at the station.

Na-nŭn tang-si-nŭl chŏng-gŏ-jang-e-sŏ pae-ung-ha-get-ssŭm-ni-da.

나는 당신을 정거장에서 배웅하겠습니다.

33. Thank. See you there.

Kam-sa-ham-ni-da. Kŭ ko-se-sŏ man-nap-ssi-da.

감사합니다. 그 곳에서 만납시다.

34. Conductor, where is the berth?

Ch'a-jang, ch'im-dae-nŭn ŏ-di it-tchi-yo?

차장, 침대는 어디 있지요?

35. Where is the dining car?

Sik-ttang-ch'a-nŭn ŏ-di it-tchi-yo?

식당차는 어디 있지요?

36. What's the next station?

Ta-ŭm yŏ-gŭn ŏ-di im-ni-kka?

다음 역은 어디 입니까?

37. Now, we have a rest stop for five minutes.

Cha, o-bun-gan hyu-sik-im-ni-da.

자, 오분간 휴식입니다.

38. What's the name of this river?

I kang-ŭi i-rŭ-mŭn mu-ŏ-sim-ni-kka?

이 강의 이름은 무엇입니까?

39. We passed Taejon se-

U-ri-nŭn myŏt ssi-gan chŏ-ne tae-jŏ

---

arrive(*to-ch'a-k'a-da*)…도착하다
temple(*sa-wŏn*)…사원
accommodation facility(*suk-ppak si-sŏl*)…숙박 시설
offer(*che-gong*)…제공

conductor(*ch'a-jang, chi-hwi-ja*)…차장, 지휘자
diningcar(*sik-ttang-ch'a*)…식당차
rest(*hyu-sik*)…휴식
station(*yŏk*)…역

veral hours ago, and we must be nearing Taegu.

nŭl chi-na tae-gu-e ka-kka-wŏ o-go it-ssŭm-ni-da.

우리는 몇 시간 전에 대전을 지나 대구에 가까워 오고 있습니다.

40. Let's get ready to get off.

Nae-ril chun-bi-rŭl hap-ssi-da.

내릴 준비를 합시다.

41. My trunk in the luggage-car.

Hwa-mul-ch'a-e che t'ŭ-rŏng-k'ŭ-ga it-ssŭm-ni-da.

화물차에 제 트렁크가 있습니다.

42. Please take this luggage down.

I chi-mŭl nae-ryŏ chu-sip-ssi-o.

이 짐을 내려 주십시오.

43. Where is the information booth?

An-nae-so-nŭn ŏ-di it-ssŭm-ni-kka?

안내소는 어디 있습니까?

44. Beautiful. What is the name of this town?

Ch'am a-rŭm-dap-ssŭm-ni-da. I ma-ŭ-rŭi i-rŭ-mŭn mu-ŏ-sim-ni-kka?

참 아름답습니다. 이 마을의 이름은 무엇입니까?

45. Please, call a taxi for me.

T'aek-ssi-rŭl ha-na pul-lŏ chu-sip-ssi-o.

택시를 하나 불러 주십시오.

46. Handle this parcel with care.

I chi-mŭl chu-ŭi-hae-sŏ ta-rwŏ chu-sip-ssi-o.

이 짐을 주의해서 다뤄 주십시오.

47. Please, take me to the Haeinsa temple.

Hae-in-sa chŏl-kka-ji te-ryŏ-da chu-sip-ssi-o.

---

ready(*chun-bi-doen*)···준비된
baggage-car(*hwa-mul-ch'a*)···화물차
information booth(*an-nae-so*)···안내소

town(*ma-ŭl*)···마을
parcel(*chim*)···짐
heavy(*mu-gŏp-tta*)···무겁다

해인사 절까지 데려다 주십시오.

48. Go a little faster.

Chom ppal-li ka-sip-ssi-o.

좀 빨리 가십시오.

49. Look out! Go slowly.

Cho-sim-ha-sip-ssi-o. Ch'ŏn-ch'ŏn-hi kap-ssi-da.

조심하십시오. 천천히 갑시다.

50. Where can I get the tourism information?

Ŏ-di-sŏ yŏ-haeng chi-si-gŭl ŏ-dŭl ssu it-ssŭl-kka-yo?

어디서 여행 지식을 얻을 수 있을 까요?

51. There are many travel agencies in Seoul.

Seŏ-u-re-nŭn ma-nŭn yŏ-haeng-sa-ga it-ssŭm-ni-da.

서울에는 많은 여행사가 있습니다.

52. Here's a complete guidebook of Seoul.

I-gŏ-si seŏ-u-re kwan-han wan-jŏn-han an-nae ch'aek-tcha-im-ni-da.

이것이 서울에 관한 완전한 안내 책자입니다.

53. Do you have an particular field of interest?

T'ŭ-k'i hŭng-mi-rŭl ka-ji-go kye-sin pun-ya-ra-do it-ssŭ-sim-ni-kka?

특히 흥미를 가지고 계신 분야라도 있으십니까?

54. You can use the sightseeing bus for the convenient travel.

Tang-si-nŭn p'yŏ-nan-han yŏ-haeng-ŭl wi-hae-sŏ kwan-gwang ppŏ-ssŭ-rŭl i-yong-ha-sil ssu it-ssŭm-ni-da.

당신은 편안한 여행을 위해서 관광 버스를 이용하실 수 있습니다.

55. What have you seen in Seoul?

Seŏ-u-re-sŏ-nŭn mwŏl po-syŏt-ssŭm-ni-kka?

서울에서는 뭘 보셨습니까 ?

56. Can I visit Panmunjom ?

P'an-mun-jŏ-mūl pang-mun-hal ssu it-ssŭm-ni-kka ?

판문점을 방문할 수 있습니까 ?

57. You need a special permission for Panmunjom tour.

P'an-mun-jŏm yŏ-haeng-ūl wi-haesŏ-nūn t'ŭk-ppyŏl-han hŏ-ga-ga p'i-ryo-ham-ni-da.

판문점 여행을 위해서는 특별한 허가가 필요합니다.

58. Let's spend summer holidays at the Haeundae beach.

Hae-un-dae hae-su-yok-tchang-e-sŏ yŏ-rūm hyu-ga-rūl po-naep-ssi-da.

해운대 해수욕장에서 여름 휴가를 보냅시다.

59. Walker Hill is a famous resort place in Seoul.

Wŏ-k'ŏ hi-rūn seŏ-u-re-sŏ yu-myŏnghan yu-wŏn-ji-im-ni-da.

워커 힐은 서울에서 유명한 유원 지입니다.

At the Post Office

U-ch'e-gu-ge-sŏ (우체국에서)

1. Where is the nearest post office ?

Ka-jang ka-kka-un u-ch'e-gu-gūn ŏdi it-ssŭm-ni-kka ?

가장 가까운 우체국은 어디 있습 니까 ?

2. You can buy stamps at the post office.

U-ch'e-gu-ge-sŏ u-p'yo-rūl sal ssu itssŭm-ni-da.

우체국에서 우표를 살 수 있습니다.

3. Please give me two one

Paek wŏn-tcha-ri u-p'yo tu chang-man

---

rosort place(*yu-wŏn-ji*) … 유원지
post office(*u-ch'e-guk*) … 우체국
stamp(*u-p'yo*) … 우표

stamp(*in-ji*) … 인지
stamp(*to-jang*) … 도장

hundred won stamps.

chu-sip-ssi-o.

백 원짜리 우표 두 장만 주십시오.

4. I would like to mail this letter by air mail.

I p'yŏn-ji-rŭl hang-gong u-p'yŏ-nŭ-ro pu-ch'i-go sip-ssŭm-ni-da.

이 편지를 항공 우편으로 부치고 싶습니다.

5. I want to mail this package.

I so-p'o-rŭl pu-ch'i-go sip-ssŭm-ni-da.

이 소포를 부치고 싶습니다.

6. I would like to send a telegram to New York.

Nyu-yo-gŭ-ro chŏn-bo-rŭl ch'i-go sip-ssŭm-ni-da.

뉴욕으로 전보를 치고 싶습니다.

7. How much is it per word?

Han cha-e ŏl-ma-im-ni-kka?

한 자에 얼마입니까?

8. Is this postage correct?

I u-p'yo-nŭn ttok-ppa-ro pu-t'ŏt-ssŭm-ni-kka?

이 우표는 똑바로 붙었습니까?

9. Please weigh this letter.

I p'yŏn-ji-rŭl ta-ra chu-sip-ssi-o.

이 편지를 달아 주십시오.

10. I want to register this letter.

I p'yŏn-ji-rŭl tŭng-gi-ro pu-ch'i-go sip-ssŭm-ni-da.

이 편지를 등기로 부치고 싶습니다.

11. How much postage for this registered letter?

I tŭng-gi p'yŏn-ji-e-nŭn ŏl-ma-tcha-ri u-p'yo-rŭl pu-ch'yŏ-ya ham-ni-kka?

이 등기 편지에는 얼마짜리 우표를

---

air mail(*hang-gong u-p'yŏn*)…항공 우편

telegram(*chŏn-bo*)…전보

correct(*pa-rŭn*)…바른

postage stamp(*u-p'yo*)…우표

붙여야 합니까?

12. Please send this parcel by registered mail.

I so-p'o-rŭl tŭng-gi u-p'yŏ-nŭ-ro po-nae chu-sip-ssi-o.

이 소포를 등기 우편으로 보내 주십시오.

13. This package will reach Seoul in about a week.

I so-p'o-nŭn yak il-tchu-i-ri-myŏn seŏ-u-re to-ch'a-k'am-ni-da.

이 소포는 약 일주일이면 서울에 도착합니다.

14. What is the local telegram rate?

Kung-nae chŏn-bo yo-gŭ-mŭn ŏl-ma-im-ni-kka?

국내 전보 요금은 얼마입니까?

15. What is the rate of telegram for Tokyo?

Tong-gyŏng-ŭ-ro ka-nŭn chŏn-bo yo-gŭ-mŭn ŏl-ma-im-ni-kka?

동경으로 가는 전보 요금은 얼마입니까?

16. I like to write letters.

P'yŏn-ji-rŭl ssŭ-go sip-ssŭm-ni-da.

편지를 쓰고 싶습니다.

17. To whom do you write letters?

Tang-si-nŭn nu-gu-e-ge p'yŏn-ji-rŭl ssŭ-sim-ni-kka?

당신은 누구에게 편지를 쓰십니까?

18. Last night, I wrote a letter to my friend.

Chi-nan-bam na-nŭn ch'in-gu-e-ge p'yŏn-ji-rŭl ssŏt-ssŭm-ni-da.

지난밤 나는 친구에게 편지를 썼습니다.

19. Do you often receive letter from your frie-

Tang-si-nŭn ch'in-gu-e-ge ka-kkŭm p'yŏn-ji-rŭl pat-ssŭm-ni-kka?

---

register(*tŭng-no-k'a-da*)···등록하다
local(*chi-bang-ŭi*)···지방의

registry(*tŭng-gi*)···등기
special delivery(*sok-ttal*)···속달

nds?

당신은 친구에게 가끔 편지를 받습니까?

20. When I finish my letter, I fold the letter.

P'yŏn-ji-rŭl ta ssŭ-myŏn, na-nŭn kŭ p'yŏn-ji-rŭl chŏp-ssŭm-ni-da.

편지를 다 쓰면, 나는 그 편지를 접습니다.

21. I address the envelope and put a stamp on it.

Na-nŭn pong-t'u-e chu-so-rŭl ssŭ-go, kŭ pong-t'u wi-e u-p'yo-rŭl pu-ch'im-ni-da.

나는 봉투에 주소를 쓰고, 그 봉투 위에 우표를 부칩니다.

22. What is the iron box with red and blue colors on the street?

Kŏ-ri-e in-nŭn pul-kko p'u-rŭn-sae-gŭi soe-sang-ja-nŭn mu-ŏ-sim-ni-kka?

거리에 있는 붉고 푸른색의 쇠상자는 무엇입니까?

23. It is the mail box.

U-ch'e-t'ong-im-ni-da.

우체통입니다.

24. May I call a taxi for you?

T'aek-ssi-rŭl pul-lŏ tŭ-ril-kka-yo?

택시를 불러 드릴까요?

At the Government Office

Kwan-ch'ŏng-e-sŏ (관청에서)

1. Can I help you?

To-wa tŭ-ril-kka-yo?

도와 드릴까요?

2. What can I do for

Mu-ŏ-sŭl to-wa tŭ-ril-kka-yo?

---

receive(*pat-tta*) … 받다
finish(*ma-ch'i-da*) … 마치다
iron(*soe*) … 쇠
government office(*kwan-ch'ŏng*) … 관청

trouble(*sa-kkŏn*) … 사건
box(*sang-ja*) … 상자
preservation(*po-jon*) … 보존

you?
3. What's the trouble?

4. Please take a seat and wait a moment.

5. I think I can help you.

6. May I have your name and address?

7. Would you fill out this form?

8. I'd like to make an appointment for an interview.

9. He is at a meeting now.

10. Where is the Immigration Office?

11. Where is the Ministry

무엇을 도와 드릴까요?
Mu-sŭn i-ri-sim-ni-kka?
무슨 일이십니까?

Cha-ri-e an-ja cho-gŭm-man ki-da-ri-sip-ssi-o.
자리에 앉아 조금만 기다리십시오.

Tang-si-nŭl to-wa tŭ-ril ssu it-tta-go saeng-ga-k'am-ni-da.
당신을 도와 드릴 수 있다고 생각합니다.

Tang-si-nŭi sŏng-ham-gwa chu-so-rŭl il-rŏ chu-si-get-ssŭm-ni-kka?
당신의 성함과 주소를 일러 주시겠습니까?

I yang-si-gŭl ki-ro-k'ae chu-si-get-ssŭm-ni-kka?
이 양식을 기록해 주시겠습니까?

Myŏn-jŏp yak-sso-gŭl ha-go sip-ssŭm-ni-da.
면접 약속을 하고 싶습니다.

Kŭ-nŭn chi-gŭm hoe-ŭi chung-im-ni-da.
그는 지금 회의 중입니다.

Ch'ul-ip-kkuk kwal-li sa-mu-so-nŭn ŏ-di it-ssŭm-ni-kka?
출입국 관리 사무소는 어디 있습니까?

Woe-mu-bu-nŭn ŏ-di it-ssŭm-ni-kka

Ministry of Foreign Affairs *(woe-mu-bu)*…외무부

form *(yang-sik)*…양식

143

of Foreign Affairs?

       ?

외무부는 어디 있습니까?

12. It is in the Government Building.

Che il chong-hap ch'ŏng-sa a-ne it-ssŭm-ni-da.

제 일 종합 청사 안에 있습니다.

13. Whom do I see about my visa extension?

Pi-ja yŏn-jang-kkŏ-ne kwan-hae-sŏ-nŭn nu-gu-rŭl man-na po-a-ya ham-ni-kka?

비자 연장건에 관해서는 누구를 만나 보아야 합니까?

14. May I have a form to report change of my address?

Chu-so pyŏn-gyŏng sin-go-e kwan-han yang-si-gŭl ŏ-dŭl ssu it-ssŭm-ni-kka?

주소 변경 신고에 관한 양식을 얻을 수 있습니까?

15. What is your Foreign Registration Number?

Tang-si-nŭi woe-gu-gin tŭng-nok pŏn-ho-nŭn mu-ŏ-sim-ni-kka?

당신의 외국인 등록 번호는 무엇입니까?

16. Is there any possibility that I could stay here a little longer?

Che-ga yŏ-gi chom-dŏ mŏ-mu-rŭl ssu in-nŭn ka-nŭng-sŏng-i it-ssŭm-ni-kka?

제가 여기 좀더 머무를 수 있는 가능성이 있습니까?

17. Did you file the income tax return?

Tang-si-nŭn so-dŭk-sse-rŭl wan-nap-ha-syŏt-ssŭm-ni-kka?

---

higher officer(*sang-gwan*)…상관
Ministry of Education(*mun-gyo-bu*)…문교부
Ministry of Home Affairs(*nae-mu-bu*)…내무부

Ministry of justice(*pŏm-mu-bu*)…법무부
Ministry of Finance(*chae-mu-bu*)…재무부
income tax(*so-dŭk-sse*)…소득세

당신은 소득세를 완납하셨습니까?

18. Is this your resume ?

I-gŏ-si tang-sin i-ryŏk-ssŏ-im-ni-kka ?

이것이 당신 이력서입니까?

19. We charge ten thousand won for your immigration visa.

I-min sa-tchŭng-e tae-han yo-gŭ-mŭn man wŏn-im-ni-da.

이민 사증에 대한 요금은 만 원입니다.

20. We will notify you the result by mail.

U-ri-nŭn kyŏl-gwa-rŭl u-p'yŏ-nŭ-ro t'ong-ji-hae tŭ-ri-get-ssŭm-ni-da.

우리는 결과를 우편으로 통지해 드리겠습니다.

At the Bank

Ŭn-haeng-e-sŏ (은행에서)

1. Where is the main office of the Hanil Bank ?

Ha-nil ŭn-haeng-ŭi pon-jŏ-mŭn ŏ-di im-ni-kka ?

한일 은행의 본점은 어디 입니

---

personal history(*i-ryŏk-ssŏ*)…이력서
immigration visa(*i-min sa-tchŭng*)…이민 사증
notify(*t'ong-ji-ha-da*)…통지하다
Ministry of Transportation(*kyo-t'ong-bu*)…교통부
Ministry of Agriculture and Fisheries (*nong-su-san-bu*)…농수산부
Ministry of Communications(*ch'e-sin-bu*)…체신부
Ministry of Commerce and Industry (*sang-gong-bu*)…상공부
Ministry of National Defense(*kuk-ppang-bu*)…국방부
Capitol(*chung-ang-ch'ŏng*)…중앙청
city hall(*si-ch'ŏng*)…시청

president(*tae-t'ong-nyŏng*)…대통령
prime minister(*kung-mu ch'ong-ni*)…국무 총리
National Assembly(*ku-k'oe*)…국회
house speaker(*ku-k'oe ŭi-jang*)…국회 의장
justice(*pŏp-kkwan*)…법관
law(*pŏp*)…법
assemblyman(*ku-k'oe ŭi-wŏn*)…국회 의원
supreme court(*tae-bŏ-bwŏn*)…대법원
embassy(*tae-sa-gwan*)…대사관
ambassador(*tae-sa*)…대사
political party(*chŏng-dang*)…정당
cabinet(*nae-gak*)…내각
minister(*chang-gwan*)…장관

2. Where is the Tongdae-mun branch office of the Commercial Bank ?

Sang-ŏp ŭn-haeng-ŭi tong-dae-mun chi-jŏ-mŭn ŏ-di im-ni-kka ?

상업 은행의 동대문 지점은 어디 입니까 ?

3. I want to make a deposit.

Ye-gŭ-mŭl ha-go sip-ssŭm-ni-da.

예금을 하고 싶습니다.

4. Fill this blank, please.

I yong-ji-e ki-i-bŭl hae chu-sip-ssi-o.

이 용지에 기입을 해 주십시오.

5. I want to withdraw 50,000 won.

O-man wŏn-ŭl ch'at-kko sip-ssŭm-ni-da.

오만 원을 찾고 싶습니다.

6. I need about ten thousand won.

Chŏ-nŭn yak man wŏn-i p'i-ryo-ham-ni-da.

저는 약 만 원이 필요합니다.

7. Go to the cashier's desk.

Chi-bul-gye-ro ka-sip-ssi-o.

지불계로 가십시오.

8. May I see your identification card ?

Sin-bun chŭng-myŏng-sŏ-rŭl po-yŏ chu-si-get-ssŭm-ni-kka ?

신분 증명서를 보여 주시겠습니까 ?

9. May I have your chomp.

To-jang chom chu-si-get-ssŭm-ni-kka ?

도장 좀 주시겠습니까 ?

10. Where is window No.

Sip ppŏn ch'ang-gu-nŭn ŏ-di im-ni-

---

cashier's desk 〈*chi-bul-gye*〉…지불계
indetification card 〈*sin-bun chŭng-myŏng-sŏ*〉…신분 증명서
bank 〈*ŭn-haeng*〉…은행
branch office 〈*chi-jŏm*〉…지점
deposit 〈*ye-gŭm*〉…예금

chomp 〈*to-jang*〉…도장
check 〈*su-p'yo*〉…수표
forgery 〈*wi-jo*〉…위조
cancellation 〈*hae-yak*〉…해약
gradual advance 〈*nu-jin*〉…누진

10?

11. I want to cash this check.

12. Please endorse your check.

13. May I have your signature here, please?

14. Today's exchange rato is 750 won to a dollar.

15. How would like your money?

16. Are you a regular depositor?

17. Yes, I am. Here is my savings account.

18. Is yours a current or a fixed account?

kka?

십 번 창구는 어디 입니까?

I su-p'yo-rŭl hyŏn-gŭ-mŭ-ro pa-kku-go sip-ssŭm-ni-da.

이 수표를 현금으로 바꾸고 싶습니다.

Tang-sin su-p'yo-e i-sŏ-rŭl hae chu-sip-ssi-o.

당신 수표에 이서를 해 주십시오.

Yŏ-gi-e sŏ-myŏng-ŭl hae chu-sil-kka-yo?

여기에 서명을 해 주실까요?

O-nŭ-rŭi hwan-yu-rŭn il pu-re ch'il-baek-o-sip wŏn-im-ni-da.

오늘의 환율은 일 불에 칠백오십 원입니다.

To-nŭn ŏ-ttŏ-k'e tŭ-rĭl-kka-yo?

돈은 어떻게 드릴까요?

Chŏng-gyu ye-gŭm-ja-i-sim-ni-kka?

정규 예금자이십니까?

Ne, kŭ-rŏt-ssŭm-ni-da. Yŏ-gi t'ong-jang-i it-ssŭm-ni-da.

네, 그렇습니다. 여기 통장이 있습니다.

Po-t'ong ye-gŭm-im-ni-kka, a-ni-myŏn chŏng-gi ye-gŭm-im-ni-kka?

보통 예금입니까, 아니면 정기 예금입니까?

---

passbook (*t'ong-jang*)…통장
instalment (*chŏk-kkŭm*)…적금

borrow (*pil-li-da*)…빌리다
guarantor (*po-jŭng-in*)…보증인

19. It's a fixed account.

Chŏng-gi ye-gŭm-im-ni-da.
정기 예금입니다.

20. Please state the amount you wish to deposit.

Ye-gŭm-ha-sil-lyŏ-nŭn   kŭ-mae-gŭl chŏ-gŏ chu-sip-ssi-o.
예금하실려는 금액을 적어 주십시오.

21. Would you like to insure it?

Po-hŏ-mŭl kŏ-si-get-ssŭm-ni-kka?
보험을 거시겠습니까?

22. Can you change this 10,000 won bill for me?

I il-man wŏn-kkwŏ-nŭl chan-do-nŭ-ro pa-kkwŏ chu-sil-kka-yo?
이 일만 원권을 잔돈으로 바꿔 주실까요?

23. Can you change this five hundred won bill?

I o-baek wŏn-ŭl chan-do-nŭ-ro pa-kkwŏ chu-si-get-ssŭm-ni-kka?
이 오백 원을 잔돈으로 바꿔 주시겠습니까?

24. Have you got any change?

Chan-do-ni it-ssŭ-sim-ni-kka?
잔돈이 있으십니까?

25. Could I borrow some money from you?

Ton chom pil-lil ssu it-ssŭl-kka-yo?
돈 좀 빌릴 수 있을까요?

26. Here are ten five hundred won bill and eight coins.

Yŏ-gi o-baek wŏn ta-sŏt kkae-wa tong-jŏn yŏ-dŏl kkae-ga it-ssŭm-ni-da.
여기 오백 원 다섯 개와 동전 여덟 개가 있습니다.

27. This will be 960 won.

Ku-baek-yuk-ssip wŏn-i toe-get-ssŭm-ni-da.
구백육십 원이 되겠습니다.

---

lending clerk(*tae-ch'ul-gye*)···대출계
lending out(*tae-ch'ul*)···대출

life insurance(*saeng-myŏng po-hŏm*)···
생명 보험

At the Bookstore

1. Where is the Donghwa Bookstore?

2. Where is the Chongno Bookstore?

3. Where can I buy Korean History book?

4. Do you have a guide-book of Korea?

5. Yes, here is. This book was issued recently.

6. How much is it?

7. It is five thousand won.

8. I will take it.

9. Is there anything else

Sŏ-jŏm-e-sŏ (서점에서)

Tong-hwa sŏ-jŏ-gŭn ŏ-di it-ssŭm-ni-kka?
동화 서적은 어디 있습니까?

Chong-no sŏ-jŏ-gŭn ŏ-di it-ssŭm-ni-kka?
종로 서적은 어디 있습니까?

Ŏ-di-sŏ han-guk yŏk-ssa-ch'ae-gŭl sal ssu it-ssŭm-ni-kka?
어디서 한국 역사책을 살 수 있습니까?

Han-guk an-nae-sŏ-ga it-ssŭm-ni-kka?
한국 안내서가 있습니까?

Ne, yŏ-gi it-ssŭm-ni-da. I ch'ae-gŭn ch'oe-gŭ-ne pal-gan-doe-ŏt-ssŭm-ni-da.
네, 여기 있습니다. 이 책은 최근에 발간되었습니다.

Ŏl-ma-im-ni-kka?
얼마입니까?

O-ch'ŏn wŏn-im-ni-da.
오천 원입니다.

Kŭ-gŏl sa-get-ssŭm-ni-da.
그걸 사겠습니다.

Po-yŏ tŭ-ril ch'ae-gi-ra-do tto it-ssŭm-

---

coin(*tong-jŏn*)···동전
bookstore(*sŏ-jŏm*)···서점
history(*yŏk-ssa*)···역사
guide-book(*an-nae-sŏ*)···안내서

issue(*pal-gan-ha-da*)···발간하다
recently(*ch'oe-gŭn*)···최근
shop clerk(*chŏm-wŏn*)···점원
sale(*p'an-mae*)···판매

I can show you, sir?

ni-kka?

보여 드릴 책이라도 또 있습니까?

10. Do you have any books on economy?

Kyŏng-je-e kwan-han ch'ae-gi it-ssŭm-ni-kka?

경제에 관한 책이 있습니까?

11. Do you have any book on politics?

Chŏng-ch'i-e kwan-han sŏ-jŏ-gi it-ssŭm-ni-kka?

정치에 관한 서적이 있습니까?

12. I want an interesting novel.

Chae-mi-in-nŭn so-sŏ-rŭl wŏn-ham-ni-da.

재미있는 소설을 원합니다.

13. Do you want a foreing novel?

Woe-guk so-sŏ-rŭl wŏn-ham-ni-kka?

외국 소설을 원합니까?

14. No, I want a novel written by a Korean writer.

A-nim-ni-da. Han-guk chak-kka-ga ssŭn so-sŏ-rŭl wŏn-ham-ni-da.

아닙니다. 한국 작가가 쓴 소설을 원합니다.

15. Yes, we have. Here is one which is very popular.

Ne, it-ssŭm-ni-da. Yŏ-gi mae-u in-kki in-nŭn so-sŏ-ri ha-na it-ssŭm-ni-da.

네, 있습니다. 여기 매우 인기 있는 소설이 하나 있습니다.

16. Do you have any philosophy books?

Ch'ŏl-hak sŏ-jŏ-gi it-ssŭm-ni-kka?

철학 서적이 있습니까?

17. Who is the author?

Chŏ-ja-nŭn nu-gu-im-ni-kka?

저자는 누구입니까?

---

contribution (*ki-go*)…기고
writer (*chak-kka*)…작가
popular (*in-kki in-nŭn*)…인기 있는
translation (*pŏ-nyŏk*)…번역
stamp duty (*in-sse*)…인세

philosophy (*ch'ŏl-hak*)…철학
author (*chŏ-ja*)…저자
sell (*p'al-da*)…팔다
new publication (*sin-gan*)…신간
old edition (*ku-gan*)…구간

18. It is Dr. Kim Kilsu of Seoul National University.

Seŏ-ul tae-hak-kkyo-ŭi kim-gil-ssu pak-ssa-im-ni-da.

서울 대학교의 김길수 박사입니다.

19. I'm sorry. They are all sold out.

Mi-an-ham-ni-da. Kŭ-gŏ-sŭn mo-du p'al-lyŏt-ssŭm-ni-da.

미안합니다. 그것은 모두 팔렸습니다.

20. Will it be reprinted?

Ta-si pal-haeng-doem-ni-kka?

다시 발행됩니까?

21. Yes, it is now in press.

Ne, chi-gŭm in-swoe chung-im-ni-da.

네, 지금 인쇄 중입니다.

22. If you should get a new supply, please keep a copy for me.

Sae-ro kong-gŭp-ttoe-myŏn chŏ-rŭl wi-hae han kwŏn-man po-gwan-hae chu-sip-ssi-o.

새로 공급되면 저를 위해 한 권만 보관해 주십시오.

Recreation

O-rak (오락)

1. What's your hobby?

Tang-si-nŭi ch'wi-mi-nŭn mu-ŏ-sim-ni-kka?

당신의 취미는 무엇입니까?

2. My hobby is stamp collecting.

Na-ŭi ch'wi-mi-nŭn u-p'yo su-jip-im-ni-da.

나의 취미는 우표 수집입니다.

3. What kind of recreation do you like?

Tang-si-nŭn ŏ-ttŏn o-ra-gŭl cho-a-ha-sim-ni-kka?

---

reprint(*chae-bal-haeng*) … 재발행
copy(*pok-ssa-ha-da*) … 복사하다
recreation(*o-rak*) … 오락
absence from stock(*p'um-jŏl*) … 품절
drama(*yŏn-gŭk*) … 연극

join(*hap-ch'i-da*) … 합치다
hobby(*ch'wi-mi*) … 취미
collection(*su-jip*) … 수집
stroll(*san-ch'aek*) … 산책

당신은 어떤 오락을 좋아하십니까?

4. I like going to the movies.

Na-nŭn yŏng-hwa ku-gyŏng-ŭl cho-a-ham-ni-da.

나는 영화 구경을 좋아합니다.

5. I like everything if it is recreational.

Na-nŭn o-rak-tchŏk-i-gi-man ha-myŏn mu-ŏ-si-na cho-a-ham-ni-da.

나는 오락적이기만 하면 무엇이나 좋아합니다.

6. We are going on a picnic tomorrow. Will you join us?

U-ri-nŭn nae-il p'i-k'ŭ-ni-gŭl kam-ni-da. Ham-kke ka-si-get-ssŭm-ni-kka?

우리는 내일 피크닉을 갑니다. 함께 가시겠습니까?

7. Where are you going?

Ŏ-di ka-sim-ni-kka?

어디 가십니까?

8. We are going to go to Mt. Tobong.

U-ri-nŭn to-bong-sa-nel kal-lyŏ-go ham-ni-da.

우리는 도봉산엘 갈려고 합니다.

9. I will go with you, with pleasure.

Chŭl-gŏ-un ma-ŭ-mŭ-ro ka-ch'i ka-get-ssŭm-ni-da.

즐거운 마음으로 같이 가겠습니다.

10. Then, let's meet at the bus terminal near the Seoul Railway Station at 10 o'clock tomorrow morning.

Kŭ-rŏ-t'a-myŏn nae-il a-ch'im yŏl-ssi-e seŏ-ul-lyŏk kŭn-ch'ŏ-ŭi ppŏ-ssŭ chŏng-gŏ-jang-e-sŏ man-nap-ssi-da.

그렇다면 내일 아침 열시에 서울역 근처의 버스 정거장에서 만납시다.

---

theater(*kŭk-tchang*)…극장
picnic(*p'i-k'ŭ-nik*)…피크닉

performance(*yŏn-gi*)…연기

11. Let's meet at seven Sunday morning at the Tajong coffee shop and go hiking.

I-ryo-il a-ch'im il-gop-ssi-e ta-jŏng ta-bang-e-sŏ man-na tŭng-sa-nŭl kap-ssi-da.

일요일 아침 일곱시에 다정 다방에서 만나 등산을 갑시다.

12. The only way to enjoy Autumn is to be outdoors.

Ka-ŭ-rŭl chŭl-gi-nŭn yu-il-han pang-bŏ-bŭn pak-kkŭ-ro na-ga-nŭn kŏ-sim-ni-da.

가을을 즐기는 유일한 방법은 밖으로 나가는 것입니다.

13. Don't forget to bring your lunch box.

To-si-ra-gŭl ka-jyŏ-o-nŭn kŏ-sŭl it-tchi ma-sip-ssi-o.

도시락을 가져오는 것을 잊지 마십시오.

14. I'll take a kettle to make coffee.

Kŏ-p'i-rŭl kkŭ-ri-gi wi-hae chu-jŏn-ja-rŭl ka-ji-go ka-get-ssŭm-ni-da.

커피를 끓이기 위해 주전자를 가지고 가겠습니다.

15. Please wear old clothes and comfortable walking shoes for hiking.

Tŭng-sa-nŭl wi-hae-sŏ-nŭn hŏn ot-kkwa p'yŏn-han sin-ba-rŭl si-nŭ-sip-ssi-o.

등산을 위해서는 헌 옷과 편한 신발을 신으십시오.

16. After supper, let's walk along the river bank.

Chŏ-nyŏ-gŭl mŏk-kko na-sŏ, kang-ttu-gŭl tta-ra san-ppo-rŭl hap-ssi-da.

---

knapsack⟨*pae-nang*⟩…배낭
hiking⟨*tŭng-san*⟩…등산
lunch box⟨*to-si-rak*⟩…도시락
wear⟨*ip-tta*⟩…입다

outdoor⟨*pa-kkat*⟩…바깥
wicker tray⟨*ch'ae-ban*⟩…채반
tray⟨*chaeng-ban*⟩…쟁반
comfortable⟨*kan-p'yŏn-han*⟩…간편한

저녁을 먹고 나서, 강뚝을 따라 산보를 합시다.

17. In the deep woods, we listened to the cuckoos and larks.

Ki-p'ŭn sup-sso-ge-sŏ u-ri-nŭn ppŏ-kkuk-ssae-wa chong-dal-ssae u-rŭm-sso-ri-rŭl tŭt-ssŭm-ni-da.

깊은 숲속에서 우리는 뻐꾹새와 종달새 울음소리를 듣습니다.

18. On the mountain, we gathered sticks and built fire.

San wi-e-sŏ u-ri-nŭn na-mu-kka-ji-rŭl mo-a pu-rŭl no-at-ssŭm-ni-da.

산 위에서 우리는 나뭇가지를 모아 불을 놓았습니다.

19. We sat on the grass and had our lunch.

U-ri-nŭn chan-di wi-e an-ja-sŏ chŏm-si-mŭl mŏ-gŏt-ssŭm-ni-da.

우리는 잔디 위에 앉아서 점심을 먹었습니다.

20. Around the campfire, we all sang together.

Mo-dak-ppul chu-wi-e-sŏ u-ri-nŭn mo-du no-rae-rŭl pul-lŏt-ssŭm-ni-da.

모닥불 주위에서 우리는 모두 노래를 불렀습니다.

21. Will you go mountain climbing next Sunday?

Ta-ŭm i-ryo-i-re tŭng-sa-nŭl ka-si-get-ssŭm-ni-kka?

다음 일요일에 등산을 가시겠습니까?

22. I like going to the mountains.

Na-nŭn sa-ne ka-gi-rŭl cho-a-ham-ni-da.

나는 산에 가기를 좋아합니다.

---

lake(*ho-su*)…호수
cuckoo(*ppŏ-kkuk-ssae*)…뻐꾹새

lark(*chong-dal-ssae*)…종달새

23. In summer, I like to go to sea for swimming.

Yŏ-rŭ-me na-nŭn su-yŏng-ŭl ha-gi wi-hae pa-da-e ka-gi-rŭl cho-a-ham-ni-da.

여름에 나는 수영을 하기 위해 바다에 가기를 좋아합니다.

24. Is there a good beach around Pusan?

Pu-san kŭn-ch'ŏ-e-nŭn cho-ŭn hae-su-yok-tchang-i it-ssŭm-ni-kka?

부산 근처에는 좋은 해수욕장이 있습니까?

25. Yes, there are several good beaches including the Haeundae.

Ne, hae-un-dae-rŭl p'o-ham-han myŏt kkae-ŭi cho-ŭn hae-su-yok-tchang-i it-ssŭm-ni-da.

네, 해운대를 포함한 몇 개의 좋은 해수욕장이 있습니다.

26. Let's go to Songdo beach this coming Sunday.

O-nŭn i-ryo-i-re song-do hae-su-yok-tchang-el kap-ssi-da.

오는 일요일에 송도 해수욕장엘 갑시다.

27. You swim very well.

Tang-si-nŭn su-yŏng-ŭl ssŏk chal-ham-ni-da.

당신은 수영을 썩 잘합니다.

28. Can you row?

No-rŭl chŏ-ŭl ssu it-ssŭm-ni-kka?

노를 저을 수 있습니까?

29. Shall we row back to the shore?

Pae-rŭl chŏ-ŏ hae-a-nŭ-ro to-ra-gal-kka-yo?

배를 저어 해안으로 돌아갈까요?

30. Life on the beach is

Hae-byŏn-kka-ŭi   saeng-hwa-rŭn

---

horizon(*chi-p'yŏng-sŏn*)…지평선
row(*no-rŭl chŏt-tta*)…노를 젓다
sea(*pa-da*)…바다

shore(*hae-an*)…해안
sun bath(*il-gwang-yok*)…일광욕

	very romantic.	*mae-u nang-man-jŏk-im-ni-da.* 해변가의 생활은 매우 낭만적입니다.

31. What's the most beautiful mountain in Korea ?

Han-gu-ge-sŏ ka-jang a-rŭm-da-un sa-nŭn mu-ŏ-sim-ni-kka ?

한국에서 가장 아름다운 산은 무엇입니까 ?

32. It's the Diamond Mountain. But it's in north Korea.

Kŭm-gang-san-im-ni-da. Kŭ-rŏ-na kŭ-gŏ-sŭn i-bu-ge it-ssŭm-ni-da.

금강산입니다. 그러나 그것은 이북에 있습니다.

33. The highest mountain in Korea is Mt. Paektu.

Han-gu-ge-sŏ ka-jang no-p'ŭn sa-nŭn paek-ttu-san-im-ni-da.

한국에서 가장 높은 산은 백두산입니다.

34. Do you like fishing ?

Nak-ssi-rŭl cho-a-ha-sim-ni-kka ?

낚시를 좋아하십니까 ?

35. I like it very much.

Na-nŭn nak-ssi-rŭl mae-u cho-a-ham-ni-da.

나는 낚시를 매우 좋아합니다.

36. How about going fishing on coming Sunday ?

O-nŭn i-ryo-i-re nak-ssi-rŭl ka-nŭn-ge ŏ-ttŏ-k'et-ssŭm-ni-kka ?

오는 일요일에 낚시를 가는게 어떻겠습니까 ?

37. Where is a famous

Nak-ssi-ro-nŭn ŏ-nŭ ko-si yu-

---

romantic(*nang-man-jŏk*)…낭만적
north(*puk*)…북
hunting gun(*yŏp-ch'ong*)…엽총
bow(*hwal*)…활
spear(*ch'ang*)…창

fishing(*ko-gi-jap-kki*)…고기잡기
hunting(*sa-nyang*)…사냥
badug(*pa-duk*)…바둑
chess(*chang-gi*)…장기
fish spear(*chak-ssal*)…작살

place for fishing?

myŏng-ham-ni-kka?

낚시로는 어느 곳이 유명합니까?

38. The Chongpyong Lake is a good place for fishing.

Ch'ŏng-p'yŏng ho-su-ga nak-ssi-t'ŏ-ro yu-myŏng-ham-ni-da.

청평 호수가 낚시터로 유명합니다.

39. Let's take a walk in the Toksu Palace.

Tŏk-ssu-gung-ŭ-ro san-ppo-rŭl kap-ssi-da.

덕수궁으로 산보를 갑시다.

40. Children like to go to the Yongin Farm Land.

A-i-dŭ-rŭn yong-in cha-yŏn nong-wŏ-ne ka-gil cho-a-ham-ni-da.

아이들은 용인 자연 농원에 가길 좋아합니다.

41. There are many theaters in Seoul.

Seŏ-u-re-nŭn ma-nŭn kŭk-tchang-i it-ssŭm-ni-da.

서울에는 많은 극장이 있습니다.

42. I would like to see a Korean play.

Han-guk yŏn-gŭ-gŭl ha-na po-go sip-ssŭm-ni-da.

한국 연극을 하나 보고 싶습니다.

43. Where can I see a Korean play?

Ŏ-di-sŏ han-guk yŏn-gŭ-gŭl pol ssu it-ssŭm-ni-kka?

어디서 한국 연극을 볼 수 있습니까?

44. You can see it at the Tongsung-dong street.

Tong-sung-dong kŏ-ri-e-sŏ ku-gyŏng-hal ssu it-ssŭm-ni-da.

동숭동 거리에서 구경할 수 있습

---

palace(*kung-jŏn*)…궁전
hook(*nak-ssi*)…낚시
motor race(*cha-dong-ch'a kyŏng-ju*)…
　자동차 경주
air gun(*kong-gi-ch'ong*)…공기총
sand bath(*mo-rae-tchim*)…모래찜
surfing(*sŏ-p'ing*)…서핑

zoo(*tong-mu-rwŏn*)…동물원
cinema house(*yŏng-hwa-gwan*)…영화
　관
seashore(*hae-byŏn*)…해변
diving(*cham-su*)…잠수
riding(*sŭng-ma*)…승마
billiards(*tang-gu*)…당구

니다.

45. There are many movie cinemas in Seoul.

Seŏ-u-re-nŭn ma-nŭn yŏng-hwa-gwa-ni it-ssŭm-ni-da.

서울에는 많은 영화관이 있습니다.

46. You can see Korean or foreign movies in Seoul movie theaters.

Tang-si-nŭn seŏ-u-rŭi yŏng-hwa-gwa-ne-sŏ han-guk yŏng-hwa-na woe-guk yŏng-hwa-rŭl pol ssu it-ssŭm-ni-da.

당신은 서울의 영화관에서 한국 영화나 외국 영화를 볼 수 있습니다.

47. Are there any good Korean movies tonight ?

O-nŭl-ppam cho-ŭn yŏng-hwa-ra-do it-ssŭm-ni-kka ?

오늘밤 좋은 영화라도 있습니까 ?

48. The Daehan Theater is running a Korean movie called "Regent Taewon."

Tae-han kŭk-tchang-ŭn han-guk yŏng-hwa tae-wŏn-gu-nŭl sang-yŏng-ha-go it-ssŭm-ni-da.

대한 극장은 한국 영화 "대원군"을 상영하고 있습니다.

49. There are many coffee shop in Seoul.

Seŏ-u-re-nŭn ma-nŭn ta-bang-i it-ssŭm-ni-da.

서울에는 많은 다방이 있습니다.

50. Let's take a rest at the coffee shop after lunch.

Chŏm-sim hu-e ta-bang-e-sŏ chom sip-ssi-da.

점심 후에 다방에서 좀 쉽시다.

At the Hospital

Pyŏng-wŏ-ne-sŏ (병원에서)

1. What's your trouble ?

Ŏ-di-ga a-p'ŭ-sim-ni-kka ?

---

movie(*yŏng-hwa*) ···영화
tonight(*o-nŭl-ppam*) ···오늘밤

rest(*swi-da*) ···쉬다

어디가 아프십니까?

2. I'm having trouble with
   my eyes.

Nu-ni a-p'ŭm-ni-da.

눈이 아픕니다.

3. I have a little fever.

Yak-kkan yŏ-ri it-ssŭm-ni-da.

약간 열이 있습니다.

4. I have a stomach ache.

Pok-t'ong-i it-ssŭm-ni-da.

복통이 있습니다.

5. I have a pain in my
   chest.

Ka-sŭ-mi a-p'ŭm-ni-da.

가슴이 아픕니다.

6. How is your appetite?

Si-gyo-gŭn ŏ-ttŏt-ssŭm-ni-kka?

식욕은 어떻습니까?

7. I'll take your temperature.

Yŏ-rŭl che-ŏ po-get-ssŭm-ni-da.

열을 재어 보겠습니다.

8. Lie down a moment.

Cham-kkan nu-u-sip-ssi-o

잠깐 누우십시오.

9. Take a deep breath.

Su-mŭl kil-ge ma-si-sip-ssi-o.

숨을 길게 마시십시오.

10. Is mine a serious
    case?

Nae pyŏng-ŭn sim-gak-ham-ni-kka?

내 병은 심각합니까?

11. Can I eat anything I
    wish?

*Mŏk-kko si-p'ŭn kŏ-sŭl mŏ-gŏ-do
toem-ni-kka?*

먹고 싶은 것을 먹어도 됩니까?

12. I was sick in the hos-
    pital for one week.

*Il-tchu-il ttong-an pyŏng-wŏ-ne-sŏ ip-
wŏn-ha-go it-ssŏt-ssŭm-ni-da.*

일주일 동안 병원에서 입원하고
있었습니다.

---

bleeding (*ch'ul-hyŏl*)…출혈
hospital (*pyŏng-wŏn*)…병원
stomach ache (*pok-t'ong*)…복통
migraine (*p'yŏn-du-t'ong*)…편두통

fever (*yŏl*)…열
heart   disease (*sim-jang-byŏng*)…심장
   병

13. Which hospital were you in?

Ŏ-nŭ pyŏng-wŏ-ne ip-wŏn-haet-ssŏt-ssŭm-ni-kka?

어느 병원에 입원했었습니까?

14. I was in the Seoul National University Hospital.

Na-nŭn seŏ-ul tae-hak-kkyo pu-sok pyŏng-wŏ-ne ip-wŏn-ha-go it-ssŏt-ssŭm-ni-da.

나는 서울 대학교 부속 병원에 입원하고 있었습니다.

15. I was operated on for appendicitis.

Na-nŭn maeng-jang-yŏ-mŭl su-sul-haet-ssŭm-ni-da.

나는 맹장염을 수술했습니다.

16. I hope you get well soon.

So-k'i hoe-bo-k'a-si-gi-rŭl pim-ni-da.

속히 회복하시기를 빕니다.

17. I progressed favorably and recovered very quickly.

Kyŏng-gwa-ga cho-a-sŏ kot hoe-bo-k'aet-ssŭm-ni-da.

경과가 좋아서 곧 회복했습니다.

18. You look pale. Have you been sick?

Ŏl-gu-ri ch'ang-bae-k'am-ni-da. A-p'at-ssŭm-ni-kka?

얼굴이 창백합니다. 아팠습니까?

19. I had a slight fever last night, and I do not feel well even this morning.

Chi-nan-bam mi-yŏ-ri it-ssŏt-ssŭm-ni-da. O-nŭl a-ch'im-kka-ji-do mo-mi cho-ch'i mo-t'am-ni-da.

지난밤 미열이 있었습니다. 오늘 아침까지도 몸이 좋지 못합니다.

---

chest(*ka-sŭm*)…가슴
appetite(*si-gyok*)…식욕
temperature(*on-do*)…온도
breath(*sum*)…숨
serious(*chung-dae-han*)…중대한
pulsation(*maek-ppak*)…맥박

headache(*tu-t'ong*)…두통
surgery(*su-sul*)…수술
appendicitis(*maeng-jang-yŏm*)…맹장염
head(*mŏ-ri*)…머리
loose bowels(*sŏl-ssa*)…설사

20. That's too bad. You had better see a doctor.

An-doet-kkun-yo. Ŭi-sa-rŭl ch'a-ja poem-nŭn kŏ-si cho-ŭl kkŏ-sim-ni-da.

안됐군요. 의사를 찾아 뵙는 것이 좋을 것입니다.

21. Do you know a good doctor around here?

I kŭn-ch'ŏ-e chal-ha-nŭn ŭi-sa-rŭl a-sim-ni-kka?

이 근처에 잘하는 의사를 아십니까?

22. Take this medicine three times a day.

I ya-gŭl ha-ru-e se pŏn-ssik chap-ssu-sip-ssi-o.

이 약을 하루에 세 번씩 잡수십시오.

23. You'll get over it soon.

Kot mo-mi cho-a-ji-sil kkŏ-sim-ni-da.

곧 몸이 좋아지실 것입니다.

24. Have you been hurt?

Ta-ch'i-syŏt-ssŭm-ni-kka?

다치셨습니까?

25. Yes. But it is only a scratch.

Ne, kŭ-rŏ-na tan-ji ka-byŏ-un sang-ch'ŏ-im-ni-da.

네, 그러나 단지 가벼운 상처입니다.

26. Are you feeling any better today?

O-nŭ-rŭn mo-mi chom na-at-ssŭm-ni-kka?

오늘은 몸이 좀 나았습니까?

---

recover(*hoe-bo-k'a-da*)…회복하다
pale(*ch'ang-bae-k'an*)…창백한
hurt(*sang-ch'ŏ*)…상처
death(*sa-mang*)…사망

doctor(*ŭi-sa*)…의사
medicine(*yak*)…약
scratch(*kyŏng-sang*)…경상
severe wound(*chung-sang*)…중상

27. I have a terrible cold.   *Sim-han kam-gi-ga tŭ-rŏt-ssŭm-ni-da.*

심한 감기가 들었습니다.

28. I feel chilly.   *O-ha-ni tŭn kŏt kat-ssŭm-ni-da.*

오한이 든 것 같습니다.

29. I'm suffering from insomnia.   *Pul-myŏn-tchŭng-ŭ-ro ko-saeng-ha-go it-ssŭm-ni-da.*

불면증으로 고생하고 있습니다.

30. I can't sleep all night.   *Pam-sae-do-rok chal ssu-ga ŏp-ssŏt-ssŭm-ni-da.*

밤새도록 잘 수가 없었습니다.

31. Take a full rest.   *P'uk swi-sip-ssi-o.*

푹 쉬십시오.

32. Your eyes are bloodshot.   *Nu-ni ch'ung-hyŏl-doe-ŏt-ssŭm-ni-da.*

눈이 충혈되었습니다.

At the Barber Shop   *I-bal-gwa-ne-sŏ*(이발관에서)

1. Haircut, sir ?   *Mŏ-ri-rŭl kka-kkŭ-si-get-ssŭm-ni-kka, sŏn-saeng-nim ?*

머리를 깎으시겠습니까, 선생님 ?

2. Yes, plus a shave.   *Ne, myŏn-do-do hae chu-sip-ssi-o.*

네, 면도도 해 주십시오.

3. Right this way. Please sit here.   *I-ri-ro o-sip-ssi-o. Yŏ-gi an-jŭ-sip-ssi-o.*

이리로 오십시오. 여기 앉으십시오.

---

terrible(*sim-han*)…심한
chilly(*ch'u-un*)…추운
suffer(*ko-t'ong-ŭl pat-tta*)…고통을 받다

bloodshot(*ch'ung-hyŏl-doen*)…충혈된
barber shop(*i-bal-gwan*)…이발관
shave(*myŏn-do-ha-da*)…면도하다
insomnia(*pul-myŏn-tchŭng*)…불면증

4. How would you like to have your hair trimmed?

Ŏ-ttŏ-k'e mŏ-ri-rŭl kka-kka tŭ-ril-kka-yo?

어떻게 머리를 깎아 드릴까요?

5. Not too short.

Nŏ-mu tchal-tchi an-k'e kka-kka chu-sip-ssi-o.

너무 짧지 않게 깎아 주십시오.

6. May I use the clipper?

I-bal ki-gye-ro kka-kkŭl-kka-yo?

이발 기계로 깎을까요?

7. Of course.

Chot-ssŭm-ni-da.

좋습니다.

8. Please shave me as lightly as possible. My skin is very sensitive.

Toel ssu in-nŭn tae-ro ka-byŏp-kke myŏn-do-rŭl hae chu-sip-ssi-o. Che sal-kka-ch'ŭn mae-u ya-k'am-ni-da.

될 수 있는 대로 가볍게 면도를 해 주십시오. 제 살갗은 매우 약합니다.

9. Please this way for your shampoo.

Se-bal-ha-rŏ i-ri-ro o-sip-ssi-o.

세발하러 이리로 오십시오.

10. And after you're through, please give me a massage.

Ta ma-ch'in hu-e ma-ssa-ji chom hae chu-sip-ssi-o.

다 마친 후에 마사지 좀 해 주십시오.

11. May I put some pomade on?

P'o-ma-dŭ-rŭl pa-rŭ-si-get-ssŭm-ni-kka?

포마드를 바르시겠습니까?

12. On which side do you

Mŏ-ri-rŭl ŏ-nŭ tcho-gŭ-ro ka-rŭ-sim-

---

chipper (*i-bal ki-gye*)…이발 기계
skin (*sal-kkat*)…살갗
sensitive (*min-gam-han*)…민감한

shampoo (*se-bal*)…세발
massage (*ma-ssa-ji*)…마사지
moustache (*k'o-ssu-yŏm*)…콧수염

part your hair, sir ? *ni-kka, sŏn-saeng-nim ?*

머리를 어느 쪽으로 가르십니까, 선생님 ?

13. On the left side please. *Woen-tcho-gŭ-ro ka-rŭm-ni-da.*

왼쪽으로 가릅니다.

14. How does that look ? *Mo-yang-i ŏ-ttŏt-ssŭm-ni-kka ?*

모양이 어떻습니까 ?

15. How much ? *Ŏl-ma-im-ni-kka ?*

얼마입니까 ?

16. It is twenty-five thousands won, sir. *I-man o-ch'ŏn wŏn-im-ni-da, sŏn-saeng-nim.*

이만 오천 원입니다, 선생님.

17. Here's a thirty thousands won. Please keep the change. *Yŏ-gi sam-man wŏn-i it-ssŭm-ni-da. Chan-do-nŭn kŭ-man tu-sip-ssi-o.*

여기 삼만 원이 있습니다. 잔돈은 그만 두십시오.

18. Thank you very much. Come again please. *Kam-sa-ham-ni-da. TTo o-sip-ssi-o.*

감사합니다. 또 오십시오.

Taking a walk *San-ppo*(산보)

1. Taking walks is good for health. *San-ppo-nŭn kŏn-gang-e chot-ssŭm-ni-da.*

산보는 건강에 좋습니다.

2. Are you fond walking ? *San-ppo-rŭl cho-a-ham-ni-kka ?*

산보를 좋아합니까 ?

3. Yes, I am. *Ne, cho-a-ham-ni-da.*

네, 좋아합니다.

---

taking a walk(*san-ppo*)…산보
walking race(*kyŏng-bo*)…경보

gymnastics(*ch'e-jo*)…체조

4. Then, let's go out together.

Kŭ-rŏ-t'a-myŏn ham-kke na-gap-ssi-da.

그렇다면 함께 나갑시다.

5. Where shall we go?

Ŏ-di-ro kal-kka-yo?

어디로 갈까요?

6. Let's go to the Toksu Palace. It's a good place for walking.

Tŏk-ssu-gung-e kap-ssi-da. San-ppo-ha-gi-e cho-ŭn chang-so-im-ni-da.

덕수궁에 갑시다. 산보하기에 좋은 장소입니다.

7. How about going to the Changchungdan Park?

Chang-ch'ung-dan kong-wŏ-nŭ-ro ka-nŭn kŏ-si ŏ-ttŏ-k'et-ssŭm-ni-kka?

장충단 공원으로 가는 것이 어떻겠습니까?

8. Anyhow, let's go out.

Ŏ-tchae-ttŭn na-gap-ssi-da.

어쨌든 나갑시다.

9. Which way shall we go?

Ŏ-nŭ kil-lo kal-kka-yo?

어느 길로 갈까요?

10. Let's go this way.

I kil-lo kap-ssi-da.

이 길로 갑시다.

11. How far is the Toksu Palace?

Tŏk-ssu-gung-ŭn ŏl-ma-na mŏm-ni-kka?

덕수궁은 얼마나 멉니까?

12. It's an hour walk from here.

Yŏ-gi-sŏ han si-gan kŏ-ri-im-ni-da.

여기서 한 시간 거리입니다.

13. What's the name of this street?

I ki-rŭi i-rŭ-mŭn mu-ŏ-sim-ni-kka?

이 길의 이름은 무엇입니까?

14. It is Kwanghwamun.

Kwang-hwa-mun-im-ni-da.

---

anyhow(*ŏ-tchae-ttŭn*)…어쨌든
medicinal waters(*yak-ssu*)…약수

park(*kong-wŏn*)…공원

광화문입니다.

15. What's the name of that tall building?

Chŏ no-p'ŭn ppil-tting-ŭi i-rŭ-mŭn mu-ŏ-sim-ni-kka?

저 높은 빌딩의 이름은 무엇입니까?

16. It's the Samil Building.

Sa-mil ppil-tting-im-ni-da.

삼일 빌딩입니다.

17. This street is really crowded.

I kŏ-ri-nŭn chŏng-mal sa-ra-mi man-ssŭm-ni-da.

이 거리는 정말 사람이 많습니다.

18. We'll reach the park soon.

U-ri-nŭn kot kong-wŏ-ne to-ch'a-k'al kkŏ-sim-ni-da.

우리는 곧 공원에 도착할 것입니다.

19. I'm getting a little tired.

Na-nŭn ya-kkan p'i-gon-hae-jyŏt-ssŭm-ni-da.

나는 약간 피곤해졌습니다.

20. Let's have lunch.

Chŏm-si-mŭl mŏ-gŭp-ssi-da.

점심을 먹읍시다.

21. Is there a good restaurant nearby?

Kŭn-ch'ŏ-e cho-ŭn sik-ttang-i it-ssŭm-ni-kka?

근처에 좋은 식당이 있습니까?

22. Many young lovers are taking walk in the park.

Ma-nŭn chŏl-mŭn yŏ-nin-dŭ-ri kong-wŏ-ne-sŏ san-ppo-rŭl ha-go it-ssŭm-ni-da.

많은 젊은 연인들이 공원에서 산보를 하고 있습니다.

---

refreshing(*sang-k'wae-ha-da*)…상쾌하다

crossroads(*kyo-ch'a-ro*)…교차로

step(*kŏt-tta*)…걷다

nearby(*kŭn-ch'ŏ*)…근처

crowd(*kun-jung*)…군중

street crossing(*hoeng-dan po-do*)…횡단 보도

23. This is the Toksu Palace.

I-gŏ-si tŏk-ssu-gung-im-ni-da.

이것이 덕수궁입니다.

24. What a beautiful architecture!

Ŏl-ma-na a-rŭm-da-un kŏn-ch'uk-im-ni-kka!

얼마나 아름다운 건축입니까!

House Rent

Se-tchip (셋집)

1. Do you have a house for rent?

Se no-ŭl tchi-bi it-ssŭm-ni-kka?

세 놓을 집이 있습니까?

2. Do you have a room for rent?

Se no-ŭl pang-i it-ssŭm-ni-kka?

세 놓을 방이 있습니까?

3. This is the house for rent.

I-gŏ-si se no-ŭl tchip-im-ni-da.

이것이 세 놓을 집입니다.

4. It looks nice.

Ch'am hul-lyung-ham-ni-da.

참 훌륭합니다.

5. Has this house a garage?

I chi-be ch'a-go-ga it-ssŭm-ni-kka?

이 집에 차고가 있습니까?

6. Yes, there is a garage and a beautiful garden too.

Ne, ch'a-go-wa a-rŭm-da-un chŏng-wŏn-do it-ssŭm-ni-da.

네, 차고와 아름다운 정원도 있습니다.

7. It will take about ten minutes from the City Hall to here.

Si-ch'ŏng-e-sŏ yŏ-gi-kka-ji yak sip-ppun-i kŏl-lim-ni-da.

시청에서 여기까지 약 십분이 걸립니다.

8. This is this main entrance and this is the lou-

I-gŏ-si hyŏn-gwa-ni-go, i-gŏ-si ŭng-jŏp-ssil-im-ni-da.

---

architecture(*kŏn-ch'uk*) ··· 건축
house rent(*se-tchip*) ··· 셋집
pond(*yŏn-mot*) ··· 연못

rent(*se-no-t'a*) ··· 세놓다
garage(*ch'a-go*) ··· 차고
garden(*chŏng-wŏn*) ··· 정원

nge room.

이것이 현관이고, 이것이 응접실입니다.

9. I like this house.

I chi-bi ma-ŭ-me tŭm-ni-da.

이 집이 마음에 듭니다.

10. How much is the rent?

Se-nŭn ŏl-ma-im-ni-kka?

세는 얼마입니까?

11. It's one million won a month.

Han ta-re paeng-man wŏn-im-ni-da.

한 달에 백만 원입니다.

12. You must pay six months rent in advance.

Yuk kkae-wŏl-ch'i-ŭi se-rŭl sŏn-bul-hae-ya toem-ni-da.

육 개월치의 세를 선불해야 됩니다.

13. When may I move in?

Ŏn-je i-sa-hal-kka-yo?

언제 이사할까요?

14. Anytime after next Friday.

Ta-ŭm kŭ-myo-il i-hu ŏ-nŭ ttae-na chot-ssŭm-ni-da.

다음 금요일 이후 어느 때나 좋습니다.

15. All right. I'll take it.

Chot-ssŭm-ni-da. I chi-be tŭl-get-ssŭm-ni-da.

좋습니다. 이 집에 들겠습니다.

16. Let's contract tomorrow.

Nae-il kye-ya-gŭl hap-ssi-da.

내일 계약을 합시다.

17. I have read your advertisement about the house in the newspaper. Is it still available?

Sin-mu-ne-sŏ chi-be kwan-han kwang-go-rŭl po-at-ssŭm-ni-da. A-jik-tto chi-bi it-ssŭm-ni-kka?

신문에서 집에 관한 광고를 보았습니다. 아직도 집이 있습니까?

18. I'm sorry. The house

Mi-an-ham-ni-da. Ŏ-je chi-bi na-

---

advertisement(*kwang-go*)…광고
company house(*sa-t'aek*)…사택

apartment(*a-p'a-t'ŭ*)…아파트
private house(*cha-t'aek*)…자택

was rented yesterday.	*gat-ssŭm-ni-da.*
	미안합니다. 어제 집이 나갔습니다.
19. Do you live in an apartment or in a house ?	*Tang-si-nŭn a-p'a-t'ŭ-e sa-sim-ni-kka, a-ni-myŏn cha-t'ae-ge sa-sim-ni-kka ?*
	당신은 아파트에 사십니까, 아니면 자택에 사십니까 ?
20. I live in an apartment.	*Na-nŭn a-p'a-t'ŭ-e sam-ni-da.*
	나는 아파트에 삽니다.

At the Stadium

Ch'e-yu-kkwa-ne-sŏ
(체육관에서)

1. Let's play table tennis.	*T'ak-kku-rŭl ch'ip-ssi-da.*
	탁구를 칩시다.
2. Can you play tennis ?	*Chŏng-gu-rŭl ch'il tchul a-sim-ni-kka ?*
	정구를 칠 줄 아십니까 ?
3. Where is Seoul Stadium ?	*Seŏ-ul un-dong-jang-ŭn ŏ-di it-ssŭm-ni-kka ?*
	서울 운동장은 어디 있습니까 ?
4. There's a baseball field in Seoul Stadium.	*Seŏ-ul un-dong-jang-e-nŭn ya-gu-jang-i it-ssŭm-ni-da.*
	서울 운동장에는 야구장이 있습니다.
5. Football games are played mostly in Hyochang Stadium.	*Ch'uk-kku kyŏng-gi-nŭn tae-gae hyo-ch'ang un-dong-jang-e-sŏ yŏl-lim-ni-da.*
	축구 경기는 대개 효창 운동장에서

---

stadium(*ch'e-yu-kkwan*)…체육관   tennis(*chŏng-gu*)…정구

열립니다.

6. The Changchung Gymnasium is a good place to play basketball.

Chang-ch'ung ch'e-yu-kkwa-nŭn nong-gu-rŭl ha-gi-e cho-ŭn chang-so-im-ni-da.

장충 체육관은 농구를 하기에 좋은 장소입니다.

7. A baseball team consists of nine players.

Ya-gu-t'i-mŭn a-hop sŏn-su-ro ku-sŏng-doem-ni-da.

야구팀은 아홉 선수로 구성됩니다.

8. Six persons play volleyball.

Yŏ-sŏt ssa-ra-mi pae-gu-rŭl ham-ni-da.

여섯 사람이 배구를 합니다.

9. Seoul Stadium has facilties for night games.

Seŏ-ul un-dong-jang-ŭn ya-gan kyŏng-gi-rŭl wi-han si-sŏ-rŭl kat-ch'u-go it-ssŭm-ni-da.

서울 운동장은 야간 경기를 위한 시설을 갖추고 있습니다.

10. Korean boxer Kim Kisu won the Oriental middle weight title by defeating a Japanese champion.

Han-guk kwŏn-t'u sŏn-su kim-gi-su-nŭn il-bon sŏn-su-rŭl mul-li-ch'i-mŭ-ro-ssŏ, tong-yang chung-nyang-kkŭp sŏn-su-kkwŏ-nŭl hoek-ttŭ-k'aet-ssŭm-ni-da.

한국 권투 선수 김기수는 일본 선수를 물리침으로써, 동양 중량급

---

facility(*si-sŏl*) ···시설
boxer(*kwŏn-t'u sŏn-su*) ···권투 선수
victory(*sŭng-ni*) ···승리
defeat(*p'ae-bae*) ···패배
champion(*u-sŭng-ja*) ···우승자
football(*ch'uk-kku*) ···축구
match(*si-hap*) ···시합

championship(*sŏn-su-kkŏn*) ···선수권
defeat(*mul-li-ch'i-da*) ···물리치다
basketball(*nong-gu*) ···농구
volleyball(*pae-gu*) ···배구
baseball(*ya-gu*) ···야구
player(*sŏn-su*) ···선수

선수권을 획득했습니다.

11. A Korean women's basketball team crushed the Indonesian team by 80 : 62.

Han-guk yŏ-ja nong-gu-t'i-mŭn in-do-ne-si-a-t'i-mŭl p'al-ssip ttae yuk-ssip-i-ro kyŏk-p'a-haet-ssŭm-ni-da.

한국 여자 농구팀은 인도네시아팀을 팔십 대 육십이로 격파했습니다.

12. The Korean team tied with Thailand it the football game.

Han-guk-t'i-mŭn t'a-i-raen-dŭ-t'im-gwa-ŭi ch'uk-kku kyŏng-gi-e-sŏ tong-tchŏ-mŭl ŏ-dŏt-ssŭm-ni-da.

한국팀은 타이랜드팀과의 축구 경기에서 동점을 얻었습니다.

13. What is the score for the tennis game betwen Korean and American champions?

Han-guk-kkwa mi-guk sŏn-su-ga pŏ-rin chŏng-gu si-ha-bŭi tŭk-tchŏ-mŭn ŏl-ma-im-ni-kka?

한국과 미국 선수가 벌인 정구 시합의 득점은 얼마입니까?

14. How about going to a baseball game?

Ya-gu si-ha-be an-ga-get-ssŭm-ni-kka?

야구 시합에 안가겠습니까?

15. Let's go to chamsil Stadium to see the Korea-Japan good will baseball game.

Ha-nil ch'in-sŏn ya-gu kyŏng-gi-rŭl po-rŏ cham-sil un-dong-jang-e kap-ssi-da.

한 · 일 친선 야구 경기를 보러 잠실 운동장에 갑시다.

16. The tickets are all sold out.

P'yo-nŭn mae-jin-im-ni-da.

표는 매진입니다.

17. The 1988 Olympic Ga-

Ch'ŏn-gu-baek-p'al-ssip-p'al-nyŏn ol-

tie(*tong-tchŏm*) …동점
score(*tŭk-tchŏm*) …득점

training(*yŏn-sŭp*) …연습
selling out(*mae-jin*) …매진

171

mes were held in Seoul, Korea.

rim-p'ik kyŏng-gi-nŭn han-gu-gŭi seŏ-u-re-sŏ yŏl-lyŏt-ssŭm-ni-da.

천구백팔십팔년 올림픽 경기는 한국의 서울에서 열렸습니다.

18. Does Korea participate in the Olympic Games?

Han-gu-gŭn ol-lim-p'ik kyŏng-gi-e ch'am-ga-ham-ni-kka?

한국은 올림픽 경기에 참가합니까?

19. In autumn, most primary schools in Korea hold athletic carnivals on their school grounds.

Ka-ŭ-ri toe-myŏn han-guk tae-bu-bun kung-min hak-kkyo-dŭ-rŭn, kŭ-dŭ-rŭi un-dong-jang-e-sŏ un-dong-hoe-rŭl yŏm-ni-da.

가을이 되면 한국 대부분 국민 학교들은, 그들의 운동장에서 운동회를 엽니다.

20. Can you fence?

P'en-sing-ŭl hal tchul a-sim-ni-kka?

펜싱을 할 줄 아십니까?

21. Korean judoists go everywhere in the world to teach their techniques.

Han-guk yu-do sŏn-su-dŭ-rŭn kŭ-dŭ-rŭi ki-su-rŭl ka-rŭ-ch'i-gi wi-hae se-gye ŏ-nŭ ko-se-na kam-ni-da.

한국 유도 선수들은 그들의 기술을 가르치기 위해 세계 어느 곳에나 갑니다.

22. The Korean football team is one of the strongest in Asia.

Han-guk ch'uk-kku-t'i-mŭn a-si-a-e-sŏ ka-jang kang-han t'i-mŭi ha-na-im-ni-da.

한국 축구팀은 아시아에서 가장

---

primary school(*kung-min hak-kkyo*)⋯ 국민 학교

fencing(*p'en-sing*)⋯펜싱
technique(*ki-sul*)⋯기술

강한 팀의 하나입니다.

At the Antique Shop

Kol-ttong-p'um ka-ge-e-sŏ
(골동품 가게에서)

1. There're many antique shops in Korea.

Han-gu-ge-nŭn ma-nŭn kol-ttong-p'um sang-jŏ-mi it-ssŭm-ni-da.

한국에는 많은 골동품 상점이 있습니다.

2. Where can I see Korean antiques ?

Ŏ-di-sŏ han-guk kol-ttong-p'um-dŭ-rŭl pol ssu it-ssŭl-kka-yo ?

어디서 한국 골동품들을 볼 수 있을까요 ?

3. I will guide you. In Insa-dong street, you can find many antique shops.

Che-ga mo-si-get-ssŭm-ni-da. In-sa-dong kŏ-ri-e-sŏ ma-nŭn kol-ttong-p'um sang-jŏ-mŭl pal-gyŏn-hal ssu-ga it-ssŭm-ni-da.

제가 모시겠습니다. 인사동 거리에서 많은 골동품 상점을 발견할 수가 있습니다.

4. Because of her long history, Korea has many valuable cultural heritages.

Han-gu-gŭn yŏk-ssa-ga kil-gi ttae-mu-ne, su-ma-nŭn kwi-jung-han mun-hwa yu-san-dŭ-rŭl ka-ji-go it-ssŭm-ni-da.

한국은 역사가 길기 때문에, 수많은

---

curio shop(*kol-ttong-p'um ka-ge*)…골동품 가게
ceramic ware(*to-ja-gi*)…도자기
potter(*to-gong*)…도공
cultural heritage(*mun-hwa yu-san*)…문화 유산

guide(*an-nae-ha-da*)…안내하다
kiln(*ka-ma*)…가마
gold crown(*kŭm-gwan*)…금관
pottery factory(*to-ja-gi kong-jang*)…도자기 공장
valuable(*ka-ch'i in-nŭn*)…가치 있는

귀중한 문화 유산들을 가지고 있습니다.

5. White celadon of the Yi dynasty is well known throughout the world.

I-jo paek-tcha-nŭn se-gye-jŏ-gŭ-ro chal al-lyŏ-jyŏ it-ssŭm-ni-da.

이조 백자는 세계적으로 잘 알려져 있습니다.

6. What is the blue pot?

Pu-rŭn-sae-gŭi chŏ hang-a-ri-nŭn mu-ŏ-sim-ni-kka?

푸른색의 저 항아리는 무엇입니까?

7. It is a famous Koryo celadon. It was produced by our ancestors during the Koryo dynasty.

Yu-myŏng-han ko-ryŏ cha-gi-im-ni-da. Kŭ-gŏ-sŭn ko-ryŏ si-dae-e u-ri sŏn-jo-dŭ-ri man-dŭ-rŏt-ssŭm-ni-da.

유명한 고려 자기입니다. 그것은 고려 시대에 우리 선조들이 만들었습니다.

8. Can I buy old coins in the antique shop?

Kol-ttong-p'um sang-jŏ-me-sŏ yen-nal tong-jŏ-nŭl sal ssu it-ssŭm-ni-kka?

골동품 상점에서 옛날 동전을 살 수 있습니까?

9. Of course. There are various old coins used by Korean ancestors.

Mul-lon-im-ni-da. Han-guk sŏn-jo-dŭ-ri sa-yong-haet-ttŏn yŏ-rŏ ka-ji yen-nal tong-jŏ-ni it-ssŭm-ni-da.

물론입니다. 한국 선조들이 사용했던 여러 가지 옛날 동전이 있습니다.

Koryo celadon(*ko-ryŏ cha-gi*)…고려 자기
nature(*cha-yŏn*)…자연
ancestor(*sŏn-jo*)…선조

tangible cultural properties(*yu-hyŏng mun-hwa-jae*)…유형 문화재
genuine article(*chin-p'um*)…진품

10. What is this statue?

I sang-ŭn mu-ŏ-sim-ni-kka?
이 상은 무엇입니까?

11. It is a Buddha image made of gold.

Kŭ-gŏ-sŭn kŭ-mŭ-ro man-dŭn pul-ssang-im-ni-da.
그것은 금으로 만든 불상입니다.

12. Where was it found?

Ŏ-di-sŏ pal-gyŏn-doe-ŏt-ssŭm-ni-kka?
어디서 발견되었습니까?

13. It was discovered in Kyongju, capital of the ancient Silla dynasty.

Yen-nal sil-la wang-jo-ŭi su-do-in kyŏng-ju-e-sŏ pal-gyŏn-doe-ŏt-ssŭm-ni-da.
옛날 신라 왕조의 수도인 경주에서 발견되었습니다.

14. Will you sell it to me?

Kŭ-gŏ-sŭl chŏ-e-ge p'a-si-get-ssŭm-ni-kka?
그것을 저에게 파시겠습니까?

15. No, I cannot sell it. But I can sell an exact imitation of it.

An-doem-ni-da. P'al ssu ŏp-ssŭm-ni-da. Kŭ-rŏ-na kŭ-wa mo-yang-i ttok-kka-t'ŭn mo-jo-p'u-mŭn p'al ssu it-ssŭm-ni-da.
안됩니다. 팔 수 없습니다. 그러나 그와 모양이 똑같은 모조품은 팔 수 있습니다.

16. Many precious cultural relics are preserved in

Su-ma-nŭn ko-gwi-han mun-hwa yu-mul-dŭ-ri kung-nip pang-mul-

Buddha image(*pul-ssang*)…불상
gold(*kŭm*)…금
capital(*su-do*)…수도
ancient(*ko-dae*)…고대
imitation(*mo-jo-p'um*)…모조품
preciousness(*chin-gwi*)…진귀

precious(*ko-gwi-han*)…고귀한
preserve(*po-gwan-ha-da*)…보관하다
museum(*pang-mul-gwan*)…박물관
silver(*ŭn*)…은
relic(*yu-mul*)…유물
statue(*tong-sang*)…동상

the National Museum.

gwa-ne po-gwan-doe-ŏ it-ssŭm-ni-da.

수많은 고귀한 문화 유물들이 국립 박물관에 보관되어 있습니다.

17. In the museum, you can learn about the brilliant Korean culture of the past by observing many valuable relics.

Pang-mul-gwa-ne ka-myŏn su-ma-nŭn ko-gwi-han yu-mul-dŭ-rŭl kwan-ch'al-ha-ma-mŭ-ro-ssŏ, kwa-gŏ-ŭi ch'al-lan-haet-ttŏn, han-guk mun-hwa-rŭl pae-ul ssu-ga it-ssŭm-ni-da.

박물관에 가면 수많은 고귀한 유물들을 관찰함으로써, 과거의 찬란했던 한국 문화를 배울 수가 있습니다.

18. Buddhism had much influence on ancient Korean culture.

Pul-gyo-nŭn ko-dae han-guk mun-hwa-e ma-nŭn yŏng-hyang-ŭl chu-ŏt-ssŭm-ni-da.

불교는 고대 한국 문화에 많은 영향을 주었습니다.

19. Korea was much influenced by Chinese culture.

Han-gu-gŭn chung-guk mun-hwa-e-sŏ ma-nŭn yŏng-hyang-ŭl pa-dat-ssŭm-ni-da.

한국은 중국 문화에서 많은 영향을 받았습니다.

20. Korea is proud of her five-thousand-year history and culture.

Han-gu-gŭn o-ch'ŏn nyŏ-nŭi yŏk-ssa-wa mun-hwa-rŭl cha-rang-ham-ni-da.

한국은 오천 년의 역사와 문화를

---

nugget(*kŭm-goe*)…금괴
pot(*hang-a-ri*)…항아리

national treasure(*kuk-ppo*)…국보
metal(*kŭm-sok*)…금속

자랑합니다.

On the Campus

Kyo-jŏng-e-sŏ(교정에서)

1. How many colleges are there in Korea?

Han-gu-ge-nŭn tae-ha-gi myŏt kkae-na it-ssŭm-ni-kka?

한국에는 대학이 몇 개나 있습니까?

2. There're more than eighty colleges.

P'al-sip kkae i-sang-ŭi tae-ha-gi it-ssŭm-ni-da.

팔십 개 이상의 대학이 있습니다.

3. When does the spring semester begin in Korea?

Han-gu-ge-sŏ pom hak-kki-nŭn ŏn-je si-ja-k'am-ni-kka?

한국에서 봄 학기는 언제 시작합니까?

4. The spring semester usually begins in March.

Po-t'ong pom hak-kki-nŭn sam-wŏ-re si-ja-k'am-ni-da.

보통 봄 학기는 삼월에 시작합니다.

5. The autumn semester starts in September.

Ka-ŭl hak-kki-nŭn ku-wŏ-re si-ja-k'am-ni-da.

가을 학기는 구월에 시작합니다.

6. There are a few colleges only for women in Seoul. Ehwa Women's University is one of them.

Seŏ-u-re-nŭn yŏ-ja-dŭl-ma-nŭl wi-han myŏt kkae-ŭi tae-ha-gi it-ssŭm-ni-da. Kŭ chung-ŭi ha-na-ga i-hwa yŏ-ja tae-hak-kkyo-im-ni-da.

서울에는 여자들만을 위한 몇 개의 대학이 있습니다. 그 중의 하나가 이화 여자 대학교입니다.

7. Would you show me the

Hak-kkyo to-sŏ-gwa-nŭ-ro ka-nŭn

---

semester(*hak-kki*)⋯학기

177

way to the school library?

ki-rŭl ka-rŭ-ch'yŏ chu-si-get-ssŭm-ni-kka?

학교 도서관으로 가는 길을 가르쳐 주시겠습니까?

8. In the auditorium, many academic seminars and lectures are held.

Kang-dang-e-sŏ-nŭn ma-nŭn hak-ssul sse-mi-na-wa kang-yŏn-i yŏl-lim-ni-da.

강당에서는 많은 학술 세미나와 강연이 열립니다.

9. When autumn comes, various carnivals are held on college campuses throughout the nation.

Ka-ŭ-ri o-myŏn yŏ-rŏ ka-ji ch'uk-tche-ga chŏn-guk tae-hak k'aem-p'ŏ-ssŭ-e-sŏ yŏl-rim-ni-da.

가을이 오면 여러 가지 축제가 전국 대학 캠퍼스에서 열립니다.

10. Where can i consult about a job?

Ŏ-di-sŏ chi-gŏ-be kwan-hae sang-ŭi-hal ssu it-ssŭl-kka-yo?

어디서 직업에 관해 상의할 수 있을까요?

11. How long have you been at this school?

I hak-kkyo-e ŏl-ma-na kye-syŏt-ssŭm-ni-kka?

이 학교에 얼마나 계셨습니까?

12. How long have you been with company?

I hoe-sa-e it-ssŭ-sin-ji ŏl-ma-na toem-ni-kka?

이 회사에 있으신지 얼마나 됩니까?

13. You can consult about

Hak-ssaeng-kkwa-e-sŏ   chi-gŏ-be

---

lecture(*kang-yŏn*)…강연
carnival(*ch'uk-tche*)…축제
consult(*sang-ŭi-ha-da*)…상의하다
consultation(*ha-bŭi*)…합의

auditorium(*kang-dang*)…강당
academic seminar(*hak-ssul sse-mi-na*)…학술 세미나

a job at the department
of student affairs.

kwan-han sang-ŭi-rŭl hal ssu it-
ssŭm-ni-da.

학생과에서 직업에 관한 상의를 할
수 있습니다.

14. Where can I see my
academic records?

Ŏ-di-sŏ sŏng-jŏ-gŭl pol ssu it-ssŭl-
kka-yo?

어디서 성적을 볼 수 있을까요?

15. You can see your aca-
demic records at the
department of academic
affairs.

Kyo-mu-kkwa-e-sŏ sŏng-jŏ-gŭl pol ssu
it-ssŭm-ni-da.

교무과에서 성적을 볼 수 있습니다.

16. How long does the su-
mmer vacation last?

Yŏ-rŭm pang-ha-gŭn ŏl-ma-na o-rae
kye-sok-doem-ni-kka?

여름 방학은 얼마나 오래 계속됩
니까?

17. Usually, the summer
vacation last for one
and a half months.

Il-ban-jŏ-gŭ-ro yŏ-rŭm pang-ha-gŭn
han tal pan ttong-an kye-sok-toem-
ni-da.

일반적으로 여름 방학은 한 달 반
동안 계속됩니다.

At the Railway Station

Chŏng-gŏ-jang-e-sŏ
(정거장에서)

1. All the railway in Korea
are operated by the go-
vernment.

Han-gu-gŭi ch'ŏl-tto-nŭn chŏn-bu
chŏng-bu-e-sŏ u-nyŏng-ha-go it-
ssŭm-ni-da.

한국의 철도는 전부 정부에서 운

---

academic record (*sŏng-jŏk*)…성적
station employee (*yŏk-wŏn*)…역원
track (*sŏl-lo*)…선로

railway station (*chŏng-gŏ-jang*)…정거
장
advance sale (*ye-mae*)…예매

영하고 있습니다.

2. Where can I get the train to Pusan?

Pu-san-haeng ki-ch'a-nŭn ŏ-di-sŏ t'al ssu it-ssŭm-ni-kka?

부산행 기차는 어디서 탈 수 있습니까?

3. You can take the train at the Seoul Railway Station.

Sŏ-ul-lyŏ-ge-sŏ ki-ch'a-rŭl t'al ssu it-ssŭm-ni-da.

서울역에서 기차를 탈 수 있습니다.

4. the ticket windows are just around the corner.

Mae-p'yo-gu-nŭn chŏ-ri-ro to-ra-ga-myŏn it-ssŭm-ni-da.

매표구는 저리로 돌아가면 있습니다.

5. Which is the train to Taejon?

Tae-jŏn-haeng ki-ch'a-nŭn ŏ-nŭ kŏ-sim-ni-kka?

대전행 기차는 어느 것입니까?

6. No. 1546 is the Taejon bound train.

Ch'ŏn-o-baek-sa-sim-yu k'o-ga tae-jŏn-haeng ki-ch'a-im-ni-da.

천오백사십육 호가 대전행 기차입니다.

7. Please give me a ticket to Pusan.

Pu-san-haeng ch'a-p'yo han chang-man chu-sip-ssi-o.

부산행 차표 한 장만 주십시오.

8. Please give me a round-trip ticket to Taegu.

Tae-gu-haeng wang-bok ch'a-p'yo-rŭl han chang-man chu-sip-ssi-o.

대구행 왕복 차표를 한 장만 주십시오.

9. How much is a firstclass ticket to Taegu?

Tae-gu-haeng il-ttŭng ch'a-p'yo-nŭn ŏl-ma-im-ni-kka?

대구행 일등 차표는 얼마입니까?

---

operate〈*un-haeng-ha-da*〉…운행하다   delayed arrival〈*yŏn-ch'ak*〉…연착

10. It is fifteen thousand and four hundred won.

Man o-ch'ŏn-sa-baek wŏn-im-ni-da.

만 오천사백 원입니다.

11. The sightseeing train is operated every day between Seoul and Pusan.

Kwan-gwang ki-ch'a-ga mae-il seŏ-ul, pu-san-ga-nŭl un-haeng-ham-ni-da.

관광 기차가 매일 서울, 부산간을 운행합니다.

12. What time does this train start?

I ki-ch'a-nŭn myŏt ssi-e ch'ul-bal-ham-ni-kka?

이 기차는 몇 시에 출발합니까?

13. There's the bell. Better run.

Pe-ri ul-lim-ni-da. PPal-li ka-syŏ-ya-get-ssŭm-ni-da.

벨이 울립니다. 빨리 가셔야겠습니다.

14. You have to have your tickets punched by the station officials at the wicket.

P'yo-nŭn kae-ch'al-gu-e-sŏ yŏ-gwŏ-ni p'ŏn-ch'i-rŭl ha-ge toe-ŏ it-ssŭm-ni-da.

표는 개찰구에서 역원이 펀치를 하게 되어 있습니다.

15. Can I reach Haeundae Beach on this train?

I ki-ch'a-ro hae-un-dae hae-su-yok-tchang-e kal ssu it-ssŭm-ni-kka?

이 기차로 해운대 해수욕장에 갈 수 있습니까?

16. You can reach Taejon within two hours on this train.

I ki-ch'a-ro tu si-ga-ni-myŏn tae-jŏ-ne kal ssu it-ssŭm-ni-da.

이 기차로 두 시간이면 대전에 갈 수 있습니다.

17. Trains are safer and faster than buses.

Ki-ch'a-nŭn ppŏ-ssŭ-bo-da an-jŏn-ha-go ppa-rŭm-ni-da.

---

safe(*an-jŏn-han*)…안전한

hindrance(*ko-jang*)…고장

기차는 버스보다 안전하고 빠릅니다.

18. Would you guide me to the dining car? *Sik-ttang-ch'a-e an-nae-hae chu-si-get-ssŭm-ni-kka?*

식당차에 안내해 주시겠습니까?

19. Condutor, here is my ticket. *Ch'a-jang, ch'a-p'yo-ga yŏ-gi it-ssŭm-ni-da.*

차장, 차표가 여기 있습니다.

At a Department Store

Pae-k'wa-jŏ-me-sŏ(백화점에서)

1. I'm looking for the toy department. · *Wan-gu-bu-rŭl ch'at-kko it-ssŭm-ni-da.*

완구부를 찾고 있습니다.

2. I'd like to see some camera. *Ka-me-ra-rŭl* ` *ku-gyŏng-ha-ryŏ-go ham-ni-da.*

카메라를 구경하려고 합니다.

3. Where do they sell men's shoes? *Nam-ja-yong ku-du-nŭn ŏ-di-sŏ p'am-ni-kka?*

남자용 구두는 어디서 팝니까?

4. You'll find them on the third floor, sir. *Sam-ch'ŭng-e-sŏ sa-sil ssu it-ssŭm-ni-da.*

삼층에서 사실 수 있습니다.

5. Where on the third floor? *Sam-ch'ŭng ŏ-di im-ni-kka?*

삼층 어디 입니까?

6. Take the escalator. You'll find the camera *Sŭng-gang-gi-rŭl t'a-sip-ssi-o. Nae-ri-si-myŏn pa-ro o-rŭn-tchok-p'yŏ-*

The Korea Tourist Service, Inc. (*kuk-tche kwan-gwang kong-sa*)··· 국제 관광 공사

department store(*pae-k'wa-jŏm*)···백화점

diningcar(*sik-ttang-ch'a*)···식당차

escalator(*e-sŭ-k'ŏl-le-i-t'ŏ*)···에스컬레이터

third floor(*sam-ch'ŭng*)···삼층

counter to the right as you get off.

ne k'a-me-ra-bu-ga it-ssŭm-ni-da.

승강기를 타십시오. 내리시면 바로 오른쪽편에 카메라부가 있습니다.

7. Books are sold on the fifth floor at the book department.

Ch'ae-gŭn o-ch'ŭng-ŭi sŏ-jŏk-ppu-e-sŏ p'al-go it-ssŭm-ni-da.

책은 오층의 서적부에서 팔고 있습니다.

8. The book department is on the fifth floor.

Sŏ-jŏk-ppu-nŭn o-ch'ŭng-e it-ssŭm-ni-da.

서적부는 오층에 있습니다.

9. Is there any bargain sale going on now?

Chi-gŭm yŏm-kka mae-ch'ul-ha-nŭn ko-si it-ssŭm-ni-kka?

지금 염가 매출하는 곳이 있습니까?

10. Yes, A special summer sale is being held on the 9th floor.

Ye, it-ssŭm-ni-da. T'ŭk-ppyŏl ha-ge tae-mae-ch'u-ri   yuk-chŭng-e-sŏ yŏl-li-go it-ssŭm-ni-da.

예, 있습니다. 특별 하계 대매출이 육층에서 열리고 있습니다.

11. Walk to the end of this aisle and turn right, please.

I t'ong-no mak-ppa-ji-kka-ji ka-sŏ o-rŭn-tcho-gŭ-ro to-sip-ssi-o.

이 통로 막바지까지 가서 오른쪽으로 도십시오.

12. What sort of commodities are being sold?

Ŏ-ttŏn chong-nyu-ŭi sang-p'u-mi it-ssŭm-ni-kka?

어떤 종류의 상품이 있습니까?

---

commodity(*sang-p'um*)…상품
goods(*mul-gŏn*)…물건
bargain sale(*yŏm-kka mae-ch'ul*)…염가 매출

export(*su-ch'ul*)…수출
import(*su-i-p'a-da*)…수입하다
fifth floor(*o-ch'ŭng*)…오층

13. It's a general sale of various types of goods, ranging from shoes to kitchen utensils.

Ku-du-e-sŏ pu-ŏk yong-gu-e i-rŭ-gi-kka-ji yŏ-rŏ ka-ji sang-p'um-dŭ-rŭl p'al-go it-ssŭm-ni-da.

구두에서 부엌 용구에 이르기까지 여러 가지 상품들을 팔고 있습니다.

14. The furniture department is on the ninth floor.

Ka-gu mae-jang-ŭn ku-ch'ŭng-e it-ssŭm-ni-da.

가구 매장은 구층에 있습니다.

15. The furniture department is on the other side of the escalator.

Ka-gu mae-jang-ŭn e-sŭ-k'a-re-i-t'ŏ chŏ-tcho-ge it-ssŭm-ni-da.

가구 매장은 에스카레이터 저쪽에 있습니다.

16. Can I help you?

Mu-ŏ-sŭl sa-si-get-ssŭm-ni-kka?

무엇을 사시겠습니까?

17. I'm just looking around.

Kŭ-jŏ ku-gyŏng-ha-nŭn kŏ-sim-ni-da.

그저 구경하는 것입니다.

18. Please help yourself.

Ne, ku-gyŏng-ha-sip-ssi-o.

네, 구경하십시오.

19. Do you have imported canned goods?

Su-i-p'an t'ong-jo-rim sang-p'u-mi it-ssŭm-ni-kka?

수입한 통조림 상품이 있습니까?

20. Yes, we do. You will find them on the shelves over there.

Ye, it-ssŭm-ni-da. Chŏ-tchok sŏn-ban wi-e it-ssŭm-ni-da.

예, 있습니다. 저쪽 선반 위에 있습니다.

21. It's just about where the pillar is.

Chŏ ki-dung kŭn-ch'ŏ-ga toe-get-ssŭm-ni-da.

---

can(*kkang-t'ong*)…깡통
shelf(*sŏn-ban*)…선반

kitchen utensil(*pu-ŏk yong-gu*)…부엌 용구

저 기둥 근처가 되겠습니다.

22. Do you keep cereals too ?

Kong-nyu sik-p'um-do it-ssŭm-ni-kka ?

곡류 식품도 있습니까 ?

23. It's beyond this counter.

K'a-un-t'ŏ chŏ-tcho-ge it-ssŭm-ni-da.

카운터 저쪽에 있습니다.

24. Yes, many varieties. What kind do you want ?

Ne, yŏ-rŏ ka-ji chong-nyu-ga it-ssŭm-ni-da. Ŏ-ttŏn chong-nyu-rŭl wŏn-ha-sim-ni-kka ?

네, 여러 가지 종류가 있습니다. 어떤 종류를 원하십니까 ?

25. How much is that watch ?

Chŏ si-gye-nŭn ŏl-ma-im-ni-kka ?

저 시계는 얼마입니까 ?

26. Fifty thousand won, sir.

O-man wŏn-im-ni-da.

오만 원입니다.

27. I'm afraid it's too expensive for me. Haven't you anything cheaper ?

Nŏ-mu pi-ssam-ni-da. Chom-dŏ ssan kŏ-sŭn ŏp-ssŭm-ni-kka ?

너무 비쌉니다. 좀더 싼 것은 없습니까 ?

28. Would you like to try this one, then ?

Kŭ-rŏ-si-da-myŏn i-gŏ-sŭl han-bŏn ssŏ po-sip-ssi-o.

그러시다면 이것을 한번 써 보십시오.

29. How about this one ? It's nine thousand won.

I-gŏ-sŭn ŏ-ttŏt-ssŭm-ni-kka ? I-gŏ-sŭn ku-ch'ŏn wŏn-im-ni-da.

이것은 어떻습니까 ? 이것은 구천 원입니다.

---

subdue(*wan-hwa-ha-da*)…완화하다
shoes(*ku-du*)…구두
cereal(*kong-nyu*)…곡류

cheaper(*kap-ssan*)…값싼
fear(*tu-ryŏ-um*)…두려움
processing(*ka-gong*)…가공

30. The price is all right for me. I'll take it.

Kap-ssi chŏk-ttang-ha-gun-yo. Kŭ-gŏl sa-get-ssŭm-ni-da.

값이 적당하군요. 그걸 사겠습니다.

31. Would you care to place an order?

Chu-mu-nŭl ha-si-get-ssŭm-ni-kka?

주문을 하시겠습니까?

32. Thank you, sir. Will you wait a moment, please? I'll have it wrapped.

Kam-sa-ham-ni-da. Cham-kkan-man ki-da-ri-si-get-ssŭm-ni-kka? P'o-jang-hae tŭ-ri-get-ssŭm-ni-da.

감사합니다. 잠깐만 기다리시겠습니까? 포장해 드리겠습니다.

33. Make it gift wrapped please.

Sŏn-mul-yong p'o-jang-ŭ-ro hae chu-sip-ssi-o.

선물용 포장으로 해 주십시오.

34. Anything I can do for you?

Mu-ŏl ch'a-jŭ-sim-ni-kka?

무얼 찾으십니까?

35. Let me call an English-speaking guide.

Yŏng-ŏ-rŭl hal ssu in-nŭn sa-ra-mŭl pul-lŏ tŭ-ri-get-ssŭm-ni-da.

영어를 할 수 있는 사람을 불러 드리겠습니다.

36. May I see that woolen necktie?

Chŏ mo-jik nek-t'a-i-rŭl chom pop-ssi-da.

저 모직 넥타이를 좀 봅시다.

37. This one?

I-gŏt mal-ssŭm-i-sim-ni-kka?

이것 말씀이십니까?

38. No. The one next to it.

A-nim-ni-da. Pa-ro kŭ yŏ-p'e in-nŭn kŏt mal-im-ni-da.

아닙니다. 바로 그 옆에 있는 것 말입니다.

---

inquiry office(*an-nae-so*) ··· 안내소   perfectly(*wan-jŏn-hi*) ··· 완전히

39. It is a subdued shade, but it matches your suit perfectly. This kind of tie appeals to everybody.

Pu-dŭ-rŏ-un pit-kkal-i-gin ha-ji-man, i-bŭ-sin yang-bo-k'a-go chal ŏ-ul-rim-ni-da. I-rŏn nek-t'a-i-nŭn ŏ-nŭ pu-ni-na ta cho-a-ha-sim-ni-da.

부드러운 빛깔이긴 하지만, 입으신 양복하고 잘 어울립니다. 이런 넥타이는 어느 분이나 다 좋아하십니다.

40. How does it compare with that brown one?

Chŏ kal-ssaek nek-t'a-i-e pi-ha-myŏn ŏ-ttŏt-ssŭm-ni-kka?

저 갈색 넥타이에 비하면 어떻습니까?

41. I think this one is much better.

Che saeng-ga-ge-nŭn i-gŏ-si hwŏl-ssin na-ŭn kŏt kat-ssŭm-ni-da.

제 생각에는 이것이 훨씬 나은 것 같습니다.

42. Can I have it delivered?

I-gŏ-sŭl pae-dal-hae chu-sil ssu it-ssŭm-ni-kka?

이것을 배달해 주실 수 있습니까?

43. In the city?

Si-nae-im-ni-kka?

시내입니까?

44. No, in the outskirts.

A-nim-ni-da. Kyo-woe-im-ni-da.

아닙니다. 교외입니다.

45. There is no charge for delivery in the city, but

Si-nae pae-da-rŭn mu-ryo-im-ni-da-man, kyo-woe pae-da-rŭn p'o-jang

---

appeal(*ho-so-ha-da*)…호소하다
compare(*pi-gyo-ha-da*)…비교하다
postage(*u-song-ryo*)…우송료
pillar(*ki-dung*)…기둥
toyshop(*wan-gu-bu*)…완구부

deliver(*pae-dal-ha-da*)…배달하다
outskirt(*kyo-woe*)…교외
add(*tŏ-ha-da*)…더하다
ready-made clothes(*ki-sŏng-bok*)…기성복

for delivery to the outskirts we ask for an additional charge of two thousand won for packing and handling.

bi-wa ch'wi-gŭp-ppi-ro i-ch'ŏn wŏn-ŭl tŏ pat-ssŭm-ni-da.

시내 배달은 무료입니다만, 교외 배달은 포장비와 취급비로 이천 원을 더 받습니다.

46. That will be fine.

Chot-ssŭm-ni-da.

좋습니다.

47. I'm looking for a suit.

Yang-bo-gŭl han pŏl sa-go sip-ssŭm-ni-da.

양복을 한 벌 사고 싶습니다.

48. Do you wish one made to order?

Han pŏl mat-ch'u-si-get-ssŭm-ni-kka?

한 벌 맞추시겠습니까?

49. I'd like a ready-made one.

Ki-sŏng-bo-gŭl sa-get-ssŭm-ni-da.

기성복을 사겠습니다.

50. This shade is quite popular this year. Why don't you try it on?

I saek-kka-ri ol-hae-nŭn a-ju yu-haeng-im-ni-da. Han-bŏn i-bŏ po-sip-ssi-o.

이 색깔이 올해는 아주 유행입니다. 한번 입어 보십시오.

51. Do you think it will fit me?

Nae-ge ma-jŭl-kka-yo?

내게 맞을까요?

52. It's very becoming.

A-ju ŏ-ul-lim-ni-da.

아주 어울립니다.

53. Please show me some cloth samples.

O-kkam kyŏn-bon chom po-yŏ chu-sip-ssi-o.

옷감 견본 좀 보여 주십시오.

---

handling(*ch'wi-gŭp*)…취급
toilet articles(*hwa-jang-p'um*)…화장품

measurement(*ch'i-su*)…치수
fitting(*ka-bong*)…가봉
sample(*kyŏn-bon*)…견본

54. Is it for a suit or a spring coat ?

Yang-bok-kkam-im-ni-kka,　a-ni-myŏn sŭ-p'ŭ-ring k'o-t'ŭ-kkam-im-ni-kka ?

양복감입니까, 아니면 스프링 코트 감입니까 ?

55. I'd like to order a suit of this cloth.

I ch'ŏ-nŭ-ro han pŏl mat-ch'wŏ chu-sip-ssi-o.

이 천으로 한 벌 맞춰 주십시오.

56. May I take your measurements ?

Chae-ŏ pol-kka-yo ?

재어 볼까요 ?

57. You can have a fitting on next Tuesday.

Ta-ŭm tchu hwa-yo-i-re ka-bong-i toe-get-ssŭm-ni-da.

다음 주 화요일에 가봉이 되겠습 니다.

58. I was told that this store is also having a special exhibition of flower arrangements.

I pae-k'wa-jŏ-me-sŏ t'ŭk-ppyŏl kkok-kko-ji chŏn-si-hoe-ga yŏl-li-go it-tta-go tŭ-rŏt-ssŭm-ni-da.

이 백화점에서 특별 꽃꽂이 전시회 가 열리고 있다고 들었습니다.

59. That's right. The flower arrangement show is being held till the end of this week on the 10th floor.

Kŭ-rŏt-ssŭm-ni-da.　KKok-kko-ji chŏn-si-hoe-ga　sip-ch'ŭng-e-sŏ kŭm-ju mal-kka-ji yŏl-li-go it-ssŭm-ni-da.

그렇습니다. 꽃꽂이 전시회가 십층 에서 금주 말까지 열리고 있습니다.

60. Can I buy a ticket for the exhibition here ?

Yŏ-gi-sŏ chŏn-si-hoe kwal-lam-kkwŏ-nŭl sal ssu it-ssŭm-ni-kka?

여기서 전시회 관람권을 살 수 있 습니까 ?

---

exhibition(*chŏn-si-hoe*)…전시회　　admission(*hŏ-ga*)…허가

61. Admission is free.	*Ip-tchang-ŭn mu-ryo-im-ni-da.* 입장은 무료입니다.
62. Does this elevator go up to the 10th floor?	*I sŭng-gang-gi-nŭn sip-ch'ŭng-ŭ-ro kam-ni-kka?* 이 승강기는 십층으로 갑니까?
63. No, it doesn't. Please take elevator No. 5.	*A-nim-ni-da. O pŏn sŭng-gang-gi-rŭl t'a-sip-ssi-o.* 아닙니다. 오 번 승강기를 타십시오.

At a Bakery

PPang-tchi-be-sŏ (빵집에서)

1. I want a loaf of bread.	*Sik-ppang han tŏng-i chu-sip-ssi-o.* 식빵 한 덩이 주십시오.
2. What kind, sir?	*Ŏ-ttŏn kŏ-sŭ-ro tŭ-ril-kka-yo?* 어떤 것으로 드릴까요?
3. Sandwich bread, please.	*Saen-dŭ-wi-ch'i ppang-ŭ-ro chu-sip-ssi-o.* 샌드위치 빵으로 주십시오.
4. Do you want it sliced?	*SSŏ-rŏ-sŏ tŭ-ril-kka-yo?* 썰어서 드릴까요?
5. How thick do you want the slices?	*Ŏ-nŭ chŏng-do-ŭi tu-kke-ro ssŏ-rŏ tŭ-ril-kka-yo?* 어느 정도의 두께로 썰어 드릴까요?
6. Rather thin, please. I want to make sandwiches.	*A-ju yŏl-kke ssŏ-rŏ chu-sip-ssi-o. Saen-dŭ-wi-ch'i-rŭl man-dŭl kkŏ-sim-ni-da.*

---

arrangement(*chŏng-ni*) … 정리
bakery(*ppang-tchip*) … 빵집
free(*mu-ryo*) … 무료

elevator(*sŭng-gang-gi*) … 승강기
brown bread(*hŭk-ppang*) … 흑빵
slice(*tcha-rŭ-da*) … 짜르다

아주 엷게 썰어 주십시오. 샌드위
치를 만들 것입니다.

7. Do you have dough-nuts, too?

To-nŏt-ch'ŭ-do it-ssŭm-ni-kka?

도넛츠도 있습니까?

8. I'm sorry they're sold out.

Choe-song-ham-ni-da. Mo-du p'al-lyŏt-ssŭm-ni-da.

죄송합니다. 모두 팔렸습니다.

9. How about buns?

Kwa-ja-ppang-ŭn it-ssŭm-ni-kka?

과자빵은 있습니까?

10. We have all kinds.

Kat-kka-ji kkŏ-si mo-du it-ssŭm-ni-da.

갖가지 것이 모두 있습니다.

11. Please try one as a sa-mple.

Ha-na tŭ-syŏ po-sip-ssi-o.

하나 드셔 보십시오.

12. I've given you a gene-rous serving.

Hu-ha-ge tŭ-ryŏt-ssŭm-ni-da.

후하게 드렸습니다.

13. Anything else, sir? We have very nice tol-lhouse cookies today.

Kŭ pak-kke ta-rŭn kŏ-sŭn p'i-ryo-ha-ji an-ssŭm-ni-kka? O-nŭ-rŭn ma-sin-nŭn t'ol-ha-u-sŭ k'u-k'i-ga it-ssŭm-ni-da.

그 밖에 다른 것은 필요하지 않습
니까? 오늘은 맛있는 톨하우스
쿠키가 있습니다.

14. Would you like to try these sweets?

I kwa-ja-rŭl han-bŏn tŭ-syŏ po-si-get-ssŭm-ni-kka?

이 과자를 한번 드셔 보시겠습니
까?

15. How much are they?

Kŭ-gŏ-sŭn ŏl-ma-im-ni-kka?

---

doughnut (*to-nŏt*)…도넛
charged (*yu-ryo*)…유료

bun (*kwa-ja-ppang*)…과자빵
thick (*tu-kkŏ-un*)…두꺼운

그것은 얼마입니까?

16. Eight hundred won per hundred grams. Please try one and see how it tastes.

Paek kkŭ-rae-me p'al-baek wŏn-im-ni-da. Tŭ-syŏ po-si-go ma-si ŏ-ttŏn-ga po-sip-ssi-o.

백 그램에 팔백 원입니다. 드셔 보시고 맛이 어떤가 보십시오.

17. All right. I'll take 500 grams.

Chot-ssŭm-ni-da. O-baek kkŭ-raem-man sa-get-ssŭm-ni-da.

좋습니다. 오백 그램만 사겠습니다.

18. What kind of bread is this wrapped up in wax paper?

I ki-rŭm chong-i-e ssa-no-ŭn ppang-ŭn mu-sŭn ppang-im-ni-kka?

이 기름 종이에 싸놓은 빵은 무슨 빵입니까?

19. How much is this loaf of rye bread?

I ho-mil-ppang-ŭn ŏl-ma-im-ni-kka?

이 호밀빵은 얼마입니까?

20. Could I have half a loaf?

Pan tŏng-i-man sal ssu it-ssŭm-ni-kka?

반 덩이만 살 수 있습니까?

21. Certainly. Here you are.

A-mu-ryŏm-yo. Yŏ-gi it-ssŭm-ni-da.

아무렴요. 여기 있습니다.

22. How long will these cream puffs keep?

I syu-k'ŭ-ri-mŭn ŏl-ma ttong-a-ni-na tu-ŏ tul ssu it-ssŭm-ni-kka?

이 슈크림은 얼마 동안이나 두어 둘 수 있습니까?

23. About three days in a refrigerator.

Naeng-jang-go so-ge nŏ-ŏ-sŏ sa mil chŏng-do tul ssu it-ssŭm-ni-da.

---

taste(*mat-ppo-da*)⋯맛보다
rye bread(*ho-mil-ppang*)⋯호밀빵
antiseptic(*pang-bu-je*)⋯방부제

refrigerator(*naeng-jang-go*)⋯냉장고
custody(*po-gwan*)⋯보관
food-tasting(*si-si-k'a-da*)⋯시식하다

냉장고 속에 넣어서 삼 일 정도 둘
수 있습니다.

24. I'll take half a dozen.

Yŏ-sŏt kkae-man sa-get-ssŭm-ni-da.

여섯 개만 사겠습니다.

25. I will wrap up the bread for you.

PPang-ŭl ssa tŭ-ri-get-ssŭm-ni-da.

빵을 싸 드리겠습니다.

26. What kind of cakes are these?

I-gŏ-sŭn mu-sŭn kwa-ja-im-ni-kka?

이것은 무슨 과자입니까?

27. They're Korean rice cakes.

Han-guk-ssik ttŏk-im-ni-da.

한국식 떡입니다.

28. What's inside?

So-ge mu-ŏ-si tŭ-rŏ it-ssŭm-ni-kka?

속에 무엇이 들어 있습니까?

29. There's sweet bean jam in it.

Tan-kko-mu-ri tŭ-rŏ it-ssŭm-ni-da.

단고물이 들어 있습니다.

30. This may be too sweet for you.

Nŏ-mu tan-ji mo-rŭ-get-ssŭm-ni-da.

너무 단지 모르겠습니다.

31. Are they good?

Ma-si chot-ssŭm-ni-kka?

맛이 좋습니까?

32. Yes, very good. Here's a small sample. Please try it.

Ne, a-ju ma-si it-ssŭm-ni-da. Yŏ-gi cho-gŭ-man si-sing-yong-i i-ssŭ-ni han-bŏn tŭ-syŏ po-sip-ssi-o.

네, 아주 맛이 있습니다. 여기 조그만 시식용이 있으니 한번 드셔 보십시오.

33. If you don't like it, please leave it.

Ma-nyak cho-a-ha-ji a-nŭ-myŏn nam-gyŏ no-ŭ-sip-ssi-o.

만약 좋아하지 않으면 남겨 놓으

---

mashed red-bean(*p'at-kko-mul*)…팥고물

steamed rice-cake(*paek-ssŏl-gi*)…백설기

cake made from glutinous rice(*in-jŏl-mi*)…인절미

mill building(*pang-a-kkan*)…방앗간

glutinous(*ch'ap-ssal*)…찹쌀

십시오.

34. It's very tasty. I'll take some.

Ch'am ma-si chot-ssŭm-ni-da. Myŏt kkae sa-get-ssŭm-ni-da.

참 맛이 좋습니다. 몇 개 사겠습니다.

35. What's mandu?

Man-du-nŭn mu-ŏ-sim-ni-kka?

만두는 무엇입니까?

36. It's a Chinese cake.

Chung-guk-ssik kwa-ja-im-ni-da.

중국식 과자입니다.

37. Where can I have some mandu?

Ŏ-di-sŏ man-du-rŭl sal ssu it-ssŭm-ni-kka?

어디서 만두를 살 수 있습니까?

38. You can buy it in the Chinese restaurant.

Chung-guk ŭm-sik-tchŏ-me-sŏ kŭ-gŏ-sŭl sal ssu it-ssŭm-ni-da.

중국 음식점에서 그것을 살 수 있습니다.

39. This sponge cake is very good. It's a specialty of Pusan.

I k'a-sŭ-t'e-ra-ga a-ju ma-si it-ssŭm-ni-da. Pu-sa-nŭi t'ŭk-ssan-p'um-i-ram-ni-da.

이 카스테라가 아주 맛이 있습니다. 부산의 특산품이랍니다.

40. I'll take a box.

Han sang-ja sa-get-ssŭm-ni-da.

한 상자 사겠습니다.

41. Do you want the large box or the small?

Kŭn sang-ja-ro tŭ-ril-kka-yo, a-ni-myŏn cha-gŭn sang-ja-ro tŭ-ril-kka-yo?

큰 상자로 드릴까요, 아니면 작은 상자로 드릴까요?

---

sponge cake(*k'a-sŭ-t'e-ra*)…카스테라
pastry(*kwa-ja*)…과자

special product(*t'ŭk-ssan-p'um*)…특산품

42. The small one, please.

Cha-gŭn sang-ja-ro chu-sip-ssi-o.
작은 상자로 주십시오.

43. How much is it?

Ŏl-ma-im-ni-kka?
얼마입니까?

44. Five thousand won, sir.

O-ch'ŏn wŏn-im-ni-da.
오천 원입니다.

45. Will you wrap it?

SSa chu-si-get-ssŭm-ni-kka?
싸 주시겠습니까?

46. Of course.

Mul-lon-i-ji-yo.
물론이지요.

At a Butcher's, Fish Shop

Chŏng-yuk-tchŏm, Saeng-sŏn ka-ge-e-sŏ
(정육점, 생선 가게에서)

1. I want some meat. Have you a fresh supply?

Ko-gi-rŭl chom sal-lyŏ-go ham-ni-da. Sin-sŏn-han kŏ-si it-ssŭm-ni-kka?
고기를 좀 살려고 합니다. 신선한 것이 있습니까?

2. Yes, we have. This meat just arrived this morning.

Ne, it-ssŭm-ni-da. I ko-gi-nŭn pa-ro o-nŭl a-ch'i-me to-ch'a-k'aet-ssŭm-ni-da.
네, 있습니다. 이 고기는 바로 오늘 아침에 도착했습니다.

3. How much is it per Kilogram?

Il k'il-lo-gŭ-rae-me ŏl-ma-im-ni-kka?
일 킬로그램에 얼마입니까?

4. Fifteen thousand won, sir. It has gone up a little since the last time.

Man o-ch'ŏn wŏn-im-ni-da. Chi-nan-bŏn-bo-da kap-ssi yak-kkan ol-lat-ssŭm-ni-da.

---

buchers shop(*chŏng-yuk-tchŏm*)…정육점

kilogram(*k'il-lo-gŭ-raem*)…킬로그램
balance(*chŏ-ul*)…저울

만 오천 원입니다. 지난번보다 값
이 약간 올랐습니다.

5. I'll take two kilograms.

*I k'il-lo-gŭ-raem-man sa-get-ssŭm-
ni-da.*

이 킬로그램만 사겠습니다.

6. Good. By the way do you want it sliced ?

*Chot-ssŭm-ni-da. SSŏ-rŏ tŭ-ril-kka-
yo ?*

좋습니다. 썰어 드릴까요 ?

7. No, I want it whole. I hope it's tender.

*A-nim-ni-da. Kŭ-nyang chu-sip-ssi-
o. Yŏn-han kŏ-sŭ-ro chu-sip-ssi-o.*

아닙니다. 그냥 주십시오. 연한 것
으로 주십시오.

8. How about this sliced beef ?

*I ssŏ-rŏ no-ŭn soe-go-gi-nŭn ŏ-ttŏt-
ssŭm-ni-kka ?*

이 썰어 놓은 쇠고기는 어떻습니
까 ?

9. They are of excellent quality.

P'um-ji-ri a-ju chot-ssŭm-ni-da.

품질이 아주 좋습니다.

10. It looks very nice. Is it imported bacon ?

*A-ju cho-k'e po-i-nŭn-gun-yo. Su-i-
p'an pe-i-k'on-im-ni-kka ?*

아주 좋게 보이는군요. 수입한 베
이콘입니까 ?

11. No. But it is just as good as imported one.

*A-nim-ni-da. Kŭ-rŏ-na su-i-p'an
mul-gŏn-man-k'ŭ-mi-na   hul-
lyung-ham-ni-da.*

아닙니다. 그러나 수입한 물건만큼
이나 훌륭합니다.

12. Give me about a dozen

Tu-kkŏp-kke ssŏn kŏ-sŭ-ro han t'a-

---

quality(*chil*)…질
tender(*yŏn-han*)…연한

bill(*pu-ri*)…부리

thick slices.

sŭ-tchŭm chu-sip-ssi-o.

두껍게 썬 것으로 한 타스쯤 주십시오.

13. We also have some good mutton.

Cho-ŭn yang-go-gi-do it-ssŭm-ni-da.

좋은 양고기도 있습니다.

14. Not for me, thanks. We don't care for mutton.

Kŭ-man tu-sip-ssi-o. Yang-go-gi-nŭn cho-a-ha-ji an-ssŭm-ni-da.

그만 두십시오. 양고기는 좋아하지 않습니다.

15. Do you also handle chicken meat?

Tak-kko-gi-do p'am-ni-kka?

닭고기도 팝니까?

16. No, I'm afraid we don't. But in the market over there, there are two or three shops that specialize in the chickens and other poultry.

Kŭ-gŏn p'al-ji an-ssŭm-ni-da. Kŭ-rŏ-na kŏn-nŏ-p'yŏn si-jang a-ne tak-kkwa ka-gŭ-mŭl chŏn-mu-nŭ-ro ch'wi-gŭ-p'a-nŭn sang-jŏ-mi tu-sŏ-nŏ ko-si it-ssŭm-ni-da.

그건 팔지 않습니다. 그러나 건너편 시장 안에 닭과 가금을 전문으로 취급하는 상점이 두서너 곳이 있습니다.

17. Please show me some sausages.

So-si-ji chom po-yŏ chu-sip-ssi-o.

소시지 좀 보여 주십시오.

18. What kind, sir? We have such a wide variety.

Ŏ-ttŏn kŏ-sŭl wŏn-ha-sim-ni-kka? Yŏ-rŏ ka-ji-ga it-ssŭm-ni-da.

어떤 것을 원하십니까? 여러 가지가 있습니다.

19. I want vienna.

Pi-en-na so-si-ji chom pop-ssi-da.

비엔나 소시지 좀 봅시다.

---

poultry(*ka-gŭm*)…가금   chicken meat(*tak-kko-gi*)…닭고기

20. Give me a few of each, please.

Kak-kak cho-gŭm-ssik chu-sip-ssi-o.
각각 조금씩 주십시오.

21. What kind of meat would you recommend for making soup?

Su-p'ŭ-rŭl man-dŭ-nŭn te-nŭn ŏ-ttŏn ko-gi-ga cho-k'et-ssŭm-ni-kka ?
수프를 만드는 데는 어떤 고기가 좋겠습니까?

22. Well, I think chicken would be the best.

Tak-kko-gi-ga che-il cho-ŭl kkŏt kat-ssŭm-ni-da.
닭고기가 제일 좋을 것 같습니다.

23. Do you have veal to-day?

O-nŭl song-a-ji ko-gi-ga it-ssŭm-ni-kka?
오늘 송아지 고기가 있습니까?

24. I'm sorry we haven't. Tomorrow, however, we may get a supply. We shall be glad to let you know by telephone as soon as it arrives.

Choe-song-ham-ni-da. Ŏp-ssŭm-ni-da. Nae-i-rŭn ol-kkŏm-ni-da. To-ch'a-k'a-nŭn tae-ro chŏn-hwa-ro al-lyŏ tŭ-ri-get-ssŭm-ni-da.
죄송합니다. 없습니다. 내일은 올 겁니다. 도착하는 대로 전화로 알려 드리겠습니다.

25. I would advise you to try trout.

Song-ŏ-rŭl tŭ-syŏ po-sip-ssi-o.
송어를 드셔 보십시오.

26. Will you take out the insides?

Nae-jang-ŭl chal-la-nae chu-sip-ssi-o.
내장을 잘라내 주십시오.

27. How do the Koreans

Han-guk ssa-ram-dŭ-rŭn po-t'ong ŏ-

---

pepper-pot soup(*mae-un-t'ang*)…매운 탕

roast fish(*saeng-sŏn ku-i*)…생선 구이

veal(*song-a-ji ko-gi*)…송아지 고기

pig meat(*twae-ji-go-gi*)…돼지고기

usually prepare tuna?

28. Tuna is usually eaten raw. It is cut into this slices and served with grated radish or horse-radish.

29. "Saengson hoe" is one of the most favorite dishes of the Korean people.

30. How much are the trout plates?

31. They are 30,000 won per plates.

32. I will take two plates full. Will you please re-

ttŏ-k'e ta-rang-ŏ-rŭl mŏk-ssŭm-ni-kka?

한국 사람들은 보통 어떻게 다랑어를 먹습니까?

Ta-rang-ŏ-nŭn po-t'ong nal kŏ-sŭ-ro mŏk-ssŭm-ni-da. Yal-kke ssŏ-rŏ-sŏ mu-ch'ae-na kyŏ-ja-ch'ae-rŭl kyŏ-ttŭ-ryŏ nae-not-ssŭm-ni-da.

다랑어는 보통 날 것으로 먹습니다. 얇게 썰어서 무채나 겨자채를 곁들여 내놓습니다.

Saeng-sŏn-hoe-nŭn han-guk ssa-ram-dŭ-ri ka-jang chŭl-gyŏ mŏng-nŭn ŭm-sik tchung-ŭi ha-na-im-ni-da.

생선회는 한국 사람들이 가장 즐겨 먹는 음식 중의 하나입니다.

Chŏp-ssi-e tam-gin i song-ŏ-nŭn ŏl-ma-im-ni-kka?

접시에 담긴 이 송어는 얼마입니까?

Han chŏp-ssi-e sam-man wŏn-im-ni-da.

한 접시에 삼만 원입니다.

Tu chŏp-ssi ka-dŭ-k'i sa-get-ssŭm-ni-da. Mŏ-ri-wa chi-nŭ-rŏ-mi-rŭl

---

trout(*song-ŏ*)…송어
tuna(*ta-rang-ŏ*)…다랑어
radish(*mu*)…무
lobster(*sae-u*)…새우

horseradish(*kyŏ-ja*)…겨자
plate(*chŏp-ssi*)…접시
fin(*chi-nŭ-rŏ-mi*)…지느러미
crab(*ke*)…게

move the heads and the fins, and take out the insides?

tte-go, nae-jang-do ppae-ju-si-get-ssŭm-ni-kka?

두 접시 가득히 사겠습니다. 머리와 지느러미를 떼고, 내장도 빼주시겠습니까?

33. Certainly, if you will wait just a moment. Have you brought something to put them in?

Kŭ-rŏ-k'e ha-jyo. Cham-kkan-man ki-da-ri-sip-ssi-o. Ta-ma ka-jyŏ-gal kkŏ-sŭl ka-ji-go o-syŏt-ssŭm-ni-kka?

그렇게 하죠. 잠깐만 기다리십시오. 담아 가져갈 것을 가지고 오셨습니까?

34. Please put them in this vinyl bag. Have you also removed the scales?

I pi-nil pong-ji-e nŏ-ŏ chu-sip-ssi-o. Pi-nŭl-do mul-lon tte-ŏ nae-syŏt-kket-tchi-yo?

이 비닐 봉지에 넣어 주십시오. 비늘도 물론 떼어 내셨겠지요?

35. May I eat oysters in this season?

Yo-jŭm ku-rŭl mŏ-gŏ-do chot-ssŭm-ni-kka?

요즘 굴을 먹어도 좋습니까?

36. It's quite all right. Oysters are specially good in cold season.

Kwaen-ch'an-k'o mal-go-yo. Kul ma-sŭn kyŏ-u-re pyŏl-mi-im-ni-da.

괜찮고 말고요. 굴 맛은 겨울에 별미입니다.

37. Can you tell me when they shouldn't be eaten in Korea?

Han-gu-ge-sŏ-nŭn ŏn-je ku-rŭl mŏ-gŭ-myŏn an toem-ni-kka?

한국에서는 언제 굴을 먹으면 안 됩니까?

---

oyster*(kul)*⋯굴　　　　　　　　vinyl bag*(pi-nil-ppaek)*⋯비닐백

38. In the months which do not have "r," oysters should be left alone.

Al-tcha-ga tŭ-rŏ it-tchi a-nŭn ta-ren mŏk-tchi an-ssŭm-ni-da.

"*r*"자가 들어 있지 않은 달엔 먹지 않습니다.

39. I see. You mean May, June, July and August.

Al-get-ssŭm-ni-da. O-wŏl, yu-wŏl, ch'i-rwŏl, p'a-rwŏ-rŭl mal-ha-si-nŭn-gun-yo.

알겠습니다. 오월, 유월, 칠월, 팔월을 말하시는군요.

40. I wonder if I'll find any pearls in these oysters.

I kul sso-ge chin-ju-ga tŭ-rŏ in-nŭn-ji-do mo-rŭ-get-kkun-yo.

이 굴 속에 진주가 들어 있는지도 모르겠군요.

At a Fruit Shop

Kwa-il-tchŏ-me-sŏ(과일점에서)

1. I want to buy some apples.

Sa-gwa-rŭl myŏt kkae sa-ryŏ-go ham-ni-da.

사과를 몇 개 사려고 합니다.

2. How about these? They are arrived from Taegu only yesterday, so I can assure you they're very fresh.

I-gŏ-si ŏ-ttŏt-ssŭm-ni-kka? Pa-ro ŏ-je tae-gu-e-sŏ on kŏ-si-gi ttae-mu-ne a-ju sing-sing-ham-ni-da.

이것이 어떻습니까? 바로 어제 대구에서 온 것이기 때문에 아주 싱싱합니다.

3. They are very sweet and exceptionally juicy.

A-ju tal-go mu-ri man-ssŭm-ni-da.

아주 달고 물이 많습니다.

4. What about the ones

Chŏ-tcho-ge in-nŭn kŏ-sŭn ŏ-ttŏ-k'e

---

pear(*pae*)···배
grapes(*p'o-do*)···포도
fruit shop(*kwa-il-tchŏm*)···과일점

apple(*sa-gwa*)···사과
berry(*ttal-gi*)···딸기
assure(*hwak-ssin-ha-da*)···확신하다

over there?

    ham-ni-kka?

저 쪽에 있는 것은 어떻게 합니까?

5. Eighty won piece.

    Han kae-e p'al-baek wŏn-im-ni-da.

한 개에 팔백 원입니다.

6. Those are thousand won a piece, for they're much larger than others.

    Chŏ-gŏt-ttŭ-rŭn ta-rŭn kŏt-ppo-da hwŏl-ssin k'ŭ-gi ttae-mu-ne han kae-e chŏn wŏn-im-ni-da.

저것들은 다른 것보다 훨씬 크기 때문에 한 개에 천 원입니다.

7. Will there be anything else?

    Kŭ pak-kke p'i-ryo-han kŏ-si ŏp-ssŭ-sim-ni-kka?

그 밖에 필요한 것이 없으십니까?

8. We have wonderful tangerines that were shipped directly to us from Cheju island.

    Che-ju-do-e-sŏ chik-tchŏp pu-ch'yŏ on hul-ryung-han kyu-ri it-ssŭm-ni-da.

제주도에서 직접 부쳐 온 훌륭한 귤이 있습니다.

9. I'll take the hundred won ones.

    Baek wŏn tcha-ri-rŭl sa-get-ssŭm-ni-da.

백 원 짜리를 사겠습니다.

10. I can assure you these are very fresh.

    I-gŏ-sŭn a-ju sing-sing-ham-ni-da.

이것은 아주 싱싱합니다.

11. How much are they per kilogram?

    Il k'il-lo-gŭ-rae-me ŏl-ma-im-ni-kka?

일 킬로그램에 얼마입니까?

12. They won't be ready for eating for another

    A-jik il-tchu-il-tchŭm tŏ i-ssŏ-ya mŏ-gŭl ssu i-ssŭl kkŏm-ni-da.

---

tangerine(*kyul*)…귤
banana(*pa-na-na*)…바나나
peach(*pok-ssung-a*)…복숭아

bunch(*ta-bal*)…다발
damage(*sang-ha-da*)…상하다

week or so.

아직 일주일쯤 더 있어야 먹을 수
있을 겁니다.

13. Are these grapes ripe ?

I p'o-do-nŭn i-gŏt-ssŭm-ni-kka ?

이 포도는 익었습니까 ?

14. These bananas look green.

I pa-na-na-nŭn tŏl i-gŭn kŏt kat-ssŭm-ni-da.

이 바나나는 덜 익은 것 같습니다.

15. How much is this bunch ?

Han ta-ba-re ŏl-ma-im-ni-kka ?

한 다발에 얼마입니까 ?

16. Give me three bunches.

Se ta-bal-man chu-sip-ssi-o.

세 다발만 주십시오.

17. These two bunches look damaged.

I tu ta-ba-rŭn sang-han kŏt kat-ssŭm-ni-da.

이 두 다발은 상한 것 같습니다.

18. I want a basket of fruit.

Kwa-il han pa-gu-ni-rŭl sa-get-ssŭm-ni-da.

과일 한 바구니를 사겠습니다.

19. Several kinds mixed.

Myŏt kka-ji-rŭl sŏk-kkŏ-sŏ chu-sip-ssi-o.

몇 가지를 섞어서 주십시오.

20. I'd like to buy some American oranges.

Mi-guk-ssan o-ren-ji-rŭl chom sa-go sip-ssŭm-ni-da.

미국산 오렌지를 좀 사고 싶습니다.

21. They're going so fast that we have two lay in a fresh stock every to or three days.

I-gŏ-sŭn a-ju chal p'al-ri-gi ttae-mu-ne i, sa mil-ma-da sae-ro tŭ-ryŏ-wa-ya ham-ni-da.

이것은 아주 잘 팔리기 때문에 이,
삼 일마다 새로 들여와야 합니다.

---

sweet taste(*tan-mat*)…단맛
mix(*sŏk-tta*)…섞다

ripe(*ik-tta*)…익다
half-done(*sŏ-rik-tta*)…설익다

22. The price ranges from 1,000 won to 3,000 won, depending on species.

Chong-nyu-e tta-ra ch'ŏn wŏn-e-sŏ sam-ch'ŏn wŏn-kka-ji pat-ssŭm-ni-da.

종류에 따라 천 원에서 삼천 원까지 받습니다.

23. That kinds of oranges cost 10,000 won per kilogram, but I can let you have them for 9,000 won, because you are a regular customer.

I-rŏn chong-nyu-ŭi o-ren-ji-nŭn il k'il-lo-gŭ-raem-dang man wŏn-im-ni-da-man, tang-si-nŭn chŏng-gyu ko-gaek-i-gi ttae-mu-ne ku-ch'ŏn wŏn-e tŭ-ri-get-ssŭm-ni-da.

이런 종류의 오렌지는 일 킬로그램당 만 원입니다만, 당신은 정규 고객이기 때문에 구천 원에 드리겠습니다.

24. Are they ripe? They still look a bit green.

I-gŏt-ssŭm-ni-kka? A-jik chom tŏl i-gŭn kŏt kat-ssŭm-ni-da.

익었습니까? 아직 좀 덜 익은 것 같습니다.

25. These won't be ready to eat for another week or so.

I-gŏ-sŭn a-jik il-tchu-il-tchŭm tŏ i-ssŏ-ya mŏ-gŭl ssu i-ssŭl kkŏ-sim-ni-da.

이것은 아직 일주일쯤 더 있어야 먹을 수 있을 것입니다.

26. Would you like to have your purchases delivered to your home?

Sa-sin mul-gŏ-nŭl taek-kka-ji pae-dal-hae tŭ-ril-kka-yo?

사신 물건을 댁까지 배달해 드릴까요?

---

orange(*o-ren-ji*)…오렌지
regular(*chŏng-gyu-ŭi*)…정규의
expense(*pi-yong*)…비용

customer(*ko-gaek*)…고객
price(*ka-gyŏk*)…가격

27. Yes, please. For I still have many other things to buy.

Kŭ-rŏ-k'e hae chu-sip-ssi-o. A-jik sal kkŏ-si ma-ni i-ssŭ-ni-kka-yo.

그렇게 해 주십시오. 아직 살 것이 많이 있으니까요.

28. I'll dispatch our delivery boy right away.

Pae-dal-ha-nŭn a-i-rŭl chŭk-ssi po-nae-get-ssŭm-ni-da.

배달하는 아이를 즉시 보내겠습니다.

29. I'll be back again tomorrow.

Nae-il ta-si o-get-ssŭm-ni-da.

내일 다시 오겠습니다.

30. Thank you.

Kam-sa-ham-ni-da.

감사합니다.

At a Furniture Store

Ka-gu-jŏ-me-sŏ(가구점에서)

1. What kinds of furniture are you looking for?

Ŏ-ttŏn chong-nyu-ŭi ka-gu-rŭl ch'a-jŭ-sim-ni-kka?

어떤 종류의 가구를 찾으십니까?

2. Could you please show me around?

Chom po-yŏ chu-si-get-ssŭm-ni-kka?

좀 보여 주시겠습니까?

3. What types of furniture are you interested in?

Ŏ-ttŏn mo-yang-ŭi ka-gu-ga ma-ŭ-me tŭ-sim-ni-kka?

어떤 모양의 가구가 마음에 드십니까?

4. What kind of curtains would you suggest for

Ch'im-sil ch'ang-mu-ne-nŭn ŏ-ttŏn chong-nyu-ŭi k'ŏ-t'ŭ-ni cho-k'et-

---

purchase(*sa-da*)…사다
furniture(*ka-gu*)…가구
furniture store(*ka-gu-jŏm*)…가구점
window(*ch'ang-mun*)…창문
trouble(*su-go*)…수고

table(*t'ak-tcha*)…탁자
suggest(*che-an-ha-da*)…제안하다
repair(*su-ri*)…수리
shape(*mo-yang*)…모양
desire(*wŏn-ha-da*)…원하다

bedroom windows?

ssŭm-ni-kka?

침실 창문에는 어떤 종류의 커튼이
좋겠습니까?

5. Here are some speci-
mens.

*Yŏ-gi myŏt kka-ji kyŏn-bo-ni it-ssŭm-
ni-da.*

여기 몇 가지 견본이 있습니다.

6. What furnishings would
I need in my bedroom?
Could you give me some
idea?

*Ch'im-si-re-nŭn ŏ-ttŏn ka-gu-ga p'i-
ryo-ha-get-ssŭm-ni-kka? Mwŏ-ga
cho-ŭn-ji mal-ssŭm-hae chu-si-get-
ssŭm-ni-kka?*

침실에는 어떤 가구가 필요하겠습
니까? 뭐가 좋은지 말씀해 주시
겠습니까?

7. First of all you will need
beds. Now, we have se-
veral kinds of them. You
will also need a dressing
table, a floor lamp, pos-
sibly a bookcase, and of
course a wardrobe. If
you have a baby, a cot
would also be necessary.

*Mu-ŏ-ppo-da-do ch'im-dae-ga p'i-ryo-
hal kkŏ-sim-ni-da. Myŏt kka-ji
chong-nyu-ŭi ch'im-dae-ga it-
ssŭm-ni-da. TTo, hwa-jang-dae,
sŭ-t'aen-dŭ, a-ma ch'aek-tchang-do
p'i-ryo-ha-get-kko, mul-ron o-
tchang-do i-ssŏ-ya hal kkŏ-sim-ni-
da. Ae-gi-ga i-ssŭ-si-myŏn yu-a-
yong ch'im-dae-do p'i-ryo-hal kkŏ-
sim-ni-da.*

무엇보다도 침대가 필요할 것입니
다. 몇 가지 종류의 침대가 있습
니다. 또, 화장대, 스탠드, 아마

---

bedroom(*ch'im-sil*)…침실
dressing table(*hwa-jang-dae*)…화장대
bookcase(*ch'aek-tchang*)…책장
ornamental(*chang-sik*)…장식

cot(*ka-ni ch'im-dae*)…간이 침대
old fashions(*ko-p'ung*)…고풍
necessary(*p'i-ryo-han*)…필요한
curtion(*k'ŏ-t'ŭn*)…커튼

책장도 필요하겠고, 물론 옷장도 있어야 할 것입니다. 애기가 있으시면 유아용 침대도 필요할 것입니다.

8. I think pale green curtains made out of silk would be ideal for the bedroom.

Che saeng-ga-gŭ-ro-nŭn kyŏn-sa-ro tchan yŏn-ch'o-rok-ssaek ch'ŏ-ni ch'im-sil ch'ang-mu-ne-nŭn cho-ŭ-ri-ra saeng-gak-doem-ni-da.

제 생각으로는 견사로 짠 연초록색 천이 침실 창문에는 좋으리라 생각됩니다.

9. I need a sideboard to keep all the tableware and silver.

Sik-ssa to-gu-wa ŭn-sik-kki tŭng-ŭl nŏ-ŏ tul ch'an-tchang-i p'i-ryo-ham-ni-da.

식사 도구와 은식기 등을 넣어 둘 찬장이 필요합니다.

10. Here's a sideboard with an exceptionally fine mirror and attractive drawers.

Yŏ-gi a-ju mŏ-tchin kŏ-ul-gwa mo-yang in-nŭn sŏ-ra-bi tal-lin ch'an-tchang-i it-ssŭm-ni-da.

여기 아주 멋진 거울과 모양 있는 서랍이 달린 찬장이 있습니다.

11. That looks very nice, but I'm afraid it is altogether too large for my dining room. I want

Mae-u mŏ-sit-kkun-yo. Kŭ-rŏ-na u-ri chip sik-ttang-e-nŭn nŏ-mu k'ŭl kkŏt kat-ssŭm-ni-da. Chom-dŏ cho-ch'ol-han kŏ-si i-ssŏt-ssŭ-myŏn

---

silk(*pi-dan*)…비단
sideboard(*ch'an-tchang*)…찬장
tableware(*sik-ssa to-gu*)…식사 도구
iron(*ch'ŏl-tche*)…철제
mirror(*kŏ-ul*)…거울

attractive(*mae-ryŏk in-nŭn*)…매력 있는
drawer(*sŏ-rap*)…서랍
dining room(*sik-ttang*)…식당
compact(*cho-ch'ol-han*)…조촐한

something far more compact.

cho-k'et-ssŭm-ni-da.

매우 멋있군요. 그러나 우리 집 식당에는 너무 클 것 같습니다. 좀더 조촐한 것이 있었으면 좋겠습니다.

12. Do you like steeltube furniture?

Ch'ŏl-tche ka-gu-rŭl cho-a-ha-sim-ni-kka?

철제 가구를 좋아하십니까?

13. No, I think it looks too special. I prefer the usual furniture.

A-nim-ni-da. Che saeng-ga-ge-nŭn nŏ-mu pyŏl-ra po-i-nŭn kŏt kat-ssŭm-ni-da. Po-t'ong ka-gu-ga tŏ chot-ssŭm-ni-da.

아닙니다. 제 생각에는 너무 별나 보이는 것 같습니다. 보통 가구가 더 좋습니다.

14. I will show you some excellent sofas and easy-chairs made of bamboo and also of rattan.

Tae-na-mu-wa tŭng-na-mu-ro man-dŭn hul-ryung-han sso-p'a-wa al-lak ŭi-ja-rŭl po-yŏ tŭ-ri-get-ssŭm-ni-da.

대나무와 등나무로 만든 훌륭한 소파와 안락 의자를 보여 드리겠습니다.

15. This living room set costs-only 500,000 won, including the cushions.

I kŏ-sil sse-t'ŭ-nŭn k'u-ssyŏn-kka-ji p'o-ham-hae-sŏ tan-ji o-sim-man wŏn-im-ni-da.

이 거실 세트는 쿠션까지 포함해서 단지 오십만 원입니다.

---

fantastic(*hwan-sang-jŏ-gin*)…환상적인
easy-chair(*al-lak ŭi-ja*)…안락 의자
stove(*nal-lo*)…난로

sofa(*so-p'a*)…소파
bamboo(*tae-na-mu*)…대나무
rattan(*tŭng-na-mu*)…등나무

16. That's very reasonable. I might order a set when my new house is ready.

Chŏk-ttang-han kap-ssim-ni-da. Sae chi-bi ma-ryŏn-doe-myŏn han sse-t'ŭ chu-mun-hae-ya toe-get-ssŭm-ni-da.

적당한 값입니다. 새 집이 마련되면 한 세트 주문해야 되겠습니다.

17. I want a stove. Do you have some good stove?

Nal-lo-rŭl ha-na sa-go sip-ssŭm-ni-da. Cho-ŭn nal-lo-ga it-ssŭm-ni-kka?

난로를 하나 사고 싶습니다. 좋은 난로가 있습니까?

18. How do you light this kerosene stove?

I sŏ-gyu nal-lo-nŭn ŏ-ttŏ-k'e pu-rŭl pu-ch'im-ni-kka?

이 석유 난로는 어떻게 불을 붙입니까?

19. It's very simple. You just turn up the wick like this and light it.

A-ju kan-ttan-ham-ni-da. I-rŏ-k'e sim-ji-rŭl t'ŭ-rŏ ol-lyŏ-sŏ pu-rŭl pu-ch'i-myŏn toem-ni-da.

아주 간단합니다. 이렇게 심지를 틀어 올려서 불을 붙이면 됩니다.

20. How often do you have to change the wick?

Ŏl-ma-ma-ne sim-ji-rŭl ka-ra-ya ham-ni-kka?

얼마만에 심지를 갈아야 합니까?

21. One wick will usually last one season for normal use.

Sim-ji ha-na-ro po-t'ong han-ch'ŏ-rŭn ssŭm-ni-da.

심지 하나로 보통 한철은 씁니다.

22. Don't you have to pump it up?

Pŏm-p'ŭ-rŭl nul-lŏ chu-ji a-na-do toem-ni-kka?

펌프를 눌러 주지 않아도 됩니까?

---

wick(*sim-ji*)···심지   normal(*po-t'ong*)···보통

23. No. There's no air pressure involved.

Ne, kong-gi am-nyŏk-kkwa-nŭn kwan-gye-ga ŏp-ssŭm-ni-da.

네, 공기 압력과는 관계가 없습니다.

24. I would like to see some padlocks that are burglarproof.

Tt-nan pang-ji-yong maeng-kkong-i cha-mul-ssoe-rŭl myŏt kkae ku-gyŏng-haet-ssŭ-myŏn ham-ni-da.

도난 방지용 맹꽁이 자물쇠를 몇 개 구경했으면 합니다.

25. Here's a patented padlock that would puzzle any burglar.

Ŏ-ttŏn to-du-gi-ra-do yŏl-gi him-dŭn t'ŭ-k'ŏ-p'um maeng-kkong-i cha-mul-ssoe-ga it-ssŭm-ni-da.

어떤 도둑이라도 열기 힘든 특허품 맹꽁이 자물쇠가 있습니다.

26. It's the very thing I want. Where is the key?

Che-ga pa-ro ch'at-ttŏn kŏ-si-ro-gun-yo. Yŏl-ssoe-nŭn ŏ-di it-ssŭm-ni-kka?

제가 바로 찾던 것이로군요. 열쇠는 어디 있습니까?

27. Right here. If you lose it, we can always supply you with another.

Yŏ-gi it-ssŭm-ni-da. I-jŏ-bŏ-ri-si-myŏn ta-rŭn kŏ-sŭ-ro tŭ-ri-get-ssŭm-ni-da.

여기 있습니다. 잊어버리시면 다른 것으로 드리겠습니다.

28. Then I'll take it.

Kŭ-rŏm kŭ-gŏl sa-get-ssŭm-ni-da.

그럼 그걸 사겠습니다.

---

padlock(*cha-mul-ssoe*)…자물쇠
burglarproof(*to-nan pang-ji-yong*)…
　도난 방지용

puzzle(*tang-hwang*)…당황
burglar(*kang-do*)…강도
pressure(*am-nyŏk*)…압력

At a Shoe Store

1. I want a pair of black shoes.

2. How do you want your shoes, custom-made or ready-made?

3. They are a little bit tight.

4. Please try this pair on.

5. I'm sure you'll find this pair very comfortable.

6. Here's a larger size.

7. How long must I wait if I want them custom-made?

8. It will take about a week, sir.

9. I won't be able to wait

Che-hwa-jŏ-me-sŏ(제화점에서)

Kŏm-jŏng-saek ku-du-rŭl han k'yŏl-le sa-go sip-ssŭm-ni-da.
검정색 구두를 한 켤레 사고 싶습니다.

Ma-ch'um ku-du-ro ha-si-get-ssŭm-ni-kka, ki-sŏng-hwa-ro ha-si-get-ssŭm-ni-kka?
맞춤 구두로 하시겠습니까, 기성화로 하시겠습니까?

Pa-ri chom cho-i-nŭn-gun-yo.
발이 좀 조이는군요.

I ku-du-rŭl han-bŏn si-nŏ po-sip-ssi-o.
이 구두를 한번 신어 보십시오.

I ku-du-ga mae-u p'yŏn-ha-sil kkŏm-ni-da.
이 구두가 매우 편하실 겁니다.

Yŏ-gi chom k'ŭn-ge it-ssŭm-ni-da.
여기 좀 큰게 있습니다.

Ma-ch'u-ŏ si-nŭ-ryŏ-myŏn ŏl-ma-na ki-da-ryŏ-ya ham-ni-kka?
맞추어 신으려면 얼마나 기다려야 합니까?

Yak il-tchu-i-ri kŏl-rim-ni-da.
약 일주일이 걸립니다.

Kŭ-rŏ-k'e o-rae-ttong-an ki-da-ril

---

shoemaker's store(*che-hwa-jŏm*)…제화점

ready-made shoes(*ki-sŏng-hwa*)…기성화

that long. Show me some ready-made shoes.

ssu-ga ŏp-ssŭm-ni-da. Ki-sŏng-hwa-rŭl myŏt k'yŏl-le po-yŏ chu-sip-ssi-o.

그렇게 오랫동안 기다릴 수가 없습니다. 기성화를 몇 켤레 보여 주십시오.

10. How do you like these?

I-gŏ-ttŭ-rŭn ŏ-ttŏt-ssŭm-ni-kka?

이것들은 어떻습니까?

11. They look very nice. Let me try this pair on.

A-ju mŏ-tchin kŏt kat-ssŭm-ni-da. Han-bŏn si-nŏ po-get-ssŭm-ni-da.

아주 멋진 것 같습니다. 한번 신어 보겠습니다.

12. Try this pair on. Here is a shoehorn.

I-gŏ-sŭl si-nŏ po-sip-ssi-o. Yŏ-gi ku-du chu-gŏ-gi it-ssŭm-ni-da.

이것을 신어 보십시오. 여기 구두 주걱이 있습니다.

13. This pair fits perfectly.

I-gŏ-si a-ju kkok mat-ssŭm-ni-da.

이것이 아주 꼭 맞습니다.

14. What are those shoes like that look like canoes?

Chŏ k'a-nu-ga-ch'ï saeng-gin sin-ba-rŭn mu-ŏ-sim-ni-kka?

저 카누같이 생긴 신발은 무엇입니까?

15. They're traditional Korean housewifes rubber shoes. They are one of the best souvenirs to take back home with. You won't find them

Chŏn-t'ong-jŏ-gin han-guk chu-bu-dŭ-rŭi ko-mu-si-ni-ra-nŭn kŏ-sim-ni-da. Chi-bŭ-ro ka-ji-go ka-sil ka-jang hul-lyung-han ki-nyŏm-p'um chung-ŭi ha-na-im-ni-da. Se-gye ŏ-nŭ ko-se-sŏ-do i-rŏn

---

shoemaker(*che-hwa-gong*)…제화공
repairman(*su-sŏn-gong*)…수선공

mending(*su-sŏn*)…수선
sole leather(*ch'ang*)…창

anywhere in the world.

sin-bal-dŭ-rŭn ch'a-ja-bo-ji mo-t'al kkŏ-sim-ni-da.

전통적인 한국 주부들의 고무신이라는 것입니다. 집으로 가지고 가실 가장 훌륭한 기념품 중의 하나입니다. 세계 어느 곳에서도 이런 신발들은 찾아보지 못할 것입니다.

16. Is there anything else we can do for you?

TTo sal kkŏ-si ŏp-ssŭ-sim-ni-kka?

또 살 것이 없으십니까?

17. Yes. I want a pair of man's rubber shoes, too. Where are they?

It-ssŭm-ni-da. Nam-ja-yong ko-mu-sin-do han k'yŏl-le sa-go sip-ssŭm-ni-da. Kŭ-gŏ-ttŭ-rŭn ŏ-di it-ssŭm-ni-kka?

있습니다. 남자용 고무신도 한 켤레 사고 싶습니다. 그것들은 어디 있습니까?

18. Let me show you. Man's rubber shoes look like LST boats.

Po-yŏ tŭ-ri-jyo. Nam-ja-dŭ-rŭi ko-mu-si-nŭn el-es-t'i po-t'ŭ-ch'ŏ-rŏm saeng-gyŏt-ssŭm-ni-da.

보여 드리죠. 남자들의 고무신은 엘. 에스. 티 보트처럼 생겼습니다.

19. May I try them on?

Han-bŏn si-nŏ pwa-do chot-ssŭm-ni-kka?

한번 신어 봐도 좋습니까?

20. Yes, you may. I'm

Chot-ssŭm-ni-da. Si-nŏ po-sip-ssi-o.

---

traditional(*chŏn-t'ong-jŏ-gin*)···전통적인

emergency repair(*ŭng-gŭp su-sŏn*)··· 응급 수선

souvenir(*ki-nyŏm-p'um*)···기념품

rubber shoes(*ko-mu-sin*)···고무신

shoelace(*ku-du-kkŭn*)···구두끈

scoks(*yang-mal*)···양말

sure you'll find them very comfortable.	*A-ju p'yŏ-nan-ha-sil kkŏm-ni-da.* 좋습니다. 신어 보십시오. 아주 편 안하실 겁니다.
21. Oh, Yes. They are very comfortable. Give me these two pairs.	*Kŭ-rŏ-k'un-yo. A-ju p'yŏ-nan-ham-ni-da. I-gŏl-ro tu k'yŏl-le-man chu-sip-ssi-o.* 그렇군요. 아주 편안합니다. 이걸 로 두 켤레만 주십시오.
22. Do you have woman's shoes?	*Yŏ-ja-yong ku-du-do it-ssŭm-ni-kka?* 여자용 구두도 있습니까?
23. Yes, we have. Do you want low heels or high?	*Ye, it-ssŭm-ni-da. Ro-u-hil-lo mal-im-ni-kka, ha-i-hil-lo mal-im-ni-kka?* 예, 있습니다. 로우힐로 말입니까, 하이힐로 말입니까?
24. High heels, please.	*Ha-i-hil-im-ni-da.* 하이힐입니다.
25. What color would you prefer?	*Mu-sŭn sae-gŭ-ro wŏn-ha-sim-ni-kka?* 무슨 색으로 원하십니까?
26. I like brown.	*Kal-ssae-gŭ-ro ha-get-ssŭm-ni-da.* 갈색으로 하겠습니다.
27. They're much too large.	*Nŏ-mu k'ŭm-ni-da.* 너무 큽니다.
28. Here's a smaller size.	*Yŏ-gi cho-gŭm cha-gŭn kŏ-si it-ssŭm-ni-da.* 여기 조금 작은 것이 있습니다.
29. These are too tight.	*Nŏ-mu cho-i-nŭn-gun-yo. Pa-rŭl*

---

footwear shop(*sin-bal ka-ge*)…신발 가게

rubbers(*tŏt-ssin*)…덧신
metal plate(*ching*)…징

They pinch.	*mum-ni-da.*
	너무 조이는군요. 발을 뭅니다.
30. Maybe these are the right size.	*A-ma i ch'i-ssu-ga chŏk-ttang-hal kkŏ-sim-ni-da.*
	아마 이 치수가 적당할 것입니다.
31. Yes, but they're too narrow. I want widen size.	*Kŭ-rŏ-k'un-yo. Ha-ji-man nŏ-mu chop-ssŭm-ni-da. Chom-dŏ nŏl-bŭn ch'i-ssu-ga i-ssŏt-ssŭ-myŏn ham-ni-da.*
	그렇군요. 하지만 너무 좁습니다. 좀더 넓은 치수가 있었으면 합니다.
32. How's this pair?	*I-gŏ-sŭn ŏ-ttŏt-ssŭm-ni-kka?*
	이것은 어떻습니까?
33. This pair is very comfortable. What's the price?	*I-gŏ-si a-ju p'yŏ-nan-ha-gun-yo. Ŏl-ma-im-ni-kka?*
	이것이 아주 편안하군요. 얼마입니까?
34. Seven thousand won. The discount is a favor we extend to foreign customers.	*Ch'il-ch'ŏn wŏn-im-ni-da. Woe-gu-gin ko-gaek-ttŭ-re-ge tŭ-ri-nŭn t'ŭk-ppyŏl ha-rin-im-ni-da.*
	칠천 원입니다. 외국인 고객들에게 드리는 특별 할인입니다.
35. Thank you. I'll take this pair.	*Kam-sa-ham-ni-da. I-gŏl sa-get-ssŭm-ni-da.*
	감사합니다. 이걸 사겠습니다.

---

pinch(*mul-da*)…물다
low heel(*ro-u-hil*)…로우힐
low shoes(*tan-hwa*)…단화
unloading sale(*chae-go-p'um ch'ong-jŏng-ni*)…재고품 총정리

narrow(*cho-bŭn*)…좁은
widen(*nŏl-p'i-da*)…넓히다
boots(*chang-hwa*)…장화
salesclerk(*p'an-mae-wŏn*)…판매원
tight(*kkok kki-nŭn*)…꼭 끼는

At a Leather Goods Store

1. I want to buy a brief-case.

2. Do you want one of a large size or a medium-size one?

3. I want one that will hold ordinary letterpaper sized documents without folding.

4. Here's quite a fancy one made of alligator skin.

5. It looks very nice. How much is it?

6. Well, as you may pro-

P'i-hyŏk-ssang-e-sŏ
(피혁상에서)

Sŏ-ryu ka-bang-ŭl ha-na sa-go sip-ssŭm-ni-da.

서류 가방을 하나 사고 싶습니다.

K'ŭn kŏ-sŭ-ro sa-si-get-ssŭm-ni-kka, a-ni-myŏn chung-gan-ch'i-ro sa-si-get-ssŭm-ni-kka?

큰 것으로 사시겠습니까, 아니면 중간치로 사시겠습니까?

Po-t'ong p'yŏn-ji k'ŭ-gi-ŭi sŏ-ryu-rŭl chŏp-tchi an-k'o nŏ-ŭl ssu in-nŭn kŏ-sŭl sa-go sip-ssŭm-ni-da.

보통 편지 크기의 서류를 접지 않고 넣을 수 있는 것을 사고 싶습니다.

Yŏ-gi a-gŏ ka-ju-gŭ-ro man-dŭn a-ju hul-lyung-han kŏ-si it-ssŭm-ni-da.

여기 악어 가죽으로 만든 아주 훌륭한 것이 있습니다.

Kwaen-ch'a-nŭn kŏt kat-ssŭm-ni-da. Ŏl-ma-im-ni-kka?

괜찮은 것 같습니다. 얼마입니까?

I-mi chal a-si-get-tchi-man, a-gŏ ka-

---

alligator skin(*a-gŏ ka-juk*)…악어 가죽

favor(*ho-ŭi*)…호의

leather(*ka-juk*)…가죽

leather goods store(*p'i-hyŏk-ssang*)…피혁상

briefcase(*sŏ-ryu ka-bang*)…서류 가방

decument(*sŏ-ryu*)…서류

synthetic leather(*in-jo p'i-hyŏk*)…인조 피혁

both(*yang-tchok*)…양쪽

fold(*chŏp-tta*)…접다

bably know, alligator
skin is about ten times
as costly as ordinary leather. This one costs 300,
000 won.

ju-gŭn po-t'ong ka-juk-ppo-da yŏl
ppae kka-ryang kap-ssi pi-ssam-ni-
da. I-gŏ-sŭn sam-sim-man wŏn-
im-ni-da.

이미 잘 아시겠지만, 악어 가죽은
보통 가죽보다 열 배 가량 값이 비
쌉니다. 이것은 삼십만 원입니다.

7. That's quite a sum. I
couldn't afford to such
luxury.

Ŏm-ch'ŏng-nan kap-ssi-gun-yo. Kŭ-
rŏ-k'e sa-ch'i-han kŏ-sŭn sal ssu-ga
ŏp-ssŭm-ni-da.

엄청난 값이군요. 그렇게 사치한
것은 살 수가 없습니다.

8. Is there any cheaper
one made of ordinary
leather ?

Po-t'ong ka-ju-gŭ-ro man-dŭn chom-
dŏ ssan kŏ-si ŏp-ssŭm-ni-kka ?

보통 가죽으로 만든 좀더 싼 것이
없습니까 ?

9. Yes, we have. We are
now on the stage of int-
roducing this new type
of briefcase to the mar-
ket for the firse time.
How about this one ?

Ye, it-ssŭm-ni-da. U-rin i-je ch'ŏ-ŭ-
mŭ-ro i sae mo-yang-ŭi sŏ-ryu ka-
bang-ŭl si-jang-e nae-no-k'i si-ja-
k'aet-ssŭm-ni-da. I-gŏ-sŭn ŏ-ttŏt-
ssŭm-ni-kka ?

예, 있습니다. 우린 이제 처음으로
이 새 모양의 서류 가방을 시장에
내놓기 시작했습니다. 이것은 어떻
습니까 ?

10. All right. I'll take it.

Chot-ssŭm-ni-da.   Kŭ-gŏl   sa-get-

---

luxury(*sa-ch'i*)…사치
charge(*yo-gŭm*)…요금
human work(*in-gong*)…인공

fancy(*hwan-sang*)…환상
shape(*mo-yang-sae*)…모양새

By the way, how do you keep this bag well-polished?

ssŭm-ni-da. Kŭ-ri-go i ka-bang-ŭl ŏ-ttŏ-k'e yu-nŭl chal nae-ji-yo?

좋습니다. 그걸 사겠습니다. 그리고 이 가방을 어떻게 윤을 잘 내지요?

11. Here's a can of polish which we will let you have free of charge. Apply a small quantity at intervals of about once a week and rub with a piece of cloth. It'll give the bag a wonderful luster.

Yŏ-gi ttang-nŭn ya-gi in-nŭn-de kŭ-nyang han t'ong tŭ-ri-get-ssŭm-ni-da. Il-tchu-il-ma-da cho-gŭm-ssik ya-gŭl pa-rŭ-go, hŏng-gŏp cho-ga-gŭ-ro mun-ji-rŭ-sip-ssi-o. Kŭ-rŏ-myŏn a-ju ka-bang-i yu-ni nal kkŏ-sim-ni-da.

여기 닦는 약이 있는데 그냥 한 통 드리겠습니다. 일주일마다 조금씩 약을 바르고, 헝겊 조각으로 문지르십시오. 그러면 아주 가방이 윤이 날 것입니다.

12. We will give you a special reduction of five percent.

O p'ŏ-sen-t'ŭ t'ŭk-ppyŏl ha-ri-nŭl hae tŭ-ri-get-ssŭm-ni-da.

오 퍼센트 특별 할인을 해 드리겠습니다.

13. The price depends on the quality of the leather.

Kap-ssŭn ka-ju-gŭi chi-re tal-lyŏt-ssŭm-ni-da.

값은 가죽의 질에 달렸습니다.

14. This is made of genuine leather and that's made of vinyl.

I-gŏ-sŭn chin-tcha ka-ju-gŭ-ro man-dŭ-rŏ-jyŏt-kko, chŏ-gŏ-sŭn pi-nil-lo man-dŭ-rŏ-jyŏ it-ssŭm-ni-da.

---

quantity(*yang*)…양
luster(*yun*)…윤
profit(*i-ik*)…이익

genuine(*chin-tcha*)…진짜
selling wholesale(*to-mae*)…도매
retail(*so-mae*)…소매

이것은 진짜 가죽으로 만들어졌고, 저것은 비닐로 만들어져 있습니다.

15. I would like to see some trunks.

T'ŭ-rŏng-k'ŭ chom ku-gyŏng-ha-go sip-ssŭm-ni-da.

트렁크 좀 구경하고 싶습니다.

16. What kind of trunk do you want to buy? The price depends on the quality of the leather and the way in which the trunk was manufactured.

Ŏ-ttŏn chong-nyu-ŭi t'ŭ-rŏng-k'ŭ-rŭl sa-sil-lyŏ-go ha-sim-ni-kka? Ka-ju-gŭi chil-gwa t'ŭ-rŏng-k'ŭ-ga man-dŭ-rŏ-jin kong-jŏng-e tta-ra kap-ssi t'ŭl-rim-ni-da.

어떤 종류의 트렁크를 사실려고 하십니까? 가죽의 질과 트렁크가 만들어진 공정에 따라 값이 틀립니다.

17. I'm tempted to buy that large one but I don't like the color.

Chŏ k'ŭn kŏ-sŭl sa-go si-p'ŭn-de, saek-kka-ri cho-ch'i an-ssŭm-ni-da.

저 큰 것을 사고 싶은데, 색깔이 좋지 않습니다.

18. We have the same trunk in several other colors. How about black?

TTo-kka-t'ŭn mo-yang-ŭi saek-kka-ri ta-rŭn kŏ-si it-ssŭm-ni-da. Kŏm-jŏng-sae-gŭn ŏ-ttŏt-ssŭm-ni-kka?

똑같은 모양의 색깔이 다른 것이 있습니다. 검정색은 어떻습니까?

19. Black color would be very nice. How do you open this trunk?

Kŏm-jŏng saek-kka-ri a-ju cho-k'et-ssŭm-ni-da. I t'ŭ-rŏng-k'ŭ-nŭn ŏ-ttŏ-k'e yŏm-ni-kka?

검정 색깔이 아주 좋겠습니다. 이

---

trunk(*t'ŭ-rŏng-k'ŭ*)…트렁크   manufacture(*che-jo-ha-da*)…제조하다

트렁크는 어떻게 엽니까?

20. All you have to do is to press this button on the lock.

Cha-mul-ssoe-e tal-lin tan-ch'u-man nu-rŭ-myŏn toem-ni-da.

자물쇠에 달린 단추만 누르면 됩니다.

21. And how do you close it?

Ta-dŭl ttae-nŭn ŏ-ttŏ-k'e ham-ni-kka?

닫을 때는 어떻게 합니까?

22. You press the button again, and snap the lock.

Tan-ch'u-rŭl ta-si nu-rŭ-go cha-mul-ssoe-rŭl cham-gŭ-si-myŏn toem-ni-da.

단추를 다시 누르고 자물쇠를 잠그시면 됩니다.

23. That red trunk is made of artifical leather.

Chŏ pul-gŭn-sae-gŭi t'ŭ-rŏng-k'ŭ-nŭn in-jo ka-ju-gŭ-ro man-dŭ-rŏt-ssŭm-ni-da.

저 붉은색의 트렁크는 인조 가죽으로 만들었습니다.

24. Do you think this bag will hold very much?

I ka-bang-ŭn ma-ni tŭ-rŏ kam-ni-kka?

이 가방은 많이 들어 갑니까?

25. Of course. You will notice that the bottom expands and contracts.

Mul-lon-i-jyo. A-si-da-si-p'i mi-ppa-da-gi p'yŏ-jyŏt-tta cho-p'yŏ-jyŏt-tta ham-ni-da.

---

artificial(*in-jo-ŭi*)…인조의
suitcase(*yŏ-haeng-yong ka-bang*)…여행용 가방
firm(*t'ŭn-t'ŭn-han*)…튼튼한
button(*tan-ch'u*)…단추
use(*sa-yong*)…사용

vinyl(*pi-nil*)…비닐
press(*nu-rŭ-da*)…누르다
amount of work(*kong-jŏng*)…공정
leather goods(*ka-juk che-p'um*)…가죽 제품

물론이죠. 아시다시피 밑바닥이 펴졌다 좁혀졌다 합니다.

26. Do you have some wallets? I need one.

Chi-gap-tto it-ssŭm-ni-kka? Chi-gap-tto p'i-ryo-han-de-yo.

지갑도 있습니까? 지갑도 필요한데요.

27. Here's a very popular wallet. It will hold all bills without folding.

Yŏ-gi mae-u yu-haeng-ha-nŭn chi-ga-bi it-ssŭm-ni-da. Mo-dŭn chi-p'ye-rŭl chŏp-tchi an-k'o nŏ-ŭl ssu it-ssŭm-ni-da.

여기 매우 유행하는 지갑이 있습니다. 모든 지폐를 접지 않고 넣을 수 있습니다.

28. I'm sure you've made a wise purchase.

A-ju chal sa-syŏt-tta-go saeng-ga-k'am-ni-da.

아주 잘 사셨다고 생각합니다.

At a Jewelry Store

Po-sŏk-ssang-e-sŏ(보석상에서)

1. I'm the manager of this store. Can I be of any assistance to you?

I sang-jŏ-mŭi chi-bae-in-im-ni-da. Mu-ŏ-sŭl sa-si-get-ssŭm-ni-kka?

이 상점의 지배인입니다. 무엇을 사시겠습니까?

2. I want to see some pearl necklaces.

Chin-ju mok-kkŏ-ri-rŭl ku-gyŏng-ha-go sip-ssŭm-ni-da.

진주 목걸이를 구경하고 싶습니다.

3. Do you want natural

Ch'ŏ-nyŏn chin-ju-rŭl po-si-get-ssŭm-

---

jewelry store(*po-sŏk-ssang*)…보석상
manager(*chi-bae-in*)…지배인
necklace(*mok-kkŏ-ri*)…목걸이
workmanship(*se-gong*)…세공

bottom(*mi-ppa-dak*)…밑바닥
satchel(*mel-ppang-i in-nŭn ka-bang*)…멜빵이 있는 가방
strap(*ka-juk-kkŭn*)…가죽끈

pearls or cultured pearls? We have both kinds.

ni-kka, yang-sik chin-ju-rŭl po-si-get-ssŭm-ni-kka? Tu ka-ji mo-du ku-bi-doe-ŏ it-ssŭm-ni-da.

천연 진주를 보시겠습니까, 양식 진주를 보시겠습니까? 두 가지 모두 구비되어 있습니다.

4. Which are more valuable?

Ŏ-ttŏn kŏ-si tŏ kap-ssi na-gam-ni-kka?

어떤 것이 더 값이 나갑니까?

5. Natural pearls, of course. However, some cultured pearls have equal luster and are just as beautiful.

Mul-lon ch'ŏ-nyŏn chin-ju-im-ni-da. Kŭ-rŏ-na sil-tche-ro yang-sik chin-ju-do kwang-t'ae-gi-na a-rŭm-da-u-mi ttok-kkat-ssŭm-ni-da.

물론 천연 진주입니다. 그러나 실제로 양식 진주도 광택이나 아름다움이 똑같습니다.

6. We have some Korean cultured pearls as well.

Han-guk-ssan yang-sik chin-ju-do it-ssŭm-ni-da.

한국산 양식 진주도 있습니다.

7. How much is this string of pearls you have on display over here?

Yŏ-gi chi-nyŏl-doen i chin-ju mok-kkŏ-ri-nŭn ŏl-ma-na ham-ni-kka?

여기 진열된 이 진주 목걸이는 얼마나 합니까?

8. I'm afraid this one is rather expensive, as it is made of over 50 pearls

Saek-kkal-gwa k'ŭ-gi-ga tto-kka-t'ŭn chin-ju-man o-sip kkae-rŭl ssŏt-kki ttae-mu-ne kap-ssi chom pi-ssam-

---

actually(*sil-tche-ro*)…실제로
string of pearls(*chin-ju mok-kkŏ-ri*)…
진주 목걸이

preserve(*po-jŏn*)…보전
store(*ka-ge*)…가게
appraisal(*kam-jŏng*)…감정

that are absolutely identical in size and color. It costs one million won.

9. That's a fortune !

10. There are many cheaper kinds. For example, this string over here costs only half the amount.

11. It looks very much the same as the other.

12. Haven't you anything cheaper ?

13. Yes, we do. We have strings that are as cheap as thirty thousand won. But I would not recommend them.

ni-da. Paeng-man wŏn-im-ni-da.
색깔과 크기가 똑같은 진주만 오십 개를 썼기 때문에 값이 좀 비쌉니다. 백만 원입니다.

Ŏm-ch'ŏng-nan kap-ssi-gun-yo.
엄청난 값이군요.

Kap-ssi chom ssan kŏt-tto ma-ni it-ssŭm-ni-da. Ye-rŭl tŭ-rŏ, yŏ-gi in-nŭn i mok-kkŏ-ri-nŭn mŏn-jŏ kkŏ-sŭi pan-kkap-ba-kke an-toem-ni-da.
값이 좀 싼 것도 많이 있습니다. 예를 들어, 여기 있는 이 목걸이는 먼저 것의 반값밖에 안됩니다.

Mŏn-jŏ kkŏ-si-na a-ju pi-sŭ-t'a-ge po-im-ni-da.
먼저 것이나 아주 비슷하게 보입니다.

Chom-dŏ ssan kŏ-sŭn ŏp-ssŭm-ni-kka ?
좀더 싼 것은 없습니까 ?

Ye, it-ssŭm-ni-da. sam-sim-man wŏn chŏng-do-ro ssan mok-kkŏ-ri-do it-ssŭm-ni-da-man, kwŏn-hae tŭ-ri-go sip-tchi an-ssŭm-ni-da.
예, 있습니다. 삼십만 원 정도로 싼 목걸이도 있습니다만, 권해 드

---

display(*chi-nyŏl-ha-da*)…진열하다
identical(*ka-t'ŭn*)…같은
similar(*pi-sŭ-t'an*)…비슷한

encourage(*kwŏn-jang*)…권장
example(*ye*)…예
string(*kkŭn*)…끈

리고 싶지 않습니다.

14. Do you have anything else?

15. How about a broach? We have some very nice specimens.

Ta-rŭn kŏ-si tto it-ssŭm-ni-kka?
다른 것이 또 있습니까?

Pŭ-ro-ch'i-nŭn ŏ-ttŏ-sim-ni-kka? A-ju hul-lyung-han mul-gŏ-ni it-ssŭm-ni-da.
브로치는 어떠십니까? 아주 훌륭한 물건이 있습니다.

16. What kind of stone is this?

17. It's a diamond. Don't you think it's very attractive? This broach is really a very fine work of art.

I-gŏ-sŭn mu-sŭn po-sŏk-im-ni-kka?
이것은 무슨 보석입니까?

Ta-i-a-mon-dŭ-im-ni-da. Mae-u a-rŭm-dap-tchi an-ssŭm-ni-kka? I pŭ-ro-ch'i-ya-mal-lo   chŏng-mal hul-lyung-han ye-sul-p'um-im-ni-da.
다이아몬드입니다. 매우 아름답지 않습니까? 이 브로치야말로 정말 훌륭한 예술품입니다.

18. I like it very much, but I'm afraid I don't like the design. Would you show me some other's?

Cho-k'in-han-de ti-ja-i-ni ma-ŭ-me tŭl-ji an-ssŭm-ni-da. Ta-rŭn kŏt tchom po-yŏ chu-si-get-ssŭm-ni-kka?
좋긴한데 디자인이 마음에 들지 않습니다. 다른 것 좀 보여 주시겠습니까?

19. How about this one, a ruby set in a gold

I-gŏ-sŭn ŏ-ttŏt-ssŭm-ni-kka? Kŭ-mŭ-ro na-bi mo-yang-ŭl ti-ja-in-

---

brooch(*pŭ-ro-ch'i*)…브로치
specimen(*kyŏn-bon*)…견본
stone(*po-sŏk*)…보석

design(*ti-ja-in*)…디자인
diamond(*ta-i-a-mon-dŭ*)…다이아몬드
unique(*t'ŭ-gi-han*)…특이한

frame designed as a butterfly. It's very unique.

20. How much is it?

21. It's only thirty thousand won.

22. That's a very steep price for a broach.

23. But you must realize that the ruby is the most precious of precious stones.

24. How about a bracelet? This silver one studded with tiny sapphires and emeralds is one of our bestselling items.

25. Does it go beyond my

hae-sŏ ru-bi-rŭl pa-gŭn kŏ-sim-ni-da. A-ju t'ŭ-gi-han kŏ-sim-ni-da.
이것은 어떻습니까? 금으로 나비 모양을 디자인해서 루비를 박은 것입니다. 아주 특이한 것입니다.

Ŏl-ma-im-ni-kka?
얼마입니까?

Tan-ji sam-sim-man wŏn-im-ni-da.
단지 삼십만 원입니다.

Pŭ-ro-ch'i kap ch'i-go-nŭn nŏ-mu pi-ssam-ni-da.
브로치 값 치고는 너무 비쌉니다.

Ha-ji-man ru-bi-ga po-sŏk chung-e-sŏ-do ka-jang kap-bi-ssan kwi-jung-p'u-mi-ra-nŭn kŏ-sŭl a-syŏ-ya ham-ni-da.
하지만 루비가 보석 중에서도 가장 값비싼 귀중품이라는 것을 아셔야 합니다.

P'al-tchi-nŭn ŏ-ttŏt-ssŭm-ni-kka? I ŭn-p'al-tchi-nŭn sa-p'a-i-ŏ-wa e-me-ral-dŭ-rŭl pa-gŭn kŏ-sin-de che-il chal p'al-lim-ni-da.
팔찌는 어떻습니까? 이 은팔찌는 사파이어와 에메랄드를 박은 것인데 제일 잘 팔립니다.

Che-ga sal ssu in-nŭn aek-ssu-rŭl

---

butterfly(*na-bi*)…나비
amethyst(*cha-su-jŏng*)…자수정

transparency(*t'u-myŏng*)…투명
opacity(*pul-t'u-myŏng*)…불투명

budget?

nŏm-nŭn-ge a-nim-ni-kka?

제가 살 수 있는 액수를 넘는게
아닙니까?

26. I hope these stones are genuine.

Chin-tcha po-sŏk-i-me-nŭn t'ŭl-ri-mi ŏp-kket-tchyo.

진짜 보석임에는 틀림이 없겠죠.

27. Well, please let me think it over. Let me try them on.

Chom saeng-ga-k'ae po-get-ssŭm-ni-da. Han-bŏn kki-wŏ po-get-ssŭm-ni-da.

좀 생각해 보겠습니다. 한번 끼워
보겠습니다.

28. I'm half persuaded to buy them.

Sa-go si-p'ŭn saeng-ga-gi tŭm-ni-da.

사고 싶은 생각이 듭니다.

29. Have you a nice case to go with them?

I-gŏ-sŭl nŏ-ŭl cho-ŭn sang-ja-ga it-ssŭm-ni-kka?

이것을 넣을 좋은 상자가 있습니
까?

30. Yes, the bracelet comes with this beautiful leather case lined with velvet.

It-ssŭm-ni-da. I pel-be-sŭ-ro chu-ri tŭn a-rŭm-da-un ka-juk sang-ja-rŭl ham-kke tŭ-rim-ni-da.

있습니다. 이 벨벳으로 줄이 든
아름다운 가죽 상자를 함께 드립
니다.

31. That's nice.

Chot-ssŭm-ni-da.

좋습니다.

---

ruby(*ru-bi*)…루비
precious(*kwi-jung-han*)…귀중한
content(*ham-nyang*)…함량
platinum(*paek-kkŭm*)…백금

bracelet(*p'al-tchi*)…팔찌
budget(*ye-san*)…예산
genuine(*chin-tcha*)…진짜
topaz(*hwang-su-jŏng*)…황수정

At a Music Store

1. Have you a list of the latest hit songs?

2. Yes, we have many.

3. I want a record of Korean folk songs.

4. Which one do you want? Here are some.

5. I want Arirang.

6. This is it. Miryang Arirang and Chindo Arirang are on the front side and on the back side are recorded Doraji and one more folk song.

Re-k'o-dŭ-sang-e-sŏ
(레코드상에서)

Ch'oe-gŭ-nŭi hi-t'ŭ ssong ri-sŭ-t'ŭ-ga it-ssŭm-ni-kka?
최근의 히트 송 리스트가 있습니까?

Ye, yŏ-rŏ ka-ji-ga it-ssŭm-ni-da.
예, 여러 가지가 있습니다.

Han-guk mi-nyo re-k'o-dŭ-rŭl han chang sal-lyŏ-go ham-ni-da.
한국 민요 레코드를 한 장 살려고 합니다.

Ŏ-nŭ kŏ-sŭl wŏn-ha-sim-ni-kka? Yŏ-gi myŏt kka-ji-ga it-ssŭm-ni-da.
어느 것을 원하십니까? 여기 몇 가지가 있습니다.

A-ri-rang-ŭl wŏn-ham-ni-da.
아리랑을 원합니다.

I-gŏ-si pa-ro kŭ-gŏ-sim-ni-da. Am-myŏ-ne-nŭn mi-ryang-a-ri-rang-gwa chin-do-a-ri-rang-i it-kko, twin-myŏ-ne-nŭn to-ra-ji-wa ta-rŭn han ka-ji mi-nyo-ga su-rok-doe-ŏ it-ssŭm-ni-da.
이것이 바로 그것입니다. 앞면에는

---

persuade(*sŏl-ttŭ-k'a-da*)···설득하다
velvet(*pel-bet*)···벨벳
music store(*re-k'o-dŭ ka-ge*)···레코드 가게

folk song(*mi-nyo*)···민요
composition(*chak-kkok*)···작곡
arrangement(*p'yŏn-gok*)···편곡
choral(*hap-ch'ang-gok*)···합창곡

밀양아리랑과 진도아리랑이 있고, 뒷면에는 도라지와 다른 한 가지 민요가 수록되어 있습니다.

7. I want to hear this one.

I-gŏ-sŭl tŭt-kko sip-ssŭm-ni-da.

이것을 듣고 싶습니다.

8. I wonder if I could hear the tune on your hi-fi.

Ha-i-p'a-i chŏn-ch'u-gŭ-ro tŭ-rŏ-bwa-ssŭ-myŏn cho-k'et-ssŭm-ni-da.

하이파이 전축으로 들어봤으면 좋겠습니다.

9. Have you a record of classical Korean Pansori?

Han-guk ko-jŏ-nin p'an-sso-ri re-k'o-dŭ-ga it-ssŭm-ni-kka?

한국 고전인 판소리 레코드가 있습니까?

10. I'm sorry. It's sold out.

Mi-an-ham-ni-da. Mo-du p'al-lyŏt-ssŭm-ni-da.

미안합니다. 모두 팔렸습니다.

11. Can you get it for me?

Ha-na ku-hae chu-si-get-ssŭm-ni-kka?

하나 구해 주시겠습니까?

12. Yes, I can.

Ye, ku-hae tŭ-ril ssu it-ssŭm-ni-da.

예, 구해 드릴 수 있습니다.

13. How soon?

Ŏn-je-tchŭm toel-kka-yo?

언제쯤 될까요?

14. In about one week.

Yak il-tchu-il nae-e toe-get-ssŭm-ni-da.

약 일주일 내에 되겠습니다.

15. Please order it for me.

KKok ha-na ku-hae chu-sip-ssi-o.

---

front side(*am-myŏn*)…앞면
stereo player(*sŭ-t'e-re-o chŏn-ch'uk*)…

스테레오 전축
back side(*twin-myŏn*)…뒷면

꼭 하나 구해 주십시오.

16. Jazz songs are sung one day and forgotten the next, but the good classical selections are evergreen and never die out.

Tchae-jŭ ŭ-ma-gŭn han-ttae yu-haeng-ha-da sa-ra-ji-ji-man, hul-lyung-han ko-jŏn ŭ-ma-gŭn nŭl han-gyŏl ka-t'a-sŏ yŏng-wŏn-hi sa-ra-ji-ji an-ssŭm-ni-da.

재즈 음악은 한때 유행하다 사라지지만, 훌륭한 고전 음악은 늘 한결 같아서 영원히 사라지지 않습니다.

17. I can't find the disk I want.

Che-ga ch'at-kko in-nŭn re-k'o-dŭ-nŭn ŏp-kkun-yo.

제가 찾고 있는 레코드는 없군요.

18. I'll take both the music sheet and the record.

Ak-ppo-wa re-k'o-dŭ-rŭl ham-kke sa-get-ssŭm-ni-da.

악보와 레코드를 함께 사겠습니다.

19. You have quite a lot of the latest hit songs.

Ch'oe-gŭ-nŭi hi-t'ŭ ssong-i koeng-jang-hi man-ssŭm-ni-da.

최근의 히트 송이 굉장히 많습니다.

20. I don't like fashionable songs. But have you the record called "Tears in Mokpo?"

Yu-haeng-ga-nŭn cho-a-ha-ji an-ch'i-man, mok-p'o-ŭi nun-mu-ri-ra-nŭn re-k'o-dŭ-ga it-ssŭm-ni-kka?

유행가는 좋아하지 않지만, 목포의

Jazz(*chae-jŭ*)…재즈
evergreen(*sang-no-gŭi*)…상록의
die out(*sa-ra-ji-da*)…사라지다
recording(*no-gŭm*)…녹음
performance(*yŏn-ju*)…연주
singer(*ka-su*)…가수

disk(*re-k'o-dŭ*)…레코드
sheet music(*ak-ppo*)…악보
fashionable song(*yu-haeng-ga*)…유행가
orchestra(*ak-ttan*)…악단
tone quality(*ŭm-jil*)…음질

229

눈물이라는 레코드가 있습니까?

21. It's sung by Miss Lee Nan-yong, one of the most well-known Korean woman singers.

Kŭ-gŏ-sŭn han-gu-ge-sŏ ka-jang yu-myŏng-han yŏ-ja ka-su-ŭi han sa-ra-min i-na-nyŏng ssi-ga pul-lŏt-ssŭm-ni-da.

그것은 한국에서 가장 유명한 여자 가수의 한 사람인 이난영 씨가 불렀습니다.

22. The song I want is a sentimental American ditty known as "Old Black Joe."

Che-ga ch'at-kko in-nŭn no-rae-nŭn ol-dŭ pŭl-laek tchyo-ra-go ha-nŭn kam-sang-jŏ-gin mi-guk mi-nyo-im-ni-da.

제가 찾고 있는 노래는 올드·블랙·죠라고 하는 감상적인 미국 민요입니다.

23. I think we have it. I'll look it up in our index.

Kŭ-gŏ-si it-tta-go saeng-ga-k'am-ni-da. Mong-no-ge-sŏ ch'a-ja-bo-get-ssŭm-ni-da.

그것이 있다고 생각합니다. 목록에서 찾아보겠습니다.

24. We have just laid in a new supply of good symphonic recordings. I would be glad to play some for you.

Hul-lyung-han kyo-hyang-gok re-k'o-dŭ-rŭl sae-ro i-p'a-haet-ssŭm-ni-da. Tang-si-ne-ge myŏt kkok t'ŭ-rŏ tŭ-ri-get-ssŭm-ni-da.

훌륭한 교향곡 레코드를 새로 입하했습니다. 당신에게 몇 곡 틀어

---

solo(*tok-tchu-gok*)···독주곡
sentimental(*kam-sang-jŏ-gin*)···감상적인
march(*haeng-jin-gok*)···행진곡

index(*mong-nok*)···목록
mili tary band(*ku-nak-ttae*)···군악대
band(*ak-ttan*)···악단

230

드리겠습니다.
Tae-dan-hi ko-map-ssŭm-ni-da.
대단히 고맙습니다.

25. I'd be very much obliged.

At a souvenir Shop

Ki-nyŏm-p'um sang-jŏ-me-sŏ
(기념품 상점에서)

1. What can I show you?

Mu-ŏ-sŭl po-yŏ tŭ-ril-kka-yo?
무엇을 보여 드릴까요?

2. I'd like to see some typical Korean dolls.

Chŏn-hyŏng-tchŏ-gin han-guk in-hyŏng-ŭl chom po-yŏ chu-sip-ssi-o.
전형적인 한국 인형을 좀 보여 주십시오.

3. We have many kinds. Here's one that is very popular. It's called "Chunhyang," after the heroine of a legendary Korean romance story.

Yŏ-rŏ ka-ji-ga it-ssŭm-ni-da. I-gŏ-si a-ju in-kki-ga it-ssŭm-ni-da. Ch'un-hyang-i-ran kŏn-de chŏn-sŏl-tchŏ-gin han-guk ae-jŏng so-sŏ-rŭi yŏ-ju-in-gong-im-ni-da.
여러 가지가 있습니다. 이것이 아주 인기가 있습니다. 춘향이란 건데 전설적인 한국 애정 소설의 여주인공입니다.

4. Oh, what an exquisite, delicate and attractive little doll!

Ŏ-ma, ch'a-mŭ-ro u-a-ha-go, sŏm-se-ha-go, mae-ryŏk-tchŏ-gin in-hyŏng-im-ni-da.
어마, 참으로 우아하고, 섬세하고,

---

symphony(*kyo-hyang-gok*) ···교향곡
musical(*yŏng-hwa ŭ-mak*) ···영화 음악
local products(*t'o-san-p'um*) ···토산품
typical(*chŏn-hyŏng-jŏ-gin*) ···전형적인
performance(*kong-yŏn*) ···공연

collection of songs(*ka-gok-tchip*) ···가곡집
pack(*kku-rŏ-mi*) ···꾸러미
doll(*in-hyŏng*) ···인형
heroine(*yŏ-ju-in-gong*) ···여주인공

매력적인 인형입니다.

5. It looks just gorgeous !

Chŏng-mal hul-lyung-ham-ni-da!
정말 훌륭합니다 !

6. Can you pack doll and send it to the United States for me ?

Kŭ in-hyŏng-ŭl p'o-jang-hae-sŏ mi-gu-gŭ-ro po-nae-jul ssu it-ssŭm-ni-kka?
그 인형을 포장해서 미국으로 보내줄 수 있습니까 ?

7. Yes, sir. But the postage will be extra.

Kŭ-rŏm-yo. Kŭ-rŏ-na u-p'yŏn-nyo-nŭn pyŏl-tto-im-ni-da.
그럼요. 그러나 우편료는 별도입니다.

8. I'll take the doll. Please ship it to the address.

Kŭ in-hyŏng-ŭl sa-get-ssŭm-ni-da. Kŭ-gŏl i chu-so-ro pu-ch'yŏ chu-sip-ssi-o.
그 인형을 사겠습니다. 그걸 이 주소로 부쳐 주십시오.

9. What is this cigarette case made of ? It isn't some kind of plastic, is it ?

I tam-bae-kka-bŭn mu-ŏ-sŭ-ro man-dŭn kŏ-sim-ni-kka? P'ŭl-la-sŭ-t'ik kka-t'ŭn kŏ-sŭ-ro man-dŭn kŏ-sŭn a-nim-ni-kka?
이 담뱃갑은 무엇으로 만든 것입니까 ? 플라스틱 같은 것으로 만든 것은 아닙니까 ?

10. Oh, no. It's genuine tortoise shell.

A-nim-ni-da. Chin-tcha kŏ-buk kkŏp-tchil-ro man-dŭn kŏ-sim-ni-da.
아닙니다. 진짜 거북 껍질로 만든

---

tortoise shell (*kŏ-buk kkŏp-tchil*)…거북 껍질

extra (*pyŏl-tto*)…별도
delicacy (*sŏm-se*)…섬세

것입니다.

11. It sounds great !

Ya, mŏt-tchim-ni-da !

야, 멋집니다 !

12. How many cigarettes will it hold ?

Kŭ so-ge tam-bae-ga myŏt kka-ch'i-na tŭ-rŏ-gam-ni-kka ?

그 속에 담배가 몇 가치가 들어갑니까 ?

13. Just twenty.

KKok sŭ-mu kae-im-ni-da.

꼭 스무 개입니다.

14. Could you engrave my name on it ?

Nae i-rŭ-mŭl kŭ wi-e sae-gil ssu it-ssŭm-ni-kka ?

내 이름을 그 위에 새길 수 있습니까 ?

15. Yes, sir. It'll take only about an hour.

Kŭ-rŏ-mŭn-yo. Han si-gan chŏng-do-ba-kke kŏl-li-ji an-ssŭm-ni-da.

그러믄요. 한 시간 정도밖에 걸리지 않습니다.

16. How much is the item ?

Kŭ-gŏ kap-ssŭn ŏl-ma-im-ni-kka ?

그거 값은 얼마입니까 ?

17. 30,000 won, plus 1,000 won for the engraving.

Sam-man wŏn ha-go, i-rŭm sae-gi-nŭn te ch'ŏn wŏn-im-ni-da.

삼만 원 하고, 이름 새기는 데 천원입니다.

18. Isn't there any discount ?

Ha-rin-hal ssu ŏp-ssŭm-ni-kka ?

할인할 수 없습니까 ?

19. Normally we do not give any discounts, for the prices have already been greatly reduced.

I-mi kap-ssŭl a-ju ssa-ge mŏ-gyŏ-nwa-sŏ e-nu-ri-rŭl hal ssu ŏp-ssŭm-ni-da-man, ta-rŭn mul-gŏ-nŭl ma-ni sa-syŏt-ssŭ-ni chŏng-

---

engrave(*sae-gi-da*)…새기다   charm(*mae-ryŏk*)…매력

But as you have made many other purchases, I will take off ten percent from the price on the tag.	*kka-p'yo-e-sŏ sip p'ŏ-sen-t'ŭ kam-hae tŭ-ri-get-ssŭm-ni-da.* 이미 값을 아주 싸게 먹여놔서 에누리를 할 수 없습니다만, 다른 물건을 많이 사셨으니 정가표에서 십 퍼센트 감해 드리겠습니다.
20. How much are these silver spoons and chopsticks?	*I ŭn-su-jŏ-nŭn ŏl-ma-im-ni-kka?* 이 은수저는 얼마입니까?
21. Those are 20,000 won and these are 25,000 won.	*Chŏ-gŏ-sŭn i-man wŏn-i-go, i-gŏ-sŭn i-man o-ch'ŏn wŏn-im-ni-da.* 저것은 이만 원이고, 이것은 이만 오천 원입니다.
22. Why is the price different?	*Wae kap-ssi ta-rŭm-ni-kka?* 왜 값이 다릅니까?
23. The higher ones are of better quality.	*Kap-ssi pi-ssan kŏ-sŭn tŏ cho-ŭn p'um-jil-im-ni-da.* 값이 비싼 것은 더 좋은 품질입니다.
24. What are these lacquered dishes used for?	*I ch'il-gi chŏp-ssi-nŭn mu-ŏ-se sa-yong-ham-ni-kka?* 이 칠기 접시는 무엇에 사용합니까?
25. In korea they are used for serving cakes and breads.	*Han-gu-ge-sŏ-nŭn kwa-ja-na ppang-ŭl tae-jŏ-p'a-nŭn te sa-yong-ham-ni-da.*

---

difference(*ch'a-i*)…차이
chopstick(*chŏt-kka-rak*)…젓가락
lacquered dish(*ch'il-gi chŏp-ssi*)…칠기 접시

price tag(*chŏng-kka-p'yo*)…정가표
receipt(*yŏng-su-jŭng*)…영수증
quality(*p'um-jil*)…품질
spoon(*sut-kka-rak*)…숟가락

한국에서는 과자나 빵을 대접하는 데 사용합니다.

26. Do you think they'll make a good souvenir to send to a friend of mine in the United States?

Mi-gu-ge in-nŭn ch'in-gu-e-ge po-nael ki-nyŏm-p'u-mŭ-ro chŏk-ttang-ha-get-ssŭm-ni-kka?

미국에 있는 친구에게 보낼 기념품으로 적당하겠습니까?

27. Oh, yes. It's one of the popular souvenir items. Korea is noted for its lacquerware.

Kŭ-rŏ-mŭn-yo. Kŭ-gŏn a-ju in-kki in-nŭn ki-nyŏm-p'um chung-ŭi ha-na-im-ni-da. Han-gu-gŭn ch'il-gi-ro yu-myŏng-ham-ni-da.

그럼요. 그건 아주 인기 있는 기념품 중의 하나입니다. 한국은 칠기로 유명합니다.

28. We will pack it and mail it for you.

Kŭ-gŏ-sŭl p'o-jang-hae-sŏ pu-ch'yŏ tŭ-ri-get-ssŭm-ni-da.

그것을 포장해서 부쳐 드리겠습니다.

29. What kind of toy would you recommend for a baby just about to celebrate its first birthday?

Ch'ŏt tto-ri toen a-gi-e-ge chul sŏn-mul-lo ŏ-ttŏn chang-nan-kka-mi cho-k'et-ssŭm-ni-kka?

첫 돐이 된 아기에게 줄 선물로 어떤 장난감이 좋겠습니까?

30. I think a rattle would be the best thing.

TTal-lang-i-ga che-il cho-ŭl kkŏt kat-ssŭm-ni-da.

딸랑이가 제일 좋을 것 같습니다.

31. And now, could you

Kŭ-ri-go kyo-yuk-tchŏk ka-ch'i-ga in-

---

souvenir(*ki-nyŏm-p'um*)…기념품
congratulatory present(*ch'u-k'a sŏn-mul*)…축하 선물

celebrate(*ki-nyŏm-ha-da*)…기념하다
toy(*chang-nan-kkam*)…장난감
rattle(*ttal-lang-i*)…딸랑이

advise me as to what sort of toy would have some educational value?

nŭn chang-nan-kka-mŭ-ro-nŭn ŏ-ttŏn kŏ-si cho-k'et-ssŭm-ni-kka?

그리고 교육적 가치가 있는 장난감으로는 어떤 것이 좋겠습니까?

32. These wooden blocks marked with all the letters of the Hangul alphabet would help to teach children letters at an early stage.

Han-gŭl al-p'a-be-sŭi kŭl-tcha-ga ssŭ-yŏ-jin i na-mu-t'o-ma-gi, ŏ-rin-a-i-dŭ-re-ge il-tchik kŭl-tcha-rŭl ka-rŭ-ch'i-nŭn te to-u-mi toel kkŏ-sim-ni-da.

한글 알파벳의 글자가 쓰여진 이 나무토막이, 어린아이들에게 일찍 글자를 가르치는 데 도움이 될 것입니다.

33. Most of the dolls made in Korea are of the unique Korean type.

Han-gu-ge-sŏ man-dŭn tae-bu-bu-nŭi in-hyŏng-ŭn han-guk ko-yu-ŭi in-hyŏng-im-ni-da.

한국에서 만든 대부분의 인형은 한국 고유의 인형입니다.

34. We have a very wide selection of dolls.

U-ri-nŭn yŏ-rŏ ka-ji in-hyŏng-ŭl mo-du kat-ch'wŏ no-k'o it-ssŭm-ni-da.

우리는 여러 가지 인형을 모두 갖춰 놓고 있습니다.

35. This is nearly the same toy as the one you described.

Tang-sin-kke-sŏ mal-ssŭm-ha-sin kŏt-kkwa kŏ-ŭi ttŏ-kka-t'ŭn chang-nan-kkam-im-ni-da.

당신께서 말씀하신 것과 거의 똑같은 장난감입니다.

---

unique(*t'ŭ-gi-han*)…특이한
hard(*tan-dan-han*)…단단한
experience(*kyŏng-hŏm*)…경험

describe(*myo-sa-ha-da*)…묘사하다
imitation(*mo-bang*)…모방

36. Please wrap up all my purchase together.

Nae-ga san kŏ-sŭl mo-du ham-kke ssa chu-sip-ssi-o.

내가 산 것을 모두 함께 싸 주십시오.

At a Camera Shop

K'a-me-ra sang-jŏ-me-sŏ
(카메라 상점에서)

1. What can I do for you?

Ŏ-ttŏ-k'e o-syŏt-ssŭm-ni-kka?
어떻게 오셨습니까?

2. I'd like to see some camera.

K'a-me-ra-rŭl chom ku-gyŏng-ha-go sip-ssŭm-ni-da.
카메라를 좀 구경하고 싶습니다.

3. What kind would you like?

Ŏ-ttŏn chong-nyu-rŭl wŏn-ha-sim-ni-kka?
어떤 종류를 원하십니까?

4. I want one that's simple to operate.

Sa-yong-ha-gi kan-ttan-han kŏ-sŭ-ro wŏn-ham-ni-da.
사용하기 간단한 것으로 원합니다.

5. This is the twin-lens reflex and it is quite easy to use. It's a fine camera for beginners.

I-gŏ-sŭn ssang-an-ren-jŭ ri-p'ŭl-rek-ssŭ-in-de, sa-yong-ha-gi-ga a-ju kan-p'yŏn-ham-ni-da. Ch'o-sim-ja-e-ge al-man-nŭn k'a-me-ra-im-ni-da.
이것은 쌍안렌즈 리플렉스인데, 사용하기가 아주 간편합니다. 초심자에게 알맞는 카메라입니다.

6. This camera is guaran-

I k'a-me-ra-nŭn il nyŏn ttong-an po-

---

use(*sa-yong-ha-da*)…사용하다
kind(*chong-nyu*)…종류
instruction(*chi-si*)…지시

simple(*kan-ttan-han*)…간단한
beginner(*ch'o-sim-ja*)…초심자
expert(*chŏn-mun-ga*)…전문가

teed for one year. We import them from the world's top makers.

jŭng-ham-ni-da. U-ri-nŭn se-gye yu-su-ŭi che-jo-ŏp-tcha-e-ge-sŏ k'a-me-ra-rŭl su-i-p'a-go it-ssŭm-ni-da.

이 카메라는 일 년 동안 보증합니다. 우리는 세계 유수의 제조업자에게서 카메라를 수입하고 있습니다.

7. Do you have a booklet of operating instructions?

Sa-yong-ppŏp sŏl-myŏng-sŏ-ga it-ssŭm-ni-kka?

사용법 설명서가 있습니까?

8. Does a case come with the camera?

K'e-i-ssŭ-nŭn k'a-me-ra-e tta-ra-om-ni-kka?

케이스는 카메라에 따라옵니까?

9. Yes. This is the case for the camera.

Kŭ-rŏt-ssŭm-ni-da. I-gŏ-si kŭ k'a-me-ra-ŭi k'e-i-ssŭ-im-ni-da.

그렇습니다. 이것이 그 카메라의 케이스입니다.

10. Let me have a roll of black and white film.

Hŭk-ppaek p'il-lŭm-do han t'ong chu-sip-ssi-o.

흑백 필름도 한 통 주십시오.

11. I need a roll of 35mm color film. I prefer a Kodak film.

Sam-sip-o mi-ri k'ŏl-lŏ p'il-lŭm han t'ong-man chu-sip-ssi-o. I-wang-i-myŏn k'o-dak p'il-lŭ-mŭ-ro chu-sip-ssi-o.

삼십오 미리 컬러 필름 한 통만 주십시오. 이왕이면 코닥 필름으로 주십시오.

---

explanatory note(*sŏl-myŏng-sŏ*)⋯설명서

guaranty(*po-jŭng*)⋯보증

12. I want this color film developed and made into slides.

I ch'ŏ-nyŏn-saek p'il-lŭ-mŭl hyŏn-sang-hae-sŏ sŭl-la-i-dŭ-ro man-dŭ-rŏ chu-sip-ssi-o.

이 천연색 필름을 현상해서 슬라이드로 만들어 주십시오.

13. I want the enlarged in cabinet size.

K'ae-bi-nit k'ŭ-gi-ro hwak-ttae-hae chu-sip-ssi-o.

캐비닛 크기로 확대해 주십시오.

14. Which kind of paper shall I use, glossy paper or grain paper?

Ŏ-ttŏn in-hwa-ji-rŭl sa-yong-hal-kka-yo? Kŭl-lo-ssi-ro hal-kka-yo, ko-gŭp yang-p'i-ji-ro hal-kka-yo?

어떤 인화지를 사용할까요? 글로씨로 할까요, 고급 양피지로 할까요?

15. Don't you want any prints?

In-hwa-nŭn an-ha-si-get-ssŭm-ni-kka?

인화는 안하시겠습니까?

16. When can I have them?

Ŏn-je ch'a-jŭl ssu it-kket-ssŭm-ni-kka?

언제 찾을 수 있겠습니까?

17. Your order will be ready in the evening the day after tomorrow.

Sŏn-saeng-ni-mi chu-mun-ha-sin kŏ-sŭn mo-re chŏ-nyŏk-kka-ji-nŭn toe-get-ssŭm-ni-da.

선생님이 주문하신 것은 모레 저녁까지는 되겠습니다.

18. I'll take the camera.

Kŭ k'a-me-ra-rŭl sa-get-ssŭm-ni-da.

그 카메라를 사겠습니다.

---

color film(*k'ŏl-lŏ p'il-lŭm*)…컬러 필름

enlarge(*hwak-ttae-ha-da*)…확대하다
grain paper(*yang-p'i-ji*)…양피지

Photo-taking

Sa-jin-tchik-kki(사진찍기)

1. Let's take picture.

Sa-ji-nŭl tchi-gŭp-ssi-da.
사진을 찍읍시다.

2. Shall I click for you?

Che-ga tchi-gŏ tŭ-ril-kka-yo?
제가 찍어 드릴까요?

3. Pardon me, would you mind if I take your picture?

Sil-lye-ji-man tae-gŭi sa-ji-nŭl tchi-gŏ-do chot-ssŭm-ni-kka?
실례지만 댁의 사진을 찍어도 좋습니까?

4. I'd like to send you copies of the pictures I took.

Che-ga tchi-gŭn sa-ji-nŭl po-nae tŭ-ri-get-ssŭm-ni-da.
제가 찍은 사진을 보내 드리겠습니다.

5. Please stay there for a moment.

Kŏ-gi cham-kkan-man sŏ kye-sip-ssi-o.
거기 잠깐만 서 계십시오.

6. Please smile.

Chom u-sŭ-sip-ssi-o.
좀 웃으십시오.

7. Don't move. I'm pushing the shutter now.

Um-ji-gi-ji ma-sip-ssi-o. Chi-gŭm syŏ-t'ŏ-rŭl nu-rŭm-ni-da.
움직이지 마십시오. 지금 셔터를 누릅니다.

8. Will you take my photo with my camera, please?

Che k'a-me-ra-ro sa-jin chom tchi-gŏ chu-si-get-ssŭm-ni-kka?
제 카메라로 사진 좀 찍어 주시겠습니까?

9. Will you pose with me

Ham-kke sa-ji-nŭl tchi-gŭ-si-jyo?

---

picture frame(*sa-jin-t'ŭl*)…사진틀
photograph(*sa-jin*)…사진

print(*in-hwa*)…인화
developing(*hyŏn-sang*)…현상

for a picture?

10. Please wait. I'll take another picture.

함께 사진을 찍으시죠?

*Cham-kkan-man ki-da-ri-sip-ssi-o.
Sa-jin han chang tŏ tchik-kket-
ssŭm-ni-da.*

잠깐만 기다리십시오. 사진 한 장
더 찍겠습니다.

11. Why don't we have something to drink at the tea room there?

*Chŏ-gi in-nŭn ta-bang-e-sŏ mwŏ-ra-
do ma-si-nŭn kŏ-si ŏ-ttŏ-k'et-
ssŭm-ni-kka?*

저기 있는 다방에서 뭐라도 마시는
것이 어떻겠습니까?

At a Florist's

1. I would like to buy a few roses.

KKot kka-ge-e-sŏ(꽃 가게에서)

*Chang-mi-kko-ch'ŭl chom sa-go sip-
ssŭm-ni-da.*

장미꽃을 좀 사고 싶습니다.

2. They are very beautiful. Were they grown in your own nursery?

*Ch'am a-rŭm-dap-ssŭm-ni-da. Tae-
gŭi hwa-wŏ-ne-sŏ ki-rŭ-sin kŏ-
sim-ni-kka?*

참 아름답습니다. 댁의 화원에서
기르신 것입니까?

3. Mind the thorns when you thouch them. They are liable to prick you.

*Man-ji-sil ttae, ka-si-e cho-sim-ha-
sip-ssi-o. Tchil-li-gi swip-ssŭm-ni-
da.*

만지실 때, 가시에 조심하십시오.
찔리기 쉽습니다.

4. I'll wrap them up in the cellophane and tie the bundle up nicely with a

*Sel-lo-p'an-ji-ro ssa-sŏ p'u-rŭn ri-bo-
nŭ-ro ye-ppŭ-ge mae-ŏ tŭ-ri-get-
ssŭm-ni-da.*

---

rose(*chang-mi*)…장미   wild rose(*tŭl-tchang-mi*)…들장미

blue ribbon.

셀로판지로 싸서 푸른 리본으로 예쁘게 매어 드리겠습니다.

5. That would be nice. Do you only handle cut flo-wers ?

Chŏt-ssŭm-ni-da. Tcha-rŭn kkon-man ch'wi-gŭ-p'a-sim-ni-kka?

좋습니다. 짜른 꽃만 취급하십니까 ?

6. We also handle various potted plants.

Yŏ-rŏ ka-ji hwa-bun-do ch'wi-gŭ-p'am-ni-da.

여러 가지 화분도 취급합니다.

7. Do you wish to write any message to accom-pany these roses ?

I chang-mi-kko-ch'e mu-sŭn in-sa-ma-ri-ra-do ssŏ tŭ-ril-kka-yo?

이 장미꽃에 무슨 인사말이라도 써 드릴까요 ?

8. No. thank you. They are not meant as a gift but merely to decorate room.

A-ni kwaen-ch'an-ssŭm-ni-da. Sŏn-mul-hal kkŏ-si a-ni-ra, che pang-e kko-ja tul kkŏ-sim-ni-da.

아니 괜찮습니다. 선물할 것이 아니라, 제 방에 꽂아 둘 것입니다.

9. Have you any nice li-lies ?

A-rŭm-da-un pae-k'ap-kko-ch'i it-ssŭm-ni-kka ?

---

flower(*kkot*)…꽃
sunflower(*hae-ba-ra-gi*)…해바라기
camellia(*tong-baek-kkot*)…동백꽃
azalea(*chin-dal-lae*)…진달래
tulip(*t'yul-lip*)…튤립
lilac(*ra-il-lak*)…라일락
lily(*pae-k'ap*)…백합
glass culture(*on-sil chae-bae*)…온실 재배
dandelion(*min-dŭl-lae*)…민들레

morning glory(*na-p'al-kkot*)…나팔꽃
seed(*ssi-at*)…씨앗
root(*ppu-ri*)…뿌리
trunk(*chul-gi*)…줄기
garden plant(*wŏ-nye sing-mul*)…원예 식물
gradening tool(*wŏ-nye yong-gu*)…원예 용구
hothouse(*on-sil*)…온실
narcissus(*su-sŏn-hwa*)…수선화

아름다운 백합꽃이 있습니까?

10. We have, but I'm afraid the flowers are still in buds.

It-kki-nŭn ha-ji-man, a-jik kko-ch'i p'i-ji a-nat-ssŭm-ni-da.

있기는 하지만, 아직 꽃이 피지 않았습니다.

11. Give me five pieces. How much are they a piece?

Ta-sŏt song-i-man chu-sip-ssi-o. Han song-i-e ŏl-ma-im-ni-kka?

다섯 송이만 주십시오. 한 송이에 얼마입니까?

12. I hope they'll last long.

O-rae ka-ssŭ-myŏn cho-k'et-ssŭm-ni-da.

오래 갔으면 좋겠습니다.

13. If you keep changing the water in the vase for several days, they'll last long.

Myŏ-ch'il ttong-an hwa-byŏng-ŭi mul-man ka-ra-ju-si-myŏn o-rae-gal kkŏ-sim-ni-da.

며칠 동안 화병의 물만 갈아주시면 오래갈 것입니다.

14. Considering that they are still in buds. I think that's rather expensive.

A-jik kko-ch'i p'i-ji-do a-nŭn-gŏn-de, chom pi-ssa-da-go saeng-ga-k'am-ni-da.

아직 꽃이 피지도 않은건데, 좀 비싸다고 생각합니다.

15. How often should I

Ŏl-ma-na mu-rŭl cha-ju ka-ra-ju-ŏ-

---

potted flower(*hwa-bun-kkot*)…화분꽃

hothouse plant(*on-sil sing-mul*)…온실 식물

maiden flower(*yŏ-rang-hwa*)…여랑화

rose of sharon(*mu-gung-hwa*)…무궁화

orchid(*nan-ch'o*)…난초

forsythis(*kae-na-ri*)…개나리

accompany(*tong-ban-ha-da*)…동반하다

decorate(*chang-si-k'a-da*)…장식하다

bud(*kkot-ppong-o-ri*)…꽃봉오리

flowering plants(*hwa-ch'o*)…화초

grafted tree(*chŏm-mok*)…접목

change the water?

16. You may change the water at least twice a day.

17. How long will it take before the buds blossom out into flowers?

18. Well, I would say in a couple of days, or even sooner, depending on the temperature.

19. What flower usually proves most popular?

20. That depends on the season, for every season brings a different crop of flowers.

21. It's quite a job to remember the different

ya ham-ni-kka?

얼마나 물을 자주 갈아주어야 합니까?

Ha-ru-e chŏ-gŏ-do tu pŏn-ssi-gŭn mu-rŭl ka-ra-ya hal kkŏ-sim-ni-da.

하루에 적어도 두 번씩은 물을 갈아야 할 것입니다.

KKo-ch'i p'i-ja-myŏn ŏl-ma-na i-ssŏ-ya ham-ni-kka?

꽃이 피자면 얼마나 있어야 합니까?

Han i-t'ŭl chŏng-do i-ssŭ-myŏn p'i-get-ssŭm-ni-da-man, ki-on-e tta-ra tŏ ppal-li p'il ssu-do i-ssŭl kkŏ-sim-ni-da.

한 이틀 정도 있으면 피겠습니다만, 기온에 따라 더 빨리 필 수도 있을 것입니다.

Mu-sŭn kko-ch'i che-il chal p'al-lim-ni-kka?

무슨 꽃이 제일 잘 팔립니까?

Kŭ-gŏn kye-jŏ-re tta-ra ta-rŭm-ni-da. Kye-jŏl-ma-da ta-rŭn kko-ch'i na-o-gi ttae-mun-im-ni-da.

그건 계절에 따라 다릅니다. 계절마다 다른 꽃이 나오기 때문입니다.

Wŏ-nak ma-nŭn kko-ch'i it-kki ttae-mu-ne, kkot i-rŭ-mŭl mo-du ki-ŏ-

---

vase(*kkot-ppyŏng*)…꽃병   temperature(*ki-on*)…기온

names of flowers there are so many.

k'a-nŭn kŏ-sŭn mae-u him-dŭn il-im-ni-da.

워낙 많은 꽃이 있기 때문에, 꽃 이름을 모두 기억하는 것은 매우 힘든 일입니다.

22. What flower is usually considered to be most expensive?

Mu-sŭn kko-ch'i ka-jang pi-ssam-ni-kka?

무슨 꽃이 가장 비쌉니까?

23. What kind of flowers would you recommend to take to a person who is convalescing in a hospital?

Pyŏng-wŏ-ne-sŏ yo-yang-ha-go in-nŭn hwan-ja-e-ge-nŭn mu-sŭn kko-ch'i cho-k'et-ssŭm-ni-kka?

병원에서 요양하고 있는 환자에게 는 무슨 꽃이 좋겠습니까?

24. Do you have any potted azaleas?

Hwa-bu-ne si-mŭn chin-dal-lae-kko-ch'i it-ssŭm-ni-kka?

화분에 심은 진달래꽃이 있습니 까?

25. I'm sorry we haven't one on hand at the moment. But we could easily get one for you if you don't mind waiting a few days.

Mi-an-ham-ni-da-man tang-jang-en ŏp-ssŭm-ni-da. Myŏ-ch'il-man ki-da-ri-sil ssu it-tta-myŏn ha-na ku-hae tŭ-ril ssu it-ssŭm-ni-da.

미안합니다만 당장엔 없습니다. 며 칠만 기다리실 수 있다면 하나 구해 드릴 수 있습니다.

26. Please order one for me. I'll pick it up sometime next week.

Ha-na ku-hae chu-sip-ssi-o. Ta-ŭm chu-il-tchŭm ka-ji-rŏ o-get-ssŭm-ni-da.

하나 구해 주십시오. 다음 주일쯤

---

flowerpot(*hwa-bun*)…화분
hospital ward(*pyŏng-dong*)…병동

recuperation(*yo-yang*)…요양
patient(*hwan-ja*)…환자

가지러 오겠습니다.

27. Aren't there some other flowers you are interested in?

Tŏ sa-go si-p'ŭn kko-ch'ŭn ŏp-ssŭ-sim-ni-kka?

더 사고 싶은 꽃은 없으십니까?

28. Lilies are my favorite flower. I'll take them.

Pae-k'ap-kko-ch'ŭn nae-ga ka-jang cho-a-ha-nŭn kko-ch'im-ni-da. Kŭ-gŏl sa-get-ssŭm-ni-da.

백합꽃은 내가 가장 좋아하는 꽃입니다. 그걸 사겠습니다.

29. The Rose of Sharon is the national flower of Republic of Korea.

Mu-gung-hwa-nŭn tae-han min-gu-gŭi ku-k'wa-im-ni-da.

무궁화는 대한 민국의 국화입니다.

At a Stationer's

Mun-bang-gu-jŏ-me-sŏ
(문방구점에서)

1. Give me a box of paper clips.

K'ŭl-lip han sang-ja-man chu-sip-ssi-o.

클립 한 상자만 주십시오.

2. Steel or plastic?

Kang-ch'ŏl-lo toen kŏ-sim-ni-kka, p'ŭl-la-sŭ-t'ik-tche-im-ni-kka?

강철로 된 것입니까, 플라스틱제입니까?

3. Either will do.

A-mu-gŏ-si-na chot-ssŭm-ni-da.

아무것이나 좋습니다.

4. Large size, medium, or small size?

Kŭn kŏ-sŭ-ro hal-kka-yo, a-ni-myŏn chung-gan-ch'ï, a-ni-myŏn a-ju cha-gŭn kŏ-sŭ-ro ha-get-ssŭm-ni-

---

pot(*hwa-bun*)…화분
favorite(*cho-a-ha-nŭn*)…좋아하는
national flower(*ku-k'wa*)…국화

box(*sang-ja*)…상자
fragrance(*hyang-gi*)…향기

kka?

큰 것으로 할까요, 아니면 중간치,
아니면 아주 작은 것으로 하겠습
니까?

5. And I want hundred sheets of letter paper.

Kŭ-ri-go p'yŏn-ji-ji paek tchang-man chu-sip-ssi-o.

그리고 편지지 백 장만 주십시오.

6. I also want an eraser, a blotter, a bottle, of blue-black ink, and a ruler.

Chi-u-gae ha-na, ap-tchi han t'ong, am-ch'ŏng-saek ing-k'ŭ han pyŏng, kŭ-ri-go cha-do ha-na chu-sip-ssi-o.

지우개 하나, 압지 한 통, 암청색
잉크 한 병, 그리고 자도 하나 주
십시오.

7. How much are these air mail envelopes?

I hang-gong u-p'yŏn pong-t'u-nŭn ŏl-ma-im-ni-kka?

이 항공 우편 봉투는 얼마입니까?

8. How many sheets are there in the box?

I sang-ja-e-nŭn myŏt tchang-i-na tŭ-rŏt-ssŭm-ni-kka?

이 상자에는 몇 장이나 들었습니
까?

9. Take any number you want. They're twenty won each.

SSŭ-sil man-k'ŭm ka-jyŏ ka-sip-ssi-o. Han chang-e i-sip wŏn-ssik-im-ni-da.

쓰실 만큼 가져 가십시오. 한 장에
이십 원씩입니다.

---

steel(*kang-ch'ŏl*)…강철
medium(*chung-gan*)…중간
eraser(*chi-u-gae*)…지우개
take(*ap-tchŏng*)…압정
letter paper(*p'yŏn-ji-ji*)…편지지

ink(*ing-k'ŭ*)…잉크
ruler(*cha*)…자
envelope(*pong-t'u*)…봉투
carbon paper(*muk-tchi*)…묵지

10. Please show me some pencil sharpeners.

Yŏn-p'il-kkak-kkae chom po-yŏ chu-sip-ssi-o.

연필깎개 좀 보여 주십시오.

11. What kind would you like to see? We have three kinds on hand. One is a small pocket sharpener which you twist with your fingers. Another is the type which you mount on your desk and work with a handle. The third kind the automatic sharpener operated by electricity.

Ŏ-ttŏn chong-nyu-ro po-si-get-ssŭm-ni-kka? Se ka-ji chong-nyu-ga it-ssŭm-ni-da. Han ka-ji-nŭn son-kka-ra-gŭ-ro pi-t'ŭ-rŏ sa-yong-ha-nŭn cha-gŭn p'o-k'en-yong-i-go, tto ha-na-nŭn ch'aek-ssang-e pu-ch'yŏ no-k'o haen-dŭl-lo tol-lyŏ ssŭ-nŭn kŏ-si-go, se pŏn-tchae kkŏ-sŭn chŏn-gi-ro um-ji-gi-nŭn cha-dong-sik yŏn-p'il-kkak-kkae-im-ni-da.

어떤 종류로 보시겠습니까? 세 가지 종류가 있습니다. 한 가지는 손가락으로 비틀어 사용하는 작은 포켓용이고, 또 하나는 책상에 붙여 놓고 핸들로 돌려 쓰는 것이고, 세 번째 것은 전기로 움직이는 자동식 연필깎개입니다.

12. This model is very popular. It costs 5,000 won.

I hyŏng-i mae-u in-kki-ga in-nŭn-de, kap-ssŭn o-ch'ŏn wŏn-im-ni-da.

이 형이 매우 인기가 있는데, 값은 오천 원입니다.

13. I want some letter paper.

P'yŏn-ji-ji chom sa-ryŏ-go ham-ni-da.

편지지 좀 사려고 합니다.

---

pencil sharpener(*yŏn-p'il-kkak-kkae*)…연필깎개

automatic(*cha-dong*)…자동

surface(*myŏn*)…면

electrity(*chŏn-gi*)…전기

paste(*p'ul*)…풀

14. What kind of paper do you want?

Ŏ-ttŏn chong-i-rŭl sa-si-ryŏm-ni-kka?

어떤 종이를 사시렵니까?

15. I want the kind with a smooth surface.

Chi-myŏ-ni mae-kkŭ-rŏ-un kŏ-sŭ-ro chu-sip-ssi-o.

지면이 매끄러운 것으로 주십시오.

16. We have the very thing for you.

KKok kŭ-rŏn-ge it-ssŭm-ni-da.

꼭 그런게 있습니다.

17. I also want some paper clips, a box of thumb tacks, a can of pins, and also some staples for my stapler.

TTo chong-i k'ŭl-lip myŏt kkae, ap-tchŏng han t'ong, p'in han t'ong, kŭ-ri-go ho-ch'i-k'i-sŭ-yong al-maeng-i-ga yak-kkan p'i-ryo-ham-ni-da.

또 종이 클립 몇 개, 압정 한 통, 핀 한 통, 그리고 호치키스용 알맹이가 약간 필요합니다.

18. I also want two kinds of ink, one for a stamp pad and the other for a fountain pen.

Kŭ-ri-go sŭ-t'aem-p'ŭ-yong ing-k'ŭ-wa man-nyŏn-p'il-yong ing-k'ŭ-rŭl han pyŏng-ssik chu-sip-ssi-o.

그리고 스템프용 잉크와 만년필용 잉크를 한 병씩 주십시오.

19. Do you have any brushes made of camel hair?

Nak-t'a-t'ŏl-lo man-dŭn pu-si it-ssŭm-ni-kka?

낙타털로 만든 붓이 있습니까?

20. I don't think we have any brushes made of camel hairs.

Nak-t'a-t'ŏl-lo man-dŭn pu-sŭn ŏp-ssŭm-ni-da.

낙타털로 만든 붓은 없습니다.

21. These Korean brushes

I han-guk-tche pu-sŭn mi-sul chŏn-

---

electronic computer(*chŏn-ja kye-san-gi*)…전자 계산기
fountain pen(*man-nyŏn-p'il*)…만년필
adhesive(*chŏp-ch'ak-tche*)…접착제
camel hair(*nak-t'a-t'ŏl*)…낙타털
brush(*put*)…붓

are used by professional artists, so I think you will find them satisfactory.

mun-ga-dŭ-ri sa-yong-ha-nŭn kŏ-si-ni-man-k'ŭm kwaen-ch'a-nŭl kkŏ-sim-ni-da.

이 한국제 붓은 미술 전문가들이 사용하는 것이니만큼 괜찮을 것입니다.

22. Do you have any good fountain pen?

Cho-ŭn man-nyŏn-p'i-ri it-ssŭm-ni-kka?

좋은 만년필이 있습니까?

23. This is an American fountain pen of the latest model.

I-gŏ-sŭn ch'oe-sin-hyŏng mi-je man-nyŏn-p'il-im-ni-da.

이것은 최신형 미제 만년필입니다.

24. Ball pens with trade mark "Mon Ami" are most popular in Korea.

Mo-na-mi sang-p'yo-ŭi pol-p'e-nŭn han-gu-ge-sŏ ka-jang yu-myŏng-ham-ni-da.

모나미 상표의 볼펜은 한국에서 가장 유명합니다.

25. I'd like to buy one of these pen and pencil sets. But I'm afraid it's a little too expensive.

I p'en-gwa yŏn-p'il sse-t'ŭ-rŭl ha-na sal-kka ha-nŭn-de, kap-ssi nŏ-mu pi-ssa-gun-yo.

이 펜과 연필 세트를 하나 살까 하는데, 값이 너무 비싸군요.

26. Perhaps we could give you a discount. I thing we can give you ten percent off.

SSa-ge hae tŭ-ril ssu-do it-ssŭm-ni-da. Sip p'ŏ-sen-t'ŭ-nŭn kam-hae tŭ-ril ssu it-tta-go saeng-ga-k'am-ni-da.

싸게 해 드릴 수도 있습니다. 십 퍼센트는 감해 드릴 수 있다고 생

---

latest model(*ch'oe-sin-hyŏng*)…최신형
best(*ch'oe-go-ŭi*)…최고의

file(*sŏ-ryu-kko-ji*)…서류꽂이
filing cabinet(*sŏ-ryu-ham*)…서류함

각합니다.

27. I'm afraid it would still be too expensive.

A-jik-tto pi-ssan-p'yŏn-im-ni-da.

아직도 비싼편입니다.

28. I'm afraid the best we can do is fifteen percent.

Ch'oe-go-ro sip-o p'ŏ-sen-t'ŭ kam-hae tŭ-ril ssu it-ssŭm-ni-da.

최고로 십오 퍼센트 감해 드릴 수 있습니다.

29. All right. I'll buy it.

Chot-ssŭm-ni-da. Sa-get-ssŭm-ni-da.

좋습니다. 사겠습니다.

30. Never mind wrapping it up. Just put in the box.

SSal kkŏt ŏp-ssŭm-ni-da. Kŭ-nyang sang-ja-e nŏ-ŏ chu-sip-ssi-o.

쌀 것 없습니다. 그냥 상자에 넣어 주십시오.

At a Beauty Parlor

Mi-jang-wŏ-ne-sŏ(미장원에서)

1. If you be so kind as to wait just a few minutes, we'll attend to you soon.

Cham-kkan-man ki-da-ryŏ chu-si-myŏn kot mo-si-get-ssŭm-ni-da.

잠깐만 기다려 주시면 곧 모시겠습니다.

2. Do you want a permanent?

Pŏ-mŏ-rŭl ha-si-get-ssŭm-ni-kka?

퍼머를 하시겠습니까?

3. Yes, I want a permanent wave.

Ne, p'ŏ-mŏ-nŏn-t'ŭ we-i-bŭ-rŭl hae chu-sip-ssi-o.

---

permanent(*p'ŏ-mŏ*)…퍼머

cold permanent(*k'ol-du p'ŏ-mŏ*)…콜드 퍼머

oil permanent(*o-il p'ŏ-mŏ*)…오일 퍼머

beauty art(*mi-yong-sul*)…미용술

black hair(*hŭk-ppal*)…흑발

hairdye(*mŏ-ri yŏm-saeng-yak*)…머리 염색약

long hair(*chang-bal*)…장발

short-cut(*tchal-bŭn mŏ-ri*)…짧은 머리

251

네, 퍼머넌트 웨이브를 해 주십시오.

4. How long will the whole procedure take?

Ta kkŭn-na-ryŏ-myŏn ŏl-ma-na kŏl-rim-ni-kka?

다 끝나려면 얼마나 걸립니까?

5. Shampoo and hair set, please.

Mŏ-ri-rŭl kam-kko sse-t'ŭ-rŭl hae chu-sip-ssi-o.

머리를 감고 세트를 해 주십시오.

6. Lemon rinse or cream rinse?

Re-mo-nŭ-ro heng-gu-si-get-ssŭm-ni-kka, k'ŭ-ri-mŭ-ro heng-gu-si-get-ssŭm-ni-kka?

레몬으로 헹구시겠습니까, 크림으로 헹구시겠습니까?

7. Shall I trim your hair a little?

Mŏ-ri-rŭl chom cha-rŭl-kka-yo?

머리를 좀 자를까요?

8. How short do you want your hair?

Mŏ-ri-rŭl ŏl-ma-na tchal-kke kka-kkŭl-kka-yo?

머리를 얼마나 짧게 깎을까요?

9. We'll begin by giving you a shampoo.

U-sŏn mŏ-ri-rŭl mŏn-jŏ ka-ma-dŭ-ri-get-ssŭm-ni-da.

우선 머리를 먼저 감아드리겠습니다.

10. Would you like to have a manicure?

Mae-ni-k'yu-ŏ-rŭl ha-si-get-ssŭm-ni-kka?

매니큐어를 하시겠습니까?

---

hair cream(*mŏ-ri k'ŭ-rim*)…머리 크림
drier(*tŭ-ra-i-ŏ*)…드라이어
golden hair(*kŭm-bal*)…금발
brunette(*kal-ssaek mŏ-ri*)…갈색 머리

head kerchief(*mŏ-rit-ssu-gŏn*)…머릿수건
perfume(*hyang-su*)…향수
curly hair(*kop-ssŭl-mŏ-ri*)…곱슬머리

11. I'm sorry to have kept you waiting. There's a place open now and we're ready for you.

Ki-da-ri-ge hae-sŏ choe-song-ham-ni-da. I-je cha-ri-ga nat-ssŭ-ni an-jŭ-sip-ssi-o.

기다리게 해서 죄송합니다. 이제 자리가 났으니 앉으십시오.

12. I'm in no rush, you may take your time.

Pa-ppŭ-ji an-ssŭm-ni-da. Ch'ŏn-ch'ŏn-hi ha-sip-ssi-o.

바쁘지 않습니다. 천천히 하십시오.

13. I would like to have my hair done in the swept fashion. I notice it's quite popular now.

Mŏ-ri-rŭl ŏp sŭ-wep-t'ŭ-hyŏng-ŭ-ro haet-ssŭ-myŏn cho-k'et-ssŭm-ni-da. Yo-jŭm a-ju yu-haeng-ha-go it-ttŏ-gun-yo.

머리를 업·스웹트형으로 했으면 좋겠습니다. 요즘 아주 유행하고 있더군요.

14. First, we will give you a shampoo. And after your hair has been thoroughly dried under the electric drier, we will begin by applying the curling irons.

U-sŏn mŏ-ri-rŭl kam-kko, kŭ-ri-go chŏn-gi tŭ-ra-i-ŏ-e mŏ-ri-rŭl chal mal-lin hu-e ko-de-rŭl si-ja-k'a-do-rok ha-get-ssŭm-ni-da.

우선 머리를 감고, 그리고 전기 드라이어에 머리를 잘 말린 후에 고데를 시작하도록 하겠습니다.

15. Your hair always has wonderful luster. You must take very good

Tae-gŭi mŏ-ri-nŭn ŏn-je-na a-rŭm-da-un yu-ni na-go it-kkun-yo. A-ma mŏ-ri son-ji-rŭl a-ju chal ha-

---

curling (*ko-de*)···고데
false hair (*ka-bal*)···가발
cosmetics (*hwa-jang-p'um*)···화장품
trimming (*son-jil*)···손질

hair dresser (*mi-yong-sa*)···미용사
hairdo (*mŏ-ri ch'i-jang*)···머리 치장
cosmetic surgery (*mi-yong chŏng-hyŏng*)···미용 정형

care of it.

si-nŭn mo-yang-i-ji-yo.

댁의 머리는 언제나 아름다운 윤이 나고 있군요. 아마 머리 손질을 아주 잘 하시는 모양이지요.

16. I hope I didn't get soap in your eyes.

Nu-ne pi-nun-mu-ri tŭ-rŏ-ga-ji a-nan-nŭn-ji mo-rŭ-get-ssŭm-ni-da.

눈에 비눗물이 들어가지 않았는지 모르겠습니다.

17. Only a little. Could you lend me a towel?

Cho-gŭm tŭ-rŏ-gat-ssŭm-ni-da. Su-gŏn chom chu-si-get-ssŭm-ni-kka?

조금 들어갔습니다. 수건 좀 주시 겠습니까?

18. I read in a magazine that the greater part of a woman's appeal lies in the way her hair looks.

Ŏ-nŭ chap-tchi-e-sŏ il-gŏn-nŭn-de, yŏ-ja-ŭi mae-ryŏ-gŭn mŏ-ri maep-ssi-ga kŏ-da-ran pi-jung-ŭl ch'a-ji-ha-go it-tta-nŭn-gun-yo.

어느 잡지에서 읽었는데, 여자의 매력은 머리 맵시가 커다란 비중을 차지하고 있다는군요.

19. After we finish with your permanent, would you also like a facial massage?

Pŏ-mŏ-rŭl kkŭn-naen hu-e ŏl-gul ma-ssa-ji-do ha-si-get-ssŭm-ni-kka?

퍼머를 끝낸 후에 얼굴 마사지도 하시겠습니까?

20. I would indeed. I al-

Hae chu-sip-ssi-o. Tŭm-man i-ssŭ-

---

dutch cut(*tan-bal*)…단발
luster(*yun*)…윤
soap(*pi-nu*)…비누
failing-out of hair(*t'al-mo*)…탈모

hair style(*mŏ-ri-hyŏng*)…머리형
facial massage(*ŏl-gul ma-ssa-ji*)…얼굴 마사지
decolorant(*t'al-ssaek-tche*)…탈색제

ways make it a rule to
get a facial as often as
I can. It's so refre-
shing.

*myŏn ŏl-gul ma-ssa-ji-nŭn kkok
ha-go it-ssŭm-ni-da. A-ju si-wŏn-
ha-gŏ-dŭn-yo.*

해 주십시오. 틈만 있으면 얼굴 마
사지는 꼭 하고 있습니다. 아주
시원하거든요.

21. I hope this cover pla-
ced over your head
won't make you dizzy.
Many of our customers
complain of the heat af-
ter a long session.

*Mŏ-ri wi-e ŏn-jŭn tŏp-kkae-ttae-mu-
ne ŏ-ji-rŏp-tchi-na a-nŭ-sil-tchi
mo-rŭ-get-ssŭm-ni-da. O-rae ŏn-
jŏ-du-ni-kka ttŭ-gŏp-tta-go mal-
ssŭm-ha-si-nŭn pu-ni man-t'ŏ-
gun-yo.*

머리 위에 얹은 덮개때문에 어지
럽지나 않으실지 모르겠습니다. 오
래 얹어두니까 뜨겁다고 말씀하시
는 분이 많더군요.

22. Your permanent is now
ready. Please look at
the mirror and tell us
if you like it.

*I-je p'ŏ-mŏ-ga kkŭn-nat-ssŭm-ni-da.
Kŏ-u-rŭl po-si-go ŏ-ttŏn-ji mal-
ssŭm-hae chu-sip-ssi-o.*

이제 퍼머가 끝났습니다. 거울을
보시고 어떤지 말씀해 주십시오.

23. If you would like us
to make any changes
we would be very ha-
ppy to do so.

*Chom tal-li ko-ch'i-go si-p'ŭ-si-myŏn
mal-ssŭm-hae chu-sip-ssi-o.*

좀 달리 고치고 싶으시면 말씀해
주십시오.

24. No, I think you have

A-nim-ni-da. A-ju chal toe-ŏt-ssŭm-

---

refleshing *(si-wŏn-han)*…시원한
headpiece *(mŏ-ri-ssŭ-gae)*…머리쓰개
cleaning *(so-je)*…소제
fingernail *(son-t'op)*…손톱

hair slide *(mŏ-ri-jip-kke)*…머리집게
hairlace *(mŏ-ri-kkŭn)*…머리끈
hairbrush *(mŏ-ri-sol)*…머리솔
baldhead *(tae-mŏ-ri)*…대머리

done an excellent job.
Thank you.

ni-da. Kam-sa-ham-ni-da.

아닙니다. 아주 잘 되었습니다. 감
사합니다.

At a Musical Instrument Shop

Ak-kki-jŏ-me-sŏ(악기점에서)

1. I want to buy a guitar. Where can I get it?

Ki-t'a-rŭl sa-go si-p'ŭn-de ŏ-di-sŏ sal ssu it-kket-ssŭm-ni-kka?

기타를 사고 싶은데 어디서 살 수
있겠습니까?

2. You can buy it in the Chungmu-ro street. On the street, there are many musical instrument shops.

Ch'ung-mu-ro-e ka-myŏn sal ssu-ga it-ssŭm-ni-da. Ch'ung-mu-ro-e-nŭn ma-nŭn ak-kki-jŏ-mi it-ssŭm-ni-da.

충무로에 가면 살 수가 있습니다.
충무로에는 많은 악기점이 있습니
다.

3. Is there any good guitar?

Cho-ŭn ki-t'a-ga it-ssŭm-ni-kka?

좋은 기타가 있습니까?

4. Yes, we have many kinds. What kind of gui-

Ne, yŏ-rŏ ka-ji chong-nyu-ga it-ssŭm-ni-da. Ŏ-ttŏn chong-nyu-ŭi

---

musical instrument(*ak-kki*)…악기
string(*chul*)…줄
clarinet(*k'ŭl-ra-li-net*)…클라리넷
saxophone(*saek-sso-p'on*)…섹소폰
ornet(*k'o-net*)…코넷
harmonica(*ha-mo-ni-k'a*)…하모니카
oboe(*o-bo-e*)…오보에
piccolo(*p'i-k'ol-lo*)…피콜로
flute(*p'ŭl-ru-t'ŭ*)…플루트
drum(*puk*)…북
ukulele(*u-k'ul-lel-le*)…우쿨렐레

bamboo flute(*t'ung-so*)…퉁소
violin(*pa-i-ol-lin*)…바이올린
guitar(*ki-t'a*)…기타
accordion(*a-k'o-di-ŏn*)…아코디언
organ(*p'ung-gŭm*)…풍금
xylophone(*sil-lo-p'on*)…실로폰
mandolion(*man-dol-lin*)…만돌린
trumpet(*t'ŭ-rŏm-p'et*)…트럼펫
harp(*ha-p'ŭ*)…하프
banjo(*paen-jo*)…밴조
keyboard(*kŏn-ban*)…건반

tars do you want？ Large size or medium size？

ki-t'a-rŭl wŏn-ha-sim-ni-kka?
K'ŭn kŏ-sŭ-ro hal-kka-yo, po-t'ong kŏ-sŭ-ro hal-kka-yo?

네, 여러 가지 종류가 있습니다. 어떤 종류의 기타를 원하십니까？ 큰 것으로 할까요, 보통 것으로 할까요？

5. Please show me a medium size one.

Po-t'ong kŏ-sŭ-ro ha-na po-yŏ chu-sip-ssi-o.

보통 것으로 하나 보여 주십시오.

6. These are purely Korean-made and they are of high quality.

I-gŏ-ttŭ-rŭn sun-jŏn-hi han-guk-ssa-nin-de, a-ju p'um-ji-ri chot-ssŭm-ni-da.

이것들은 순전히 한국산인데, 아주 품질이 좋습니다.

7. This organ with the trade mark "Yamaha" is imported from Japan. But in Korea, many kinds of good organs are produced.

Ya-ma-ha sang-p'yo-ŭi i o-rŭ-ga-nŭn il-bo-ne-sŏ su-i-p'an kŏ-sim-ni-da. Kŭ-rŏ-na han-gu-ge-sŏ yŏ-rŏ ka-ji chong-nyu-ŭi cho-ŭn o-rŭ-gan-dŭ-ri saeng-san-doe-go it-ssŭm-ni-da.

야마하 상표의 이 오르간은 일본 에서 수입한 것입니다. 그러나 한 국에서 여러 가지 종류의 좋은 오 르간들이 생산되고 있습니다.

8. The "Samik" piano is locally made and it's quality better than those Japanese-made.

Kung-nae-e-sŏ saeng-san-doe-nŭn sa-mik p'i-a-no-do, p'um-ji-ri il-bon-tche-bo-da chot-ssŭm-ni-da.

국내에서 생산되는 삼익 피아노도,

---

trademark(*sang-p'yo*)···상표   timbre(*ŭm-saek*)···음색

품질이 일본제보다 좋습니다.

9. What's the price of the Korean-made piano?

Chŏ han-guk-tche p'i-a-no-nŭn ŏl-ma-im-ni-kka?

저 한국제 피아노는 얼마입니까?

10. It is cheaper than those foreign pianos imported from Japan and the United States. It costs only 1,500,000 won.

Il-bo-ni-na mi-gu-ge-sŏ su-i-p'an woe-guk-tche p'i-a-no-bo-da kap-ssi ssam-ni-da. Tan-ji paek-o-sim-man wŏn-im-ni-da.

일본이나 미국에서 수입한 외국제 피아노보다 값이 쌉니다. 단지 백 오십만 원입니다.

11. Harmonica is a good musical instrument for children.

Ha-mo-ni-k'a-nŭn a-i-dŭ-re-ge cho-ŭn ak-kki-im-ni-da.

하모니카는 아이들에게 좋은 악기 입니다.

12. Can you play violin?

Pa-i-ol-li-nŭl k'yŏl tchul a-sim-ni-kka?

바이올린을 켤 줄 아십니까?

13. No, I cannot. But I can play guitar very well.

K'i-ji mo-t'am-ni-da-man, ki-t'a-nŭn chal ch'il tchul am-ni-da.

키지 못합니다만, 기타는 잘 칠 줄 압니다.

14. What's Komungo?

Kŏ-mun-go-ran mu-ŏ-sim-ni-kka?

거문고란 무엇입니까?

15. It is a traditional Korean musical instrument. It has twelve strings. The musical ins-

Kŭ-gŏ-sŭn chŏn-t'ong-jŏ-gin han-guk ak-kki-im-ni-da. Yŏl-ttu kae-ŭi chu-ri in-nŭn-de, kŭ ak-kki-nŭn ko-gu-ryŏ si-dae-ŭi wang-sa-na-

---

ceremonial music(*a-ak*)···아악
mother country(*mo-guk*)···모국

fatherland(*cho-guk*)···조국
ancestor(*cho-sang*)···조상

trument was invented
by Wang San-ak of the
Koguryo dynasty.

*gi-ran sa-ra-mi pal-myŏng-haet-
ssŭm-ni-da.*

그것은 전통적인 한국 악기입니다.
열두 개의 줄이 있는데, 그 악기는
고구려 시대의 왕산악이란 사람이
발명했습니다.

16. You can buy those
unique Korean musical
instruments only in a
special shop in down-
town Seoul.

*Kŭ-rŏ-han tok-t'ŭ-k'an han-guk ak-
kki-dŭ-rŭn tan-ji seŏ-ul si-nae-ŭi
t'ŭk-ppyŏl-han sang-jŏ-me-sŏ-man
sa-sil ssu it-ssŭm-ni-da.*

그러한 독특한 한국 악기들은 단지
서울 시내의 특별한 상점에서만
사실 수 있습니다.

17. Usually in Korea, the
musical instrument
shops deal with tickets
for various music con-
certs.

*Han-gu-ge-sŏ-nŭn il-ban-jŏ-gŭ-ro
ak-kki-jŏm-dŭ-ri yŏ-rŏ ŭ-ma-k'oe-
ŭi p'yo-rŭl ch'wi-gŭ-p'a-go it-ssŭm-
ni-da.*

한국에서는 일반적으로 악기점들이
여러 음악회의 표를 취급하고 있
습니다.

18. Guitar is one of the
most popular musical
instruments in Korea.

*Ki-t'a-nŭn han-gu-ge-sŏ ka-jang in-
kki in-nŭn ak-kki chung-ŭi ha-na-
im-ni-da.*

기타는 한국에서 가장 인기 있는
악기 중의 하나입니다.

19. Which musical instru-
ment do you like best?

*Ŏ-ttŏn ak-kki-rŭl ka-jang cho-a-ha-
sim-ni-kka?*

어떤 악기를 가장 좋아하십니까?

20. I like trumpet best.

*T'ŭ-rŏm-p'e-sŭl ka-jang cho-a-ham-
ni-da.*

트럼펫을 가장 좋아합니다.

At a Clock Shop

1. I want to see some wrist watch.

2. Would you show me some good watches?

3. What's the price of the clock over there?

4. Which is the most popular wrist watches in Korea?

5. I think it is Orient wirst watch. Many types of wrist watches and clocks with the trade mark "Orient" are produced in Korea under the technical cooperation with a Japanese firm.

Si-gye-tchŏ-me-sŏ(시계점에서)

Son-mok-si-gye-rŭl ku-gyŏng-ha-go sip-ssŭm-ni-da.

손목시계를 구경하고 싶습니다.

SSŭl-man-han si-gye-rŭl po-yŏ chu-si-get-ssŭm-ni-kka?

쓸만한 시계를 보여 주시겠습니까?

Chŏ-tcho-ge in-nŭn si-gye-nŭn kap-ssi ŏl-ma-im-ni-kka?

저쪽에 있는 시계는 값이 얼마입니까?

Han-gu-ge-sŏ ka-jang in-kki in-nŭn son-mok-si-gye-nŭn ŏ-nŭ kŏ-sim-ni-kka?

한국에서 가장 인기 있는 손목시계는 어느 것입니까?

O-ri-en-t'ŭ son-mok-si-gye-ra-go saeng-ga-k'am-ni-da. O-ri-en-t'ŭ sang-p'yo-ŭi yŏ-rŏ ka-ji mo-yang-ŭi son-mok-si-gye-wa pyŏk-si-gye-dŭ-ri il-bon hoe-sa-wa-ŭi ki-sul hyŏm-nyŏ-gŭ-ro han-gu-ge-sŏ saeng-san-doe-go it-ssŭm-ni-da.

오리엔트 손목시계라고 생각합니다. 오리엔트 상표의 여러 가지 모양의 손목시계와 벽시계들이 일

---

clock(*si-gye*)…시계
wrist watch(*son-mok-si-gye*)…손목시계

clock shop(*si-gye-jŏm*)…시계점
music concert(*ŭ-ma-k'oe*)…음악회
reaction(*pa-nŭng*)…반응

본 회사와의 기술 협력으로 한국에서 생산되고 있습니다.

6. Does this watch keep good time?

I si-gye-nŭn si-ga-ni chal mat-ssŭm-ni-kka?

이 시계는 시간이 잘 맞습니까?

7. We have many kinds of good woman's wrist watches.

SSŭl-man-han yŏ-ja-yong son-mok-si-gye-do yŏ-rŏ ka-ji chong-nyu-ga it-ssŭm-ni-da.

쓸만한 여자용 손목시계도 여러 가지 종류가 있습니다.

8. Watches are widely used as engagement gift in this country.

I na-ra-e-sŏ-nŭn ya-k'on sŏn-mul-lo si-gye-ga nŏl-li sa-yong-doem-ni-da.

이 나라에서는 약혼 선물로 시계가 널리 사용됩니다.

9. What's the most expensive watch?

Ka-jang kap-bi-ssan si-gye-nŭn mu-ŏ-sim-ni-kka?

가장 값비싼 시계는 무엇입니까?

10. I think it's Enica. It's the famous Swiss-made watch.

E-ni-k'a-ra-go saeng-ga-k'am-ni-da. Kŭ-gŏ-sŭn yu-myŏng-han sŭ-wi-sŭ-tche si-gye-im-ni-da.

에니카라고 생각합니다. 그것은 유명한 스위스제 시계입니다.

11. What will you recommend me as a present for my boy who will graduate from school

Kŭm-nyŏn pom hak-kkyo-rŭl cho-rŏp'a-nŭn nae a-i-e-ge chul sŏn-mul-lo mu-ŏ-si cho-k'et-ssŭm-ni-kka?

금년 봄 학교를 졸업하는 내 아이

---

technical cooperation(*ki-sul hyŏm-nyŏk*)…기술 협력
watch glass(*si-gye yu-ri*)…시계 유리
hour hand(*si-ch'im*)…시침

dial plate(*mun-ja-p'an*)…문자판
table clock(*t'ak-ssang-si-gye*)…탁상시계
minute hand(*pun-ch'im*)…분침

this spring?

에게 줄 선물로 무엇이 좋겠습니까?

12. I think the alarm clock is one of the best presents for a student like your boy.

Tae-gŭi a-i-wa ka-t'ŭn hak-ssaeng-dŭ-re-ge-nŭn cha-myŏng-jong-i ka-jang cho-ŭn sŏn-mul chung-ŭi ha-na-ra-go saeng-ga-k'am-ni-da.

댁의 아이와 같은 학생들에게는 자명종이 가장 좋은 선물 중의 하나라고 생각합니다.

13. My watchband is cut. Would you show me a good one made of skin? I don't like any iron made watchband.

Si-gye-tchu-ri tchal-la-jyŏt-ssŭm-ni-da. Ka-ju-gŭ-ro man-dŭn ssŭl-man-han kŏ-sŭl po-yŏ chu-si-get-ssŭm-ni-kka? Chŏ-nŭn ch'ŏl-tche si-gye-tchu-rŭl cho-a-ha-ji an-ssŭm-ni-da.

시계줄이 짤라졌습니다. 가죽으로 만든 쓸만한 것을 보여 주시겠습니까? 저는 철제 시계줄을 좋아하지 않습니다.

14. My watch doesn't work. Where can I repair my watch?

Che si-gye-ga ka-ji an-ssŭm-ni-da. Ŏ-di-sŏ su-ri-rŭl hal ssu i-ssŭl-kka-yo?

제 시계가 가지 않습니다. 어디서 수리를 할 수 있을까요?

15. You can do it at the clock shop. They also do repair works.

Si-gye-tchŏ-me-sŏ su-ri-rŭl hal ssu-ga it-ssŭm-ni-da. Si-gye-tchŏ-me-sŏ-nŭn su-ri-do ha-ni-kka-yo.

시계점에서 수리를 할 수가 있습

---

alarm clock(*cha-myŏng-jong*)…자명종
watchband(*si-gye-jul*)…시계줄

defect(*ko-jang*)…고장
machine(*ki-gye*)…기계

니다. 시계점에서는 수리도 하니까
요.

16. Would you clean the dial of my wrist watch? It's very dusty.

Che si-gye-ŭi mun-tcha-p'an chom so-je-hae chu-si-get-ssŭm-ni-kka? Mŏn-ji-ga mae-u ma-ni kki-ŏt-ssŭm-ni-da.

제 시계의 문자판 좀 소제해 주시
겠습니까? 먼지가 매우 많이 끼
었습니다.

17. Please replace this clock's hands with new ones.

I si-gye pa-nŭl-ŭl sae kŏt-kkwa pa-kkwŏ chu-sip-ssi-o.

이 시계 바늘을 새 것과 바꿔 주
십시오.

18. There have been produced an electronic clock which works without winding spring.

T'ae-yŏ-bŭl kam-tchi an-k'o-sŏ-do ka-nŭn chŏn-ja-si-gye-ga saeng-san-doe-ŏt-ssŭm-ni-da.

태엽을 감지 않고서도 가는 전자
시계가 생산되었습니다.

19. The electronic clocks are usually used in big offices.

Chŏn-ja-si-gye-nŭn tae-ch'e-ro k'ŭn sa-mu-si-re-sŏ sa-yong-doem-ni-da.

전자시계는 대체로 큰 사무실에서
사용됩니다.

20. What's the price of the electronic watch?

Chŏ chŏn-ja-si-gye-nŭn ŏl-ma-im-ni-kka?

저 전자시계는 얼마입니까?

21. I'll take the clock. Is there a case for the clock?

Chŏ si-gye-rŭl sa-get-ssŭm-ni-da. Kŭ si-gye-e ttal-lin sang-ja-ga it-ssŭm-ni-kka?

---

recently(*kŭl-lae*)…근래   produced(*saeng-san*)…생산

263

저 시계를 사겠습니다. 그 시계에
딸린 상자가 있습니까?

General About Korea

Han-gu-ge kwan-ha-yŏ
(한국에 관하여)

1. How long is the Korean history?

   Han-gu-gŭi yŏk-ssa-nŭn ŏl-ma-na o-rae toe-ŏt-ssŭm-ni-kka?

   한국의 역사는 얼마나 오래 되었습니까?

2. It's more than five thousand years.

   O-ch'ŏn nyŏn i-sang-i toe-ŏt-ssŭm-ni-da.

   오천 년 이상이 되었습니다.

3. Really, it's one of the oldest countries in the world.

   Chŏng-mal se-gye-e-sŏ ka-jang o-rae-doen na-ra chung-ŭi ha-na-i-gun-yo.

   정말 세계에서 가장 오래된 나라 중의 하나이군요.

4. Who's the founder of Korea?

   Han-gu-gŭl se-un i-nŭn nu-gu-im-ni-kka?

   한국을 세운 이는 누구입니까?

---

history(*yŏk-ssa*)…역사
geography(*chi-ri*)…지리
politics(*chŏng-ch'i*)…정치
economy(*kyŏng-je*)…경제
culture(*mun-hwa*)…문화
society(*sa-hoe*)…사회
mountain(*san*)…산
river(*kang*)…강
population(*in-gu*)…인구
capital city(*su-do*)…수도
founder(*ch'ang-nip-tcha*)…창립자
independence(*cha-rip*)…자립

dynasty(*wang-jo*)…왕조
king(*wang*)…왕
queen(*yŏ-wang*)…여왕
prince(*wang-ja*)…왕자
princess(*kong-ju*)…공주
royal family(*wang-jok*)…왕족
throne(*wang-jwa*)…왕좌
classic(*ko-jŏn*)…고전
classic novel(*ko-jŏn so-sŏl*)…고전 소설
ground(*ttang*)…땅
creation(*ch'ang-jo*)…창조

5. According to the Korean mythology, Dankun is the founder of this country. They say that he first established Dankun Chosun on the top of Mt. Paektu.

Han-guk sin-hwa-e tta-rŭ-myŏn tan-gu-ni i na-ra-ŭi si-jo-im-ni-da. Kŭ-ga maen ch'ŏ-ŭm paek-ttu-san kkok-ttae-gi-e tan-gun cho-sŏ-nŭl se-wŏt-tta-go mal-ha-dŏ-gun-yo.

한국 신화에 따르면 단군이 이 나라의 시조입니다. 그가 맨 처음 백두산 꼭대기에 단군 조선을 세웠다고 말하더군요.

6. How wide is the Korean territory?

Han-guk yŏng-t'o-nŭn ŏl-ma-na nŏl-ssŭm-ni-kka?

한국 영토은 얼마나 넓습니까?

7. It's 220,000 square kilometers.

I-sip-i-man p'yŏng-bang k'il-lo-mi-t'ŏ-im-ni-da.

이십이만 평방 킬로미터입니다.

8. What's the population of Korea?

Han-gu-gŭi in-gu-nŭn ŏl-ma-im-ni-kka?

한국의 인구는 얼마입니까?

9. The population of Korea is about fifty million.

Han-gu-gŭi in-gu-nŭn yak o-ch'ŏn-man-im-ni-da.

한국의 인구는 약 오천만입니다.

10. Which is the capital city of Korea?

Han-gu-gŭi su-do-nŭn ŏ-di im-ni-kka?

한국의 수도는 어디 입니까?

11. The capital city of Korea is Seoul. It's population is nearly twelve

Han-gu-gŭi su-do-nŭn Seŏ-ul-im-ni-da. Seŏ-u-rŭi in-gu-nŭn kŏ-ŭi ch'ŏn-i-baeng-man-i-na toem-ni-

---

mythology(*sin-hwa*)…신화
territory(*yŏng-t'o*)…영토
high(*no-p'i*)…높이

port(*hang-gu*)…항구
bay(*man*)…만
low(*na-jŭn*)…낮은

265

million.

da.

한국의 수도는 서울입니다. 서울의 인구는 거의 천이백만이나 됩니다.

12. Is Pusan city a port ?

Pu-san-si-nŭn hang-gu-im-ni-kka?

부산시는 항구입니까?

13. Yes, it is. It's the second largest city in Korea.

Kŭ-rŏt-ssŭm-ni-da. Pu-sa-nŭn han-gu-ge-sŏ tu pŏn-tchae-ro k'ŭn to-si-im-ni-da.

그렇습니다. 부산은 한국에서 두 번째로 큰 도시입니다.

14. What's the highest mountain in Korea ?

Han-gu-ge-sŏ ka-jang no-p'ŭn sa-nŭn mu-ŏ-sim-ni-kka?

한국에서 가장 높은 산은 무엇입니까?

15. Mt. Paektu is the highest mountain, but it's in North Korea. In South Korea, the highest mountain is Mt. Halla on Cheju island.

Paek-ttu-sa-ni ka-jang no-p'ŭn san-im-ni-da-man, pu-k'a-ne it-ssŭm-ni-da. Nam-ha-ne-sŏ ka-jang no-p'ŭn sa-nŭn che-ju-do-e in-nŭn hal-la-san-im-ni-da.

백두산이 가장 높은 산입니다만, 북한에 있습니다. 남한에서 가장 높은 산은 제주도에 있는 한라산입니다.

16. What's longest river in

Han-gu-ge-sŏ ka-jang kin kang-ŭn

---

administration(*haeng-jŏng*)…행정
language(*ŏ-nŏ*)…언어
treatise(*non-mun*)…논문
island(*sŏm*)…섬
science(*kwa-hak*)…과학
gravel(*cha-gal*)…자갈

province(*to*)…도
governor(*chi-sa*)…지사
province(*chi-bang*)…지방
long(*kin*)…긴
world(*se-gye*)…세계
earth(*chi-gu*)…지구

Korea?

mu-ŏ-sim-ni-kka?

한국에서 가장 긴 강은 무엇입니까?

17. It's Apnok river in North Korea. In the South, Nakdong is the longest river.

Pu-k'a-ne in-nŭn am-nok-kkang-im-ni-da. Nam-ha-ne-sŏ-nŭn nak-ttong-gang-i ka-jang kin kang-im-ni-da.

북한에 있는 압록강입니다. 남한에서는 낙동강이 가장 긴 강입니다.

18. What's the largest island in Korea?

Han-gu-ge-sŏ ka-jang k'ŭn sŏ-mŭn mu-ŏ-sim-ni-kka?

한국에서 가장 큰 섬은 무엇입니까?

19. It's Cheju island. Administratively, it is a province.

Che-ju-do-im-ni-da. Haeng-jŏng-jŏ-gŭ-ro che-ju-do-nŭn han to-im-ni-da.

제주도입니다. 행정적으로 제주도는 한 도입니다.

20. What's the language of Korea?

Han-gu-gŭi ŏ-nŏ-nŭn mu-ŏ-sim-ni-kka?

한국의 언어는 무엇입니까?

21. It's Hangul. It is said that the Hangul is one of the most scientific language in the world. King Sejong of the Yi dynasty invented the

Han-gŭl-im-ni-da. Han-gŭ-rŭn se-gye-e-sŏ ka-jang kwa-hak-tchŏ-gin ŏ-nŏ chung-ŭi ha-na-ra-go ham-ni-da. I-jo si-dae-ŭi se-jong tae-wang-i yak o-baek-sa-sip-o nyŏn chŏ-ne han-gŭ-rŭl pal-myŏng-ha-

---

traditional(*chŏn-t'ong-ŭi*)…전통의
classic novel(*ko-jŏn so-sŏl*)…고전 소설

court music(*kung-jung ŭ-mak*)…궁중 음악
old house(*ko-ok*)…고옥

language about five hundred forty five years ago.

syŏt-ssŭm-ni-da.

한글입니다. 한글은 세계에서 가장 과학적인 언어 중의 하나라고 합니다. 이조 시대의 세종 대왕이 약 오백사십오 년 전에 한글을 발명하셨습니다.

22. What's the most famous Korean classic novel ?

Ka-jang yu-myŏng-han han-guk ko-jŏn so-sŏ-rŭn mu-ŏ-sim-ni-kka ?

가장 유명한 한국 고전 소설은 무엇입니까 ?

23. It's Chunhyang-jon. It is a love story between a man from noble class and a girl from humble class.

Ch'un-hyang-jŏn-im-ni-da. Kŭ-gŏ-sŭn yang-ban kye-gŭ-bŭi nam-ja-wa ssang-nom kye-gŭ-bŭi han yŏ-ja sa-i-ŭi sa-rang i-ya-gi-im-ni-da.

춘향전입니다. 그것은 양반 계급의 남자와 상놈 계급의 한 여자 사이의 사랑 이야기입니다.

24. What's A-ak ?

A-a-gŭn mu-ŏ-sim-ni-kka ?

아악은 무엇입니까 ?

25. It's a traditional Korean court music.

A-a-gŭn chŏn-t'ong-jŏ-gin han-guk kung-jung ŭ-mak-im-ni-da.

아악은 전통적인 한국 궁중 음악입니다.

26. Are there many folk songs in Korea ?

Han-gu-ge-nŭn ma-nŭn min-sok no-rae-ga it-ssŭm-ni-kka ?

한국에는 많은 민속 노래가 있습니까 ?

---

ancient time(*yen-nal*)…옛날
construction(*kŏn-ch'uk*)…건축
culture(*mun-hwa*)…문화

orient(*tong-yang*)…동양
east(*tong-tchok*)…동쪽
scenery(*p'ung-gyŏng*)…풍경

27. Yes, there are many. Arirang and Toraji are most famous ones among them.

Ne, ma-ni it-ssŭm-ni-da. A-ri-rang-gwa to-ra-ji-nŭn kŭ-dŭl chung-ŭi ka-jang yu-myŏng-han no-rae-im-ni-da.

네, 많이 있습니다. 아리랑과 도라지는 그들 중의 가장 유명한 노래입니다.

28. Why are the Korean people called frequently as "people of white clothes?"

Han-guk ssa-ram-dŭ-rŭn wae chong-jong pae-gŭi min-jo-gi-ra-go pul-li-wŏ-jim-ni-kka?

한국 사람들은 왜 종종 백의 민족이라고 불리워집니까?

29. It's because they like to wear white clothes from the ancient times.

Yen-nal-bu-t'ŏ han-guk ssa-ram-dŭ-rŭn hwin-o-sŭl ip-kki cho-a-ha-gi ttae-mun-im-ni-da.

옛날부터 한국 사람들은 흰옷을 입기 좋아하기 때문입니다.

30. Where is the Pulguksa temple?

Pul-guk-ssa-nŭn ŏ-di it-ssŭm-ni-kka?

불국사는 어디 있습니까?

31. It is in Kyongju, capital city of the old Silla dynasty. The temple is the most well-known architecture in the Orient.

Yen-nal sil-la wang-jo-ŭi su-do-in kyŏng-ju-e it-ssŭm-ni-da. Kŭ chŏ-rŭn tong-yang-e-sŏ ka-jang i-rŭm-nan kŏn-ch'ung-mul-im-ni-da.

옛날 신라 왕조의 수도인 경주에 있습니다. 그 절은 동양에서 가장 이름난 건축물입니다.

32. Korea has been called

Han-gu-gŭn p'ung-gyŏng, cho-ŭn ki-

---

take pleasure(*chŭl-gi-da*)…즐기다   instant(*chŭk-ssi*)…즉시

a "land of morning calm" for its scenery, good weather and people.

hu-wa sa-ram-dŭl ttae-mu-ne, cho-yong-han a-ch'i-mŭi na-ra-ra-go pul-lyŏ-o-go it-ssŭm-ni-da.

한국은 풍경, 좋은 기후와 사람들 때문에, 조용한 아침의 나라라고 불려오고 있습니다.

At a Tavern

Sul-tchi-be-sŏ(술집에서)

1. Would you drink with me tonight?

O-nŭl-ppam na-wa ham-kke sul-ma-si-get-ssŭm-ni-kka?

오늘밤 나와 함께 술마시겠습니까?

2. Yes, I'll go with you.

Ne, ham-kke kap-ssi-da.

네, 함께 갑시다.

3. What is the most famous place for drinking in Korea?

Han-gu-ge-sŏ ka-jang yu-myŏng-ha-ge sul-ma-si-nŭn ko-sŭn ŏ-di im-ni-kka?

한국에서 가장 유명하게 술마시는 곳은 어디 입니까?

4. In Mukyo-dong street, there are many makkoli houses.

Mu-gyo-dong-e-nŭn ma-nŭn mak-kkŏl-li sul-tchi-bi it-ssŭm-ni-da.

무교동에는 많은 막걸리 술집이 있습니다.

5. What's makkoli?

Mak-kkŏl-li-ran mu-ŏ-sim-ni-kka?

---

tavern(*sul-tchip*)…술집
wine(*sul*)…술
makkoli(*mak-kkŏl-li*)…막걸리
night club(*na-i-t'ŭ-k'ŭl-lŏp*)…나이트 클럽
hard liquor(*tok-tchu*)…독주

bean curd(*tu-bu*)…두부
brandy(*pŭ-raen-di*)…브랜디
variety(*ta-yang-han*)…다양한
whisky(*wi-sŭ-k'i*)…위스키
side dish(*an-ju*)…안주
beer(*maek-tchu*)…맥주

막걸리란 무엇입니까?

6. It's the most famous traditional Korean wine made from rice. It's not too strong.

SSal-lo pi-jŭn ka-jang yu-myŏng-ha-go chŏn-t'ong-jŏ-gin han-guk ssul-im-ni-da. Pyŏl-lo to-k'a-ji an-ssŭm-ni-da.

쌀로 빚은 가장 유명하고 전통적인 한국 술입니다. 별로 독하지 않습니다.

7. What are the proper side dishes for makkoli?

Mak-kkŏl-li-e-nŭn ŏ-ttŏn an-ju-ga chŏk-ttang-ham-ni-kka?

막걸리에는 어떤 안주가 적당합니까?

8. Boiled octopus, cooked bean curd, and various raw fish are served with makkoli.

Sal-mŭn nak-tchi, yo-ri-doen tu-bu, kŭ-ri-go kak-tchong saeng-sŏn-hoe-ga mak-kkŏl-li-wa ham-kke chŏp-ttae-doem-ni-da.

삶은 낙지, 요리된 두부, 그리고 각종 생선회가 막걸리와 함께 접대됩니다.

9. How much is a kettle of makkoli?

Mak-kkŏl-li han chu-jŏn-ja-nŭn ŏl-ma-im-ni-kka?

막걸리 한 주전자는 얼마입니까?

10. Usually, It's 800 won.

Po-t'ong p'al-baek wŏn-im-ni-da.

보통 팔백 원입니다.

11. What's the price of that side dish?

Chŏ an-ju-ŭi kap-ssŭn ŏl-ma-im-ni-kka?

저 안주의 값은 얼마입니까?

12. It's 4,000 won.

Sa-ch'ŏn wŏn-im-ni-da.

사천 원입니다.

---

kettle *(chu-jŏn-ja)*…주전자   liquor *(sul)*…술

13. Many Korean office workers rush to the taverns after finishing their work.

Su-ma-nŭn han-guk hoe-sa-wŏn-dŭ-rŭn i-rŭl ma-ch'in hu-e sul-tchi-bŭ-ro mol-lyŏ-gam-ni-da.

수많은 한국 회사원들은 일을 마친 후에 술집으로 몰려갑니다.

14. Soju is stronger than makkoli.

SSo-ju-nŭn mak-kkŏl-li-bo-da to-k'am-ni-da.

소주는 막걸리보다 독합니다.

15. Jinro soju is one of the most famous liquor in Korea.

Chil-lo sso-ju-nŭn han-gu-ge-sŏ ka-jang yu-myŏng-han sul chung-ŭi ha-na-im-ni-da.

진로 소주는 한국에서 가장 유명한 술 중의 하나입니다.

16. In the cafes of hotels in downtown Seoul, you can get various kinds of foreign made drinks.

Seŏ-u-re in-nŭn ho-t'e-rŭi k'a-p'e-e-sŏ yŏ-rŏ ka-ji chong-nyu-ŭi woe-guk ssu-rŭl ma-sil ssu-ga it-ssŭm-ni-da.

서울에 있는 호텔의 카페에서 여러 가지 종류의 외국 술을 마실 수가 있습니다.

17. Do you know the "nakchi alley" in Seoul?

Seŏ-u-re in-nŭn nak-tchi kol-mo-gŭl a-sim-ni-kka?

---

flat(*sing-gŏp-tta*)…싱겁다
salty(*tcha-da*)…짜다
hot(*maep-tta*)…맵다
burning(*ttŭ-gŏp-tta*)…뜨겁다
cold(*ch'a-da*)…차다
water(*mul*)…물
spring water(*saeng-su*)…생수
poisonous(*to-k'an*)…독한
frail(*ya-k'an*)…약한

mix(*sŏk-tta*)…섞다
salt(*so-gŭm*)…소금
sugar(*sŏl-t'ang*)…설탕
red pepper(*ko-ch'u*)…고추
pepper(*hu-ch'u*)…후추
seasonings(*cho-mi-ryo*)…조미료
season(*mu-ch'i-da*)…무치다
parboil(*te-ch'i-da*)…데치다
greens(*ch'ae-so*)…채소

서울에 있는 낙지 골목을 아십니까?

18. It's in Mukyo-dong, and the place is famous for the octopus dish seasoned with hot pepper powder.

Mu-gyo-dong-e in-nŭn-de, kŭ ko-sŭn mae-un ko-ch'u-ro mu-ch'in nak-tchi an-ju-ro yu-myŏng-ham-ni-da.

무교동에 있는데, 그 곳은 매운 고추로 무친 낙지 안주로 유명합니다.

19. Drinking makkoli is cheaper than having foreign-made liquors.

Mak-kkŏl-li-rŭl ma-si-myŏn woe-guk ssu-rŭl ma-si-nŭn kŏt-ppo-da ssam-ni-da.

막걸리를 마시면 외국 술을 마시는 것보다 쌉니다.

20. Last night, I went from tavern to tavern with a few of my close friends.

Chi-nan-bam na-nŭn ch'in-han ch'in-gu myŏn myŏng-gwa ma-nŭn sul-tchi-bŭl to-ra-da-nyŏt-ssŭm-ni-da.

지난밤 나는 친한 친구 몇 명과 많은 술집을 돌아다녔습니다.

PART IV
Dialogue

Thank you very much.

Kam-sa-ham-ni-da.
(감사합니다.)

1. Excuse me. Where is the Capitol Building?

Sil-lye-ji-man chung-ang-ch'ŏng-i ŏ-di it-ssŭm-ni-kka?

실례지만 중앙청이 어디 있습니까?

2. Cross the street and turn left. You can't miss it.

Ki-rŭl kŏn-nŏ-sŏ oen-tcho-gŭ-ro ka-sip-ssi-o. Swip-kke ch'a-jŭl kkŏm-ni-da.

길을 건너서 왼쪽으로 가십시오. 쉽게 찾을 겁니다.

3. Thank you very much.

Kam-sa-ham-ni-da.

감사합니다.

4. Not at all.

Ch'ŏn-ma-ne-yo.

천만에요.

5. Thanks for the coffee. I really enjoyed it.

Kŏ-p'i kam-sa-ham-ni-da. Chal ma-syŏt-ssŭm-ni-da.

커피 감사합니다. 잘 마셨습니다.

6. You're welcome.

Ch'ŏn-ma-ne-yo.

천만에요.

7. Thank you for the flowers.

KKo-ch'ŭl po-nae-jwŏ-sŏ kam-sa-ham-ni-da.

꽃을 보내줘서 감사합니다.

8. I hope you get well soon.

PPal-li k'wae-yu-ha-si-gi-rŭl pa-ram-ni-da.

빨리 쾌유하시기를 바랍니다.

9. Thank you for coming to see me off.

Chŏn-song-ŭl na-wa chu-syŏ-sŏ kam-sa-ham-ni-da.

전송을 나와 주셔서 감사합니다.

10. I hope you enjoy your trip.

Chal ta-nyŏ o-si-gi-rŭl pa-ram-ni-da.

잘 다녀 오시기를 바랍니다.

11. Thanks for inviting me.

Ch'o-dae-hae chu-syŏ-sŏ kam-sa-ham-ni-da.

초대해 주셔서 감사합니다.

12. I hope you enjoyed the party.

P'a-t'i-ga chŭl-gŏ-u-syŏt-kki-rŭl pa-ram-ni-da.

파티가 즐거우셨기를 바랍니다.

13. Thank you for your gift.

Sŏn-mul kam-sa-ham-ni-da.

선물 감사합니다.

14. I hope you like it.

Ma-ŭ-me tŭ-sil-lŏn-ji-yo.

마음에 드실런지요.

When is your birth-day?

Saeng-i-ri ŏn-je-im-ni-kka?
(생일이 언제입니까?)

1. Can I use the car this afternoon? I have to go to the dentist.

O-nŭl o-hu-e ch'a chom ssŭl ssu it-ssŭm-ni-kka? Ch'i-kkwa-e pol li-li it-ssŭm-ni-da.

오늘 오후에 차 좀 쓸 수 있습니까? 치과에 볼 일이 있습니다.

2. Certainly. When is your appointment?

Chot-ssŭm-ni-da. Yak-ssok si-ga-ni ŏn-je-i-ji-yo?

좋습니다. 약속 시간이 언제이지요?

3. At two o'clock.

Tu-si-im-ni-da.

두시입니다.

4. I'll send the car over at one thirty.

Han-si pa-ne ch'a-rŭl po-nae-get-ssŭm-ni-da.

한시 반에 차를 보내겠습니다.

5. When is your birth-day?

Saeng-i-ri ŏn-je-im-ni-kka?

생일이 언제입니까?

6. October fifteenth.

Si-wŏl sip-o-il-im-ni-da.

시월 십오일입니다.

7. When is your first class?

Ch'ŏt si-ga-ni ŏn-je it-ssŭm-ni-kka?

첫 시간이 언제 있습니까?

8. At nine o'clock.

A-hop-ssi-e it-ssŭm-ni-da.

아홉시에 있습니다.

9. When is your annual vacation?

Hyu-ga-ga ŏn-je-im-ni-kka?

휴가가 언제입니까?

10. I hope to take it during August.

P'a-rwŏl chung-ŭ-ro t'ae-k'al saeng-gak-im-ni-da.

팔월 중으로 택할 생각입니다.

11. When is U.N. Day?

Yu-e-nŭi na-ri ŏn-je-im-ni-kka?

유엔의 날이 언제입니까?

12. October twenty fourth.

Si-wŏl i-sip-sa-il-im-ni-da.

시월 이십사일입니다.

13. When is your lunch hour?

Chŏm-sim si-ga-ni ŏn-je-im-ni-kka?

점심 시간이 언제입니까?

14. Usually between one and two o'clock.

Po-t'ong han-si-bu-t'ŏ tu-si-kka-ji-im-ni-da.

보통 한시부터 두시까지입니다.

How soon will it be over?

Ŏl-ma-na i-ssŭ-myŏn kkŭn-nam-ni-kka?

(얼마나 있으면 끝납니까?)

1. Hi! Is Mr. Kim in?

An-nyŏng-ha-sim-ni-kka? Kim sŏn-saeng chi-be kye-si-na-yo?

안녕하십니까? 김 선생 집에 계시나요?

2. I'm sorry. He's at a meeting.

Mi-an-ham-ni-da. Chi-gŭm hoe-ŭi chung-im-ni-da.

미안합니다. 지금 회의 중입니다.

3. How soon will it be over?

Ŏl-ma-na i-ssŭ-myŏn kkŭn-nam-ni-kka?

얼마나 있으면 끝납니까?

4. It'll be over in about twenty minutes. Do you think you can wait?

Yak i-sip-ppun hu-myŏn kkŭn-nam-ni-da. Ki-da-ri-si-get-ssŭm-ni-kka?

약 이십분 후면 끝납니다. 기다리시겠습니까?

5. Suppose I drop by in the afternoon.

O-hu-e tŭl-lŭ-get-ssŭm-ni-da.

오후에 들르겠습니다.

6. How soon is he expected?

Ŏl-ma-na i-ssŭ-myŏn kŭ-ga ol-kka-yo?

얼마나 있으면 그가 올까요?

7. We expect him any minute.

Kot ol-kkŏm-ni-da.

곧 올겁니다.

8. How soon will you be back?

Ŏl-ma-na i-ssŭ-myŏn to-ra-o-si-get-ssŭm-ni-kka?

얼마나 있으면 돌아오시겠습니까?

9. I'll be back before noon.

Yŏl-ttu-si chŏ-ne to-ra-o-get-ssŭm-ni-da.

열두시 전에 돌아오겠습니다.

10. How soon will you be ready?

Chun-bi-nŭn a-jik mŏ-rŏt-ssŭm-ni-kka?

준비는 아직 멀었습니까?

11. I'll be with you in a minute.

Kŭm-bang toem-ni-da.

금방 됩니다.

12. How soon can you come over?

Ŏl-ma-na i-ssŭ-myŏn ol ssu it-kket-ssŭm-ni-kka?

얼마나 있으면 올 수 있겠습니까?

13. Just as soon as I change my clothes.

O-sŭl ka-ra-im-nŭn tae-ro ka-get-ssŭm-ni-da.

옷을 갈아입는 대로 가겠습니다.

14. How soon are you lea-
ving for Seoul?

Ŏn-je-tchŭm seŏ-ul-lo ttŏ-na-sim-ni-
kka?

언제쯤 서울로 떠나십니까?

15. Early next week.

Nae-ju ch'o-e ttŏ-nam-ni-da.

내주 초에 떠납니다.

You don't have to finish it today.

O-nŭl kkŭn-nael p'i-ryo-nŭn
ŏp-ssŭm-ni-da.

(오늘 끝낼 필요는 없습니다.)

1. Have you finished the letters?

P'yŏn-ji ta ssŭ-syŏt-ssŭm-ni-kka?

편지 다 쓰셨습니까?

2. Yes. They're ready to mail.

Ne, pu-ch'i-gi-man ha-myŏn toem-ni-
da.

네, 부치기만 하면 됩니다.

3. Would you type this, please?

I-gŏ t'a-ja chom ch'yŏ chu-si-get-ssŭm-
ni-kka?

이거 타자 좀 쳐 주시겠습니까?

4. Certainly. I'll have it ready this afternoon.

Ne, o-nŭl o-hu-e hae tŭ-ri-get-ssŭm-
ni-da.

네, 오늘 오후에 해 드리겠습니다.

5. You don't have to finish it today. I won't need it until Saturday.

O-nŭl kkŭn-nae-ji a-na-do toem-ni-
da. T'o-yo-il-kka-ji-nŭn p'i-ryo-
ha-ji an-ssŭm-ni-da.

오늘 끝내지 않아도 됩니다. 토요
일까지는 필요하지 않습니다.

6. Do you want me to pick you up?

Che ch'a-ro mo-si-rŏ kal-kka-yo?

제 차로 모시러 갈까요?

7. No. You don't have to.

A-ni, kŭ-rŏl p'i-ryo ŏp-ssŭm-ni-da.

아니, 그럴 필요 없습니다.

8. Do I have to come back

Yŏl-ttu-si-kka-ji to-ra-wa-ya ham-ni-

by noon?
kka?

열두시까지 돌아와야 합니까?

9. No. You don't have to.   *A-ni, kŭ-rŏl p'i-ryo ŏp-ssŭm-ni-da.*

아니, 그럴 필요 없습니다.

10. You don't have to return it.   *Kŭ-gŏ tol-lyŏ chu-ji a-na-do chot-ssŭm-ni-da.*

그거 돌려 주지 않아도 좋습니다.

11. You mean I can keep it for good?   *A-ju ka-jyŏ-do cho-t'a-nŭn mal-ssŭm-im-ni-kka?*

아주 가져도 좋다는 말씀입니까?

12. You don't have to come all the way.   *Il-bu-rŏ o-sil p'i-ryo-nŭn ŏp-ssŭm-ni-da.*

일부러 오실 필요는 없습니다.

13. That's all right. I'm free now.   *Kwaen-ch'an-ssŭm-ni-da. Chi-gŭm pa-ppŭ-ji a-nŭ-ni-kka-yo.*

괜찮습니다. 지금 바쁘지 않으니까요.

14. Hurry up. It's already eleven.   *PPal-li kap-ssi-da. Pŏl-ssŏ yŏl-han-si-im-ni-da.*

빨리 갑시다. 벌써 열한시입니다.

15. Take it easy. We don't have to rush.   *Ch'ŏn-ch'ŏn-hi ha-sip-ssi-o. Sŏ-du-rŭl p'i-ryo-nŭn ŏp-ssŭm-ni-da.*

천천히 하십시오. 서두를 필요는 없습니다.

Have you ever tried kimchi?   *Kim-ch'i-rŭl mŏ-gŏ pon chŏ-gi it-ssŭm-ni-kka?*

(김치를 먹어 본 적이 있습니까?)

1. Have you ever tried ki-   *Kim-ch'i-rŭl mŏ-gŏ pon chŏ-gi it-*

mchi ?

ssŭm-ni-kka ?

김치를 먹어 본 적이 있습니까 ?

2. Oh, yes. I eat it very often.

Ne, cha-ju mŏk-ssŭm-ni-da.

네, 자주 먹습니다.

3. What's it like ?

Kim-ch'i-nŭn ŏ-ttŏn kŏ-sim-ni-kka ?

김치는 어떤 것입니까 ?

4. It's a pickled cabbage with lots of red pepper.

Pae-ch'u-rŭl chŏ-ryŏ-sŏ ko-ch'u-rŭl nŏ-ŭn kŏ-sim-ni-da.

배추를 절여서 고추를 넣은 것입니다.

5. I heard it's very hot.

A-ju maep-tta-dŏn-de-yo.

아주 맵다던데요.

6. It sure is, but you get used to it.

Maep-tchi-man ik-ssu-k'ae chim-ni-da.

맵지만 익숙해 집니다.

7. Have you ever visited the Kyongbok Palace ?

Kyŏng-bok-kkung-e ka pon chŏ-gi it-ssŭ-sim-ni-kka ?

경복궁에 가 본 적이 있으십니까 ?

8. Yes. I took my children there in May.

Ne, o-wŏ-re a-i-dŭl-gwa ham-kke kat-ssŭm-ni-da.

네, 오월에 아이들과 함께 갔습니다.

9. Have you ever taken piano lessons ?

P'i-a-no re-ssŭ-nŭl pa-da pon chŏ-gi it-ssŭm-ni-kka ?

피아노 레슨을 받아 본 적이 있습니까 ?

10. No, but I have studied the guitar.

A-ni-o, ki-t'a-rŭl pae-wŏt-ssŭm-ni-da.

아니오, 기타를 배웠습니다.

11. Have you ever studied Spanish ?

Sŏ-ba-na ŏ-rŭl pae-wŏ pon chŏ-gi it-ssŭm-ni-kka ?

서반아 어를 배워 본 적이 있습니까?

12. Yes, for three years in high school.

Ne, ko-dŭng hak-kkyo ttae sam nyŏn pae-wŏt-ssŭm-ni-da.

네, 고등 학교 때 삼 년 배웠습니다.

13. Have you ever eaten pulkoki?

Pul-go-gi-rŭl mŏ-gŏ pon chŏ-gi it-ssŭm-ni-kka?

불고기를 먹어 본 적이 있습니까?

14. Yes. It's very tasty.

Ne, a-ju ma-si chot-ssŭm-ni-da.

네, 아주 맛이 좋습니다.

15. Have you ever read this book?

I ch'ae-gŭl il-gŏ po-syŏt-ssŭm-ni-kka?

이 책을 읽어 보셨습니까?

16. Yes. I found it very interesting.

Ne, p'ŏk chae-mi-it-kke il-gŏt-ssŭm-ni-da.

네, 퍽 재미있게 읽었습니다.

Where else did you go?

Ŏ-di-rŭl tto ka-syŏt-ssŭm-ni-kka?

(**어디를 또 가셨습니까?**)

1. How was your trip?

Yŏ-haeng-ŭn chŭl-gŏ-wŏt-ssŭm-ni-kka?

여행은 즐거웠습니까?

2. It was really delightful. We went swimming at Taechon.

Mae-u chŭl-gŏ-wŏt-ssŭm-ni-da. Tae-ch'ŏ-ne-sŏ su-yŏng-ŭl haet-ssŭm-ni-da.

매우 즐거웠습니다. 대천에서 수영을 했습니다.

3. Where else did you go?

Ŏ-di-rŭl tto ka-syŏt-ssŭm-ni-kka?

어디를 또 가셨습니까?

4. We spent two days in Cheju island.

Che-ju-do-e-sŏ i-t'ŭ-rŭl mŏ-mul-lŏt-ssŭm-ni-da.

제주도에서 이틀을 머물렀습니다.

5. We spent three nights in Mokpo.

Mok-p'o-e-sŏ sa-hŭl-ppam mu-gŏt-ssŭm-ni-da.

목포에서 사흘밤 묵었습니다.

6. No wonder you've got such a tan.

Kŭ-rae-sŏ kŭ-rŏ-k'e ŏl-gu-ri t'al ssu-ba-kke ŏp-ssŏt-kkun-yo.

그래서 그렇게 얼굴이 탈 수밖에 없었군요.

7. What else do you need?

TTo mu-ŏ-si p'i-ryo-ham-ni-kka?

또 무엇이 필요합니까?

8. Just one more thing. Do you have a camera?

Han ka-ji in-nŭn-de-yo. K'a-me-ra-ga it-ssŭm-ni-kka?

한 가지 있는데요. 카메라가 있습니까?

9. What else do you want to know?

TTo al-go si-p'ŭn kŏ-si mu-ŏ-sim-ni-kka?

또 알고 싶은 것이 무엇입니까?

10. That's about all I can think of now.

Chi-gŭm saeng-gang-na-nŭn kŏ-sŭn kŭ-gŏt ppun-im-ni-da.

지금 생각나는 것은 그것 뿐입니다.

11. Who eles was at the meeting?

Kŭ hoe-ŭi-e-nŭn tto nu-ga ch'am-ssŏ-k'aet-ssŏt-ssŭm-ni-kka?

그 회의에는 또 누가 참석했었습니까?

12. Several businessmen from the United States.

Mi-gu-ge-sŏ on myŏn myŏng-ŭi si-rŏp-kka-ga it-ssŏt-ssŭm-ni-da.

미국에서 온 몇 명의 실업가가 있었습니다.

13. Where else can you

Not-kkŭ-rŭ-sŭl tto ŏ-di ka-myŏn sal

buy brassware?

ssu it-ssŭm-ni-kka?

놋그릇을 또 어디 가면 살 수 있
습니까?

14. Some of the department stores have good brassware.

Pae-k'wa-jŏ-me ka-myŏn cho-ŭn kŏ-si it-ssŭm-ni-da.

백화점에 가면 좋은 것이 있습니다.

How about tomorrow night?

Nae-il ppa-mŭn ŏ-ttŏt-ssŭm-ni-kka?

(내일 밤은 어떻습니까?)

1. Would you like to go bowling this evening?

O-nŭl chŏ-nyŏ-ge pol-ling ka-si-get-ssŭm-ni-kka?

오늘 저녁에 볼링 가시겠습니까?

2. I'm sorry but I have to meet someone.

Mi-an-ham-ni-da-man, man-nal ssa-ra-mi i-ssŏ-sŏ-yo.

미안합니다만, 만날 사람이 있어서
요.

3. How about tomorrow evening?

Nae-il chŏ-nyŏ-gen ŏ-ttŏt-ssŭm-ni-kka?

내일 저녁엔 어떻습니까?

4. Fine. I'm free tomorrow night.

Chot-ssŭm-ni-da. Nae-il chŏ-nyŏ-gen han-ga-ham-ni-da.

좋습니다. 내일 저녁엔 한가합니
다.

5. Shall we have supper together first?

U-ri chŏ-nyŏk-bu-t'ŏ mŏn-jŏ mŏ-gŭl-kka-yo?

우리 저녁부터 먼저 먹을까요?

6. Okay. I'll be ready at seven.

Chot-ssŭm-ni-da. Il-gop-ssi-e chun-bi-ha-get-ssŭm-ni-da.

좋습니다. 일곱시에 준비하겠습니
다.

7. How about tonight?

O-nŭl chŏ-nyŏ-gŭn ŏ-ttŏt-ssŭm-ni-kka?

오늘 저녁은 어떻습니까?

8. Sorry, but I have a date tonight. How about the day after tomorrow?

Mi-an-ham-ni-da. O-nŭl chŏ-nyŏ-ge te-i-t'ŭ-ga it-ssŭm-ni-da. Nae-il mo-re-nŭn ŏ-ttŏt-ssŭm-ni-kka?

미안합니다. 오늘 저녁에 데이트가 있습니다. 내일 모레는 어떻습니까?

9. How about this one?

I-gŏn ŏ-ttŏt-ssŭm-ni-kka?

이건 어떻습니까?

10. No. I like the one next to it.

An toe-get-ssŭm-ni-da. Kŭ yŏ-p'e kkŏ-si ma-ŭ-me tŭm-ni-da.

안 되겠습니다. 그 옆에 것이 마음에 듭니다.

11. How about going to the movies?

Yŏng-hwa ku-gyŏng ka-nŭn kŏ-si ŏ-ttŏt-ssŭm-ni-kka?

영화 구경 가는 것이 어떻습니까?

12. Sounds wonderful!

Cho-ŭn yae-gi-im-ni-da.

좋은 얘기입니다.

13. How about something to drink?

Mwŏt tchom ma-si-get-ssŭm-ni-kka?

뭣 좀 마시겠습니까?

14. No thanks. I've just had some coffee.

A-nim-ni-da. Kŭm-bang k'ŏ-p'i-rŭl ma-syŏt-ssŭm-ni-da.

아닙니다. 금방 커피를 마셨습니다.

15. What record would you like to hear?

Mu-sŭn re-k'o-dŭ-rŭl tŭt-kko sip-ssŭm-ni-kka?

무슨 레코드를 듣고 싶습니까?

16. How about the Ari-

A-ri-rang-ŭn ŏ-ttŏt-ssŭm-ni-kka?

rang? 아리랑은 어떻습니까?

They're worth trying. *Mŏ-gŏ pol man-ham-ni-da.*
(먹어 볼 만합니다.)

1. I think I'll have a steak. *Nan sŭ-t'e-i-k'ŭ-rŭl mŏk-kket-ssŭm-ni-da.*

난 스테이크를 먹겠습니다.

2. What do you suggest I order? *Nan mu-ŏ-sŭl chu-mun-hal-kka-yo?*

난 무엇을 주문할까요?

3. If you like seafood, order some shrimp. They are worth trying. *Hae-mu-rŭl chŭl-gi-sin-da-myŏn sae-u-rŭl tŭ-sip-ssi-o. Mŏ-gŭl man-ham-ni-da.*

해물을 즐기신다면 새우를 드십시오. 먹을 만합니다.

4. Good idea! I haven't had shrimp for ages. *Chot-ssŭm-ni-da! Sae-u mŏ-gŏ pon chi-ga a-ju o-rae toe-ŏt-ssŭm-ni-da.*

좋습니다! 새우 먹어 본 지가 아주 오래 되었습니다.

5. Did you like the movie? *Kŭ yŏng-hwa cho-at-ssŭm-ni-kka?*

그 영화 좋았습니까?

6. Yes. I think it's worth seeing. *Ne, pol man-ha-da-go saeng-ga-k'am-ni-da.*

네, 볼 만하다고 생각합니다.

7. What do you think of this book? *I ch'ae-gŭl ŏ-ttŏ-k'e saeng-ga-k'a-sim-ni-kka?*

이 책을 어떻게 생각하십니까?

8. It's worth reading. *Il-gŭl man-ham-ni-da.*

읽을 만합니다.

9. Was the game worth *Kŭ si-hap pol man haet-ssŭm-ni-kka?*

watching?

10. It sure was.

Hul-lyung-haet-ssŭm-ni-da.

훌륭했습니다.

11. Do you think the zoo is worth visiting?

Tong-mu-rwŏ-ne ka pol man-ha-da-go saeng-ga-k'am-ni-kka?

동물원에 가 볼 만하다고 생각합니까?

12. Oh yes. Especially. in the spring.

A ne, t'ŭ-k'i po-me chot-ssŭm-ni-da.

아 네, 특히 봄에 좋습니다.

13. Is it worth buying a summer suit now?

Chi-gŭm ha-bo-gŭl sa-do toe-get-ssŭm-ni-kka?

지금 하복을 사도 되겠습니까?

14. No. Why don't you wait till next year?

An-dwae-yo. Nae-nyŏn-kka-ji ki-da-ri-ji kŭ-rŏ-se-yo?

안돼요. 내년까지 기다리지 그러세요?

Let me take it for you.

Che-ga tae-sin kat-tta tŭ-ri-get-ssŭm-ni-da.

(제가 대신 갖다 드리겠습니다.)

1. Hi! Going somewhere?

An-nyŏng-ha-se-yo? Ŏ-di ka-sim-ni-kka?

안녕하세요? 어디 가십니까?

2. Yes, I'm taking this to Mr. Kim. He forgot it this morning.

I-gŏ-sŭl kim sŏn-saeng-e-ge ka-ji-go ka-nŭn kil-im-ni-da. O-nŭl a-ch'i-me i-jŏ-bŏ-ri-go kŭ-nyang kat-ssŭm-ni-da.

이것을 김 선생에게 가지고 가는 길입니다. 오늘 아침에 잊어버리고 그냥 갔습니다.

3. I'll be going right by his

Nan kŭ-ŭi sa-mu-si-rŭl chi-na-gam-

office. Let me take it for
you.

*ni-da. Che-ga tae-sin kat-tta tŭ-ri-
get-ssŭm-ni-da.*

난 그의 사무실을 지나갑니다. 제
가 대신 갖다 드리겠습니다.

4. Thanks. It will save me
a trip.

*Ko-map-ssŭm-ni-da. Kŭ-rŏm an ka-
do toe-get-kkun-yo.*

고맙습니다. 그럼 안 가도 되겠군
요.

5. Have you finished with
the newspaper?

Sin-mun ta il-gŭ-syŏt-ssŭm-ni-kka?

신문 다 읽으셨습니까?

6. Yes. Why don't you
take it with you?

Ne, ka-jyŏ-da il-gŭ-sip-ssi-o.

네, 가져다 읽으십시오.

7. Will you take this book
to Mr. Kim on your
way?

*Ka-nŭn ki-re i ch'ae-gŭl kim sŏn-
saeng-e-ge chŏn-hae chu-si-get-
ssŭm-ni-kka?*

가는 길에 이 책을 김 선생에게
전해 주시겠습니까?

8. Sure, I'll be glad to.

Ne, kŭ-rŏ-ji-yo.

네, 그러지요.

9. Do you want me to take
this to her?

*Che-ga i-gŏ-sŭl kŭ yŏ-ja-e-ge ka-jyŏ-
da chul-kka-yo?*

제가 이것을 그 여자에게 가져다
줄까요?

10. I'll be grateful if you
would.

*Kŭ-rŏ-k'e hae chu-si-myŏn ko-map-
kket-ssŭm-ni-da.*

그렇게 해 주시면 고맙겠습니다.

11. Are you going to take
her to the zoo?

*Kŭ yŏ-ja-rŭl tong-mu-rwŏ-ne te-ri-go
ka-sil-kkŏm-ni-kka?*

그 여자를 동물원에 데리고 가실
겁니까?

12. Yes. I'm taking my

Ne, u-ri a-i-dŭl-do ka-ch'i te-ri-go

children along too.

kal-kkŏm-ni-da.

네, 우리 아이들도 같이 데리고 갈겁니다.

13. Thank you for lending me this book.

I ch'ae-gŭl pil-lyŏ chwŏ-sŏ ko-map-ssŭm-ni-da.

이 책을 빌려 줘서 고맙습니다.

14. Take this one with you too.

I-gŏ-tto ham-kke ka-ji-go ka-sip-ssi-o.

이것도 함께 가지고 가십시오.

I must have lost them.

I-rŏ-bŏ-rin kŏ-si t'ŭl-rim-ŏp-ssŭm-ni-da.

(잃어버린 것이 틀림없습니다.)

1. I can't find my keys. I must have lost them.

Nae yŏl-swoe-rŭl ŏ-di tu-ŏn-nŭn-ji mot ch'at-kket-ssŭm-ni-da. I-rŏ-bŏ-rin kŏ-si pun-myŏng-ham-ni-da.

내 열쇠를 어디 두었는지 못 찾겠습니다. 잃어버린 것이 분명합니다.

2. Did you look your handbag?

Haen-dŭ-ppaek a-nŭl ch'a-ja po-at-ssŭm-ni-kka?

핸드백 안을 찾아 보았습니까?

3. Yes, but I'll look again.

Ne, ta-si ch'a-ja po-ji-yo.

네, 다시 찾아 보지요.

4. Look carefully this time!

I-bŏ-ne-nŭn chal ch'a-ja po-sip-ssi-o!

이번에는 잘 찾아 보십시오!

5. Oh! Here they are.

A! Yŏ-gi it-ssŭm-ni-da.

아! 여기 있습니다.

6. I must have seen you somewhere.

Ŏ-di-sŏ pun-myŏng-hi pon kŏt kat-ssŭm-ni-da.

어디서 분명히 본 것 같습니다.

7. You did. We met last summer.

Kŭ-rŏt-ssŭm-ni-da. Chang-nyŏn yŏ-rŭ-me man-nat-ssŭm-ni-da.

그렇습니다. 작년 여름에 만났습니다.

8. I must have left it at home.

Kŭ-gŏ-sŭl pun-myŏng-hi chi-be tu-go wat-ssŭm-ni-da.

그것을 분명히 집에 두고 왔습니다.

9. Don't forget to bring it tomorrow.

Nae-i-rŭn it-tchi mal-go ka-jyŏ o-sip-ssi-o.

내일은 잊지 말고 가져 오십시오.

10. I must have met him before.

Pun-myŏng-hi kŭ-wa-nŭn chŏ-ne man-nan chŏ-gi it-ssŭm-ni-da.

분명히 그와는 전에 만난 적이 있습니다.

11. I don't think you did.

Na-nŭn kŭ-rŏ-k'e saeng-ga-k'a-ji an-ssŭm-ni-da.

나는 그렇게 생각하지 않습니다.

12. I must have told you about it.

Pun-myŏng-hi nan tang-si-ne-ge kŭ yae-gi-rŭl haet-ssŭm-ni-da.

분명히 난 당신에게 그 얘기를 했습니다.

13. No, you didn't.

A-ni-o, an-haet-ssŭm-ni-da.

아니오, 안했습니다.

14. He must have missed the train.

Kŭ-nŭn t'ŭl-lim-ŏp-ssi ki-ch'a-rŭl no-ch'yŏt-ssŭl kkŏm-ni-da.

그는 틀림없이 기차를 놓쳤을 겁니다.

15. No doubt about it.

Ŭi-sim-hal yŏ-ji-do ŏp-ssŭm-ni-da.

의심할 여지도 없습니다.

You'd better stop smoking.

1. I have a terrible cough. I can't get rid of it.

2. You'd better stop smoking.

3. I tried but I just can't.

4. Well, try smoking less every day. That's how I stopped.

5. You'd better take some exercise.

6. I go hiking every Sunday.

7. You'd better take care of yourself.

8. I'm going to get some rest this weekend.

Tam-bae-rŭl kkŭn-nŭn p'yŏ-ni cho-k'et-ssŭm-ni-da.
(담배를 끊는 편이 좋겠습니다.)

Ki-ch'i-mi tae-dan-hi sim-ham-ni-da. A-mu-rae-do an ttŏ-rŏ-ji-nŭn-de-yo.
기침이 대단히 심합니다. 아무래도 안 떨어지는데요.

Tam-bae-rŭl kkŭn-nŭn p'yŏ-ni cho-k'et-ssŭm-ni-da.
담배를 끊는 편이 좋겠습니다.

KKŭ-nŭ-ryŏ-go hae-do an toem-ni-da.
끊으려고 해도 안 됩니다.

Tam-bae-rŭl mae-il cho-gŭm-ssik chu-ryŏ po-sip-ssi-o. Chŏ-do kŭ-rŏ-k'e kkŭ-nŏt-ssŭm-ni-da.
담배를 매일 조금씩 줄여 보십시오. 저도 그렇게 끊었습니다.

Un-dong chom ha-nŭn p'yŏ-ni cho-k'et-ssŭm-ni-da.
운동 좀 하는 편이 좋겠습니다.

I-ryo-il-ma-da tŭng-sa-nŭl ha-go it-ssŭm-ni-da.
일요일마다 등산을 하고 있습니다.

Mom cho-sim-hae-ya-get-ssŭm-ni-da.
몸 조심해야겠습니다.

I-bŏn chu-ma-ren chom swil-kka ham-ni-da.
이번 주말엔 좀 쉴까 합니다.

9. I'm better phone my wife.

A-nae-e-ge chŏn-hwa-rŭl ha-nŭn p'yŏ-ni cho-k'et-ssŭm-ni-da.

아내에게 전화를 하는 편이 좋겠습니다.

10. Yes. She might be waiting for you.

Ne, ki-da-ri-go i-ssŭl-tchi-do mo-rŭ-ji-yo.

네, 기다리고 있을지도 모르지요.

11. I'd better not stay too long.

Nŏ-mu o-rae it-tchi an-nŭn p'yŏ-ni cho-k'et-ssŭm-ni-da.

너무 오래 있지 않는 편이 좋겠습니다.

12. That's all right. I have plenty of time.

Kwaen-ch'an-ssŭm-ni-da. Si-ga-nŭn ŏl-ma-dŭn-ji it-ssŭm-ni-da.

괜찮습니다. 시간은 얼마든지 있습니다.

13. We'd better not stay out too late.

Nŏ-mu nŭt-kke-kka-ji to-ra-da-ni-ji an-nŭn p'yŏ-ni cho-k'et-ssŭm-ni-da.

너무 늦게까지 돌아다니지 않는 편이 좋겠습니다.

14. It's almost curfew time.

T'ong-gŭm si-ga-ni kŏ-ŭi ta toe-ŏt-ssŭm-ni-da.

통금 시간이 거의 다 되었습니다.

May I ask where you bought it?

Ŏ-di-sŏ sa-syŏt-ssŭm-ni-kka?
(어디서 사셨습니까?)

1. I like your necktie very much. May I ask where you bought it?

Nek-t'a-i-ga p'ŏk ma-ŭ-me tŭm-ni-da. Sil-lye-ji-man ŏ-di-sŏ sa-syŏt-ssŭm-ni-kka?

넥타이가 퍽 마음에 듭니다. 실례지만 어디서 사셨습니까?

2. I bought it in the Bando Arcade. There's a tie shop on the third floor.

Pan-do a-k'e-i-dŭ-e-sŏ sat-ssŭm-ni-da. Sam-ch'ŭng-e nek-t'a-i ka-ge-ga it-ssŭm-ni-da.

반도 아케이드에서 샀습니다. 삼층에 넥타이 가게가 있습니다.

3. I'd like to buy one for my husband.

Na-do nam-p'yŏn kkŏ-sŭl ha-na sa-go sip-ssŭm-ni-da.

나도 남편 것을 하나 사고 싶습니다.

4. Let me take you there now.

Che-ga chi-gŭm an-nae-hae tŭ-ri-ji-yo.

제가 지금 안내해 드리지요.

5. May I ask how old you are?

Sil-lye-ji-man na-i-ga ŏ-ttŏ-k'e twaet-ssŭm-ni-kka?

실례지만 나이가 어떻게 됐습니까?

6. I just turned forty.

Ma-hŭ-ni kat nŏ-mŏt-ssŭm-ni-da.

마흔이 갓 넘었습니다.

7. May I ask what business you're in?

Sil-lye-ji-man mu-sŭn sa-ŏ-bŭl ha-sim-ni-kka?

실례지만 무슨 사업을 하십니까?

8. I'm an exporter.

Su-ch'u-rŏ-bŭl ha-go it-ssŭm-ni-da.

수출업을 하고 있습니다.

9. May I ask where you are from?

Sil-lye-ji-man ko-hyang-i ŏ-di-sim-ni-kka?

실례지만 고향이 어디십니까?

10. I'm from the Chung-chong-do.

Ch'ung-ch'ŏng-do-im-ni-da.

충청도입니다.

11. May I ask how much you paid for it?

Sil-lye-ji-man ŏl-ma-e sa-syŏt-ssŭm-ni-kka?

실례지만 얼마에 사셨습니까?

12. I paid 35,000 won.

Sam-man o-ch'ŏn wŏn-ŭl chu-ŏt-ssŭm-ni-da.

삼만 오천 원을 주었습니다.

13. May I asked how far you're going?

Sil-lye-ji-man ŏ-di-kka-ji ka-sim-ni-kka?

실례지만 어디까지 가십니까?

14. I'm going as far as Pusan.

Pu-san-kka-ji kam-ni-da.

부산까지 갑니다.

15. May I ask how often you come here?

Sil-lye-ji-man yŏ-gi cha-ju o-sim-ni-kka?

실례지만 여기 자주 오십니까?

16. About twice a month.

Han ta-re tu pŏn chŏng-do om-ni-da.

한 달에 두 번 정도 옵니다.

I hope you like it.

Ma-ŭ-me tŭl-gi-rŭl pa-ram-ni-da.

(마음에 들기를 바랍니다.)

1. Have you seen my report? I can't find it on my desk.

Nae po-go-sŏ-rŭl po-syŏt-ssŭm-ni-kka? Ch'aek-ssang wi-e tu-ŏn-nŭn-de ŏp-ssŭm-ni-da.

내 보고서를 보셨습니까? 책상 위에 두었는데 없습니다.

2. Here it is. I retyped it.

Yŏ-gi it-ssŭm-ni-da. Che-ga t'a-ja-rŭl ta-si ch'yŏt-ssŭm-ni-da.

여기 있습니다. 제가 타자를 다시 쳤습니다.

3. Thanks. Mr. Park just asked for it.

Kam-sa-ham-ni-da. Pak sŏn-saeng-i tal-la-go hae-sŏ-yo.

감사합니다. 박 선생이 달라고 해서요.

4. I hope he likes it.

Kŭ pun ma-ŭ-me tŭl-gi-rŭl pa-ram-

ni-da.
그 분 마음에 들기를 바랍니다.

5. I'm on my way to a party.

P'a-t'i-e ka-nŭn kil-im-ni-da.
파티에 가는 길입니다.

6. I hope you have a good time.

Chal nol-go o-si-gi pa-ram-ni-da.
잘 놀고 오시기 바랍니다.

7. I'm getting ready for my vacation.

Nan hyu-ga kal chun-bi-rŭl ha-go it-ssŭm-ni-da.
난 휴가 갈 준비를 하고 있습니다.

8. I hope you have a nice trip.

Chal ta-nyŏ o-si-gil pa-ram-ni-da.
잘 다녀 오시길 바랍니다.

9. I still have a slight fever.

A-jik yŏ-ri chom it-ssŭm-ni-da.
아직 열이 좀 있습니다.

10. I hope you get well soon.

Kot nat-kki-rŭl pa-ram-ni-da.
곧 낫기를 바랍니다.

11. See you on Monday.

Wŏ-ryo-i-re ta-si poep-kket-ssŭm-ni-da.
월요일에 다시 뵙겠습니다.

12. I hope you have a nice weekend.

Chu-ma-rŭl chal chi-nae-si-gil pa-ram-ni-da.
주말을 잘 지내시길 바랍니다.

13. I hope you like hot food.

Mae-un ŭm-si-gŭl cho-a-ha-si-nŭn-ji mo-rŭ-get-ssŭm-ni-da.
매운 음식을 좋아하시는지 모르겠습니다.

14. I eat it all the time.

Hang-sang mŏk-ssŭm-ni-da.
항상 먹습니다.

15. It looks like rain.

Pi-ga ol kkŏt kat-ssŭm-ni-da.
비가 올 것 같습니다.

16. I hope she brought her

Kŭ-nyŏ-ga u-sa-nŭl ka-ji-go wat-

umbrella.

ssŭ-myŏn cho-k'en-nŭn-de-yo.
그녀가 우산을 가지고 왔으면 좋
겠는데요.

Just one copy will do.

*Tan han chang-i-myŏn toe-get
-ssŭm-ni-da.*
(단 한 장이면 되겠습니다.)

1. Will you do me a fa-
vor?

Pu-t'a-gi han ka-ji in-nŭn-de-yo?
부탁이 한 가지 있는데요?

2. Sure, what is it?

Ne, mu-ŏ-sim-ni-kka?
네, 무엇입니까?

3. Would you type this letter for me, please?

*I p'yŏn-ji chom t'a-ja ch'yŏ chu-si-get-
ssŭm-ni-kka?*
이 편지 좀 타자 쳐 주시겠습니까?

4. Certainly. I'll do it right
away. How many copies
shall I make?

*Chot-ssŭm-ni-da. Chi-gŭm kot hae
tŭ-ri-get-ssŭm-ni-da.   Myŏt
tchang-i-na man-dŭl-kka-yo?*
좋습니다. 지금 곧 해 드리겠습니
다. 몇 장이나 만들까요?

5. Just one copy will do.

Han chang-i-myŏn toem-ni-da.
한 장이면 됩니다.

6. Is this big enough?

*I chŏng-do k'ŭ-gi-myŏn toe-get-ssŭm-
ni-kka?*
이 정도 크기면 되겠습니까?

7. No, that won't do. Get
me a bigger one.

*Kŭ-gŏn   an   toe-get-ssŭm-ni-da.
Chom-dŏ k'ŭn kŏl-lo chu-sip-ssi-o.*
그건 안 되겠습니다. 좀더 큰 걸로
주십시오.

8. Will this do?

I-gŏ-myŏn toe-get-ssŭm-ni-kka?
이거면 되겠습니까?

9. I'm afraid not.

An toe-get-ssŭm-ni-da.

안 되겠습니다.

10. Any special brand you'd like ?

Tŭ-k'i cho-a-ha-nŭn chong-nyu-ga it-ssŭm-ni-kka ?

특히 좋아하는 종류가 있습니까 ?

11. Any brand will do.

Mwŏ-dŭn-ji chot-ssŭm-ni-da.

뭐든지 좋습니다.

12. Do you need a new one ?

Sae kŏ-si p'i-ryo-ham-ni-kka ?

새 것이 필요합니까 ?

13. No, an old one will do.

A-nim-ni-da. Nal-gŭn kŏt-tto chot-ssŭm-ni-da.

아닙니다. 낡은 것도 좋습니다.

14. Will a red one do ?

PPal-gan-sae-gi-myŏn toem-ni-kka ?

빨간색이면 됩니까 ?

15. No, I need a blue one.

A-nim-ni-da. Ch'ŏng-sae-gi i-ssŏ-ya ham-ni-da.

아닙니다. 청색이 있어야 합니다.

I'm afraid we're going to be late.

Nŭ-jŭl kkŏt kat-ssŭm-ni-da.
(늦을 것 같습니다.)

1. I'm afraid we're going to be late.

Nŭ-jŭl kkŏt kat-ssŭm-ni-da.

늦을 것 같습니다.

2. How much time is left ?

Si-ga-ni ŏl-ma-na na-mat-ssŭm-ni-kka ?

시간이 얼마나 남았습니까 ?

3. We've got about thirty minutes.

Yak sam-sip-ppun na-mat-ssŭm-ni-da.

약 삼십분 남았습니다.

4. That should be plenty of time.

Kŭ-man-ha-myŏn si-ga-nŭn ch'ung-bun-ha-get-ssŭm-ni-da.

그만하면 시간은 충분하겠습니다.

5. Let's step on it.

PPal-li sŏ-du-rŭp-ssi-da.
빨리 서두릅시다.

6. Be right with you.

Kot na-ga-get-ssŭm-ni-da.
곧 나가겠습니다.

7. Am I late?

Nŭ-jŏt-ssŭm-ni-kka?
늦었습니까?

8. No, You're right on time.

A-nim-ni-da. Chŏng-ga-ge o-syŏt-ssŭm-ni-da.
아닙니다. 정각에 오셨습니다.

9. He's ten minutes late already.

Kŭ sa-ra-mŭn pŏl-ssŏ sip-ppu-ni-na nŭ-jŏt-ssŭm-ni-da.
그 사람은 벌써 십분이나 늦었습니다.

10. Didn't you know he's always late?

Kŭ sa-ra-mŭn ŏn-je-na nŭn-nŭn kŏl mo-rŭ-sim-ni-kka?
그 사람은 언제나 늦는 걸 모르십니까?

11. Aren't we going to be late for the meeting?

U-ri hoe-ŭi-e nŭt-tchi a-nŭl-kka-yo?
우리 회의에 늦지 않을까요?

12. I hope not. Let's hurry.

Nŭt-tchi ma-ra-ya ham-ni-da. PPal-li kap-ssi-da.
늦지 말아야 합니다. 빨리 갑시다.

13. Were you late for school?

Hak-kkyo-e chi-ga-gŭl haet-ssŭm-ni-kka?
학교에 지각을 했습니까?

14. No. I just made it.

A-nim-ni-da. Cha-ch'i-t'a-myŏn nŭ-jŭl ppŏn haet-ssŭm-ni-da.
아닙니다. 자칫하면 늦을 뻔 했습니다.

15. Don't be late for the party.

Pa-t'i-e nŭt-tchi ma-sip-ssi-o.
파티에 늦지 마십시오.

16. No. I won't.

Ne, an nŭt-kket-ssŭm-ni-da.
네, 안 늦겠습니다.

17. What if we're late for the meeting?

Ma-nil hoe-ŭi-e nŭ-jŭ-myŏn ŏ-ttŏ-k'e ha-ji-yo?
만일 회의에 늦으면 어떻게 하지 요?

18. Don't worry. No one will be on time.

Kŏk-tchŏng ma-sip-ssi-o. Che si-ga-ne ol ssa-ra-mŭn a-mu-do ŏp-ssŭl kkŏ-sim-ni-da.
걱정 마십시오. 제 시간에 올 사 람은 아무도 없을 것입니다.

How did you know I was coming?

Nae-ga o-nŭn kŏl ŏ-ttŏ-k'e a-rat-ssŭm-ni-kka?
(내가 오는 걸 어떻게 알았습니 까?)

1. Good evening. Hope I am not too late.

An-nyŏng-ha-sim-ni-kka. Nŏ-mu nŭt-tchi a-nan-nŭn-ji mo-rŭ-get-ssŭm-ni-da.
안녕하십니까. 너무 늦지 않았는지 모르겠습니다.

2. No, we've been expecting you.

A-nim-ni-da. Ki-da-ri-go it-ssŏt-ssŭm-ni-da.
아닙니다. 기다리고 있었습니다.

3. How did you know I was coming?

Nae-ga o-nŭn kŏl ŏ-ttŏ-k'e a-rat-ssŭm-ni-kka?
내가 오는 걸 어떻게 알았습니까?

4. Your wife called. She said you were on your way over.

Pu-in-kke-sŏ chŏn-hwa-rŭl kŏ-rŏt-ssŭm-ni-da. TTŏ-nat-tta-go mal-ssŭm-ha-si-dŏ-gun-yo.
부인께서 전화를 걸었습니다. 떠났

301

5. How did you know he was there ?

Kŭ sa-ra-mi kŏ-gi in-nŭn kŏl ŏ-ttŏ-k'e a-rat-ssŭm-ni-kka ?

그 사람이 거기 있는 걸 어떻게 알았습니까 ?

6. His brother told me.

Kŭ-ŭi tong-saeng-i nae-ge mal-ha-dŏ-gun-yo.

그의 동생이 내게 말하더군요.

7. How did you know I got promoted ?

Nae-ga sŭng-jin-han kŏ-sŭl ŏ-ttŏ-k'e a-rat-ssŭm-ni-kka ?

내가 승진한 것을 어떻게 알았습니까 ?

8. I read it in the newspaper.

Sin-mu-ne-sŏ po-at-ssŭm-ni-da.

신문에서 보았습니다.

9. How did you know she was back from her trip ?

Kŭ-nyŏ-ga yŏ-haeng-e-sŏ to-ra-on kŏ-sŭl ŏ-ttŏ-k'e a-rat-ssŭm-ni-kka?

그녀가 여행에서 돌아온 것을 어떻게 알았습니까 ?

10. I met her downtown yesterday.

Ŏ-je si-nae-e-sŏ man-nat-ssŭm-ni-da.

어제 시내에서 만났습니다.

11. How did she know I bought a colcor TV set ?

Nae-ga k'ŏl-lŏ t'el-le-bi-jŏ-nŭl san kŏ-sŭl kŭ-nyŏ-ga ŏ-ttŏ-k'e a-rat-ssŭm-ni-kka ?

내가 컬러 텔레비전을 산 것을 그녀가 어떻게 알았습니까 ?

12. She saw your antenna.

Tang-si-nŭi an-t'e-na-rŭl po-at-ssŭm-ni-da.

당신의 안테나를 보았습니다.

13. How did your wife

Nae-ga p'ŭ-ra-i-dŭ ch'i-k'i-nŭl cho-a-

know I like fried chicken?

ha-nŭn kŏ-sŭl tang-sin pu-i-ni ŏ-ttŏ-k'e a-rat-tchi-yo?

내가 프라이드 치킨을 좋아하는 것을 당신 부인이 어떻게 알았지요?

14. She just guessed.

Chim-ja-gŭ-ro a-ra ma-ch'un kŏ-sim-ni-da.

짐작으로 알아 맞춘 것입니다.

Shall I phone him now?

Chi-gŭm chŏn-hwa-rŭl kŏl-kka-yo?

(지금 전화를 걸까요?)

1. Mr. Kim phoned at five o'clock.

Ta-sŏt-ssi-e kim sŏn-saeng-i chŏn-hwa-haet-ssŏt-ssŭm-ni-da.

다섯시에 김 선생이 전화했었습니다.

2. Did he leave any message?

Mu-sŭn chŏn-ha-nŭn ma-ri ŏp-ssŏt-ssŭm-ni-kka?

무슨 전하는 말이 없었습니까?

3. He asked you to call him.

Chŏn-hwa kŏ-rŏ tal-la-go ha-si-dŏ-gun-yo.

전화 걸어 달라고 하시더군요.

4. It must be something urgent.

Kin-gŭ-p'an i-rin mo-yang-i-gun-yo.

긴급한 일인 모양이군요.

5. Shall I phone him now?

Chi-gŭm chŏn-hwa-rŭl kŏl-kka-yo?

지금 전화를 걸까요?

6. Please do.

Ne. Kŭ-rŏ-k'e ha-sip-ssi-o.

네. 그렇게 하십시오.

7. Shall I answer the phone?

Che-ga chŏn-hwa pa-dŭl-kka-yo?

제가 전화 받을까요?

8. Please don't bother. I will.

Kwaen-ch'an-ssŭm-ni-da.   Che-ga pat-tchi-yo.

괜찮습니다. 제가 받지요.

9. Shall I have him call you back?

Chŏn-hwa-rŭl kŏ-rŏ tal-la-go hal-kka-yo?

전화를 걸어 달라고 할까요?

10. No thanks. I'll call again later.

A-nim-ni-da. Na-jung-e tto kŏl-get-ssŭm-ni-da.

아닙니다. 나중에 또 걸겠습니다.

11. Shall I answer the door?

Mu-ne na-ga pol-kka-yo?

문에 나가 볼까요?

12. I'll see who it is.

Nu-gun-ga nae-ga a-ra-bo-get-ssŭm-ni-da.

누군가 내가 알아보겠습니다.

13. Shall I get you a glass of water?

Mul han chan tŭ-ril-kka-yo?

물 한 잔 드릴까요?

14. Yes, please.

Ne, chu-sip-ssi-o.

네, 주십시오.

15. Shall I come back to-morrow?

Nae-il ta-si ol-kka-yo?

내일 다시 올까요?

16. Yes, I'm busy right now.

Ne, chi-gŭ-mŭn pa-ppŭm-ni-da.

네, 지금은 바쁩니다.

17. Shall I type your report?

Po-go-sŏ-rŭl t'a-ja-hae tŭ-ril-kka-yo?

보고서를 타자해 드릴까요?

18. I'd be grateful if you would.

Kŭ-rŏ-k'e hae chu-myŏn ko-map-kket-ssŭm-ni-da.

그렇게 해 주면 고맙겠습니다.

That's why I didn't invite him.

Kŭ-rae-sŏ kŭ sa-ra-mŭl ch'o-dae-ha-ji a-nat-ssŭm-ni-da.

(그래서 그 사람을 초대하지 않

았습니다.）

1. Here's the list of guests.

Son-nim myŏng-da-ni yŏ-gi it-ssŭm-ni-da.

손님 명단이 여기 있습니다.

2. Why didn't you invite Mr. Lee?

Wae i sŏn-saeng-ŭn ch'o-dae-ha-ji a-nat-ssŭm-ni-kka?

왜 이 선생은 초대하지 않았습니까?

3. He's never on time. That's why I didn't invite him.

Si-ga-nŭl chi-k'i-ji an-ssŭm-ni-da. Kŭ-rae-sŏ kŭ sa-ra-mŭn ch'o-dae-ha-ji a-nat-ssŭm-ni-da.

시간을 지키지 않습니다. 그래서 그 사람은 초대하지 않았습니다.

4. I don't blame you. He kept me waiting one hour yesterday.

Chal-haet-ssŭm-ni-da. Ŏ-jŏ-kke-do nal han si-ga-ni-na ki-da-ri-ge haet-ssŭm-ni-da.

잘했습니다. 어저께도 날 한 시간이나 기다리게 했습니다.

5. She always exaggerates.

Kŭ yŏ-ja-nŭn hang-sang kwa-jang-ŭl ham-ni-da.

그 여자는 항상 과장을 합니다.

6. That's why I don't like her.

Kŭ-rae-sŏ nan kŭ yŏ-ja-rŭl cho-a-ha-ji an-ssŭm-ni-da.

그래서 난 그 여자를 좋아하지 않습니다.

7. He drinks very heavily.

Kŭ sa-ra-mŭn su-rŭl nŏ-mu ma-ni ma-sim-ni-da.

그 사람은 술을 너무 많이 마십니다.

8. That's why he's always broke.

Kŭ-rae-sŏ kŭ-nŭn hang-sang to-ni ttŏ-rŏ-jim-ni-da.

9. He's an honest man.

그래서 그는 항상 돈이 떨어집니다.

Kŭ sa-ra-mŭn ch'am chŏng-ji-k'am-ni-da.

그 사람은 참 정직합니다.

10. That's why he is respected by everyone.

Kŭ-rae-sŏ kŭ-nŭn mo-dŭn sa-ra-mŭi chon-gyŏng-ŭl pat-ssŭm-ni-da.

그래서 그는 모든 사람의 존경을 받습니다.

11. His father is ill.

Kŭ-ŭi pu-ch'i-nŭn p'yŏn-ch'a-nŭ-sim-ni-da.

그의 부친은 편찮으십니다.

12. Is that why he couldn't come?

Kŭ-rae-sŏ kŭ pu-nŭn mot o-syŏt-ssŭm-ni-kka?

그래서 그 분은 못 오셨습니까?

13. My watch is broken.

Nae si-gye-ga ko-jang-i nat-ssŭm-ni-da.

내 시계가 고장이 났습니다.

14. Is that why you're late?

Kŭ-rae-sŏ nŭ-jŭ-syŏt-kkun-yo?

그래서 늦으셨군요?

15. This food is delicious!

I ŭm-si-gŭn ma-si it-ssŭm-ni-da.

이 음식은 맛이 있습니다.

16. That's why I always eat here.

Kŭ-rae-sŏ hang-sang na-nŭn yŏ-gi wa-sŏ mŏk-ssŭm-ni-da.

그래서 항상 나는 여기 와서 먹습니다.

Will you have him call me back?

Chŏn-hwa chom kŏ-rŏ tal-la-go ha-sip-ssi-o.

(전화 좀 걸어 달라고 하십시오.)

1. This is Mr. Kim speaking. May I speak to

Kim-im-ni-da. Pak sŏn-saeng chom pa-kkwŏ chu-sip-ssi-o.

Mr. Park, please.

김입니다. 박 선생 좀 바꿔 주십
시오.

2. I'm sorry, he's working now. Is there any message ?

Mi-an-ha-ji-man chi-gŭm il-ha-go kye-sim-ni-da. Chŏn-hal mal-ssŭ-mi it-ssŭ-sim-ni-kka ?

미안하지만 지금 일하고 계십니다.
전할 말씀이 있으십니까 ?

3. Will you have him call me back, please ?

Chŏn-hwa chom kŏ-rŏ tal-la-go chŏn-hae chu-si-get-ssŭm-ni-kka?

전화 좀 걸어 달라고 전해 주시겠
습니까 ?

4. I'll be glad to.

Ne, kŭ-rŏ-k'e ha-get-ssŭm-ni-da.

네, 그렇게 하겠습니다.

5. Will you have her mail this letter ?

Kŭ yŏ-ja-e-ge i p'yŏn-ji chom pu-ch'yŏ tal-la-go hae chu-si-get-ssŭm-ni-kka ?

그 여자에게 이 편지 좀 부쳐 달
라고 해 주시겠습니까 ?

6. Certainly. She's going to the post office now.

Ne. Kŭ yŏ-ja-nŭn chi-gŭm u-ch'e-gu-ge ka-nŭn kil-im-ni-da.

네. 그 여자는 지금 우체국에 가는
길입니다.

7. Will you have her bring me a cup of coffee ?

Kŭ yŏ-ja-e-ge k'ŏ-p'i han chan ka-jyŏ-o-ra-go ha-si-get-ssŭm-ni-kka ?

그 여자에게 커피 한 잔 가져오라고
하시겠습니까 ?

8. Yes. I'll tell her right away.

Ne, kot chŏn-ha-get-ssŭm-ni-da.

네, 곧 전하겠습니다.

9. Will you have him come into my office ?

Kŭ pu-nŭl nae sa-mu-si-re tŭ-ryŏ po-nae chu-si-get-ssŭm-ni-kka ?

그 분을 내 사무실에 들여 보내

주시겠습니까?

10. I'll tell him as soon as he comes.

Kŭ pu-ni o-si-nŭn tae-ro kŭ-rŏ-k'e ha-get-ssŭm-ni-da.

그 분이 오시는 대로 그렇게 하겠습니다.

11. Mr. Kim is here to see you.

Kim sŏn-saeng-i ch'a-ja wat-ssŭm-ni-da.

김 선생이 찾아 왔습니다.

12. Will you have him wait a moment, please?

Chom ki-da-ryŏ tal-la-go hae chu-se-yo?

좀 기다려 달라고 해 주세요?

13. Everyone is present.

Chŏ-nwŏn ch'am-ssŏ-k'aet-ssŭm-ni-da.

전원 참석했습니다.

14. Will you have them start the meeting?

Hoe-ŭi-rŭl si-ja-k'al-kka-yo?

회의를 시작할까요?

I don't know what to do.

Ŏ-ttŏ-k'e hae-ya hal tchi mo-rŭ-get-ssŭm-ni-da.

(어떻게 해야 할 지 모르겠습니다.)

1. Where are you going for your vacation?

Ŏ-di-ro hyu-ga-rŭl kal saeng-gak-im-ni-kka?

어디로 휴가를 갈 생각입니까?

2. I don't know what to do. Should I go to Pusan or Cheju island?

Ŏ-ttŏ-k'e hae-ya hal tchi mo-rŭ-get-ssŭm-ni-da. Pu-sa-nŭ-ro kal-kka-yo, che-ju-do-ro kal-kka-yo?

어떻게 해야 할 지 모르겠습니다. 부산으로 갈까요, 제주도로 갈까요?

3. Why not go to Cheju is-

Che-ju-do-ro mŏn-jŏ ka-si-ji kŭ-rŏm-

land first? Then you can return by way of Pusan.

ni-kka? Kŭ-rŏm to-ra-o-nŭn ki-re pu-sa-ne tŭl-lŭl ssu it-ssŭm-ni-da.

제주도로 먼저 가시지 그럽니까? 그럼 돌아오는 길에 부산에 들를 수 있습니다.

4. Good idea! That way I can visit both places.

Cho-ŭn saeng-gak-im-ni-da. Kŭ-rŏ-k'e ha-myŏn tu kun-de-rŭl ta tŭl-lŭl ssu it-kket-kkun-yo.

좋은 생각입니다. 그렇게 하면 두 군데를 다 들를 수 있겠군요.

5. What are you going to do about your cough?

Ki-ch'i-mŭl ŏ-ttŏ-k'e ha-get-ssŭm-ni-kka?

기침을 어떻게 하겠습니까?

6. I don't know what to do about it.

Ŏ-ttŏ-k'e hae-ya hal tchi na-do chal mo-rŭ-get-ssŭm-ni-da.

어떻게 해야 할 지 나도 잘 모르겠습니다.

7. Did you make up your mind?

Kyŏl-ssi-mŭl haet-ssŭm-ni-kka?

결심을 했습니까?

8. No, I can't decide what to do.

A-ni, ŏ-ttŏ-k'e hae-ya hal tchi na-do chal mo-rŭ-get-ssŭm-ni-da.

아니, 어떻게 해야 할 지 나도 잘 모르겠습니다.

9. Tell me what to do?

Ŏ-ttŏ-k'e ha-myŏn cho-ŭn-ji nae-ge mal-hae chu-se-yo?

어떻게 하면 좋은지 내게 말해 주세요?

10. I wish I knew myself.

Nae cha-si-nŭl mo-rŭ-get-ssŭm-ni-da.

내 자신을 모르겠습니다.

11. Did you tell him about

Kŭ sa-ra-me-ge kŭ yae-gi-rŭl haet-

it ?

ssŭm-ni-kka?

그 사람에게 그 얘기를 했습니까?

12. No, I'm at a loss what to do.

A-ni, ŏ-tchi-hae-ya cho-ŭl-tchi na-do mo-rŭ-get-ssŭm-ni-da.

아니, 어찌해야 좋을지 나도 모르겠습니다.

13. Does he know what to do ?

Kŭ sa-ram hae-ya hal ri-rŭl al-go it-ssŭm-ni-kka?

그 사람 해야 할 일을 알고 있습니까?

14. Yes, I told him this morning.

Ne, o-nŭl a-ch'i-me mal-hae chu-ŏt-ssŭm-ni-da.

네, 오늘 아침에 말해 주었습니다.

I don't think he can make it.

Kŭ pu-nŭn ŏ-ryŏ-ul kkŏt kat-ssŭm-ni-da.

(그 분은 어려울 것 같습니다.)

1. Are you going to the opera tomorrow night ?

Nae-il chŏ-nyŏ-ge o-p'e-ra ku-gyŏng ka-si-get-ssŭm-ni-kka?

내일 저녁에 오페라 구경 가시겠습니까?

2. Yes. I want to see it very much.

Ne, kkok po-go sip-ssŭm-ni-da.

네, 꼭 보고 싶습니다.

3. How about Mr. Park ? Is he going too ?

Pak sŏn-saeng-ŭn? Kŭ pun-do ka-sil kkŏm-ni-kka?

박 선생은? 그 분도 가실 겁니까?

4. I don't think he can make it. He may have to work overtime.

Mot kkal kkŏt kat-ssŭm-ni-da. Kŭ pu-nŭn nŭt-kke-kka-ji kŭn-mu-hae-ya hal kkŏm-ni-da.

못 갈 것 같습니다. 그 분은 늦게

까지 근무해야 할 겁니다.

5. I don't think he's home.

Kŭ pu-nŭn chi-be an kye-sil kkŏt kat-ssŭm-ni-da.

그 분은 집에 안 계실 것 같습니다.

6. Neither do I.

Che saeng-gak-tto kŭ-rŏt-ssŭm-ni-da.

제 생각도 그렇습니다.

7. How about this one?

I-gŏn ŏ-ttŏ-sim-ni-kka?

이건 어떠십니까?

8. I don't think he likes that color.

Kŭ pu-ni kŭ sae-gŭl cho-a-hal kkŏt kat-tchi an-ssŭm-ni-da.

그 분이 그 색을 좋아할 것 같지 않습니다.

9. Does she speak Korea?

Kŭ yŏ-ja han-gung-mal ha-na-yo?

그 여자 한국말 하나요?

10. I don't think she does.

Mo t'al kkŏt kat-ssŭm-ni-da.

못 할 것 같습니다.

11. Can you be here by 10?

Yŏl-ssi-kka-ji yŏ-gi ol ssu it-kket-ssŭm-ni-kka?

열시까지 여기 올 수 있겠습니까?

12. I don't think I can make it by then.

Ku ttae-kka-ji-nŭn mot kkal kkŏt kat-ssŭm-ni-da.

그 때까지는 못 갈 것 같습니다.

13. Where's Miss Lee?

I yang-ŭn wat-ssŭm-ni-kka?

이 양은 왔습니까?

14. I don't think she's coming.

Kŭ-nyŏ-nŭn an ol kkŏt kat-ssŭm-ni-da.

그녀는 안 올 것 같습니다.

15. I don't think I met your friend.

Tang-sin ch'in-gu-wa-nŭn in-sa-ga ŏm-nŭn kŏt kat-ssŭm-ni-da.

당신 친구와는 인사가 없는 것 같

습니다.

16. She's my next door neighbor.

Kŭ-nyŏ-nŭn chŏ-ŭi i-u-se sa-nŭn pun-im-ni-da.

그녀는 저의 이웃에 사는 분입니다.

I'll be there in a few minutes.

Myŏt ppun hu-e ka-get-ssŭm-ni-da.
(몇 분 후에 가겠습니다.)

1. Hello, Miss Park. Are you busy now?

Pak yang. Chi-gŭm pa-ppŭ-sim-ni-kka?

박 양. 지금 바쁘십니까?

2. No. Just doing the dishes.

A-nim-ni-da. Chi-gŭm sŏl-gŏ-ji chung-im-ni-da.

아닙니다. 지금 설겆이 중입니다.

3. Mr. Kim and his wife just dropped in. Would you like to come over?

Kim sŏn-saeng pu-bu-ga chi-gŭm mak tŭl-lŏt-ssŭm-ni-da. O-si-get-ssŭm-ni-kka?

김 선생 부부가 지금 막 들렀습니다. 오시겠습니까?

4. I'd love to. I'll be there in a few minutes.

Ne. Myŏt ppun hu-e ka-get-ssŭm-ni-da.

네. 몇 분 후에 가겠습니다.

5. Be there at nine o'clock sharp, then.

Kŭ-rŏm a-hop-ssi chŏng-ga-ge kŭ ko-se ka-get-ssŭm-ni-da.

그럼 아홉시 정각에 그 곳에 가겠습니다.

6. I'll try to get there before that.

Kŭ si-gan chŏn-e ka-do-rok ae-ssŏ po-get-ssŭm-ni-da.

그 시간 전에 가도록 애써 보겠습니다.

7. I'll be there by noon.

Yŏl-ttu-si-kka-ji-nŭn ka-get-ssŭm-

ni-da.

열두시까지는 가겠습니다.

8. Fine. I'll be expecting you then.

Chot-ssŭm-ni-da. Kŭ-rŏm ki-da-ri-go it-kket-ssŭm-ni-da.

좋습니다. 그럼 기다리고 있겠습니다.

9. I'll be there around ten.

Yŏl-ssi kyŏng-e kŭ ko-se ka-get-ssŭm-ni-da.

열시 경에 그 곳에 가겠습니다.

10. Ten is too late. Make it nine.

Yŏl-ssi-myŏn nŏ-mu nŭt-ssŭm-ni-da. A-hop-ssi-ro hap-ssi-da.

열시면 너무 늦습니다. 아홉시로 합시다.

11. Can I see you this morning?

O-nŭl a-ch'i-me chom poel ssu it-ssŭm-ni-kka?

오늘 아침에 좀 뵐 수 있습니까?

12. Sure. I'll be over right away.

Chot-ssŭm-ni-da. Kot ka-get-ssŭm-ni-da.

좋습니다. 곧 가겠습니다.

13. Don't forget the party tonight.

O-nŭl chŏ-nyŏk p'a-t'i it-tchi ma-sip-ssi-o.

오늘 저녁 파티 잊지 마십시오.

14. I'll be there right after work.

T'oe-gŭn chŭk-ssi ka-get-ssŭm-ni-da.

퇴근 즉시 가겠습니다.

Will you have them wrapped?

P'o-jang chom hae chu-sip-ssi-o.

(포장 좀 해 주십시오.)

1. Is there anything else you'd like?

Tŏ sa-sil kkŏ-si it-ssŭm-ni-kka?

더 사실 것이 있습니까?

2. No. I think that's all.

A-nim-ni-da. Ta sat-ssŭm-ni-da.

아닙니다. 다 샀습니다.

3. That's five thousand won.

O-ch'ŏn wŏn-im-ni-da.

오천 원입니다.

4. Here you are. Will you have them wrapped, please?

Yŏ-gi it-ssŭm-ni-da. P'o-jang chom hae chu-si-get-ssŭm-ni-kka?

여기 있습니다. 포장 좀 해 주시겠습니까?

5. Certainly. I'll put them in a box, too.

Ne, p'o-jang-ŭl hae-sŏ sang-ja-e nŏ-ŏ tŭ-ri-get-ssŭm-ni-da.

네, 포장을 해서 상자에 넣어 드리겠습니다.

6. Will you have it mailed to my house?

Kŭ-gŏ-sŭl u-ri chi-bŭ-ro u-song-hae chu-si-get-ssŭm-ni-kka?

그것을 우리 집으로 우송해 주시겠습니까?

7. Certainly. What's your address?

Kŭ-rŏ-ji-yo. Chu-so-rŭl mal-ssŭm-ha-sip-ssi-o.

그러지요. 주소를 말씀하십시오.

8. Will you have them delivered, please?

Kŭ-gŏl pae-dal-hae chu-si-get-ssŭm-ni-kka?

그걸 배달해 주시겠습니까?

9. Yes, of course. They'll arrive in five days.

Mul-lon-i-jyo. O il nae-e to-ch'a-k'al kkŏ-sim-ni-da.

물론이죠. 오 일 내에 도착할 것입니다.

10. Will you have this letter typed?

Nu-gu-rŭl si-k'yŏ-sŏ i p'yŏn-ji-rŭl t'a-ja ch'yŏ chu-si-get-ssŭm-ni-kka?

누구를 시켜서 이 편지를 타자 쳐 주시겠습니까?

11. I'll ask Miss Nam right

Ne, kot nam yang-e-ge pu-t'ak-dŭ-ri-

	away.	*get-ssŭm-ni-da.*
		네, 곧 남 양에게 부탁드리겠습니다.
12.	Will you have my watch fixed?	*Nae si-gye chom ko-ch'yŏ-da chu-se-yo?*
		내 시계 좀 고쳐다 주세요?
13.	I'll take it to a watch store after work.	*T'oe-gŭn hu-e si-gye-ppang-e kat-tta chu-get-ssŭm-ni-da.*
		퇴근 후에 시계방에 갖다 주겠습니다.
14.	Will you have my shoes polished?	*Nu-gu-rŭl si-k'yŏ-sŏ nae ku-du chom tak-kka chu-sip-ssi-o.*
		누구를 시켜서 내 구두 좀 닦아 주십시오.
15.	Sure. I'll call a shoe shine boy.	*Ne. Ku-du-dak-kki-rŭl pul-lŏ o-ji-yo.*
		네. 구두닦이를 불러 오지요.

That's the same as mine.

Nae kŏt-kkwa kkok kat-ssŭm-ni-da.

(내 것과 꼭 같습니다.)

1. Mr. Lee bought a new car last month.

I sŏn-saeng-ŭn chi-nan chu-e sae ch'a-rŭl sat-ssŭm-ni-da.

이 선생은 지난 주에 새 차를 샀습니다.

2. Oh. What kind did he buy?

Kŭ-rae-yo. Mu-sŭn ch'a-rŭl sat-ssŭm-ni-kka?

그래요. 무슨 차를 샀습니까?

3. A Sonata.

So-na-t'a-im-ni-da.

소나타입니다.

4. That's the same as

Kŭ-gŏn nae kŏt-kkwa ka-t'ŭn kŏ-si-

mine.

gun-yo.

그건 내 것과 같은 것이군요.

5. Yes, but the color is different from yours. His is grey.

Kŭ-rŏ-na saek-kka-ri ta-rŭm-ni-da.
   I sŏn-saeng ch'a-nŭn hoe-saek-im-ni-da.

그러나 색깔이 다릅니다. 이 선생 차는 회색입니다.

6. Is your pen the same as mine ?

Tang-sin yŏn-p'i-ri nae kŏt-kkwa kat-ssŭm-ni-kka ?

당신 연필이 내 것과 같습니까 ?

7. No, it's different from yours.

A-ni, tang-sin kŏt-kkwa ta-rŭm-ni-da.

아니, 당신 것과 다릅니다.

8. I'm thirty one years old.

Na-nŭn sŏ-rŭn han sal-im-ni-da.

나는 서른 한 살입니다.

9. Oh, you're the same age as I.

A, kŭ-rae-yo. Na-wa tong-gap-i-gun-yo.

아, 그래요. 나와 동갑이군요.

10. Your shoes are the same as mine.

Tang-sin ku-du-nŭn nae kŏt-kkwa kat-ssŭm-ni-da.

당신 구두는 내 것과 같습니다.

11. I think my design is a little different from yours.

Tang-sin kŏt-kkwa ti-ja-i-ni chom ta-rŭn kŏt kat-ssŭm-ni-da.

당신 것과 디자인이 좀 다른 것 같습니다.

12. My car is the same as yours.

Nae ch'a-ga tang-sin ch'a-wa kat-ssŭm-ni-da.

내 차가 당신 차와 같습니다.

13. Yes, but mine looks newer.

Kŭ-rŏ-na nae ch'a-ga tŏ sae-gŏm-ni-da.

그러나 내 차가 더 새껍니다.

14. This is my new television set.

Nae-ga sae-ro san t'el-le-bi-jŏn-im-ni-da.

내가 새로 산 텔레비전입니다.

15. I have one the same as yours.

Na-do tang-sin kŏt-kkwa ka-t'ŭn kŏ-sŭl ka-ji-go it-ssŭm-ni-da.

나도 당신 것과 같은 것을 가지고 있습니다.

What kind of programs do you like?

Mu-sŭn p'ŭ-ro-rŭl cho-a-ha-sim-ni-kka?

(무슨 프로를 좋아하십니까?)

1. Do you watch much television?

T'el-le-bi-jŏ-nŭl ma-ni po-sim-ni-kka?

텔레비전을 많이 보십니까?

2. Just a few hours a week.

Il-tchu-i-re kyŏ-u myŏt ssi-gan pom-ni-da.

일주일에 겨우 몇 시간 봅니다.

3. What kind of program do you watch?

Mu-sŭn p'ŭ-ro-rŭl po-sim-ni-kka?

무슨 프로를 보십니까?

4. Usually sports programs. What kind of program do you like?

Tae-gae sŭ-p'o-ch'ŭ p'ŭ-ro-rŭl pom-ni-da. Tang-si-nŭn mu-sŭn p'ŭ-ro-rŭl cho-a-ha-sim-ni-kka?

대개 스포츠 프로를 봅니다. 당신은 무슨 프로를 좋아하십니까?

5. I like to watch dramas.

Na-nŭn yŏn-sok-kkŭ-gŭl cho-a-ham-ni-da.

나는 연속극을 좋아합니다.

6. What kind of dictionary do you have?

Mu-sŭn sa-jŏ-nŭl ka-ji-go kye-sim-ni-kka?

무슨 사전을 가지고 계십니까?

7. An English-Korean

Yŏng-han sa-jŏn-im-ni-da.

one.

영한 사전입니다.

8. What kind of flower do you like best?

Mu-sŭn kko-ch'ŭl cho-a-ha-sim-ni-kka?
무슨 꽃을 좋아하십니까?

9. I like roses best of all.

Nan chang-mi-rŭl che-il cho-a-ham-ni-da.
난 장미를 제일 좋아합니다.

10. What kind of book are you looking for?

Mu-sŭn ch'ae-gŭl ch'at-kko kye-sim-ni-kka?
무슨 책을 찾고 계십니까?

11. One about computers.

K'ŏm-p'yu-t'ŏ-e kwan-han ch'aek-im-ni-da.
컴퓨터에 관한 책입니다.

12. What kind of coffee do you use?

Mu-sŭn k'ŏ-p'i-rŭl ssŭ-sim-ni-kka?
무슨 커피를 쓰십니까?

13. I use instant coffee.

Ka-ru k'ŏ-p'i-rŭl ssŭm-ni-da.
가루 커피를 씁니다.

14. What kind of music do you like?

Mu-sŭn ŭ-ma-gŭl cho-a-ha-sim-ni-kka?
무슨 음악을 좋아하십니까?

15. I like classical music.

Ko-jŏn ŭ-ma-gŭl cho-a-ham-ni-da.
고전 음악을 좋아합니다.

How long have you been waiting?

Ki-da-rin chi ŏl-ma-na toe-ŏt-ssŭm-ni-kka?
(기다린 지 얼마나 되었습니까?)

1. I'm sorry I'm late.

Nŭ-jŏ-sŏ mi-an-ham-ni-da.
늦어서 미안합니다.

2. That's all right.

Kwaen-ch'an-ssŭm-ni-da.
괜찮습니다.

3. How long have you

Ŏl-ma-na ki-da-ri-syŏt-ssŭm-ni-kka

been waiting ?

4. About fifteen minutes. Did you get caught in traffic ?

5. Yes. There's always a traffic jam at this hour.

6. How long have you been married ?

7. About five years.

8. How long have they been married ?

9. They had their silver anniversary last month.

10. How long had she been gone ?

11. Since ten o'clock.

12. How long has Mr. Kim been away from home ?

?

얼마나 기다리셨습니까 ?

Yak sip-o-bun-gan im-ni-da. Ch'a-ga ma-k'yŏt-ssŭm-ni-kka ?

약 십오분간 입니다. 차가 막혔습니까 ?

Ne, i si-ga-ni-myŏn nŭl kyo-t'ong hon-ja-bi saeng-gim-ni-da.

네, 이 시간이면 늘 교통 혼잡이 생깁니다.

Kyŏl-hon-han chi ŏl-ma-na toe-syŏt-ssŭm-ni-kka ?

결혼한 지 얼마나 되셨습니까 ?

Yak o nyŏn toem-ni-da.

약 오 년 됩니다.

Kŭ pun-dŭ-rŭn kyŏl-hon-han chi ŏl-ma-na toe-ŏt-ssŭm-ni-kka ?

그 분들은 결혼한 지 얼마나 되었습니까 ?

Chi-nan-da-re ŭn-hon-si-gŭl ka-jyŏt-ssŭm-ni-da.

지난달에 은혼식을 가졌습니다.

Kŭ yŏ-ja-nŭn na-gan chi ŏl-ma-na toe-ŏt-ssŭm-ni-kka ?

그 여자는 나간 지 얼마나 되었습니까 ?

Yŏl-ssi-e na-gat-ssŭm-ni-da.

열시에 나갔습니다.

Kim sŏn-saeng-i ko-hyang-ŭl ttŏ-nan chi ŏl-ma-na toe-ŏt-ssŭm-ni-kka ?

김 선생이 고향을 떠난 지 얼마나

되었습니까?

13. Nearly six months.
Kŏ-ŭi yuk kkae-wŏ-ri toe-ŏt-ssŭm-ni-da.

거의 육 개월이 되었습니다.

14. How long have you been in Korea?
Han-gu-ge kye-sin chi ŏl-ma-na toe-ŏt-ssŭm-ni-kka?

한국에 계신 지 얼마나 되었습니까?

15. About three years.
Yak sam nyŏ-ni toem-ni-da.

약 삼 년이 됩니다.

He's just stepped out.
Chi-gŭm mak na-gat-ssŭm-ni-da.

(**지금 막 나갔습니다.**)

1. May I speak to Mr. Moon, please?
Mun sŏn-saeng chom pa-kkwŏ chu-si-get-ssŭm-ni-kka?

문 선생 좀 바꿔 주시겠습니까?

2. I'm sorry. He's just stepped out.
Mi-an-ham-ni-da. Chi-gŭm mak na-gat-ssŭm-ni-da.

미안합니다. 지금 막 나갔습니다.

3. Do you have any idea where the went to?
Ŏ-di ka-syŏn-nŭn-ji a-sim-ni-kka?

어디 가셨는지 아십니까?

4. He's in a tea room nearby.
Kŭn-ch'ŏ ta-bang-e kye-sim-ni-da.

근처 다방에 계십니다.

5. Let me have the phone number, if you know it.
Chŏn-hwa pŏn-ho-rŭl al-myŏn chom ka-rŭ-ch'yŏ chu-sip-ssi-o.

전화 번호를 알면 좀 가르쳐 주십시오.

6. Just a moment, Please.
Ne, cho-gŭm-man ki-da-ri-sip-ssi-o.

네, 조금만 기다리십시오.

7. Is Mr. Moon home?
Mun sŏn-saeng chi-be kye-sim-ni-

kka?

문 선생 집에 계십니까?

8. He's just left for work.

Chi-gŭm mak ch'ul-gŭn-haet-ssŭm-ni-da.

지금 막 출근했습니다.

9. I've just come back from a trip.

Chi-gŭm mak yŏ-haeng-gat-tta to-ra-wat-ssŭm-ni-da.

지금 막 여행갔다 돌아왔습니다.

10. Have you? Where did you go?

Kŭ-rae-yo? Ŏ-di kat-ssŏt-ssŭm-ni-kka?

그래요? 어디 갔었습니까?

11. May I take another look at your picture?

Tang-sin sa-jin han pŏn-man tŏ pop-ssi-da.

당신 사진 한 번만 더 봅시다.

12. I've just mailed it home.

Chi-gŭm mak chip-e-da pu-ch'yŏt-ssŭm-ni-da.

지금 막 집에다 부쳤습니다.

13. Do you still need my dictionary?

Nae sa-jŏ-ni a-jik-tto p'i-ryo-ham-ni-kka?

내 사전이 아직도 필요합니까?

14. I've just bought one. Thanks anyway.

Ha-na sat-ssŭm-ni-da. Ko-ma-wŏt-ssŭm-ni-da.

하나 샀습니다. 고마웠습니다.

15. I've just finished reading that book.

Chi-gŭm mak kŭ ch'ae-gŭl ta il-gŏt-ssŭm-ni-da.

지금 막 그 책을 다 읽었습니다.

16. I'm only half way through mine.

Nan kyŏ-u pan il-gŏt-ssŭm-ni-da.

난 겨우 반 읽었습니다.

Do you have much snow in winter?

Kyŏ-u-re nu-ni ma-ni om-ni-kka?

321

1. How is the weather in Korea?

Han-gu-gŭi nal-ssi-nŭn ŏ-ttŏt-ssŭm-ni-kka?

한국의 날씨는 어떻습니까?

2. Just like New York.

Nyu-yok-kkwa kkok kat-ssŭm-ni-da.

뉴욕과 꼭 같습니다.

3. Do you have much snow in winter?

Kyŏ-u-re-nŭn nu-ni ma-ni om-ni-kka?

겨울에는 눈이 많이 옵니까?

4. No. Only a few inches at a time. But it does get very cold.

A-nim-ni-da. Han-bŏn ol ttae i, sam in-ch'i chŏng-do-im-ni-da. Kŭ-rŏ-na nal-ssi-nŭn mop-ssi ch'u-wŏ-jim-ni-da.

아닙니다. 한번 올 때 이, 삼 인치 정도입니다. 그러나 날씨는 몹시 추워집니다.

5. I hope it doesn't get too cold this winter.

Ol kyŏ-u-ren nŏ-mu ch'up-tchi a-nat-ssŭ-myŏn cho-k'et-ssŭm-ni-da.

올 겨울엔 너무 춥지 않았으면 좋겠습니다.

6. Do you have much rain in June?

Yu-wŏ-re pi-ga ma-ni om-ni-kka?

유월에 비가 많이 옵니까?

7. No, not in June. But we do get a lot in July.

A-ni-o. Yu-wŏ-re-nŭn an o-ji-man, ch'i-rwŏ-re-nŭn ma-ni om-ni-da.

아니오. 유월에는 안 오지만, 칠월에는 많이 옵니다.

8. Do you have snow in March?

Sam-wŏ-re-nŭn nu-ni om-ni-kka?

삼월에는 눈이 옵니까?

9. Yes, but not much.

Ne, kŭ-rŏ-na ma-ni-nŭn an om-ni-da.

네, 그러나 많이는 안 옵니다.

322

10. Do you have snow in your country?

Tang-sin na-ra-e-nŭn nu-ni om-ni-kka?

당신 나라에는 눈이 옵니까?

11. We have no winter.

U-ri na-ra-e-nŭn kyŏ-u-ri ŏp-ssŭm-ni-da.

우리 나라에는 겨울이 없습니다.

12. Did you have rain here yesterday?

Ŏ-je pi-ga wat-ssŭm-ni-kka?

어제 비가 왔습니까?

13. Only in the morning.

A-ch'i-me chom wat-ssŭm-ni-da.

아침에 좀 왔습니다.

14. Did you have heavy snow last year?

Chang-nyŏ-ne nu-ni ma-ni wat-ssŏt-ssŭm-ni-kka?

작년에 눈이 많이 왔었습니까?

15. No. It was a very mild winter.

A-nim-ni-da. Chi-nan kyŏ-u-rŭn mae-u p'o-gŭn-haet-ssŏt-ssŭm-ni-da.

아닙니다. 지난 겨울은 매우 포근했었습니다.

Some of them are hot.

Kŭ chung myŏt kka-ji-nŭn maep-ssŭm-ni-da.

(그 중 몇 가지는 맵습니다.)

1. Are all Korean dishes very hot?

Han-guk ŭm-si-gŭn ta maep-ssŭm-ni-kka?

한국 음식은 다 맵습니까?

2. No. Only some of them are hot. Have you eaten much Korean food?

A-nim-ni-da. Kŭ chung myŏt kka-ji-man maep-ssŭm-ni-da. Han-guk ŭm-si-gŭl ma-ni mŏ-gŏ po-at-ssŭm-ni-kka?

아닙니다. 그 중 몇 가지만 맵습니다. 한국 음식을 많이 먹어 보

323

왔습니까?

3. No, but I'd like to very much.

A-nim-ni-da. Kŭ-rŏ-na mŏ-gŏ po-go sip-ssŭm-ni-da.

아닙니다. 그러나 먹어 보고 싶습니다.

4. How about coming over for dinner Saturday night?

To-yo-il pa-me u-ri chi-be wa-sŏ chŏ-nyŏ-gi-na ham-kke ha-si-get-ssŭm-ni-kka?

토요일 밤에 우리 집에 와서 저녁이나 함께 하시겠습니까?

5. I'd love to. About seven?

Chot-ssŭm-ni-da. Il-gop-ssi-tchŭ-me kal-kka-yo?

좋습니다. 일곱시쯤에 갈까요?

6. Are they all in favor of the plan?

Kŭ sa-ram-dŭ-rŭn mo-du kŭ kye-hoe-ge ch'an-sŏng-ham-ni-kka?

그 사람들은 모두 그 계획에 찬성합니까?

7. No. Three of them are against it.

A-nim-ni-da. Kŭ chung se sa-ra-mŭn pan-dae-im-ni-da.

아닙니다. 그 중 세 사람은 반대입니다.

8. Are these all your books?

I-gŏ-si mo-du tang-sin ch'aek-im-ni-kka?

이것이 모두 당신 책입니까?

9. No. Some of them belongs to my father.

A-nim-ni-da. Kŭ chung myŏt kkwŏ-nŭn a-bŏ-ji ch'aek-im-ni-da.

아닙니다. 그 중 몇 권은 아버지 책입니다.

10. Most of my friends are crazy about jazz.

Nae ch'in-gu-dŭ-rŭn kŏ-ŭi ta chae-jŭ-gwang-im-ni-da.

내 친구들은 거의 다 재즈광입니

다.

11. So are most of mine.

Nae ch'in-gu-dŭl-do ma-ch'an-ga-ji-im-ni-da.

내 친구들도 마찬가지입니다.

12. None of the students have ever been abroad.

Kŭ hak-ssaeng-dŭl chung-e woe-gu-ge ka pon hak-ssaeng-ŭn ha-na-do ŏp-ssŭm-ni-da.

그 학생들 중에 외국에 가 본 학생은 하나도 없습니다.

13. Really? But most of them speak English very well.

Kŭ-rŏt-ssŭm-ni-kka? Kŭ-rŏ-na mo-du yŏng-ŏ-nŭn mae-u chal ha-dŏ-gun-yo.

그렇습니까? 그러나 모두 영어는 매우 잘 하더군요.

14. Some of them look second hand.

Chung-go-p'um ka-ch'i po-i-nŭn kŏt-tto myŏt it-kkun-yo.

중고품 같이 보이는 것도 몇 있군요.

15. Actuall all of them are second hand.

Sa-si-rŭn ta chung-go-im-ni-da.

사실은 다 중고입니다.

It will get cooler.

Sŏ-nŭl-hae chil-kkŏm-ni-da.
(서늘해 질겁니다.)

1. You must be thirsty. Would you like something cold to drink?

Mok ma-rŭ-si-get-ssŭm-ni-da. Mwŏ si-wŏn-han kŏt tchom ma-si-get-ssŭm-ni-kka?

목 마르시겠습니다. 뭐 시원한 것 좀 마시겠습니까?

2. A cold beer would be wonderful. Is it always this warm in Seoul?

Si-wŏn-han maek-tchu-ga cho-k'et-ssŭm-ni-da. Seŏ-u-rŭn nŭl i-rŏ-k'e tŏp-ssŭm-ni-kka?

시원한 맥주가 좋겠습니다. 서울은
늘 이렇게 덥습니까?

3. It will get cooler in a few days.

Myŏ ch'il chi-na-myŏn si-wŏn-hae chil-kkŏm-ni-da.

몇 일 지나면 시원해 질겁니다.

4. I sure hope so.

Chŏng-mal kŭ-raet-ssŭ-myŏn cho-k'et-ssŭm-ni-da.

정말 그랬으면 좋겠습니다.

5. It's getting warmer everyday.

Chŏm-jŏm nal-ssi-ga tta-ttŭ-t'ae-jim-ni-da.

점점 날씨가 따뜻해집니다.

6. It sure is. It's May already.

Chŏng-mal kŭ-rŏt-ssŭm-ni-da. Pŏl-ssŏ o-wŏl-im-ni-da.

정말 그렇습니다. 벌써 오월입니다.

7. It's getting darker. Let's get going.

Chŏm-jŏm ŏ-du-wŏ-jim-ni-da. Kap-ssi-da.

점점 어두워집니다. 갑시다.

8. Just a moment. I'll be ready in a minute.

Cham-kkan-man kye-sip-ssi-o. Cho-gŭm-man i-ssŭ-myŏn toem-ni-da.

잠깐만 계십시오. 조금만 있으면 됩니다.

9. It's getting chilly. I'd better put my sweater on.

Chŏm-jŏm ssal-ssal-hae-jyŏ kam-ni-da. Swe-t'a-rŭl im-nŭn kŏ-si cho-k'et-ssŭm-ni-da.

점점 쌀쌀해져 갑니다. 쉐타를 입는 것이 좋겠습니다.

10. Oh, it's not that cold.

Mwŏ-ga kŭ-rŏ-k'e ch'up-ssŭm-ni-kka?

뭐가 그렇게 춥습니까?

11. The weather is getting

Nal-ssi-ga ch'u-wŏ-jyŏ kam-ni-da.

colder.

12. Yes. Winter is around the corner.

날씨가 추워져 갑니다.

Ne, kyŏ-u-ri ŏl-ma nam-tchi a-nat-ssŭm-ni-da.

네, 겨울이 얼마 남지 않았습니다.

13. Is it always this hot?

Nŭl i-rŏ-k'e tŏp-ssŭm-ni-kka?

늘 이렇게 덥습니까?

14. It gets cooler in the evening.

Chŏ-nyŏk-i-myŏn si-wŏn-hae-jim-ni-da.

저녁이면 시원해집니다.

What makes you so certain?

Ŏ-ttŏ-k'e kŭ-rŏ-k'e cha-si-ni i-ssŭ-sim-ni-kka?

(어떻게 그렇게 자신이 있으십니까?)

1. Why don't we leave now? I don't think she's coming.

I-je kŭ-man ka po-nŭn-ge ŏ-ttŏt-ssŭm-ni-kka? Kŭ yŏ-ja-nŭn an ol kkŏt kat-ssŭm-ni-da.

이제 그만 가 보는게 어떻습니까? 그 여자는 안 올 것 같습니다.

2. She'll be here.

Kŭ yŏ-ja-nŭn ol kkŏm-ni-da.

그 여자는 올 겁니다.

3. What makes you so certain?

Ŏ-ttŏ-k'e kŭ-rŏ-k'e cha-si-ni i-ssŭ-sim-ni-kka?

어떻게 그렇게 자신이 있으십니까?

4. She called just before you came. She's waiting for Mr. Kim.

Sŏn-saeng-ni-mi o-si-gi chik-tchŏ-ne chŏn-hwa-ga wat-ssŭm-ni-da. Kim sŏn-saeng-ni-mŭl ki-da-ri-go it-tta-go mal-im-ni-da.

선생님이 오시기 직전에 전화가 왔습니다. 김 선생님을 기다리고 있다고 말입니다.

5. What makes you so happy?

Mwŏ-ga kŭ-rŏ-k'e chot-ssŭm-ni-kka?

뭐가 그렇게 좋습니까?

6. I just got a long a waited letter.

O-raet-ttong-an ki-da-ri-dŏn p'yŏn-ji-ga wat-ssŭm-ni-da.

오랫동안 기다리던 편지가 왔습니다.

7. What makes you so angry?

Wae kŭ-rŏ-k'e hwa-ga nat-ssŭm-ni-kka?

왜 그렇게 화가 났습니까?

8. He stood me up.

Kŭ-i-ga yak-sso-gŭl ŏ-gyŏt-ssŭm-ni-da.

그이가 약속을 어겼습니다.

9. What makes you so sure of it?

Ŏ-ttŏ-k'e kŭ-rŏ-k'e cha-si-ni it-ssŭm-ni-kka?

어떻게 그렇게 자신이 있습니까?

10. I just have a hunch.

Kŭ-jŏ yuk-kka-mi kŭ-rŏt-ssŭm-ni-da.

그저 육감이 그렇습니다.

11. What makes you so worried?

Mwŏ-ga kŭ-rŏ-k'e kŏk-tchŏng-i toe-sim-ni-kka?

뭐가 그렇게 걱정이 되십니까?

12. My baby is sick.

Ŏ-rin-ae-ga a-p'ŭm-ni-da.

어린애가 아픕니다.

13. What makes you so serious?

Wae kŭ-rŏ-k'e sim-ga-k'am-ni-kka?

왜 그렇게 심각합니까?

14. I'm worried about the exam.

Si-hŏ-mi kŏk-tchŏng-doem-ni-da.

시험이 걱정됩니다.

I feel like having a drink.

1. You'll like this restaurant.

2. The atmosphere is wonderful.

3. I feel like having a drink. How about you?

4. Good idea. I'll join you.

5. I feel like going on a trip.

6. Want to come along?

7. I feel like taking a walk.

8. So do I. Let's go.

9. I feel like going swimming.

10. I do too. But it's too cold.

Han chan ha-go sip-ssŭm-ni-da.

(한 잔 하고 싶습니다.)

I sik-ttang-i ma-ŭ-me tŭl-kkŏm-ni-da.

이 식당이 마음에 들겁니다.

Pu-nwi-gi-ga p'ŏk chot-ssŭm-ni-da.

분위기가 퍽 좋습니다.

Han chan ha-go si-p'ŭn-de ŏ-ttŏt-ssŭm-ni-kka?

한 잔 하고 싶은데 어떻습니까?

Kŭ-gŏ cho-ŭn saeng-gak-im-ni-da. Chŏ-do ka-ch'i han chan ha-get-ssŭm-ni-da.

그거 좋은 생각입니다. 저도 같이 한 잔 하겠습니다.

Yŏ-haeng ttŏ-na-go sip-ssŭm-ni-da.

여행 떠나고 싶습니다.

Ka-ch'i ka-si-get-ssŭm-ni-kka?

같이 가시겠습니까?

San-ch'ae-gŭl ha-go si-p'ŭn saeng-ga-gi tŭm-ni-da.

산책을 하고 싶은 생각이 듭니다.

Chŏ-do kŭ-rŏt-ssŭm-ni-da. Ka-si-ji-yo.

저도 그렇습니다. 가시지요.

Su-yŏng-ŭl ha-go si-p'ŭn saeng-ga-gi tŭm-ni-da.

수영을 하고 싶은 생각이 듭니다.

Chŏ-do kŭ-rŏ-ch'i-man nŏ-mu ch'up-ssŭm-ni-da.

저도 그렇지만 너무 춥습니다.

11. I feel like going to bed.

Cha-go sip-ssŭm-ni-da.
자고 싶습니다.

12. It's after midnight.

Cha-jŏng-i nŏ-mŏt-ssŭm-ni-da.
자정이 넘었습니다.

13. How about going to the movies ?

Yŏng-hwa ku-gyŏng an ka-si-get-ssŭm-ni-kka ?
영화 구경 안 가시겠습니까 ?

14. I don't feel like going out.

Pak-kke na-ga-go si-p'ŭn saeng-ga-gi ŏp-ssŭm-ni-da.
밖에 나가고 싶은 생각이 없습니다.

15. I don't feel like eating anything.

A-mu-gŏt-tto mŏk-kko si-p'ŭn saeng-ga-gi ŏp-ssŭm-ni-da.
아무것도 먹고 싶은 생각이 없습니다.

16. You must be sick.

Mo-mi pul-p'yŏn-han mo-yang-i-sim-ni-da.
몸이 불편한 모양이십니다.

I met him on my way home.

Chi-be ka-nŭn ki-re man-nat-ssŭm-ni-da.
(집에 가는 길에 만났습니다.)

1. I met Mr. Kim yesterday.

Kim sŏn-saeng-ŭl ŏ-je man-nat-ssŭm-ni-da.
김 선생을 어제 만났습니다.

2. Did he drop by your house ?

Chi-be tŭl-lyŏt-ssŏt-ssŭm-ni-kka ?
집에 들렸었습니까 ?

3. No, I met him my way to the office.

A-ni, che-ga sa-mu-si-re ka-nŭn to-jung-e man-nat-ssŭm-ni-da.
아니, 제가 사무실에 가는 도중에 만났습니다.

4. I met him also. He was on his way to work.

Chŏ-do man-nat-ssŭm-ni-da. Ch'ul-gŭn-ha-nŭn ki-ri-si-dŏ-gun-yo.

저도 만났습니다. 출근하는 길이시 더군요.

5. He dropped in on his way home.

Kŭ sa-ra-mi chi-be ka-nŭn ki-re cham-kkan tŭl-lŏt-ssŭm-ni-da.

그 사람이 집에 가는 길에 잠깐 들렀습니다.

6. I should have dropped by, too.

Chŏ-do tŭl-lŭl kkŏl kŭ-raet-ssŭm-ni-da.

저도 들를 걸 그랬습니다.

7. Did you mail my letter?

Che p'yŏn-ji-rŭl pu-ch'yŏt-ssŭm-ni-kka?

제 편지를 부쳤습니까?

8. Yes, on my way to work.

Ne, ch'ul-gŭn-ha-nŭn ki-re pu-ch'yŏt-ssŭm-ni-da.

네, 출근하는 길에 부쳤습니다.

9. When are you going to pick up your suit?

O-sŭn ŏn-je ch'a-jŭ-si-get-ssŭm-ni-kka?

옷은 언제 찾으시겠습니까?

10. On my way home this evening.

O-nŭl chŏ-nyŏk chi-be ka-nŭn ki-re ch'at-kket-ssŭm-ni-da.

오늘 저녁 집에 가는 길에 찾겠습니다.

11. Where did she lose her handbag?

Kŭ yŏ-ja-nŭn ŏ-di-sŏ ppae-gŭl pun-sil-haet-ssŭm-ni-kka?

그 여자는 어디서 백을 분실했습니까?

12. She lost it on her way to school.

Hak-kkyo ka-nŭn to-jung-e i-rŏt-ssŭm-ni-da.

학교 가는 도중에 잃었습니다.

13. When did you meet him ?

Ŏn-je kŭ sa-ra-mŭl man-nat-ssŭm-ni-kka?

언제 그 사람을 만났습니까?

14. On my way back from school.

Hak-kkyo kat-tta o-nŭn ki-re man-nat-ssŭm-ni-da.

학교 갔다 오는 길에 만났습니다.

APPENDIX I

ENGLISH-KOREAN DICTIONARY

A

abandon *vt.* *pŏ-ri-da* 버리다
abdomen *n.* *pae* 배
ability *n.* *nŭng-nyŏk* 능력
abolition *n.* *p'ye-ji* 폐지
abortion *n.* *yu-san* 유산
absolute *adj.* *chŏl-ttae-ŭi* 절대의
abundance *n.* *p'ung-bu* 풍부
academy *n.* *hak-wŏn* 학원
accommodation *n.* *su-yong* 수용
accompany *vt.* *ka-ch'i ka-da* 같이
　가다
account *n.* *kye-san* 계산
accuracy *n.* *chŏng-hwak* 정확
achieve *vt.* *sŏng-ch'wi-ha-da* 성취하
　다
action *n.* *tong-jak* 동작
addition *n.* *pu-ga* 부가
administration *n.* *haeng-jŏng* 행정
admiration *n.* *kam-t'an* 감탄
admission *n.* *ip-tchang* 입장
adolescence *n.* *ch'ŏng-nyŏn-gi* 청년
　기

adopted-son *n.* *yang-ja* 양자
adultery *n.* *kan-t'ong* 간통
advantage *n.* *i-ik* 이익
adventure *n.* *mo-hŏm* 모험
advertisement *n.* *kwang-go* 광고
advise *vt.* *ch'ung-go-ha-da* 충고하
　다
affection *n.* *ae-jŏng* 애정
agent *n.* *tae-ri-in* 대리인
aggresion *n.* *ch'im-nyak* 침략
agitate *vi.* *sŏn-dong-ha-da* 선동하다
agreement *n.* *hyŏp-yak* 협약
agriculture *n.* *nong-ŏp* 농업
alarm *n.* *kyŏng-go* 경고
alteration *n.* *pyŏn-gyŏng* 변경
ambassador *n.* *tae-sa* 대사
ambition *n.* *ya-sim* 야심
amendment *n.* *su-jŏng* 수정
ammunition *n.* *t'a-nyak* 탄약
amnesty *n.* *t'ŭk-ssa* 특사
amusement *n.* *o-rak* 오락
ancestor *n.* *sŏn-jo* 선조

anecdote *n.* *il-hwa* 일화

annals *n.* *yŏn-bo* 연보

anniversary *n.* *ki-nyŏ-mil* 기념일

anxiety *n.* *kŭn-sim* 근심

application *n.* *sin-ch'ŏng* 신청

apply *vi.* *sin-ch'ŏng-ha-da* 신청하
다

appointment *n.* *yak-ssok* 약속

archbishop *n.* *tae-ju-gyo* 대주교

architect *n.* *kŏn-ch'uk-kka* 건축가

armistice *n.* *hyu-jŏn* 휴전

arrest *vt.* *ch'e-p'o-ha-da* 체포하다

arrival *n.* *to-ch'ak* 도착

artist *n.* *ye-sul-ga* 예술가

assassin *n.* *am-sal-tcha* 암살자

astrology *n.* *chŏm-sŏng-hak* 점성학

atmosphere *n.* *tae-gi* 대기

audience *n.* *ch'ŏng-jung* 청중

autobiography *n.* *cha-sŏ-jŏn* 자서전

aviator *n.* *pi-haeng-ga* 비행가

azalea *n.* *chin-dal-lae* 진달래

B

bachelor *n.* *ch'ong-gak* 총각

balance *n.* *kyun-hyŏng* 균형

ballot *n.* *t'u-p'yo* 투표

balmy *adj.* *hyang-gi-ro-un* 향기로운

bankuptcy *n.* *p'a-san* 파산

barbarian *n.* *ya-ma-nin* 야만인

barley *n.* *po-ri* 보리

basis *n.* *ki-ch'o* 기초

basket *n.* *pa-gu-ni* 바구니

battle *n.* *ssa-um* 싸움

battleship *n.* *chŏn-t'u-ham* 전투함

bawl *vt.* *ko-ham-ch'i-da* 고함치다

bear *n.* *kom* 곰

beginner *n.* *ch'o-bo-ja* 초보자

behave *vi.* *haeng-dong-ha-da* 행동하
다

behavior *n.* *haeng-sil* 행실

beloved *adj.* *sa-rang-ha-nŭn* 사랑하
는

benediction *n.* *ch'uk-ppok* 축복

benefactor *n.* *ŭ-nin* 은인

beneficial *adj.* *yu-i-k'an* 유익한

benefit *n.* *i-ik* 이익

betray *vt.* *pae-ban-ha-da* 배반하다

Bible *n.* *sŏng-sŏ* 성서

bidding *n.* *ip-ch'al* 입찰

bier *n.* *sang-yŏ* 상여

big *adj.* *kŭn* 큰

bill *n.* ①*kye-san-sŏ* 계산서 ②*pu-ri*
부리

billiards *n.* *tang-gu* 당구

blacken *vt.* *kka-ma-k'e ha-da* 까맣
게 하다

blasphemy *vt.*, *vi.* *mo-do-k'a-da* 모
독하다

blast *vt.* *p'ok-p'a-ha-da* 폭파하다

blindman *n.* *chang-nim* 장님

blockade *n.* *pong-swae* 봉쇄

blueprint *n.* *ch'ŏng-sa-jin* 청사진

blunder *n.* *sil-ssu* 실수

boast *vi.* *cha-rang-ha-da* 자랑하다

boastful *adj.* *cha-rang-ha-nŭn* 자랑하는

bodyguard *n.* *ho-wi-byŏng* 호위병

bomb *n.* *p'ok-t'an* 폭탄

bonfire *n.* *hwaet-ppul* 횃불

bonus *n.* *sang-yŏ-gŭm* 상여금

book *n.* *ch'aek* 책

book-keeping *n.* *pu-gi* 부기

borrow *vt.* *pil-li-da* 빌리다

botanical garden *n.* *sing-mu-rwŏn* 식물원

botany *n.* *sing-mul-hak* 식물학

bother *vt.* *kwi-ch'an-k'e ha-da* 귀찮게 하다

boundary *n.* *kyŏng-gye* 경계

boundless *adj.* *ha-ni ŏm-nŭn* 한이 없는

bountiful *adj.* *kwan-dae-han* 관대한

bower *n.* *chŏng-ja* 정자

box-office *n.* *mae-p'yo-so* 매표소

brazier *n.* *hwa-ro* 화로

brethren *n.* *tong-p'o* 동포

bribe *n.* *noe-mul* 뇌물

brighten *vt.* *pin-na-ge ha-da* 빛나게 하다

brim *n.* *ka-jang-ja-ri* 가장자리

brisk *adj.* *hwal-bal-han* 활발한

broadcasting station *n.* *pang-song-guk* 방송국

bronchitis *n.* *ki-gwan-ji-yŏm* 기관지염

bubble *n.* *kŏ-p'um* 거품

Buddhism *n.* *pul-gyo* 불교

burglar *n.* *kang-do* 강도

burial *n.* *mae-jang* 매장

butterfly *n.* *na-bi* 나비

bystander *n.* *ku-gyŏng-kkun* 구경꾼

C

cab *n.* *t'aek-ssi* 택시

cadet *n.* *sa-gwan-saeng-do* 사관생도

cage *n.* *sae-jang* 새장

calamity *n.* *chae-nan* 재난

calculation *n.* *kye-san* 계산

calendar *n.* *tal-lyŏk* 달력

campaign *n.* *un-dong* 운동

cancel *vt.* *ch'wi-so-ha-da* 취소하다

canyon *n.* *hyŏp-kkok* 협곡

capitalism *n.* *cha-bon-ju-ŭi* 자본주의

captive *n.* *p'o-ro* 포로

career *n.* *kyŏng-nyŏk* 경력

carnival *n.* *ch'uk-tche* 축제

catalogue *n.* *mong-nok* 목록

catastrophe *n.* *chae-nan* 재난

cathedral *n.* *tae-sŏng-dang* 대성당

Catholicism *n.* *ch'ŏn-ju-gyo* 천주교

caution *n.* *cho-sim* 조심

celebrate *vt.* *kyŏng-ch'u-k'a-da* 경축하다

celebrity *n.* *myŏng-sa* 명사

cemetery *n.* *kong-dong myo-ji* 공동묘지

census n. *kuk-sse cho-sa* 국세 조사

certificate n. *chŭng-myŏng-sŏ* 증명서

chairman n. *ŭi-jang* 의장

charity n. *cha-bi* 자비

chemise n. *sok-ch'i-ma* 속치마

chrysanthemun n. *ku-k'wa* 국화

circulation n. *sun-hwan* 순환

citizenship n. *si-min-kkwŏn* 시민권

civilian n. *min-ga-nin* 민간인

civilization n. *mun-myŏng* 문명

classify vt. *pul-ryu-ha-da* 분류하다

clay n. *chin-hŭk* 진흙

clench vt. *kkwak chwi-da* 꽉 쥐다

clergyman n. *mok-ssa* 목사

clever adj. *yŏng-ni-han* 영리한

climax n. *chŏl-tchŏng* 절정

clown n. *ik-ssal-kkun* 익살꾼

coalition n. *yŏn-hap* 연합

coast n. *yŏn-an* 연안

coffin n. *kwan* 관

coincide vi. *il-ch'i-ha-da* 일치하다

collapse vi. *mu-nŏ-ji-da* 무너지다

collection n. *su-jip* 수집

comedian n. *hŭi-gŭk pae-u* 희극 배우

comedy n. *hŭi-gŭk* 희극

commencement n. *cho-rŏp-ssik* 졸업식

comment vi. *pi-p'yŏng-ha-da* 비평하다

commonwealth n. *yŏn-bang* 연방

commotion n. *tong-yo* 동요

communism n. *kong-san-ju-ŭi* 공산주의

companion n. *tong-mu* 동무

competition n. *kyŏng-jaeng* 경쟁

complain vi. *pul-p'yŏng-ha-da* 불평하다

comprehend vt. *i-hae-ha-da* 이해하다

compromise n. *t'a-hyŏp* 타협

conceal vt. *kam-ch'u-da* 감추다

concentrate vt. *chip-tchung-ha-da* 집중하다

concession n. *yang-bo* 양보

conclusion n. *chong-gyŏl* 종결

concubine n. *ch'ŏp* 첩

confess vi. *ko-bae-k'a-da* 고백하다

confidence n. *si-nim* 신임

conqueror n. *chŏng-bok-tcha* 정복자

conscience n. *yang-sim* 양심

consciousness n. *ŭi-sik* 의식

consequence n. *kyŏl-gwa* 결과

consonant n. *cha-ŭm* 자음

constitution n. *hŏn-ppŏp* 헌법

construction n. *kŏn-sŏl* 건설

consumption n. *so-bi* 소비

contribution n. *ki-bu* 기부

create vt. *ch'ang-jo-ha-da* 창조하다

creature n. *saeng-mul* 생물

crossroad n. *ne-gŏ-ri* 네거리

crowd n. *kun-jung* 군중

cruiser n. *su-nyang-ham* 순양함

customs n. *kwan-se* 관세

D

damage *n.* *son-hae* 손해
dandelion *n.* *min-dŭl-le* 민들레
daughter‒in‒law *n.* *myŏ-nŭ-ri* 며
느리
dealer *n.* *chang-sa-kkun* 장사꾼
decent *n.* *chŏm-ja-nŭn* 점잖은
declaration *n.* *sŏ-nŏn* 선언
decoration *n.* *chang-sik* 장식
dedicate *vt.* *pa-ch'i-da* 바치다
defend *vt.* *pang-ŏ-ha-da* 방어하다
defendant *n.* *p'i-go* 피고
deficient *adj.* *pu-jo-k'an* 부족한
delegate *n.* *tae-p'yo* 대표
delicious *adj.* *ma-sin-nŭn* 맛있는
delivery *n.* *pae-dal* 배달
democracy *n.* *min-ju-ju-ŭi* 민주주
의
demonstration *n.* *te-mo* 데모
dentist *n.* *ch'i-kkwa ŭi-sa* 치과 의
사
departure *n.* *ch'ul-bal* 출발
descedant *n.* *cha-son* 자손
destitute *adj.* *ka-nan-han* 가난한
description *n.* *myo-sa* 묘사
desperate *adj.* *kyŏl-ssa-jŏk* 결사적
destruction *n.* *p'a-goe* 파괴
development *n.* *pal-tchŏn* 발전
devotion *n.* *hŏn-sin* 헌신
dialogue *n.* *tae-hwa* 대화
dictator *n.* *tok-tchae-ja* 독재자

dictionary *n.* *sa-jŏn* 사전
diploma *n.* *cho-rŏp-tchang* 졸업장
diplomat *n.* *woe-gyo-gwan* 외교관
disappointment *n.* *sil-mang* 실망
disapproval *n.* *pul-ch'an-sŏng* 불찬
성
discontent *n.* *pul-man* 불만
discouragement *n.* *nak-ssim* 낙심
discrimination *n.* *ch'a-byŏl* 차별
disgraceful *adj.* *su-ch'i-sŭ-rŏ-un* 수
치스러운
dishonesty *n.* *pu-jŏng-jik* 부정직
disobedience *n.* *pul-ssun-jong* 불순
종
disorder *n.* *mu-jil-ssŏ* 무질서
distress *n.* *ko-min* 고민
distribution *n.* *pun-bae* 분배
divine *adj.* *sŏng-sŭ-rŏ-un* 성스러운
dominate *vt.* *chi-bae-ha-da* 지배하다
doubtful *adj.* *ŭi-sim-sŭ-rŏ-un* 의심
스러운
doze *vi.* *chol-da* 졸다
dragon *n.* *yong* 용
drizzle *n.* *i-sŭl-bi* 이슬비
drunkard *n.* *chu-jŏng-kkun* 주정꾼
dual *adj.* *i-jung-ŭi* 이중의
dust *n.* *mŏn-ji* 먼지
duty *n.* *ŭi-mu* 의무
dynasty *n.* *wang-jo* 왕조

E

eagerness *n.* *yŏl-ssim* 열심

earnings *n.* *su-ip* 수입

earthquake *n.* *chi-jin* 지진

Easter *n.* *pu-hwal-tche* 부활제

ebb *n.* *ssŏl-mul* 썰물

eclipse *n.* *il-ssik* 일식

economics *n.* *kyŏng-je-hak* 경제학

ecstasy *n.* *hwang-hol* 황홀

editor *n.* *p'yŏn-jip-tcha* 편집자

efficiency *n.* *nŭng-nyul* 능률

egoism *n.* *i-gi-ju-ŭi* 이기주의

election *n.* *sŏn-gŏ* 선거

electricity *n.* *chŏn-gi* 전기

elementary school *n.* *kung-min hak-kkyo* 국민 학교

embassy *n.* *tae-sa-gwan* 대사관

embroider *vi.* *su-no-t'a* 수놓다

emergency *n.* *ŭi-gi* 의기

emigrate *vi.* *i-ju-ha-da* 이주하다

emperor *n.* *hwang-je* 황제

employee *n.* *chong-ŏ-bwŏn* 종업원

enchant *vt.* *hwang-hol-ha-ge ha-da* 황홀하게 하다

encyclopaedia *n.* *paek-kkwa sa-jŏn* 백과 사전

endless *adj.* *kkŭt-ŏm-nŭn* 끝없는

endurance *n.* *ch'a-mŭl-ssŏng* 참을성

enemy *n.* *chŏk* 적

energy *n.* *him* 힘

engaged *adj.* *ye-yak-ttoen* 예약된

engagement *n.* *ya-k'on* 약혼

engrave *vt.* *cho-ga-k'a-da* 조각하다

enjoyment *n.* *hyang-nak* 향락

enlarge *vt.* *hwak-ttae-ha-da* 확대하다

enmity *n.* *chŭng-o* 증오

enroll *vt.* *tŭng-no-k'a-da* 등록하다

enterprise *n.* *ki-ŏp* 기업

entertainment *n.* *chŏp-ttae* 접대

enthusiastic *adj.* *yŏl-gwang-jŏ-gin* 열광적인

entrance *n.* *ip-kku* 입구

enumerate *vt.* *he-a-ri-da* 헤아리다

environment *n.* *hwan-gyŏng* 환경

epidemic *n.* *yu-haeng-ppyŏng* 유행병

equality *n.* *p'yŏng-dŭng* 평등

essay *n.* *su-p'il* 수필

establishment *n.* *sŏl-lip* 설립

eternity *n.* *yŏng-wŏn* 영원

ethics *n.* *yul-li-hak* 윤리학

evidence *n.* *chŭng-gŏ* 증거

excitement *n.* *hŭng-bun* 흥분

excursion *n.* *so-p'ung* 소풍

exhibition *n.* *chŏl-lam-hoe* 전람회

existence *n.* *chon-jae* 존재

expedition *n.* *t'am-hŏm* 탐험

expense *n.* *chi-ch'ul* 지출

experience *n.* *kyŏng-hŏm* 경험

exterior *n.* *woe-bu* 외부

extraordinary *adj.* *t'ŭk-ppyŏl-han* 특별한

extreme *adj.* *kŭk-tta-nŭi* 극단의

eyesight *n.* *si-ryŏk* 시력

F

fable *n.* *tong-hwa* 동화
factory *n.* *kong-jang* 공장
failure *n.* *sil-p'ae* 실패
faith *n.* *mi-dŭm* 믿음
faithfulness *n.* *ch'ung-sil* 충실
famine *n.* *kum-ju-rim* 굶주림
fancy *n.* *kong-sang* 공상
farmhouse *n.* *nong-ga* 농가
fasting *n.* *tan-sik* 단식
fate *n.* *un-myŏng* 운명
fatigue *n.* *p'i-gon* 피곤
fertilizer *n.* *pi-ryo* 비료
fiction *n.* *so-sŏl* 소설
finance *n.* *chae-jŏng* 재정
fisherman *n.* *ŏ-bu* 어부
flattery *n.* *a-ch'ŏm* 아첨
flock *n.* *tte* 떼
flood *n.* *hong-su* 홍수
flourish *vi.* *pŏ-nyŏng-ha-da* 번영하
다
football *n.* *ch'uk-kku* 축구
foreigner *n.* *woe-gu-gin* 외국인
forest *n.* *sup* 숲
forgery *n.* *wi-jo* 위조
forgive *vt.* *yong-sŏ-ha-da* 용서하다
formation *n.* *ku-sŏng* 구성
founder *n.* *ch'ang-nip-tcha* 창립자
fraud *n.* *hyŏp-tchap* 협잡
freedom *n.* *cha-yu* 자유
friendship *n.* *u-jŏng* 우정

frontier *n.* *kuk-kkyŏng* 국경
frugality *n.* *kŏm-nyak* 검약
full *adj.* *ka-dŭ-k'an* 가득한
full-moon *n.* *po-rŭm-ttal* 보름달
fullness *n.* *ch'ung-man* 충만
function *n.* *ki-nŭng* 기능
funeral *n.* *chang-nye* 장례
furious *adj.* *kyŏk-ppun-han* 격분한
futile *adj.* *mu-i-k'an* 무익한

G

gaiety *n.* *myŏng-nang* 명랑
gallant *adj.* *hul-lyung-han* 훌륭한
garage *n.* *ch'a-go* 차고
garbage *n.* *ssŭ-re-gi* 쓰레기
gardener *n.* *chŏng-wŏn-sa* 정원사
garland *n.* *hwa-hwan* 화환
garment *n.* *ot* 옷
gender *n.* *sŏng* 성
genealogy *n.* *chok-ppo* 족보
generation *n.* *se-dae* 세대
generous *adj.* *kwan-dae-han* 관대한
geometry *n.* *ki-ha-hak* 기하학
ghost *n.* *kwi-sin* 귀신
gigantic *adj.* *kŏ-dae-han* 거대한
glisten *vi.* *pan-tchak-kkŏ-ri-da* 반짝
거리다
gloomy *adj.* *ŏ-du-un* 어두운
glory *n.* *yŏng-gwang* 영광
goodness *n.* *ch'a-k'am* 착함
gorgeous *adj.* *ch'al-lan-han* 찬란한

gospel *n.* *po-gŭm* 복음

government *n.* *chŏng-bu* 정부

governor *n.* *chi-sa* 지사

graceful *adj.* *in-ja-han* 인자한

graduation *n.* *cho-rŏp* 졸업

grammar *n.* *mun-ppŏp* 문법

grand *adj.* *ung-dae-han* 웅대한

gratitude *n.* *kam-sa* 감사

graveyard *n.* *myo-ji* 묘지

greedy *adj.* *yok-ssim ma-nŭn* 욕심
많은

grumble *vi.* *pul-p'yŏng-ha-da* 불평
하다

guardian *n.* *po-ho-ja* 보호자

gymnastics *n.* *ch'e-jo* 체조

H

habit *n.* *pŏ-rŭt* 버릇

hammer *n.* *mang-ch'i* 망치

hand-bag *n.* *son-kka-bang* 손가방

handkerchief *n.* *son-ssu-gŏn* 손수건

happiness *n.* *haeng-bok* 행복

harmony *n.* *cho-hwa* 조화

harsh *adj.* *kŏ-ch'i-rŭn* 거칠은

harvest *n.* *ch'u-su* 추수

haughty *adj.* *kŏ-man-han* 거만한

hazard *n.* *wi-hŏm* 위험

headache *n.* *tu-t'ong* 두통

headline *n.* *che-mok* 제목

headquarters *n.* *pon-bu* 본부

healthy *adj.* *kŏn-gang-han* 건강한

heaven *n.* *ch'ŏn-guk* 천국

hedge *n.* *ul-t'a-ri* 울타리

helmet *n.* *ch'ŏl-mo* 철모

helpful *adj.* *to-u-mi toe-nŭn* 도움이
되는

heredity *n.* *yu-jŏn* 유전

hero *n.* *yŏng-ung* 영웅

heroine *n.* *yŏ-jang-bu* 여장부

highland *n.* *ko-ji* 고지

historian *n.* *yŏk-ssa-ga* 역사가

hobby *n.* *ch'wi-mi* 취미

homesickness *n.* *hyang-su* 향수

honeymoon *n.* *sin-hon yŏ-haeng* 신
혼 여행

horizon *n.* *chi-p'yŏng-sŏn* 지평선

horse race *n.* *kyŏng-ma* 경마

hospitality *n.* *hwan-dae* 환대

hot spring *n.* *on-ch'ŏn* 온천

housekeeper *n.* *ka-jŏng-bu* 가정부

humble *n.* *kyŏm-son-han* 겸손한

hypocrite *n.* *wi-sŏn-ja* 위선자

I

identification *n.* *sin-bun* 신분

idleness *n.* *ke-ŭ-rŭm* 게으름

ignorance *n.* *mu-ji* 무지

illiteracy *n.* *mu-sik* 무식

illness *n.* *pyŏng* 병

illumination *n.* *cho-myŏng* 조명

imagination *n.* *sang-sang* 상상

imitation *n.* *mo-bang* 모방

impatient *adj.* *ch'a-mŭl ssu ŏm-nŭn* 참을 수 없는

imperialism *n.* *che-guk-ju-ŭi* 제국주의

improvement *n.* *kae-sŏn* 개선

inauguration *n.* *ch'wi-im* 취임

income *n.* *su-ip* 수입

independent *adj.* *tong-ni-bŭi* 독립의

indignant *adj.* *hwa-ga nan* 화가 난

individualism *n.* *kae-in-ju-ŭi* 개인주의

industrious *adj.* *pu-ji-rŏn-han* 부지런한

industry *n.* *sa-nŏp* 산업

infantry *n.* *po-byŏng* 보병

influence *n.* *yŏng-hyang* 영향

information *n.* *chŏng-bo* 정보

inhabitant *n.* *chu-min* 주민

injustice *n.* *pu-jŏng* 부정

inn *n.* *yŏ-gwan* 여관

insignia *n.* *hwi-jang* 휘장

inspection *n.* *si-ch'al* 시찰

insurance *n.* *po-hŏm* 보험

intent *n.* *ŭi-hyang* 의향

international *adj.* *kuk-tche-jŏ-gin* 국제적인

interpreter *n.* *t'ong-yŏk-tcha* 통역자

invention *n.* *pal-myŏng* 발명

investigation *n.* *cho-sa* 조사

irregular *adj.* *pul-gyu-ch'i-k'an* 불규칙한

island *n.* *sŏm* 섬

itinerary *n.* *sun-hwoe* 순회

J

jacket *n.* *chŏ-go-ri* 저고리

jail *n.* *kam-ppang* 감방

janitor *n.* *su-wi* 수위

jaw *n.* *t'ŏk* 턱

jaunty *adj.* *kyŏng-k'wae-han* 경쾌한

jealousy *n.* *chil-t'u* 질투

joke *n.* *nong-dam* 농담

judge *n.* *p'an-sa* 판사

justification *n.* *chŏng-dang-hwa* 정당화

K

kettle *n.* *chu-jŏn-ja* 주전자

kindergarten *n.* *yu-ch'i-wŏn* 유치원

kingdom *n.* *wang-guk* 왕국

knight *n.* *ki-sa* 기사

knitting *n.* *ttŭ-ge-jil* 뜨게질

knowledge *n.* *chi-sik* 지식

L

labor *n.* *no-dong* 노동

laboratory *n.* *sil-hŏm-sil* 실험실

lack *n.* *pu-jok* 부족

lake *n.* *ho-su* 호수

lament *vt.* *sŭl-p'ŏ-ha-da* 슬퍼하다

lass *n.* *so-nyŏ* 소녀

lavatory *n.* *hwa-jang-sil* 화장실

lawn *n.* *chan-di* 잔디

lawyer *n.* *pyŏn-ho-sa* 변호사

lecture *n.* *kang-ŭi* 강의

legation *n.* *kong-sa-gwan* 공사관

legislation *n.* *ip-ppŏp* 입법

leisure *n.* *yŏ-ga* 여가

lenient *adj.* *nŏ-gŭ-rŏ-un* 너그러운

liaison *n.* *yŏl-lak* 연락

liberate *vt.* *hae-bang-ha-da* 해방하다

librarian *n.* *sa-sŏ-in* 사서인

library *n.* *to-sŏ-gwan* 도서관

license *n.* *myŏn-hŏ* 면허

lid *n.* *ttu-kkŏng* 뚜껑

lightning *n.* *pŏn-gae* 번개

livelihood *n.* *saeng-gye* 생계

locomotive *n.* *ki-gwan-ch'a* 기관차

lonesome *n.* *ssŭl-ssŭl-han* 쓸쓸한

longevity *n.* *chang-su* 장수

luminous *adj.* *pin-na-nŭn* 빛나는

lusty *adj.* *t'ŭn-t'ŭn-han* 튼튼한

luxuriant *adj.* *pŏn-sŏng-han* 번성한

luxury *n.* *sa-ch'i* 사치

M

machine *n.* *ki-gye* 기계

magistrate *n.* *ch'i-an-gwan* 치안관

magnificient *adj.* *chang-ŏm-han* 장엄한

magnify *vt.* *hwak-ttae-ha-da* 확대하다

maiden *n.* *ch'ŏ-nyŏ* 처녀

majority *n.* *ta-su* 다수

malady *n.* *chil-byŏng* 질병

maltreat *vt.* *hak-ttae-ha-da* 학대하다

management *n.* *kwal-li* 관리

manager *n.* *kwal-li-in* 관리인

manner *n.* *pang-bŏp* 방법

mansion *n.* *tae-jŏ-t'aek* 대저택

manufacturer *n.* *che-jo-ŏp-tcha* 제조업자

manuscript *n.* *wŏn-go* 원고

marriage *n.* *kyŏl-hon* 결혼

martyr *n.* *sun-gyo-ja* 순교자

marvellous *adj.* *nol-la-un* 놀라운

massacre *n.* *hak-ssal* 학살

mathematics *n.* *su-hak* 수학

maximum *adj.* *ch'oe-dae-ha-nŭi* 최대의

mayor *n.* *si-jang* 시장

medicine *n.* *yak* 약

memorandum *n.* *me-mo* 메모

merchant *n.* *sang-in* 상인

meteorology *n.* *ki-sang-hak* 기상학

millionaire *n.* *paeng-man-jang-ja* 백만장자

minimum *adj.* *ch'oe-so-ŭi* 최소의

ministry *n.* *sŏng-jik* 성직

minority *n.* *so-su-p'a* 소수파

miracle *n.* *ki-jŏk* 기적

misfortune *n.* *pul-haeng* 불행

moment *n.* *sun-gan* 순간

monotonous *adj.* *tan-jo-ro-un* 단조
로운

monument *n.* *ki-nyŏm-bi* 기념비

mother country *n.* *mo-guk* 모국

movie *n.* *yŏng-hwa* 영화

murder *n.* *sa-rin* 살인

Museum *n.* *pang-mul-gwan* 박물관

mystery *n.* *sin-bi* 신비

myth *n.* *sin-hwa* 신화

N

nationalism *n.* *min-jok-ju-ŭi* 민족주
의

nature *n.* *cha-yŏn* 자연

navigation *n.* *hang-hae* 항해

necessity *n.* *p'il-ssu-p'um* 필수품

negotiation *n.* *kyo-sŏp* 교섭

neighbor *n.* *i-ut ssa-ram* 이웃 사
람

New Year *n.* *sae-hae* 새해

nobleman *n.* *kwi-jok* 귀족

nominate *vt.* *chi-myŏng-ha-da* 지명
하다

nourish *vt.* *ki-rŭ-da* 기르다

novelist *n.* *so-sŏl-ga* 소설가

nullify *vt.* *mu-hyo-ro ha-da* 무효로
하다

nutrition *n.* *yŏng-yang* 영양

nymph *n.* *yo-jŏng* 요정

O

oak *n.* *ch'am-na-mu* 참나무

obedience *n.* *pok-tchong* 복종

obligation *n.* *ŭi-mu* 의무

observation *n.* *kwan-ch'al* 관찰

observatory *n.* *ch'ŏn-mun-dae* 천문
대

obvious *adj.* *myŏng-bae-k'an* 명백한

occupation *n.* *chik-ŏp* 직업

opinion *n.* *ŭi-gyŏn* 의견

opponent *n.* *pan-dae-ja* 반대자

opportunity *n.* *ki-hoe* 기회

optimism *n.* *nak-ch'ŏn-ju-ŭi* 낙천주
의

orchestra *n.* *kwan-hyŏn-ak-ttan* 관현
악단

ornament *n.* *chang-sik* 장식

orphan *n.* *ko-a* 고아

outline *n.* *yun-gwak* 윤곽

owner *n.* *so-yu-ja* 소유자

P

Pacific Ocean *n.* *t'ae-p'yŏng-yang* 태
평양

pagan *n.* *i-gyo-do* 이교도

palace *n.* *kung-jŏn* 궁전

parachute *n.* *na-k'a-san* 낙하산

paradise *n.* *na-gwŏn* 낙원

paramount *adj.* *ch'oe-go-ŭi* 최고의

parliament *n.* *ŭi-hoe* 의회

passion *n.* *chŏng-yŏl* 정열

pastor *n.* *mok-ssa* 목사

pasture *n.* *mok-tchang* 목장

patience *n.* *in-nae* 인내

patriotism *n.* *ae-guk-ssim* 애국심

pavement *n.* *p'o-jang* 포장

payment *n.* *chi-bul* 지불

peasant *n.* *nong-bu* 농부

penalty *n.* *hyŏng-bŏl* 형벌

permanent *adj.* *yŏng-gu-ŭi* 영구의

permission *n.* *hŏ-ga* 허가

pessimism *n.* *yŏm-se-ju-ŭi* 염세주의

petition *n.* *t'a-nwŏn* 탄원

pharmacist *n.* *yak-tche-sa* 약제사

philanthrophy *n.* *pak-ae* 박애

philosopher *n.* *ch'ŏl-hak-tcha* 철학자

physician *n.* *nae-kkwa ŭi-sa* 내과 의사

pigeon *n.* *pi-dul-gi* 비둘기

pilgrimage *n.* *sul-lye yŏ-haeng* 순례여행

pioneer *n.* *kae-ch'ŏk-tcha* 개척자

pirate *n.* *hae-jŏk* 해적

planet *n.* *yu-sŏng* 유성

plateau *n.* *ko-wŏn* 고원

plunder *n.* *yak-t'al-ha-da* 약탈하다

pneumonia *n.* *p'ye-ryŏm* 폐렴

poem *n.* *si* 시

poet *n.* *si-in* 시인

policeman *n.* *kyŏng-gwan* 경관

politician *n.* *chŏng-ch'i-in* 정치인

popularity *n.* *in-kki* 인기

porcelain *n.* *cha-gi* 자기

portrait *n.* *ch'o-sang-hwa* 초상화

poverty *n.* *ka-nan* 가난

praise *n.* *ch'ing-ch'an* 칭찬

prank *n.* *chang-nan* 장난

preparation *n.* *chun-bi* 준비

prince *n.* *wang-ja* 왕자

princess *n.* *kong-ju* 공주

privilege *n.* *t'ŭk-kkwŏn* 특권

proclamation *n.* *sŏ-nŏn* 선언

production *n.* *saeng-san* 생산

professor *n.* *kyo-su* 교수

promotion *n.* *sŭng-jin* 승진

prosecutor *n.* *kŏm-sa* 검사

protestant *n.* *sin-gyo-do* 신교도

province *n.* *to* 도

psychology *n.* *sim-ni-hak* 심리학

puritan *n.* *ch'ŏng-gyo-do* 청교도

purity *n.* *sun-su* 순수

pursuit *n.* *ch'u-jŏk* 추적

Q

quail *n.* *me-ch'u-ra-gi* 메추라기

qualification *n.* *cha-gyŏk* 자격

quality *n.* *p'um-jil* 품질

quantity *n.* *yang* 양

quarantine *n.* *kyŏng-ni* 격리

quarrel *n.* *ssa-um* 싸움

quarters *n.* *suk-sso* 숙소

queen *n.* *yŏ-wang* 여왕

quiet *adj.* *ko-yo-han* 고요한

quotation *n.* *in-nyong* 인용

R

rabbit *n.* *t'o-kki* 토끼

railroad *n.* *ch'ŏl-tto* 철도

rainbow *n.* *mu-ji-gae* 무지개

ransom *n.* *sok-tchoe-gŭm* 속죄금

ratification *n.* *pi-jun* 비준

ration *n.* *pae-gŭp* 배급

rationalism *n.* *ham-ni-ju-ŭi* 합리주의

realization *n.* *sil-hyŏn* 실현

rebellion *n.* *pa-nyŏk* 반역

reception *n.* *chŏp-ttae* 접대

recollection *n.* *hoe-sang* 회상

recommendation *n.* *ch'u-ch'ŏn* 추천

reconaissance *n.* *chŏng-ch'al* 정찰

recovery *n.* *hoe-bok* 회복

recreation *n.* *o-rak* 오락

referee *n.* *sim-p'an-gwan* 심판관

refinement *n.* *se-ryŏn* 세련

reformation *n.* *kae-hyŏk* 개혁

refrigerator *n.* *naeng-jang-go* 냉장고

refugee *n.* *p'i-nan-min* 피난민

registration *n.* *tŭng-nok* 등록

regret *n.* *yu-gam* 유감

reinforce *vt.* *po-gang-ha-da* 보강하다

religion *n.* *chong-gyo* 종교

reanissance *n.* *mu-nye pu-hŭng* 문예 부흥

replacement *n.* *kyo-ch'e* 교체

representative *n.* *tae-p'yo* 대표

reputation *n.* *myŏng-sŏng* 명성

reservation *n.* *ye-yak* 예약

resignation *n.* *sa-jik* 사직

resistance *n.* *chŏ-hang* 저항

responsibility *n.* *ch'ae-gim* 책임

resurrection *n.* *pu-hwal* 부활

retirement *n.* *ŭn-t'oe* 은퇴

revolution *n.* *hyŏng-myŏng* 혁명

romantic *adj.* *nang-man-jŏ-gin* 낭만적인

route *n.* *kil* 길

ruler *n.* *t'ong-ch'i-ja* 통치자

rumor *n.* *so-mun* 소문

rural *adj.* *si-go-rŭi* 시골의

rye *n.* *ho-mil* 호밀

S

sabbath *n.* *an-si-gil* 안식일

sabotage *n.* *t'ae-ŏp* 태업

sacrifice *n.* *hŭi-saeng* 희생

sadness *n.* *sŭl-p'ŭm* 슬픔

safety *n.* *an-jŏn* 안전

sailor *n.* *sŏ-nwŏn* 선원

saint *n.* *sŏng-in* 성인

salary *n.* *pong-gŭp* 봉급

sanitation *n.* *wi-saeng* 위생

satire *n.* *p'ung-ja* 풍자

satisfaction *n.* *man-jok* 만족

savage *n.* *ya-ma-nin* 야만인

scandal *n.* *ch'u-mun* 추문

scarcity *n.* *pu-jok* 부족

schedule *n.* *si-gan-p'yo* 시간표

scheme *n.* *kye-hoek* 계획

scientist *n.* *kwa-hak-tcha* 과학자

scoundrel *n.* *ak-ttang* 악당

scripture *n.* *sŏng-gyŏng* 성경

sea-gull *n.* *kal-mae-gi* 갈매기

secret *n.* *pi-mil* 비밀

security *n.* *an-jŏn* 안전

semester *n.* *hak-kki* 학기

senator *n.* *sang-wŏn ŭi-wŏn* 상원 의
원

sentimental *adj.* *kam-sang-jŏ-gin* 감
상적인

serpent *n.* *paem* 뱀

servant *n.* *ha-in* 하인

sex *n.* *sŏng* 성

shameful *adj.* *su-ch'i-sŭ-rŏ-un* 수치
스러운

sheep *n.* *yang* 양

shelter *n.* *p'i-nan-ch'ŏ* 피난처

shin *n.* *chŏng-gang-i* 정강이

shipwreck *n.* *nan-p'a* 난파

shock *n.* *ch'ung-gyŏk* 충격

shooting *n.* *sa-gyŏk* 사격

shower *n.* *so-nak-ppi* 소낙비

shrine *n.* *sa-dang* 사당

sickness *n.* *pyŏng* 병

sightseeing *n.* *kwan-gwang* 관광

signboard *n.* *kan-p'an* 간판

sin *n.* *choe* 죄

singer *n.* *ka-su* 가수

sky scraper *n.* *ma-ch'ŏn-nu* 마천루

slander *n.* *chung-sang* 중상

smuggler *n.* *mil-ssu-ja* 밀수자

snowman *n.* *nun-ssa-ram* 눈사람

society *n.* *sa-hoe* 사회

soften *vt.* *pu-dŭ-rŏp-kke ha-da* 부드
럽게 하다

solemn *adj.* *ŏm-su-k'an* 엄숙한

solitude *n.* *ko-dok* 고독

sorcerer *n.* *ma-sul-ssa* 마술사

sovereign *n.* *chu-kkwŏn-ja* 주권자

space *n.* *kong-gan* 공간

speaker *n.* *yŏn-sa* 연사

specimen *n.* *kyŏn-bon* 견본

spectator *n.* *ku-gyŏng-kkun* 구경꾼

speech *n.* *yŏn-sŏl* 연설

spider *n.* *kŏ-mi* 거미

spiritual *adj.* *chŏng-sin-jŏ-gin* 정신적
인

spokesman *n.* *tae-byŏ-nin* 대변인

sponge *n.* *hae-myŏn* 해면

sponsor *n.* *hu-wŏ-nin* 후원인

spool *n.* *sil-p'ae* 실패

sportsman *n.* *un-dong-ga* 운동가

stability *n.* *an-jŏng* 안정

starvation *n.* *kum-ju-rim* 굶주림

steal *n.* *hum-ch'i-da* 훔치다

steamship *n.* *ki-sŏn* 기선

stepmother *n.* *yang-bu-mo* 양부모

stimulate *vt.* *cha-gŭ-k'a-da* 자극하
다

stomach *n.* *wi* 위

storm *n.* *p'ok-p'ung* 폭풍

street-car *n.* *chŏn-ch'a* 전차

strife *n.* *ssa-um* 싸움

strong *adj.* *t'ŭn-t'ŭn-han* 튼튼한

submission *n.* *pok-tchong* 복종

success *n.* *sŏng-gong* 성공

successor *n.* *hu-gye-ja* 후계자

suggestion *n.* *am-si* 암시

sunflower *n.* *hae-ba-ra-gi* 해바라기

superstition *n.* *mi-sin* 미신

supporter *n.* *chi-ji-ja* 지지자

surgeon *n.* *oe-kkwa ŭi-sa* 외과 의사

surrender *vi.* *hang-bo-k'a-da* 항복
하다

survey *vt.* *cho-sa-ha-da* 조사하다

suspicion *n.* *ŭi-sim* 의심

symbol *n.* *sang-jing* 상징

sympathy *n.* *tong-jŏng* 동정

symphony *n.* *kyo-hyang-ak* 교향악

system *n.* *ch'e-gye* 체계

T

target *n.* *p'yo-jŏk* 표적

tavern *n.* *sul-tchip* 술집

tearoom *n.* *ta-bang* 다방

telegram *n.* *chŏn-bo* 전보

temperature *n.* *on-do* 온도

temptation *n.* *yu-hok* 유혹

tenant *n.* *so-ja-gin* 소작인

terminal *n.* *chŏng-gŏ-jang* 정거장

territory *n.* *yŏng-t'o* 영토

testimony *n.* *chŭng-ŏn* 증언

textbook *n.* *kyo-gwa-sŏ* 교과서

thanksgiving *n.* *kam-sa-je* 감사제

thermometer *n.* *han-nan-gye* 한난계

thermos *n.* *po-on-ppyŏng* 보온병

thirst *n.* *mong-ma-rŭm* 목마름

thought *n.* *saeng-gak* 생각

throne *n.* *wang-wi* 왕위

throng *n.* *kun-jung* 군중

thunder *n.* *ch'ŏn-dung* 천둥

tidings *n.* *so-sik* 소식

tiger *n.* *ho-rang-i* 호랑이

toilet *n.* *pyŏn-so* 변소

torment *n.* *ko-t'ong* 고통

torture *n.* *ko-mun* 고문

totalitarianism *n.* *chŏn-ch'e-ju-ŭi* 전
체주의

tourist *n.* *kwan-gwang-gaek* 관광객

tower *n.* *t'ap* 탑

trace *n.* *hŭn-jŏk* 흔적

tradition *n.* *chŏn-t'ong* 전통

tragedy *n.* *pi-gŭk* 비극

tranquil *adj.* *cho-yong-han* 조용한

translate *vt.* *pŏ-nyŏ-k'a-da* 번역하
다

transportation *n.* *su-song* 수송

trap *n.* *ol-ga-mi* 올가미

treasure *n.* *po-mul* 보물

trench *n.* *ch'am-ho* 참호

trial *n.* *chae-p'an* 재판

tribe *n.* *chong-jok* 종족

triumph *n.* *sŭng-ni* 승리

tuberculosis *n.* *kyŏl-haek* 결핵

tumult *n.* *so-dong* 소동

twin *n.* *ssang-dong-i* 쌍동이

typhoid *n.* *chang-jil-bu-sa* 장질부사

tyrant *n.* *p'ok-kkun* 폭군

U

ugly *adj.* *ch'u-a-k'an* 추악한

ultimatum *n.* *ch'oe-hu t'ong-ch'ŏp* 최후 통첩

unconcious *adj.* *mu-ŭi-si-gŭi* 무의식의

underclothes *n.* *so-got* 속옷

unemployment *n.* *si-rŏp* 실업

unfavorable *adj.* *pul-li-han* 불리한

unfortunate *adj.* *pul-haeng-han* 불행한

universe *n.* *u-ju* 우주

unreasonable *adj.* *pu-dang-han* 부당한

unsuccessful *adj.* *sil-p'ae-han* 실패한

useful *adj.* *yu-yong-han* 유용한

utensil *n.* *ki-gu* 기구

utopia *n.* *i-sang-hyang* 이상향

V

vacancy *n.* *kong-hŏ* 공허

vacation *n.* *hyu-ga* 휴가

vagabond *n.* *pu-rang-ja* 부랑자

vain *adj.* *hŏt-ttoen* 헛된

value *n.* *ka-ch'i* 가치

vanity *n.* *hŏ-yŏng* 허영

variety *n.* *pyŏn-hwa* 변화

vegetation *n.* *sing-mul* 식물

vengeance *n.* *pok-ssu* 복수

vibration *n.* *chin-dong* 진동

vigor *n.* *chŏng-nyŏk* 정력

violence *n.* *p'ong-nyŏk* 폭력

virtue *n.* *tŏk* 덕

vitality *n.* *saeng-myŏng-nyŏk* 생명력

volcano *n.* *hwa-san* 화산

volleyball *n.* *pae-gu* 배구

volume *n.* *kwŏn* 권

voluntary *adj.* *cha-bal-tchŏ-gin* 자발적인

vowel *n.* *mo-ŭm* 모음

voyage *n.* *hang-hae* 항해

W

wage *n.* *im-gŭm* 임금

wagon *n.* *ma-ch'a* 마차

wander *vi.* *to-ra-da-ni-da* 돌아다니다

warrior *n.* *chŏn-sa* 전사

waterfall *n.* *p'ok-p'o* 폭포

watergap *n.* *kye-gok* 계곡

watermill *n.* *mul-bang-a* 물방아

wealth *n.* *chae-san* 재산

weapon *n.* *mu-gi* 무기

wedding *n.* *kyŏl-hon-sik* 결혼식

weed *n.* *chap-ch'o* 잡초

welfare *n.* *hu-saeng* 후생

whale *n.* *ko-rae* 고래

wheat *n.* *mil* 밀

wig *n.* *ka-bal* 가발

willow *n.* *pŏ-dŭl* 버들

wisdom *n.* *chi-hye* 지혜

witchcraft *n.* *ma-bŏp* 마법

workshop *n.* *kong-jang* 공장

worship *n.* *sung-bae* 숭배

worthy *adj.* *hul-lyung-han* 훌륭한

wound *n.* *pu-sang* 부상

wreath *n.* *hwa-hwan* 화환

wrist *n.* *son-mok* 손목

X

Xmas *n.* *sŏng-t'an-jŏl* 성탄절

X－ray *n.* *ek-ssŭ kwang-sŏn* 엑스 광선

Y

yacht *n.* *yo-t'ŭ* 요트

Yalu *n.* *am-nok-kkang* 압록강

yard *n.* *an-ma-dang* 안마당

yarn *n.* *sil* 실

yearly *adj.* *hae-ma-da* 해마다

yoke *n.* *mŏng-e* 멍에

youth *n.* *chŏl-mŭm* 젊음

Z

zeal *n.* *yŏl-ssim* 열심

zebra *n.* *ŏl-lung-mal* 얼룩말

zenith *n.* *chŏng-tchŏm* 정점

zest *n.* *mat* 맛

zone *n.* *ku-yŏk* 구역

zoo *n.* *tong-mu-rwŏn* 동물원

zoology *n.* *tong-mul-hak* 동물학

APPENDIX II

KOREAN – ENGLISH DICTIONARY

ㄱ

가게 *ka-ge* Shop
가격 *ka-gyŏk* Price
가난뱅이 *ka-nan-baeng-i* Poor man
가능한 *ka-nŭng-han* Possible
가락지 *ka-rak-tchi* Ring
가루 *ka-ru* Powder
가방 *ka-bang* Bag
가볍다 *ka-byŏp-tta* Light
가수 *ka-su* Singer
가슴 *ka-sŭm* Breast
가옥 *ka-ok* House
가요 *ka-yo* Song
가을 *ka-ŭl* Autumn
가족 *ka-jok* Family
가치 *ka-ch'i* Value
각도 *kak-tto* Angle
각료 *kang-nyo* Cabinet Minister
각본 *kak-ppon* Scenario
각서 *kak-ssŏ* Memorandum
각성 *kak-ssŏng* Awakening
각축 *kak-ch'uk* Competition
간계 *kan-gye* Trick

간주곡 *kan-ju-gok* Interlude
간첩 *kan-ch'ŏp* Spy, Agent
간통 *kan-t'ong* Adultery
간판 *kan-p'an* Signboard
간행하다 *kan-haeng-ha-da* Publish,
  Issue
간호사 *kan-ho-sa* Nurse
갈등 *kal-ttŭng* Conflict, Troube
갈매기 *kal-mae-gi* Sea gull
갈색 *kal-ssaek* Brown
갈증 *kal-tchŭng* thirst
감 *kam* persimon
감각 *kam-gak* Sense, Feeling
감금 *kam-gŭm* Confinement, Deten-
  tion
감기 *kam-gi* Cold
감방 *kam-ppang* Cell, Ward
감사 *kam-sa* Thanks
감사장 *kam-sa-tchang* Letter of appreciation
감상 *kam-sang* Appreciation
감소 *kam-so* Decrease, Diminution

감시 *kam-si* Watch, Lookout

감염 *kam-yŏm* Infection

감옥 *ka-mok* Prison

감정 *kam-jŏng* Feeling, Emotion

감추다 *kam-ch'u-da* Hide, Conceal

감회 *kam-hoe* Thought, Impression

갑부 *kap-ppu* Rich man

강간 *kang-gan* Rape

강경한 *kang-gyŏng-han* Strong, Firm, Resolute

강단 *kang-dan* Platform

강사 *kang-sa* Lecturer

강연 *kang-yŏn* Lecture, Speech

강의 *kang-ŭi* Lecture

강장제 *kang-jang-je* Tonic

강조 *kang-jo* Stress, Emphasis

강좌 *kang-jwa* Lecture

강직한 *kang-ji-k'an* Upright

강철 *kang-ch'ŏl* Steel

강탈 *kang-t'al* Seizure, extortion

강화하다 *kang-hwa-ha-da* Strengthen, Consolidate

개 *kae* Dog

개념 *kae-nyŏm* Notion, General idea

개미 *kae-mi* Ant

개관 *kae-gwan* Opening

개괄 *kae-gwal* Summary

개구리 *kae-gu-ri* Frog

개선 *kae-sŏn* Triumphant return

개설 *kae-sŏl* Establishment, Opening

개성 *kae-sŏng* Individual character

개울 *kae-ul* Stream

개입 *kae-ip* Intervention

개조 *kae-jo* Remolding

개척 *kae-ch'ŏk* Exclamation

개축 *kae-ch'uk* Reconstruction

개탄하다 *kae-t'an-ha-da* Deplore, Lament

개편 *kae-p'yŏn* Reorganization

개표 *kae-p'yo* Ballot accounting

개혁 *kae-hyŏk* Reform, Reformation

객차 *kaek-ch'a* Passenger train

갱생 *kaeng-saeng* Rebirth

갱신 *kaeng-sin* Renewal

거간 *kŏ-gan* Broker

거래 *kŏ-rae* Trading, Dealing

거리 *kŏ-ri* ①Street ②Distance

거만 *kŏ-man* Arrogance, Haughtiness

거미 *kŏ-mi* Spider

거부 *kŏ-bu* Refusal, Rejection

거북 *kŏ-buk* Turtle

거장 *kŏ-jang* Great master

건강 *kŏn-gang* Health

건전한 *kŏn-jŏn-han* Healthy, Sound

건축 *kŏn-ch'uk* Construction

걸인 *kŏ-rin* Beggar

걸작 *kŏl-tchak* Masterpiece

검사 *kŏm-sa* Prosecutor

검열 *kŏm-nyŏl* Censorship

검찰청 *kŏm-ch'al-ch'ŏng* Prosecutor's office

게으름뱅이 *ke-ŭ-rŭm-baeng-i* Idle

Man

게재 *ke-jae* Publication, Printing

경영 *kyŏng-yŏng* Management

경제 *kyŏng-je* Economy

경험 *kyŏng-hŏm* Experience

경황 *kyŏng-hwang* Situation

계급 *kye-gŭp* Class, Order

계승 *kye-sŭng* Succession

계획 *kye-hoek* Plan, Project

고객 *ko-gaek* Customer, Client

고고학 *ko-go-hak* Archaelogy

고관 *ko-gwan* High official, Dignitary

고국 *ko-guk* Fatherland, Motherland

고궁 *ko-gung* Ancient palace

고기 *ko-gi* Meat, Beef, Fish

고난 *ko-nan* Distress, Suffering

고단하다 *ko-dan-ha-da* Tired, Fatigued

고담 *ko-dam* Old tale, Folklore

고독 *ko-dok* Solitude, Loneliness

고등학교 *ko-dŭng hak-kkyo* High school

고래 *ko-rae* Whale

고립 *ko-rip* Isolation, Helplessness

고무 *ko-mu* Encouragement

고무신 *ko-mu-sin* Rubber shoes

고문 *ko-mun* Torture

고민 *ko-min* Agony, Anguish

고백 *ko-baek* Confession, Admission

고별 *ko-byŏl* Farewell

고상한 *ko-sang-han* Lofty, Noble

고생 *ko-saeng* Hardships, Difficulties

고소 *ko-so* Accusation, Complaint

고속 도로 *ko-sok tto-ro* High way, expressway

고시 *ko-si* Examination

고아 *ko-a* Orphan

고압 *ko-ap* High pressure

고양이 *ko-yang-i* Cat

고옥 *ko-ok* Old House

고용 *ko-yong* Hire, employment

고장 *ko-jang* Hindrance, Trouble

고전 *ko-jŏn* Classics

고집 *ko-jip* Persistence, Adherence

고통 *ko-t'ong* Agony, Pain

곡마단 *kong-ma-dan* Circus troupe

곡식 *kok-ssik* Cereals, Crain

골동품 *kol-ttong-p'um* Antique

공간 *kong-gan* Space, Room

공갈 *kong-gal* Threat, Blackmail

공급 *kong-gŭp* Supply

공기 *kong-gi* Air

공동 변소 *kong-dong pyŏn-so* Public lavatory

공산주의 *kong-san-ju-ŭi* Communism

공세 *kong-se* Offensive

공수 *kong-su* Air transport, Airlift

공습 *kong-sŭp* Air raid

공업 *kong-ŏp* Industry

공연 *kong-yŏn* Performance

공원 *kong-wŏn* Park

공장 *kong-jang* Factory, Plant

공정 *kong-jŏng* Justice, Fairness, Impartiality

공주 *kong-ju* Princess

공중 전화 *kong-jung chŏn-hwa* Public telephone

공천 *kong-ch'ŏn* Nomination

공청회 *kong-ch'ŏng-hoe* Public Hearing

공포 *kong-p'o* Fear, Terror

공화국 *kong-hwa-guk* Republic

관광 *kwan-gwang* Tourism

관중 *kwan-jung* Audience, Spectator

관청 *kwan-ch'ŏng* Government office

광고 *kwang-go* Advertisement

괴뢰 *kwe-roe* Puppet

교회 *kyo-hoe* Church

구교 *ku-gyo* Roman Catholic

구독 *ku-dok* Subscription

구사일생 *ku-sa-il-ssaeng* Narrow escape

구제 *ku-je* Relif, Help

구축함 *ku-ch'u-k'am* Destroyer

국가 *kuk-kka* Nation, State, Country

국경일 *kuk-kkyŏng-il* National holiday

국방 *kuk-ppang* National defense

국보 *kuk-ppo* National treasure

국적 *kuk-tchŏk* Nationality

국회 *ku-k'oe* National Assembly

권투 *kwŏn-t'u* Boxing

귀화 *kwi-hwa* Naturalization

귀향 *kwi-hyang* Homecoming

균등 *kyun-dŭng* Equality

그림자 *kŭ-rim-ja* Shadow

급행 버스 *kŭ-p'aeng ppŏ-ssŭ* Express bus

기 *ki* Flag

기계 *ki-gye* Machine, Machinery

기관총 *ki-gwan-ch'ong* Machine gun

기근 *ki-gŭn* Famine

기념 *ki-nyŏm* Commemoration

기능 *ki-nŭng* Function, Faculty

기대 *ki-dae* Expectation, Anticipation

기도 *ki-do* Prayer

기만 *ki-man* Deception, Imposition

기밀 *ki-mil* Secrecy

기본 *ki-bon* Foundation, Basis

기부 *ki-bu* Contribution

기분 *ki-bun* Feeling, Mood

기술 *ki-sul* Technique, Art

기억 *ki-ŏk* Memory, Remembrance

기여 *ki-yŏ* Contribution

기온 *ki-on* Temperature

기자 *ki-ja* Journalist, Reporter

기절 *ki-jŏl* Fainting, Swoon

기준 *ki-jun* Standard, Basis

기지 *ki-ji* Wit, Tact

기질 *ki-jil* Disposition, Nature

기차 *ki-ch'a* Train

기호 *ki-ho* Liking, Taste

기후 *ki-hu* Climate, Weather

까마귀 *kka-ma-gwi* Crow, Raven
까치 *kka-ch'i* Magpie
꼭대기 *kkok-ttae-gi* Top, Summit
꿈 *kkum* Dream
끝 *kkŭt* End

ㄴ

나 *na* I
나귀 *na-gwi* Donkey
나그네 *na-gŭ-ne* Traveller, Stranger
나누다 *na-nu-da* Divide, Share
나들이 *na-dŭ-ri* Outing, Going out
나라 *na-ra* Country, Land
나루 *na-ru* Ferry
나무 *na-mu* Tree
나물 *na-mul* Greens, Eatable grasses
나비 *na-bi* Butterfly
나사 *na-sa* Screw
나사점 *na-sa-jŏm* Taylor
나아가다 *na-a-ga-da* Advance, Proceed
나이 *na-i* age
나중에 *na-jung-e* Naked
나체 *na-ch'e* Later body
나침판 *na-ch'im-p'an* Compess
나팔 *na-p'al* Trumper
나팔꽃 *na-p'al-kkot* Morning Flower
낙 *nak* Pleasure, Delight
낙관 *nak-kkwan* Optimism, Optimistic view
낙담 *nak-ttam* Discouragement
낙서 *nak-ssŏ* Scribbling, scrawling
낙선 *nak-ssŏn* Failure in election
낙성식 *nak-ssŏng-sik* Completion Cermony
낙엽 *nak-yŏp* Fallen leaves
낙오하다 *nak-o-ha-da* Drop behind
낙원 *nak-wŏn* Paradise
낙인 *nak-in* Stigma
낙제 *nak-tche* Elimination
낙지 *nak-tchi* Octopus
낙천적 *nak-ch'ŏn-jŏk* Optimistic
낙타 *nak-t'a* Camel
낙태 *nak-t'ae* Abortion
낙하산 *na-k'a-san* Parachute
낙후 *na-k'u* Falling behind
난국 *nan-guk* Difficult Sisituation
난로 *nal-lo* Stove
날 *nal* Day
날개 *nal-gae* Wing
날다 *nal-da* Fly
날씨 *nal-ssi* Weather
날씬한 *nal-ssin-han* Slender, Slim
날짐승 *nal-tchim-sŭng* Fowls, Birds
낡은 *nal-gŭn* Old, Outdated
남극 *nam-gŭk* Southern pole
남녀 *nam-nyŏ* Man and woman
남북 *nam-buk* South and north
남자 *nam-ja* Man
남쪽 *nam-tchok* South
남편 *nam-p'yŏn* Husband

남해 *nam-hae* Southern Sea

납 *nap* Lead

납세하다 *nap-sse-ha-da* Pay one's tax

낫다 *nat-tta* Recover, Get well

낭만적 *nang-man-jŏk* Romantic

낭만주의 *nang-man-ju-ŭi* Romanticism

낭비 *nang-bi* Waste

내각 *nae-gak* Cabinet

내기 *nae-gi* Betting, Staking

내력 *nae-ryŏk* History

내막 *nae-mak* Inside facts, Inside story

내방 *nae-bang* Visit, Call

내부 *nae-bu* Inside, Interior

내실 *nae-sil* Inner room, Women's quarters

내용 *nae-yong* Contents, Substance

내일 *nae-il* Tomorrow

내핍 *nae-p'ip* Austerity

냉대 *naeng-dae* Cold treatment

냉방 장치 *naeng-bang chang-ch'i* Air Conditioning

냉장고 *naeng-jang-go* Refrigerator

너 *nŏ* You

넉넉하다 *nŏng-nŏ-k'a-da* Enough, Sufficient

네거리 *ne-gŏ-ri* Crossroads

녀석 *nyŏ-sŏk* Fellow

노곤한 *no-gon-han* Tired

노동 *no-dong* Labor

노랑 *no-rang* Yellow

노래 *no-rae* Song

노력 *no-ryŏk* Endeavor, Effort

노련한 *no-ryŏn-han* Experienced

노름 *no-rŭm* Gambling

노여움 *no-yŏ-um* Anger

노예 *no-ye* Slave

노인 *no-in* Old man

노파 *no-p'a* Old woman

녹다 *nok-tta* Melt

뇌물 *noe-mul* Bribe

논문 *non-mun* Article, Thesis

놈 *nom* Fellow, Guy

농민 *nong-min* Peasant

농부 *nong-bu* Farmer

농업 *nong-ŏp* Agriculture

농장 *nŏng-jang* Farm

농촌 *nong-ch'on* Farm Village

높이 *no-p'i* Height

누이 *nu-i* Sister

눈 *nun* ①Eye ②Snow

눈물 *nun-mul* Tear

눕다 *nup-tta* Lie down

느낌 *nŭ-kkim* Impression, Feeling

늙은이 *nŭl-gŭ-ni* Old man

능금 *nŭng-gŭm* Crab apple

ㄷ

다갈색 *ta-gal-ssaek* Brown

다감한 *ta-gam-han* Emotional, Sensitive

다과 *ta-gwa* Tea and cake

다다르다 *ta-da-rŭ-da* Arrive, Reach

다달이 *ta-da-ri* Every month

다람쥐 *ta-ram-jwi* Squirrel

다량 *ta-ryang* Large quantity

다리 *ta-ri* ①Bridge ②Leg

다망한 *ta-mang-han* Busy

다방 *ta-bang* Tea room

다섯 *ta-sŏt* Five

다채로운 *ta-ch'ae-ro-un* Colorful

다행한 *ta-haeng-han* Lucky, Fortunate

단념 *tan-nyŏm* Abandonment, Give-up

단결 *tan-gyŏl* Unity, Solidarity

단속 *tan-sok* Control, Regulation

단순한 *tan-sun-han* Simple, Plain

단조한 *tan-jo-han* Monotonous

단편 *tan-p'yŏn* Short piece

단편 소설 *tan-p'yŏn so-sŏl* Short stroy

단풍 *tan-p'ung* Maple

달 *tal* Moon

달걀 *tal-gyal* Egg

달력 *tal-lyŏk* Calendar

달빛 *tal-ppit* Moonlight, Moonbeam

닭 *tak* Hen

담배 *tam-bae* Cigarette, Tobacco

답변 *tap-ppyŏn* Reply, Answer

답안 *ta-ban* Examination paper

당 *tang* Party, Clique

당구 *tang-gu* Billiards

당신 *tang-sin* You

대결 *tae-gyŏl* Confrontation

대금 *tae-gŭm* Price

대나무 *tae-na-mu* Bamboo

대담 *tae-dam* Talk, Conversation

대령 *tae-ryŏng* Colonel

대륙 *tae-ryuk* Continent

대리석 *tae-ri-sŏk* Marble

대머리 *tae-mŏ-ri* Boldheaded man

대법원 *tae-bŏp-wŏn* Supreme Court

대부 *tae-bu* Loan

대비 *tae-bi* Preparation

대사 *tae-sa* ①Ambassador ②Dialogue

대양 *tae-yang* Ocean

대우 *tae-u* Treatment

대장 *tae-jang* General, Admiral

대전 *tae-jŏn* Great war

대접 *tae-jŏp* Treatment, Reception

대조 *tae-jo* Contrast, Comparision

대주교 *tae-ju-gyo* Archibishop

대중 *tae-jung* People, Mass

대지 *tae-ji* Earth

대책 *tae-ch'aek* Countermeasure

대출 *tae-ch'ul* Lending out

대표 *tae-p'yo* Representative

대학 *tae-hak* University, College
대한 민국 *tae-han min-guk* Republic of Korea
대합실 *tae-hap-ssil* Waiting room
대화 *tae-hwa* Conversation, Chatting
대회 *tae-hoe* Meeting, Rally
더러운 *tŏ-rŏ-un* Dirty
덕 *tŏk* Virtue, Merit
도끼 *to-kki* Axe, Hatchet
도덕 *to-dŏk* Virtue, Morality
도둑 *to-duk* Thief
도매 *to-mae* Wholesale
도보 *to-bo* Walking
도서관 *to-sŏ-gwan* Library
도시 *to-si* City
도움 *to-um* Help, Assistance
도장 *to-jang* Stamp
도전 *to-jŏn* Challenge
도주하다 *to-ju-ha-da* Run Away, Flee
도착 *to-ch'ak* Arrival
도해 *to-hae* Diagram
독립 *tong-nip* Independence
독백 *tok-ppaek* Soliloquy, Monologue
독서 *tok-ssŏ* Reading
독신자 *tok-ssin-ja* Bachelor, Spinster
독약 *tok-yak* Poisonous Drug
독자 *tok-tcha* Reader, Subscriber
독재 *tok-tchae* Dictatorship
독점 *tok-tchŏm* Monopoly, Exclusive Possession
독학 *to-k'ak* Self−Study
돈 *ton* Money
돌 *tol* Stone
돌격 *tol-gyŏk* Charge, Rush
돌려주다 *tol-lyŏ-ju-da* Return, Give back
동무 *tong-mu* Friend, Companion
동물 *tong-mul* Animal
동양 *tong-yang* Orient
동작 *tong-jak* Action, Movement
동정 *tong-jŏng* Sympathy, Compassion
동쪽 *tong-tchok* East
동창생 *tong-ch'ang-saeng* Alumnai
동포 *tong-p'o* Brethren
동화 *tong-hwa* Fairy Tale
따님 *tta-nim* Daughter
딸기 *ttal-gi* Strawberry
뛰다 *ttwi-da* Run
뜰 *ttŭl* Garden
뜻 *ttŭt* Meaning, Will, Mind

ㄹ

라디오 *ra-di-o* Radio
랑데브 *rang-de-bŭ* Rendezvous
로터리 *ro-t'ŏ-ri* Rotary
리더 *ri-dŏ* Leader
리듬 *ri-dŭm* Rythm

ㅁ

마귀 *ma-gwi* Devil, Demon

마님 *ma-nim* Lady, Madam

마당 *ma-dang* Yard, Court

마법 *ma-bŏp* Magic, Witchcraft

마부 *ma-bu* Coachman, Horse driver

마비 *ma-bi* Paralysis

마을 *ma-ŭl* Town, Village

마음 *ma-ŭm* Mind

마차 *ma-ch'a* Coach, Carriage

마취 *ma-ch'wi* Anesthesia

마흔 *ma-hŭn* Forty

만년필 *man-nyŏn-p'il* Fountain-pen

만족 *man-jok* Satisfaction, Gratification

만행 *man-haeng* Brutality, Outrage

말 *mal* ①Horse ②Language

말썽 *mal-ssŏng* Trouble

맛 *mat* Taste, Flavor

망상 *mang-sang* Fancy

매독 *mae-dok* Syphilis

매력 *mae-ryŏk* Charm

매매 *mae-mae* Buying and selling

매미 *mae-mi* Cicada

매우 *mae-u* Very

매일 *mae-il* Every day

매장 *mae-jang* Burial, Interment

맹렬한 *maeng-nyŏl-han* Furious, Fierce, Violent

맹세 *maeng-se* Oath, Vow, Pledge

맹수 *maeng-su* Wild animal

머슴 *mŏ-sŭm* Farmhand, Servant

먼동 *mŏn-dong* Dawn

며느리 *myŏ-nŭ-ri* Daughter-in-law

면담 *myŏn-dam* Interview

면제 *myŏn-je* Exemption

면허 *myŏn-hŏ* License

명물 *myŏng-mul* Specialty

명상 *myŏng-sang* Meditation

명승 *myŏng-sŭng* Scenic spot

명예 *myŏng-ye* Honor, Glory

모란 *mo-ran* Peony

모래 *mo-rae* Sand

모발 *mo-bal* Hair

모방 *mo-bang* Imitation, Copy

모순 *mo-sun* Contradiction

모습 *mo-sŭp* Appearance

모욕 *mo-yok* Insult, Contempt

모험 *mo-hŏm* Adventure, Risk

목걸이 *mok-kkŏ-ri* Necklace

목사 *mok-ssa* Pastor, Clergyman

목장 *mok-tchang* Pasture

목적 *mok-tchŏk* Purpose, Aim

목축 *mok-ch'uk* Cattle breeding, Stock raising

몫 *mok* Share, Portion

묘지 *myo-ji* Graveyard

무기 *mu-gi* Arms, Weapon

무관심 *mu-gwan-sim* Indifference

무덤 *mu-dŏm* Grave

359

무도회 *mu-do-hoe* Dancing Party
무식 *mu-sik* Ignorance, Illiteracy
무용 *mu-yong* Dancing
무지개 *mu-ji-gae* Rainbow
무효 *mu-hyo* Invalidity
묵상 *muk-ssang* Meditation, Reverie
문 *mun* Door, Gate
문명 *mun-myŏng* Civilization
문법 *mun-ppŏp* Grammar
문제 *mun-je* Question, Problem
문학 *mun-hak* Literature
물건 *mul-gŏn* Thing, Goods, Article
미덕 *mi-dŏk* Virtue
미망인 *mi-mang-in* Widow
미소 *mi-so* Smile
미술 *mi-sul* Art, Fine arts
미인 *mi-in* Beautiful Woman
미치다 *mi-ch'i-da* Go mad
미혼의 *mi-ho-nŭi* Single
민간인 *min-ga-nin* Civilian
민속 *min-sok* Ethnic customs
민요 *mi-nyo* Folk Song
민족주의 *min-jok-ju-ŭi* Nationalism
밀담 *mil-ttam* Secret talks
밀회 *mil-hoe* Secret Meeting

ㅂ

바늘 *pa-nŭl* Pin, Needle
바다 *pa-da* Sea, Ocean
바닷가 *pa-dat-kka* Shore, Coast
바람 *pa-ram* Wind

바보 *pa-bo* Fool, Idiot
바위 *pa-wi* Rock
바지 *pa-ji* Trousers, Pants
바퀴 *pa-k'wi* Wheel
박람회 *pang-nam-hoe* Exhibition, Fair
박물관 *pang-mul-gwan* Museum
박사 *pak-ssa* Doctor
박애주의 *pak-ae-ju-ŭi* Philanthropism
반 *pan* Half
반경 *pan-gyŏng* Radius
반대 *pan-dae* Opposition, Objection
반란 *pal-ran* Revolt, Rebellion
반사 *pan-sa* Reflection, Reverberation
반역 *pa-nyŏk* Treason, Rebellion
반응 *pa-nŭng* Reaction
반항 *pan-hang* Resistance
반환 *pan-hwan* Return
발가락 *pal-kka-rak* Toe
발달 *pal-ttal* Development, Growth
발명 *pal-myŏng* Invention
발표 *pal-p'yo* Announcement
밤 *pam* ①Night ②Chest nut
방법 *pang-bŏp* method
방송 *pang-song* Broadcasting
방학 *pang-hak* Vacation
방해 *pang-hae* Disturbance, Hindrance
배 *pae* ①Ship ②Pear ③Stomach
배경 *pae-gyŏng* Background

배구 *pae-gu* Volleyball

배달 *pae-dal* Delivery, Distribution

배상 *pae-sang* Compensation, Reparation

배추 *pae-ch'u* Cabbage

백 *paek* Hundred

백묵 *paeng-muk* Chalk

백성 *paek-ssŏng* People

백인 *paek-in* White people

백주 *paek-tchu* Daytime

백합 *pae-k'ap* lily

버릇 *pŏ-rŭt* Habit

번개 *pŏn-gae* Lightning

번역 *pŏ-nyŏk* Translation

번영 *pŏ-nyŏng* Prosperity

벌 *pŏl* ①Bee ②Punishment

범 *pŏm* Tiger

법 *pŏp* Law

법원 *pŏp-wŏn* Court

벙어리 *pŏng-ŏ-ri* Dumb

벼랑 *pyŏ-rang* Cliff

병 *pyŏng* ①Illness ②Bottle

병역 *pyŏng-yŏk* Military service

병자 *pyŏng-ja* Patient, Sick person

병풍 *pyŏng-p'ung* Folding screen

보도 *po-do* Report

보병 *po-byŏng* Infantry

보물 *po-mul* Treasure

보수 *po-su* Reward

보증 *po-jŭng* Guarantee

보험 *po-hŏm* Insurance

복수 *pok-ssu* Revenge, Vengeance

본능 *pon-nŭng* Instinct

봉급 *pong-gŭp* Salary, Pay

부부 *pu-bu* Couple

부정 *pu-jŏng* Injustice, Unfairness

부족 *pu-jok* Scarcity, Shortage

부친 *pu-ch'in* Father

부패 *pu-p'ae* Decomposition, Corruption

부활 *pu-hwal* Resurreciton

북쪽 *puk-tchok* North

불면증 *pul-myŏn-tchŭng* Insomnia

비 *pi* Rain

비관 *pi-gwan* Pessimism

비극 *pi-gŭk* Tragedy

비난 *pi-nan* Criticism

비누 *pi-nu* Soap

비둘기 *pi-dul-gi* Dove, Pigeon

비밀 *pi-mil* Secrecy

비보 *pi-bo* Sad news

비상 *pi-sang* Emergency

비애 *pi-ae* Sorrow, Grief, Sadness

비용 *pi-yong* Expense, Expenditure

비인도적 *pi-in-do-jŏk* Inhuman

비평 *pi-p'yŏng* Criticism, Comment

빈곤 *pin-gon* Poverty

빚 *pit* Debt, Loan

ㅅ

사건 *sa-kkŏn* Event, Incident

사기 *sa-gi* Morale

사랑 *sa-rang* Love, Affection

361

사망 *sa-mang* Death
사방 *sa-bang* All directions
사병 *sa-byŏng* Soldier
사슴 *sa-sŭm* Deer
사월 *sa-wŏl* April
사임 *sa-im* Resignation
사전 *sa-jŏn* Dictionary
사춘기 *sa-ch'un-gi* Puberty
사치 *sa-ch'i* Luxury, Extravagence
사형 *sa-hyŏng* Capital Punishment
산문 *san-mun* Prose
산업 *sa-nŏp* Industry
살인 *sa-rin* Murder, Killing
삼월 *sam-wŏl* March
상 *sang* ①Prize ②Table
상금 *sang-gŭm* Prize, Reward
상식 *sang-sik* Common sense
상인 *sang-in* Merchant
상징 *sang-jing* Symbol, Emblem
새벽 *sae-byŏk* Dawn, Daybreak
새우 *sae-u* Shrimp
샘 *saem* Spring, Fountain
생각 *saeng-gak* Thinking, Thought
생계 *saeng-gye* Livelihood, Living
생명 *saeng-myŏng* Life
생산 *saeng-san* Production
생활비 *saeng-hwal-bi* Living Expense
서류 *sŏ-ryu* Document, Papers
서양 *sŏ-yang* West
석방 *sŏk-ppang* Release
석유 *sŏk-yu* Petroleum

선거 *sŏn-gŏ* Election
선동 *sŏn-dong* Instigation
선전 *sŏn-jŏn* Propaganda
설계 *sŏl-gye* Plan, Design
설비 *sŏl-bi* Equipment, Installation
설사 *sŏl-ssa* Diarrhea
설탕 *sŏl-t'ang* Sugar
성냥 *sŏng-nyang* Match
성서 *sŏng-sŏ* Bible
성의 *sŏng-ŭi* Sincerity, Good faith
세계 *se-gye* World
세관 *se-gwan* Custom house
세금 *se-gŭm* Tax
세력 *se-ryŏk* Power
세무서 *se-mu-sŏ* Tax office
소년 *so-nyŏn* Boy
소리 *so-ri* Sound, Noise
소방서 *so-bang-sŏ* Fire Station
소설 *so-sŏl* Novel
소집 *so-jip* Call, Sermon
소포 *so-p'o* Package, Parcel
속달 *sok-ttal* Express Delivery
손녀 *son-nyŏ* Granddaughter
손자 *son-ja* Grandson
솜씨 *som-ssi* Skill, Workmanship
송금 *song-gŭm* Remittance
쇠고기 *soe-go-gi* Beef
수도 *su-do* ①Capital city ②Water pipe ③asceticism
수상 *su-sang* ①Prime Minister ② water surface ③Receivint ④suspiciousness ⑤occasional ⑥image

수재 *su-jae* Genius
수확 *su-hwak* Harvest, Crop
술집 *sul-tchip* Bar, Public house
쉰 *swin* Fifty
스물 *sŭ-mul* Twenty
시간표 *si-gan-p'yo* Time table
시골 *si-gol* Countryside, Rural district
시내 *si-nae* ①Downtown ②Stream
시월 *si-wŏl* October
시인 *si-in* Poet
시장 *si-jang* ①Market ②Mayor
시찰 *si-ch'al* Inspection
시청 *si-ch'ŏng* City, Hall
시합 *si-hap* Match, Game
시행 *si-haeng* Operation, Enforcement
식당 *sik-ttang* Restaurant
식량 *sing-nyang* Food
식물 *sing-mul* Plant, Vegetation
신경질 *sin-gyŏng-jil* Nervousness
신고 *sin-go* Report, Statement
신년 *sin-nyŏn* New Year
신도 *sin-do* Believer
신문 *sin-mun* Newspaper
신비 *sin-bi* Mystery
신앙 *si-nang* Belief, Faith
실망 *sil-mang* Disappointment, Discouragement
실연 *sil-yŏn* Unrequited love
실직 *sil-tchik* Unemployment
실천 *sil-ch'ŏn* Practice

실패 *sil-p'ae* Failure, Blunder
심부름 *sim-bu-rŭm* Errand
십이월 *sip-i-wŏl* December
십일월 *sip-i-rwŏl* November

ㅇ

아가씨 *a-ga-ssi* Young lady, Girl
아기 *a-gi* Baby
아내 *a-nae* Wife
아들 *a-dŭl* Son
아량 *a-ryang* Generosity, Magnanimity
아버지 *a-bŏ-ji* Father
아씨 *a-ssi* Young mistress
아악 *a-ak* Court music
아우 *a-u* Young brother
아우성 *a-u-sŏng* Shouting, Battle cry
아저씨 *a-jŏ-ssi* Uncle
아주머니 *a-ju-mŏ-ni* Aunt
아침 *a-ch'im* Morning
아편 *a-p'yŏn* Opium
아홉 *a-hop* Nine
아흔 *a-hŭn* Ninety
악몽 *ang-mong* Nightmare, Bad dream
악한 *a-k'an* Rascal, Rogue, Scoundrel
안경 *an-gyŏng* Glasses
안녕 *an-nyŏng* Peace, Good health
안락 *al-lak* Ease, Comfort

안마 *an-ma* Massage
안색 *an-saek* Complexion
안식 *an-sik* Rest
안심 *an-sim* Ease of Mind
안전 *an-jŏn* Safety, Security
안정 *an-jŏng* Stability
알 *al* Egg
암 *am* Cancer
암거래 *am-gŏ-rae* Black market dealing
암살 *am-sal* Assassination
암탉 *am-t'ak* Hen
압력 *am-nyŏk* Pressure
압수 *ap-ssu* Confiscation, Seizure
앙갚음 *ang-ga-p'ŭm* Revenge
앙탈 *ang-t'al* Evasion, Elusion
애교 있는 *ae-gyo in-nŭn* Charming, Lovable
애국심 *ae-guk-ssim* Patriotism
애도 *ae-do* Condolence, Mourning
애로 *ae-ro* Difficulties, Bottleneck
애수 *ae-su* Sorrow, Sadness
애숭이 *ae-sung-i* Green youth
애인 *ae-in* Lover, Sweetheart
액체 *aek-ch'e* Liquid
야구 *ya-gu* Baseball
야만 *ya-man* Barbarism
야수 *ya-su* Wild beast
약품 *yak-p'um* Medicines, Drugs
양 *yang* Sheep
양친 *yang-ch'in* Parents
어린이 *ŏ-ri-ni* Children

어머니 *ŏ-mŏ-ni* Mother
어부 *ŏ-bu* Fisherman
어제 *ŏ-je* Yesterday
억울한 *ŏ-gul-han* Resentful, Regrettable
언론 *ŏl-lon* Speech, Journalism
언약 *ŏ-nyak* Verbal promise
언쟁 *ŏn-jaeng* Verbal Dispute
얼굴 *ŏl-gul* Face
얼음 *ŏ-rŭm* Ice
엊저녁 *ŏt-tchŏ-nyŏk* Last night
여름 *yŏ-rŭm* Summer
여성 *yŏ-sŏng* Woman, Female
역사 *yŏk-ssa* History
예산 *ye-san* Budget
예술 *ye-sul* Art
예의 *ye-ŭi* Courtesy
예절 *ye-jŏl* Etiquette
오 *o* Five
오락 *o-rak* Amusement, Entertainment
오막살이 *o-mak-ssa-ri* Cottage
오월 *o-wŏl* May
오이 *o-i* Cucumber
오전 *o-jŏn* Forenoon
오해 *o-hae* Misunderstanding
오후 *o-hu* Afternoon
올해 *ol-hae* This year
완고한 *wan-go-han* Stubborn, Obstinate
완성 *wan-sŏng* Completion, Perfection

완전한 *wan-jŏn-han* Perfect, Complete

왕자 *wang-ja* Prince

왕후 *wang-hu* Empress, Queen

외교 *oe-gyo* Diplomacy

외국 *oe-guk* Foreign Country

외빈 *oe-bin* Foreign Visitor

외상 *oe-sang* Credit

외인 *oe-in* Foreigner

외출 *oe-ch'ul* Outing

요구 *yo-gu* Demand

요금 *yo-gŭm* Charge, Fee, Fare

우기 *u-gi* Rainy Season

우량한 *u-ryang-han* Excellent

우물 *u-mul* Well

우박 *u-bak* Hail

우비 *u-bi* Raincoat

우산 *u-san* Umbrella

우승 *u-sŭng* Victory

우유 *u-yu* Milk

우정 *u-jŏng* Friendship

우편 *u-p'yŏn* Mail

운동장 *un-dong-jang* Playground

운명 *un-myŏng* Fate, Destiny

운영 *u-nyŏng* Management, Operation

운전 *un-jŏn* Operation, Driving

운하 *un-ha* Canal

원수 *wŏn-su* ①Army general ② Enemy

원숭이 *wŏn-sung-i* Monkey

원조 *wŏn-jo* Support, Aid, Help

원한 *wŏn-han* Grudge, Resentment

위반 *wi-ban* Violation, Infringement

위생 *wi-saeng* Sanitation

위안 *wi-an* Comfort, Consolation

유람 *yu-ram* Sightseeing, Excursion

유언 *yu-ŏn* Will

유월 *yu-wŏl* June

유흥 *yu-hŭng* Pleasure, Merry making

유희 *yu-hŭi* Play

은막 *ŭn-mak* Screen

은인 *ŭ-nin* Benefactor

은퇴 *ŭn-t'oe* Retirement, Retreat

은하수 *ŭn-ha-su* Milky way, Galaxy

음력 *ŭm-nyŏk* Lunar Calendar

음료 *ŭm-nyo* Beverage, Drink

음모 *ŭm-mo* Plot, Conspiracy

음주 *ŭm-ju* Drinking

응모 *ŭng-mo* Application

의복 *ŭi-bok* Clothes, Dress

의사당 *ŭi-sa-dang* Assembly Hall

의식 *ŭi-sik* Consciousness, Sense

의장 *ŭi-jang* Chairman, President

이국 *i-guk* Foreign Country

이념 *i-nyŏm* Ideology

이달 *i-dal* This month

이별 *i-byŏl* Separation, Parting

이슬비 *i-sŭl-bi* Drizzle, Mizzle

이십 *i-sip* Twenty

이웃 *i-ut* Neighborhood

이월 *i-wŏl* February

이익 *i-ik* Profit
이해 *i-hae* Understanding
이혼 *i-hon* Divorce
익살 *ik-ssal* Humor
일기 *il-gi* Diary
일월 *i-rwŏl* January
일지 *il-tchi* Journal, Diary

ㅈ

자 *cha* Ruler, Yardstick
자갈 *cha-gal* Gravel, Pebble
자격 *cha-gyŏk* Qualification
자극 *cha-gŭk* Stimulus, Impetus
자급 *cha-gŭp* Self—support
자기 *cha-gi* ①Porcelain ②Himself
　③Self—register ④Magnetism
자네 *cha-ne* You
자다 *cha-da* Sleep
자동차 *cha-dong-ch'a* Automobile
자랑 *cha-rang* Pride, Boast
자료 *cha-ryo* Material, Data
자매 *cha-mae* Sisters
자명종 *cha-myŏng-jong* Alarm Clock
자백 *cha-baek* Confession
자본 *cha-bon* Fund, Capital
자본가 *cha-bon-ga* Capitalist
자부심 *cha-bu-sim* Self—confidence
자비 *cha-bi* Mercy, Pity
자살 *cha-sal* Suicide
자서전 *cha-sŏ-jŏn* Autobiography
자식 *cha-sik* Child, Son, Daughter
자신 *cha-sin* Self—confidence

자연 *cha-yŏn* Nature
자원 *cha-wŏn* Resources
자유 *cha-yu* Freedom, Liberty
자장가 *cha-jang-ga* Lullaby
자전거 *cha-jŏn-gŏ* Bicycle
자정 *cha-jŏng* Midnight
자주 *cha-ju* Independence
자책 *cha-ch'aek* Selfreproach(accusa-
　tion)
자취 *cha-ch'wi* Trace, Mark, Sign
자치 *cha-ch'i* Self—government
자포자기 *cha-p'o-ja-gi* Self—aban-
　donment
자화상 *cha-hwa-sang* Self—portrait
작곡 *chak-kkok* Composition
작년 *chang-nyŏn* Last Year
작업 *cha-gŏp* Work, Labor
작자 *chak-tcha* Author
작전 *chak-tchŏn* Operation
작품 *chak-p'um* Work
잔 *chan* Cup, Glass
잔돈 *chan-don* Small change
잔디 *chan-di* Lawn
잔소리 *chan-so-ri* Scolding, Rebuke
잔액 *cha-naek* Remainder
잔인한 *cha-nin-han* Cruel
잔치 *chan-ch'i* Banquet, Feast
잘못 *chal-mot* Mistake, Error,
　Fault
잠 *cham* Sleep, Nap
잠수부 *cham-su-bu* Diver
잠수함 *cham-su-ham* Sub marine

잡비 *chap-ppi* Sundry Expenses
잡지 *chap-tchi* Magazine
잡초 *chap-ch'o* Weed
잡화 *cha-p'wa* Miscellaneous goods
장 *chang* ①Sheet ②Soy ③Chapter
④Head, Chief⑤Fair ⑥Guts ⑦
Vitals
장갑 *chang-gap* Glove
장관 *chang-gwan* Minister
장교 *chang-gyo* Officer
장군 *chang-gun* General
장난감 *chang-nan-kkam* Toy
장녀 *chang-nyŏ* First daughter
장님 *chang-nim* Blind Man
장독 *chang-dok* Soy jar
장래 *chang-nae* Future
장례 *chang-nye* Funeral service
장마 *chang-ma* Long rain
장모 *chang-mo* Mother－in－law
장면 *chang-myŏn* Scene, Place
장미 *chang-mi* Rose
장병 *chang-byŏng* Soldier
장부 *chang-bu* Account book
장성 *chang-sŏng* Generals
장식 *chang-sik* Decoration
장애 *chang-ae* Obstacle
장인 *chang-in* Father－in－Law
장자 *chang-ja* First son
장치 *chang-ch'i* Equipment, Setting
장학금 *chang-hak-kkŭm* Scholarship
장학생 *chang-hak-ssaeng* Scholarship
student

재 *chae* ①Ash ②Hill
재건 *chae-gŏn* Reconstruction
재능 *chae-nŭng* Talent, Ability
재단 *chae-dan* Foundation
재료 *chae-ryo* Material
재목 *chae-mok* Wood, Timber, Lumber
재물 *chae-mul* Riches, Property, Wealth.
재미 *chae-mi* Fun, Interest
재발 *chae-bal* Recurrence
재벌 *chae-bŏl* Financial Combine, Tycoon
재산 *chae-san* Fortune, Assets
재선 *chae-sŏn* Reelection
재정 *chae-jŏng* Finance
재치 *chae-ch'i* Wit
재판 *chae-p'an* ①Trial ②Reprint
재해 *chae-hae* Calamity, Disaster
재향 군인 *chae-hyang ku-nin* Reservists
재혼 *chae-hon* Remarriage
쟁반 *chaeng-ban* Tray
저금 *chŏ-gŭm* Saving, Deposit
저녁 *chŏ-nyŏk* Evening
저수지 *chŏ-su-ji* Reservoir
저택 *chŏ-t'aek* Residence
적 *chŏk* Enemy
절망 *chŏl-mang* Despair
절약 *chŏl-lyak* Economy, Saving
절제 *chŏl-tche* Moderation
점 *chŏm* ①Fortune－telling ②Spot,

367

Point

점령 *chŏm-nyŏng* Occupation

점심 *chŏm-sim* Lunch

점원 *chŏ-mwŏn* Sales clerk

정리 *chŏng-ni* Arrangement

정력 *chŏng-nyŏk* Energy, Stamina, Vigour

정복 *chŏng-bok* Conquest

정부 *chŏng-bu* ①Government ②Secret lover

정의 *chŏng-ūi* ①Friendship ②Definition ③Jutice

정조 *chŏng-jo* Chastity

정찰 *chŏng-ch'al* Reconnaissance

정치 *chŏng-ch'i* Politics

제국 *che-guk* Empire

제단 *che-dan* Altar

제대 *che-dae* Discharge from Military Service

제도 *che-do* ①System ②Drawing

제막 *che-mak* Unveiling Theme, Title

제복 *che-bok* Uniform

제비 *che-bi* Swallow

제안 *che-an* Proposal, Suggestion

제자 *che-ja* Disciple, Pupil

제정 *che-jŏng* Establishment

제한 *che-han* Restriction, limit

조간 *cho-gan* Morning Paper

조개 *cho-gae* Shellfish

조국 *cho-guk* Fatherland

조기 *cho-gi* ①Mourning flag ②Early rising ③Early stage

조난 *cho-nan* Shipwreck

조사 *cho-sa* Investigation

조상 *cho-sang* Ancestor

조직 *cho-jik* Organization

존중 *chon-jung* Respect

졸업 *chol-ŏp* Graduation

죄 *choe* Sin, Crime

죄수 *choe-su* Prisoner, Convict

죄인 *choe-in* Criminal, Offender

지각 *chi-gak* Lateness, Being late

지구 *chi-gu* ①Earth, Globe ②District

지급한 *chi-gŭ-p'an* Urgent

지대 *chi-dae* Zone, Region

지도 *chi-do* ①Map ②Atlas ③Guidance, Leadership

지렁이 *chi-rŏng-i* Earthworm

지령 *chi-ryŏng* Instruction, Order, Directive

지리 *chi-ri* Geography

지배인 *chi-bae-in* Manager

지불 *chi-bul* Payment

지붕 *chi-bung* Roof

지사 *chi-sa* Governor

지옥 *chi-ok* Hell, Inferno

지점 *chi-jŏm* Branch Office

지정 *chi-jŏng* ①Appointment, Assignment ②Sincerity

지주 *chi-ju* Land Owner

지진 *chi-jin* Earthquake

지팡이 *chi-p'ang-i* Stick, Cane

지폐 *chi-p'ye* Note, Paper Money
지하 *chi-ha* Underground
지혜 *chi-hye* Wisdom
지휘 *chi-hwi* Command
직감 *chik-kkam* Intuition
직공 *chik-kkong* Worker
직업 *chik-öp* Occupation
직장 *chik-tchang* Working place
직책 *chik-ch'aek* Duty, Function
진달래 *chin-dal-rae* Azalea
진리 *chil-ri* Truth
진미 *chin-mi* Delicate Flavor
진보 *chin-bo* Progress
진상 *chin-sang* Real Facts, Truth
진술 *chin-sul* Statement
진주 *chin-ju* Pearl
진통 *chin-t'ong* Labor Pains
질병 *chil-byöng* Disease
질서 *chil-ssö* Order
질의 *chi-rüi* Inquiuy, Question
집단 *chip-ttan* Group, Mass
집회 *chi-p'oe* Meeting, Gathering
징집 *ching-jip* Conscription, Recruiting

ㅊ

차 *ch'a* ①Coffee ②Car, Vehicle
차고 *ch'a-go* Garage
차관 *ch'a-gwan* ①Loan ②Vice Minister
차단 *ch'a-dan* Interception
차도 *ch'a-do* Roadway
차례 *ch'a-rye* Order, Turn
차림 *ch'a-rim* Outflt
차별 *ch'a-byöl* Discrimination
차압 *ch'a-ap* Attachment, Seizure
차용 *ch'a-yong* Loan, Borrowing
차이 *ch'a-i* Difference
차장 *ch'a-jang* (bus, train) Conductor
차표 *ch'a-p'yo* (bus, train) Ticket
착륙 *ch'ang-nyuk* Landing
착수 *ch'ak-ssu* Start, Commencement
착오 *ch'ak-o* Mistake, Error
찬성 *ch'an-söng* Approval, Agreement
찬송 *ch'an-song* Glory, Praise
찬양 *ch'a-nyang* Commendation, Praise
찬조 *ch'an-jo* Support
찰과상 *ch'al-gwa-sang* Graze
참가 *ch'am-ga* Participation
참고 *ch'am-go* Reference
참배 *ch'am-bae* Worship
참새 *ch'am-sae* Sparrow
참석 *ch'am-sök* Attendance
참을성 *ch'a-mül-ssöng* Patience
참전 *ch'am-jön* Participation in war
참패 *ch'am-p'ae* Crushing defeat
참회 *ch'am-hoe* Repentance
찹쌀 *ch'ap-ssal* Glutinous
창 *ch'ang* ①Window ②Spear

창고 *ch'ang-go* Warehouse, Ban
창공 *ch'ang-gong* Blue Sky
창극 *ch'ang-gŭk* Classical Korean opera
창녀 *ch'ang-nyŏ* Prostitute
창립 *ch'ang-nip* Establishment
창문 *ch'ang-mun* Window
창안 *ch'ang-an* Original Idea
창작 *ch'ang-jak* Creative work
창조 *ch'ang-jo* Creation
창피 *ch'ang-p'i* Disgrace, Shame
채권 *ch'ae-kkwŏn* ①Credit claim ② Bond, Debenture
채소 *ch'ae-so* Vegetable
채식 *ch'ae-sik* Vegetable diet
채용 *ch'ae-yong* Employment
책상 *ch'aek-ssang* Desk
처 *ch'ŏ* Wife
처남 *ch'ŏ-nam* Brother—in—law
처녀 *ch'ŏ-nyŏ* Virgin, Maid
처방 *ch'ŏ-bang* Prescription
처벌 *ch'ŏ-bŏl* Punishment
처신 *ch'ŏ-sin* Behaviour, Conduct
처자 *ch'ŏ-ja* Wife and Children
처형 *ch'ŏ-hyŏng* Execution
천 *ch'ŏn* ①Thousand ②Cloth
천국 *ch'ŏn-guk* Heaven, Paradise
천기 *ch'ŏn-gi* Weather
천당 *ch'ŏn-dang* Heaven, Paradise
천대 *ch'ŏn-dae* Cold Treatment
천둥 *ch'ŏn-dung* Thunder
천사 *ch'ŏn-sa* Angel

천재 *ch'ŏn-jae* Genius
천주교 *ch'ŏn-ju-gyo* Roman Catholic
천천히 *ch'ŏn-ch'ŏn-hi* Slowly
철 *ch'ŏl* ①Season ②Iron
철거 *ch'ŏl-gŏ* Withdrawal, Removal
철도 *ch'ŏl-tto* Railroad
철모 *ch'ŏl-mo* Helmet
철사 *ch'ŏl-ssa* Wire
철수 *ch'ŏl-ssu* Withdrawal
철자 *ch'ŏl-tcha* Spelling
철학 *ch'ŏl-hak* Philosophy
첩 *ch'ŏp* Concubine
첩보 *ch'ŏp-ppo* Intelligence
청년 *ch'ŏng-nyŏn* Youth, Young man
청소 *ch'ŏng-so* Cleaning
청중 *ch'ŏng-jung* Audience
청첩 *ch'ŏng-ch'ŏp* Invitation
체육관 *ch'e-yuk-kkwan* Gymnasium
초 *ch'o* ①Second ②Vinegar ③Candle
초가 *ch'o-ga* Thatched—house
초면 *ch'o-myŏn* First Meeting
초빙 *ch'o-bing* Invitation
초상 *ch'o-sang* ①Portrait ②Mourning
초음속 *ch'o-ŭm-sok* Supersonic speed
초저녁 *ch'o-jŏ-nyŏk* Early Evening
촉각 *ch'ok-kkak* Tactual sense
촉감 *ch'ok-kkam* Touch, Feel
촉망 *ch'ong-mang* Expectation

촌 *ch'on* Village, Country

촌놈 *ch'on-nom* Country man

촛불 *ch'ot-ppul* Candle−light

총각 *ch'ong-gak* Bachelor

총선거 *ch'ong-sŏn-gŏ* General election

총액 *ch'ong-aek* Total amount

총장 *ch'ong-jang* President

총회 *ch'ong-hoe* General−Meeting

최대의 *ch'oe-dae-ŭi* Largest, Greatest

최루탄 *ch'oe-ru-t'an* Tear bomd

최선 *ch'oe-sŏn* Best

최초의 *ch'oe-ch'o-ŭi* First, Original

최후의 *ch'oe-hu-ŭi* Last, Final

추가 *ch'u-ga* Addition, Supplement

추도 *ch'u-do* Mourning

추문 *ch'u-mun* Scandal

추수 *ch'u-su* Harvest

추억 *ch'u-ŏk* Remembrance, Memory

축구 *ch'uk-kku* Football

축복 *ch'uk-ppok* Blessing

출발 *ch'ul-bal* Start, Departure

출생 *ch'ul-ssaeng* Brith

출판 *ch'ul-p'an* Publication

취미 *ch'wi-mi* Taste, Hobby

층계 *ch'ŭng-gye* Stair, Step

치과 *ch'i-kkwa* Dentistry

치료 *ch'i-ryo* Medical treatment

치마 *ch'i-ma* Skirt

치명적 *ch'i-myŏng-jŏk* Fatal, Critical

치욕 *ch'i-yok* Disgrace, Shame

친교 *ch'in-gyo* Friendship

친근 *ch'in-gŭn* Intimacy

친밀 *ch'in-mil* Intimacy

친분 *ch'in-bun* Acquaintance

친선 *ch'in-sŏn* Goodwill

친숙 *ch'in-suk* Familiarity

친절 *ch'in-jŏl* Kindness

친척 *ch'in-ch'ŏk* Relative, Kin

칠 *ch'il* ①Paint ②Seven

칠기 *ch'il-gi* Lacquer−ware

칠면조 *ch'il-myŏn-jo* Turkey

칠월 *ch'i-rwŏl* July

침 *ch'im* ①Needle, Thorn ②Acupuncture

침구 *ch'im-gu* Bedding, Bedclothes

침대 *ch'im-dae* Bed, Berth

침략 *ch'im-nyak* Invasion

침몰 *ch'im-mol* Sinking

침묵 *ch'im-muk* Silence

침범 *ch'im-bŏm* Invasion

침소 *ch'im-so* Bedroom

침입 *ch'i-mip* Invasion, Intrusion

ㅋ

칼 *k'al* Knife, Sword

칼국수 *k'al-guk-ssu* Knife−cut noodles

코 *k'o* Nose

코끼리 *k'o-kki-ri* Elephant

콩 *k'ong* Bean

371

콩가루 *k'ong-kka-ru* Bean flour
콩나물 *k'ong-na-mul* Sprouting
쾌감 *k'wae-gam* Pleasant Sensation
쾌락 *k'wae-rak* Pleasure, Delight
쾌활 *k'wae-hwal* Cheerful, Merry
키 *k'i* ①Stature, Height ②Rudder
③Winnow

ㅌ

타격 *t'a-gyŏk* Blow, Shock
타국 *t'a-guk* Foreign country
타당한 *t'a-dang-han* Proper, Appropriate
타락 *t'a-rak* Degradation, Corruption
타살 *t'a-sal* Murder
타향 *t'a-hyang* Foreign Land
타협 *t'a-hyŏp* Compromise
탁월한 *t'a-gwŏl-han* Excellent, Eminent
탄광 *t'an-gwang* Mine
탄약 *t'a-nyak* Ammunition
탈세 *t'al-sse* Tax Evasion
탈출 *t'al-ch'ul* Escape
탐구 *t'am-gu* Research
탐욕 *t'am-yok* Greed
탐정 *t'am-jŏng* Detective
탐험 *t'am-hŏm* Exploration, Expedition
태도 *t'ae-do* ①Attitude ②Mien, Bearing

태양 *t'ae-yang* Sun
태평양 *t'ae-p'yŏng-yang* Pacific Ocean
태풍 *t'ae-p'ung* Typoon
토끼 *t'o-kki* Rabbit, Hare
토대 *t'o-dae* Foundation
토론 *t'o-ron* Discussion, Debate
토요일 *t'o-yo-il* Saturday
토지 *t'o-ji* Land, Estate
통고 *t'ong-go* Notification, Notice
통곡 *t'ong-gok* Wailing
통과 *t'ong-gwa* Passage
통계 *t'ong-gye* Statistics
통로 *t'ong-no* Path, Passage
통상 *t'ong-sang* Trade, Commerce
통신 *t'ong-sin* Communication, Correspondence
통역 *t'ong-yŏk* Interpretation
통일 *t'ong-il* Unification
통제 *t'ong-je* Control
통첩 *t'ong-ch'ŏp* Note, Notification
통치 *t'ong-ch'i* Rule, Reign
통합 *t'ong-hap* Merger, Unification
퇴각 *t'oe-gak* Retreat, Withdrawal
퇴보 *t'oe-bo* Retrogression
퇴역 *t'oe-yŏk* Retirement
퇴원 *t'oe-wŏn* Discharge from hospital
퇴직 *t'oe-jik* Retirement, Resignation
퇴학 *t'oe-hak* Leave school
투고 *t'u-go* Contribution

투자 *t'u-ja* Investment
투표 *t'u-p'yo* Vote
특권 *t'ŭk-kkwŏn* Privilege
특급 *t'ŭk-kkŭp* Express
특집 *t'ŭk-tchip* Special edition
특파원 *t'ŭk-p'a-wŏn* Correspondent

ㅍ

파견 *p'a-gyŏn* Dispatch
파도 *p'a-do* Waves
파랑 *p'a-rang* Blue color
파리 *p'a-ri* Fly
파면 *p'a-myŏn* Dismissal, Discharge
파산 *p'a-san* Bankruptcy
파선 *p'a-sŏn* Shipwreck
파악 *p'a-ak* Grasp, Understanding
폐 *p'ye* ①Lungs ②Trouble
폐병 *p'ye-ppyŏng* Lung disseases
포고 *p'o-go* Decree, Proclamation
포도 *p'o-do* Grape
포로 *p'o-ro* Pirsoner of war
포병 *p'o-byŏng* Artillery
포옹 *p'o-ong* Embrace
폭력 *p'ong-nyŏk* Violence
폭로 *p'ong-no* Exposure, Disclosure
폭탄 *p'ok-t'an* Bomb
폭포 *p'ok-p'o* Waterfalls
폭풍 *p'ok-p'ung* Storm
폭행 *p'o-k'aeng* Violence, Assault
표시 *p'yo-si* Indication, Mark
표준 *p'yo-jun* Standard, Norm

표지 *p'yo-ji* Cover
표현 *p'yo-hyŏn* Expression
품삯 *p'um-ssak* Hire, Wages
품팔이 *p'um-p'a-ri* Labor
풍경 *p'ung-gyŏng* Scenery, Landscape
풍금 *p'ung-gŭm* Organ
풍년 *p'ung-nyŏn* Abundant year
풍습 *p'ung-sŭp* Custom, Practice
풍자 *p'ung-ja* Satire, Sarcasm
풍채 *p'ung-ch'ae* Appearance, Presence, Mien
피 *p'i* Blood
피고 *p'i-go* Defendant, Accused
피난 *p'i-nan* Refuge
피로 *p'i-ro* Fatigue, Exhaustion
피리 *p'i-ri* Pipe, Flute
피부 *p'i-bu* Skin
피임 *p'i-im* Contraception
피해 *p'i-hae* Damage, Injury
필수품 *p'il-ssu-p'um* Necessity
필요 *p'i-ryo* Need, Necessity
필자 *p'il-tcha* Writer, Author
핑계 *p'ing-gye* Pretext, Exucuse

ㅎ

하객 *ha-gaek* Congratulator
하기 *ha-gi* Summer
하녀 *ha-nyŏ* Housemaid, Female servant
하늘 *ha-nŭl* Sky

373

하루 *ha-ru* One day
하물 *ha-mul* Baggage, Cargo
하숙 *ha-suk* Lodging
하오 *ha-o* Afternoon
하인 *ha-in* Servant
학 *hak* Crane
학계 *hak-kkye* Academic circle
학대 *hak-ttae* Cruel treatment
학설 *hak-ssŏl* Theory, Doctrine
학우 *hak-u* Schoolmate
학원 *hak-wŏn* Educational institution
학위 *hak-wi* Degree
학자 *hak-tcha* Scholar
학회 *ha-k'oe* Academic Society
한밤중 *han-bam-tchung* Midnight
한식 *han-sik* ①Korean dish ②Korean cuisine
한약 *ha-nyak* ①Oriental medicine ②Ferocity
한자 *han-tcha* Chinese character
할머니 *hal-mŏ-ni* Grandma
할아버지 *ha-ra-bŏ-ji* Grandpa
합의 *hap-ŭi* Agreement
합창 *hap-ch'ang* Chorus
해 *hae* ①Sun ②Year
해고 *hae-go* Discharge, Dismissal
해결 *hae-gyŏl* Solution, Settlement
해군 *hae-gun* Navy
해바라기 *hae-ba-ra-gi* Sunflower
해방 *hae-bang* Liberation
해변 *hae-byŏn* Beach
해병 *hae-byŏng* Marine

해안 *hae-an* Seashore
해외 *hae-woe* Overseas, Foreign
해적 *hae-jŏk* Pirate
핵 *haek* Nucleus, Core
햅쌀 *haep-ssal* New rice
행동 *haeng-dong* Action, Conduct
행사 *haeng-sa* Event
행인 *haeng-in* Passer—by
행정 *haeng-jŏng* Administration
행진 *haeng-jin* March, Parade
향 *hyang* Incense
향기 *hyang-gi* Scent, Odour
향락 *hyang-nak* Enjoyment, Pleasure
향로 *hyang-no* Incense burner
향수 *hyang-su* ①Perfume ②Nostalgia
허가 *hŏ-ga* Permission
허공 *hŏ-gong* Empty Air
허기 *hŏ-gi* Hunger
허락 *hŏ-rak* Consent, Approval
허무 *hŏ-mu* Nothingness
허물 *hŏ-mul* Fault, Blame
허세 *hŏ-se* Bluff
허약 *hŏ-yak* Weakness
허영 *hŏ-yŏng* Vanity
허위 *hŏ-wi* Falsehood, Lie
허풍 *hŏ-p'ung* Exaggeration
혁명 *hyŏng-myŏng* Revolution
현금 *hyŏn-gŭm* Cash
형 *hyŏng* ①Elder brother ②Type, Model ③Form ④Penalty

형법 *hyŏng-ppŏp* Criminal law
형수 *hyŏng-su* Brother's wife
형제 *hyŏng-je* Brother
호기심 *ho-gi-sim* Curiosity
호랑이 *ho-rang-i* Tiger
호롱 *ho-rong* Oil Lamp
호밀 *ho-mil* Rye
호박 *ho-bak* Pumpkin
호반 *ho-ban* Lakeside
호수 *ho-su* Lake
호출 *ho-ch'ul* Call
황금 *hwang-gŭm* Gold
황새 *hwang-sae* Stork
황야 *hwang-ya* Deserted Land
황제 *hwang-je* Emperor
황혼 *hwang-hon* Twilight, Dusk
회고 *hoe-go* Reflection, Recollection

회담 *hoe-dam* Meeting, Talks
회상 *hoe-sang* Recollection
회원 *hoe-wŏn* Member
회장 *hoe-jang* Chairman, President
회화 *hoe-hwa* ①Painting ②Conversation
효과 *hyo-kkwa* Effect
효도 *hyo-do* Filial duty
휘발유 *hwi-bal-ryu* Gasoline
휘장 *hwi-jang* Badge, Insignia
휘파람 *hwi-p'a-ram* Whistle
휴가 *hyu-ga* Holiday, Vacation
휴전 *hyu-jŏn* Truce, Armistice
휴지 *hyu-ji* Waste paper
흉내 *hyung-nae* Imitation
흥미 *hŭng-mi* Interest, Zest
희망 *hŭi-mang* Hope, Wish

APPENDIX III

ANNUAL EVENTS IN KOREA

1. New Year's Day(*sŏl-nal*)······설날(Jan. 1)
2. Lunar New Year's Day(*ŭm-nyŏk sŏl-nal*)······음력 설날(Jan. 1 by lunar calendar)
3. March 1 Independence Movement Day(*sa-mil-tchŏl*)······삼일절(March 1)
4. Labor Day(*no-dong-jŏl*)······노동절(March 10)
5. Arbor Day(*sing-mo-gil*)······식목일(April 10)
6. Student Uprising(*sa il-gu hak-ssaeng hyŏng-myŏng*)······4.19 학생 혁명 (April 19)
7. Children's Day(*ŏ-ri-ni-nal*)······어린이날(May 5)
8. Parents Day(*ŏ-bŏ-i-nal*)······어버이날(May 8)
9. Memorial Day(*hyŏn-ch'ung-il*)······현충일(June 6)
10. Korean War(*yu-gi-o chŏn-jaeng*)······6.25 전쟁(June 25)
11. Constitution Day(*che-hŏn-jŏl*)······제헌절(July 17)
12. Liberation Day(*kwang-bok-tchŏl*)······광복절(August 15)
13. Moon Festival or Korean Thanksgiving(*ch'u-sŏk*)······추석(August 15 by lunar calendar)
14. Armed Forces Day(*kuk-kku-nŭi nal*)······국군의 날(Oct. 1)
15. National Foundation Day(*kae-ch'ŏn-jŏl*)······개천절(Oct. 3)
16. Korean Alphabet Day(*han-gŭl-nal*)······한글날(Oct. 9)
17. U.N. Day(*yu-e-nŭi nal*)······유엔의 날(Nov. 3)
18. Student's Day(*hak-ssaeng-ŭi nal*)······학생의 날(Nov. 3)
19. Christmas(*sŏng-t'an-jŏl*)······성탄절(Dec. 25)

SIGNS

1. Admission Free(*mu-ryo ip-tchang*)······무료 입장
2. Blockade(*p'ye-swae*)······폐쇄
3. Bridge Ahead(*kyo-ryang-ju-ŭi*)······교량주의
4. Bus Stop(*pŏ-sŭ chŏng-gŏ-jang*)······버스 정거장
5. Caution(*chu-ŭi*)······주의
6. Closed(*hyu-ŏp*)······휴업
7. No Nuisance here(*so-byŏn kŭm-ji*)······소변 금지
8. Danger(*wi-hŏm*)······위험
9. Don't Disturb(*myŏn-hoe sa-jŏl*)······면회 사절
10. Engaged(*sa-yong chung*)······사용 중
11. Entrance(*ip-kku*)······입구
12. Exit(*ch'ul-gu*)······출구
13. Fire Alarm(*hwa-jae sin-ho*)······화재 신호
14. Fire Caution(*pul-jo-sim*)······불조심
15. Fire Exit(*hwa-jae pi-sang-gu*)······화재 비상구
16. Information(*an-nae*)······안내
17. For Sale(*p'an-mae*)······판매
18. Go Slow(*sŏ-haeng*)······서행
19. Men(*nam-ja pyŏn-so*)······남자 변소
20. Hands Off(*son-dae-ji ma-si-o*)······손대지 마시오
21. Keep Off the grass(*chan-di-ba-t'e tŭ-rŏ-ga-ji ma-si-o*)······잔디밭에 들
    어가지 마시오
22. Keep Out(*tŭ-rŏ-o-ji ma-si-o*)······들어오지 마시오
23. Knock(*yo no-k'ŭ*)······요! 노크
24. Ladies(*yŏ-ja pyŏn-so*)······여자 변소
25. No Admission(*ip-tchang pul-hŏ*)······입장 불허
26. No interviews during(*chim-mu si-gan chung myŏn-hoe sa-jŏl*)······집무
    시간 중 면회 사절

27. No Left Turn(*chwa-hae-jŏn kŭm-ji*) ······ 좌회전 금지

28. No Parking(*chu-ch'a kŭm-ji*) ······ 주차 금지

29. No Scribbing Allowed(*nak-ssŏ kŭm-ji*) ······ 낙서 금지

30. No Smoking(*kŭ-myŏn*) ······ 금연

31. No Spitting(*ch'im paet-tchi ma-si-o*) ······ 침 뱉지 마시오

32. No Through fare(*t'ong-haeng kŭm-ji*) ······ 통행 금지

33. No Turn(*hoe-jŏn kŭm-ji*) ······ 회전 금지

34. No visitors are allowed(*chong-nam sa-jŏl*) ······ 종람 사절

35. On Sale(*p'an-mae chung*) ······ 판매 중

36. One Way(*il-bang t'ong-haeng*) ······ 일방 통행

37. Passengers Zone(*sŭng-ch'a chi-yŏk*) ······ 승차 지역

38. Please don't disturb(*cho-yong-hi ha-si-o*) ·····조용히 하시오

39. Please don't touch(*so-nŭl tae-ji ma-si-o*) ······ 손을 대지 마시오

40. Please wipe your feet(*sin-ba-rŭl tta-kkŭ-si-o*) ······ 신발을 닦으시오

41. Do not post bill(*kwang-go-ji-rŭl pu-ch'i-ji ma-si-o*) ······ 광고지를 붙이지 마시오

42. Private(*kae-in*) ······ 개인

43. Public notice(*kong-go*) ······ 공고

44. Pull(*tang-gi-si-o*) ······ 당기시오

45. Push(*mi-si-o*) ······ 미시오

46. Reserved(*ye-yak-ssŏk*) ······ 예약석

47. Road Closed(*t'ong-haeng kŭm-ji*) ······ 통행 금지

48. Slow(*ch'ŏn-ch'ŏn-hi*) ······ 천천히

49. Sold(*ye-yak-p'um*) ······ 예약품

50. Speed Limit(*sok-tto che-han*) ·····속도 제한

51. Stop(*chŏng-ji*) ······ 정지

52. Under repair(*su-ri chung*) ······ 수리 중

53. Vacant(*pin-ja-ri*) ······ 빈자리

54. Warning(*kyŏng-go*) ······ 경고

55. Welcome(*hwa-nyŏng*) ······ 환영

56. Wet Paint(*ch'il-ju-ŭi*) ······ 칠주의

MEMO

MEMO

MEMO

MEMO

MEMO

MEMO

	ㄱ K(G)	ㄴ N	ㄷ T(D)	ㄹ R(L)	ㅁ M	ㅂ P(B)
ㅏ a	가 K(G)a	나 Na	다 T(D)a	라 R(L)a	마 Ma	바 P(B)a
ㅑ ya	갸 K(G)ya	냐 Nya	댜 T(D)ya	랴 R(L)ya	먀 Mya	뱌 P(B)ya
ㅓ ŏ	거 K(G)ŏ	너 Nŏ	더 T(D)ŏ	러 R(L)ŏ	머 Mŏ	버 P(B)ŏ
ㅕ yŏ	겨 K(G)yŏ	녀 Nyŏ	뎌 T(D)yŏ	려 R(L)yŏ	며 Myŏ	벼 P(B)yŏ
ㅗ o	고 K(G)o	노 No	도 T(D)o	로 R(L)o	모 Mo	보 P(B)o
ㅛ yo	교 K(G)yo	뇨 Nyo	됴 T(D)yo	료 R(L)yo	묘 Myo	뵤 P(B)yo
ㅜ u	구 K(G)u	누 Nu	두 T(D)u	루 R(L)u	무 Mu	부 P(B)u
ㅠ yu	규 K(G)yu	뉴 Nyu	듀 T(D)yu	류 R(L)yu	뮤 Myu	뷰 P(B)yu
ㅡ ŭ	그 K(G)ŭ	느 Nŭ	드 T(D)ŭ	르 R(L)ŭ	므 Mŭ	브 P(B)ŭ
ㅣ i	기 K(G)i	니 Ni	디 T(D)i	리 R(L)i	미 Mi	비 P(B)i

lphabet

(McCune-Reischauer System)

ㅇ	ㅈ	ㅊ	ㅋ	ㅌ	ㅍ	ㅎ
ng	Ch(J)	Ch'	K'	T'	P'	H
아	자	차	카	타	파	하
A	Ch(J)a	Ch'a	K'a	T'a	P'a	Ha
야	쟈	챠	캬	탸	퍄	햐
Ya	Ch(J)ya	Ch'ya	K'ya	T'ya	P'ya	Hya
어	저	처	커	터	퍼	허
Ŏ	Ch(J)ŏ	Ch'ŏ	K'ŏ	T'ŏ	P'ŏ	Hŏ
여	져	쳐	켜	텨	펴	혀
Yŏ	Ch(J)yŏ	Ch'yŏ	K'yŏ	T'yŏ	P'yŏ	Hyŏ
오	조	초	코	토	포	호
O	Ch(J)o	Ch'o	K'o	T'o	P'o	Ho
요	죠	쵸	쿄	툐	표	효
Yo	Ch(J)yo	Ch'yo	K'yo	T'yo	P'yo	Hyo
우	주	추	쿠	투	푸	후
U	Ch(J)u	Ch'u	K'u	T'u	P'u	Hu
유	쥬	츄	큐	튜	퓨	휴
Yu	Ch(J)yu	Ch'yu	K'yu	T'yu	P'yu	Hyu
으	즈	츠	크	트	프	흐
Ŭ	Ch(J)ŭ	Ch'ŭ	K'ŭ	T'ŭ	P'ŭ	Hŭ
이	지	치	키	티	피	히
i	Ch(J)i	Ch'i	K'i	T'i	P'i	Hi